The Japanese Adult Video Industry

Unlike many other books on pornography which concentrate on arguments about restricting or not restricting pornography, this book focuses on the production of adult videos. It outlines and examines the industrial dynamics of the industry, its strategies, technological capabilities and organizational structure. It discusses the socialization of those who participate in the industry, the role of censorship, the nature of markets and the wider cultural impact of the industry.

Heung-wah Wong is Program Director of Global Creative Industries in the School of Modern Languages and Cultures at the University of Hong Kong.

Hoi-yan Yau is Senior Lecturer in the Department of Cultural Studies at Lingnan University.

Routledge Culture, Society, Business in East Asia Series

To view more titles in the series, follow this link: www.routledge.com/Routledge-Culture-Society-Business-in-East-Asia-Series/book-series/CSBEA

Editorial Board:
Heung-wah Wong (Executive Editor), *The University of Hong Kong, Hong Kong, China*
Chris Hutton, *The University of Hong Kong, Hong Kong, China*
Wayne Cristaudo, *The University of Hong Kong, Hong Kong, China*
Harumi Befu (Emeritus Professor), *Stanford University, USA*
Shao-dang Yan, *Peking University, China*
Andrew Stewart MacNaughton, *Reitaku University, Japan*
William Kelly, *Independent Researcher*
Keiji Maegawa, *Tsukuba University, Japan*
Kiyomitsu Yui, *Kobe University, Japan*

How and what are we to examine if we wish to understand the commonalities across East Asia without falling into the powerful fictions or homogeneities that dress its many constituencies? By the same measure, can East Asian homogeneities make sense in any way outside the biases of East-West personation?

For anthropologists familiar with the societies of East Asia, there is a rich diversity of work that can potentially be applied to address these questions within a comparative tradition grounded in the region as opposed to the singularizing outward encounter. This requires us to broaden our scope of investigation to include all aspects of intra-regional life, trade, ideology, culture and governance, while at the same time dedicating ourselves to a complete and holistic understanding of the exchange of identities that describe each community under investigation. An original and wide-ranging analysis will be the result, one that draws on the methods and theory of anthropology as it deepens our understanding of the interconnections, dependencies and discordances within and among East Asia.

The book series includes three broad strands within and between which to critically examine the various insides and outsides of the region. The first is about the globalization of Japanese popular culture in East Asia, especially in greater China. The second strand presents comparative studies of major social institutions in Japan and China, such as family, community and other major concepts in Japanese and Chinese societies. The final strand puts forward cross-cultural studies of business in East Asia.

7 **Japanese Encounters**
  The Structure and Dynamics of Cultural Frames
  Eyal Ben-Ari

8 **The Japanese Adult Video Industry**
  Heung-wah Wong and Hoi-yan Yau

The Japanese Adult Video Industry

Heung-wah Wong and Hoi-yan Yau

LONDON AND NEW YORK

First published 2018
by Routledge
2 Park Square, Milton Park, Abingdon, Oxon OX14 4RN

and by Routledge
711 Third Avenue, New York, NY 10017

Routledge is an imprint of the Taylor & Francis Group, an informa business

© 2018 Heung-wah Wong and Hoi-yan Yau

The right of Heung-wah Wong and Hoi-yan Yau to be identified as authors of this work has been asserted by them in accordance with sections 77 and 78 of the Copyright, Designs and Patents Act 1988.

All rights reserved. No part of this book may be reprinted or reproduced or utilized in any form or by any electronic, mechanical, or other means, now known or hereafter invented, including photocopying and recording, or in any information storage or retrieval system, without permission in writing from the publishers.

Trademark notice: Product or corporate names may be trademarks or registered trademarks, and are used only for identification and explanation without intent to infringe.

British Library Cataloguing in Publication Data
A catalogue record for this book is available from the British Library

Library of Congress Cataloging in Publication Data
A catalog record for this book has been requested

ISBN: 978-0-415-70378-9 (hbk)
ISBN: 978-0-203-76249-3 (ebk)

Typeset in Times New Roman
by Wearset Ltd, Boldon, Tyne and Wear

Contents

List of figures viii
List of tables x
Acknowledgements xi
A note on Japanese translation xiii

1 Introduction 1

Salvage ideology 4
Production and consumption perspectives 6
Transcending production-consumption opposition 10
Porn studies 12
Methodological difficulties 18
Organization of chapters 24

2 From pink film and *binibon* to Japanese AVs: pornographic culture in postwar Japan 27

Introduction 27
A brief history of sexual-cum-pornographic culture in modern Japan 27
The road to Japanese adult videos 34
The two traditions of AV production: binibon-*style and pink film-style 41*
Conclusion 46

3 Production, regulation and circulation of adult videos 49

Introduction 49
AV makers 50
Model agencies 53
Postproduction 56

Regulatory body 57
Wholesalers, rental and retail shops 64
Conclusion 68

4 The production of *tantai* and *kikaku*   71

Introduction 71
Narrative 71
AV genres 86
Production system 87
Cover design 94
Market price 97
Circulation/acquisition methods 98
Clientele 99
Conclusion 100

5 Who wants to be an AV girl?   104

Introduction 104
AV actresses 104
Who are the AV girls? 105
Several observations 116
*Japanese corporate system (*kaisha system*) 123*
Women's right in selling their bodies 128
Conclusion 130

6 AV girl job interview: an inventive production process   132

Introduction 132
AV girl interview: meeting the actress 133
Interview sheet 133
Interview process 140
Taking photographs and videos 148
Analysis 152
Conclusion 161

7 The reel thing: a lecture on infinite female orgasm   163

Introduction 163
Pre-filming negotiations 164
Shooting 167
Authentication of the story and the 'female character' in the AV 174

Pornographic realism as a discourse 177
Conclusion 183

8 The 'censorship' of Japanese adult videos 186

Introduction 186
Resistance against Biderin 186
Medirin getting recognition 188
Arrest of Biderin members in 2008 189
The new 'censoring' body: Eizōrin 191
One day in Eizōrin's office 199
Consequences for AV production 208
Conclusion 210

9 Conclusion 213

Mediation of production and consumption of Japanese AVs by the salvage ideology 213
Sustaining the salvage ideology in the 'censorship' of Japanese AVs 217
Retrieval of the endangered specificities 220
Production of the objectification of women in pornography 221
Politics of the sexual being of men and women 223
Pornographic realism 226

Chinese glossary	228
Japanese glossary	229
References	232
Index	244

Figures

3.1	Production, circulation and regulation of AVs in Japan	49
4.1	The cover of Yoshikawa Aimi's debut AV	72
4.2	She is portrayed looking into the camera	73
4.3	The scene where she is portrayed drawing a heart on the blackboard	74
4.4	The interview scene	75
4.5	The beginning of the second part of the movie	75
4.6	A new section where the actress is portrayed sitting on a bed	76
4.7	The actress is depicted looking into the camera	77
4.8	A scene where she is portrayed sitting in a huge hotel room facing the sea	77
4.9	Two men are depicted reading comics in a bedroom setting	80
4.10	The thin man is filmed leaving the room	81
4.11	The fat man is filmed spying on them	81
4.12	The fat man is depicted talking to the thin man	82
4.13	A *tantai* AV featuring Tokunaga Shiori released by Alice Japan in February 2016	94
4.14	A *kikaku* AV featuring sexual pranks on women who are asleep by Japan Home Video	95
4.15	A *tantai* AV featuring Uehara Ai	96
4.16	A *tantai* AV featuring Itoh Beni by Alice Japan	97
4.17	A *kikaku* AV on sale on DMM, captured on 21 February 2016	99
5.1	Age distribution of the actresses	107
5.2	Birthplace distribution	108
5.3	Birthplace distribution	109
5.4	Occupation distribution	110
5.5	Actresses' dreams	111
5.6	Reasons for becoming an AV girl	111
5.7	Recruitment methods of AV girls	112
5.8	The average age of actresses at first sexual intercourse	113
5.9	The sexual experiences of the actresses	114
5.10	The most important things in life	115
5.11	The happiest thing about being an actress	116

6.1	Original Japanese profile card filled in by the actress	134
6.2	Translated profile card filled in by the actress	135
6.3	English version of the questionnaire	136
6.4	Original questionnaire part filled in by the actress	137
6.5	Translated questionnaire part filled in by the actress	138
6.6	Publicity checklist	139
8.1	The internal structure of Eizōrin for the inspection of adult videos	197
8.2	The PC, screen, headphone and mobile hard drive for screening	200
8.3	The inspection form	200
8.4	One of the DVD inserts distributed to us for examination	202

Tables

4.1	Comparison of the market prices of *tantai* and *kikaku* AVs	97
5.1	The profile card of the interview sheet	106
5.2	The differentiating pricing system of *tantai*, *kikatan* and *kikaku* actresses	117
5.3	Comparison among *tantai*, *kikaku* and *kikatan* actresses	119
6.1	13 themes that repeatedly appeared in the interview	153
6.2	Rationale and logics of AV production I	154
6.3	Rationale and logics of AV production II	155
7.1	The content of *kotoba-zeme* by Shiranai	166
7.2	The ideology of *kotoba-zeme*	180

Acknowledgements

This is the second volume produced out of a long and difficult journey of our research on Japanese adult videos. It goes without saying that this journey would not have been possible without the help, guidance and assistance from various people. We are very grateful to Professor Eyal Ben-Ari, the well-known expert of Japanese studies, and Professor Emeritus of the Department of Sociology and Anthropology at the Hebrew University, Israel as well as to Professor Wayne Cristaudo, an all-round philosopher and Professor of Political Science at Charles Darwin University, Australia for reviewing the manuscript in spite of their busy schedules. Both of them made several important suggestions and comments without which this book would not have been possible.

We would also like to express our gratitude to Professor Mark McLelland, Professor of Gender and Sexuality Studies, University of Wollongong, Australia, who read the whole manuscript and provided very useful suggestions; and Professor Satoshi Tanahashi, Professor of Cultural Anthropology and Gender/Sexuality Studies, Ochanomizu University, Tokyo, Japan who also agreed to read our manuscript. Special thanks go to Professor Brian Moeran, Professor Emeritus of Business Anthropology at Copenhagen Business School and Honorary Professor of Global Creative Industries, The University of Hong Kong, who not only copyedited the manuscript but also gave us many criticisms and suggestions to make it much better. Also as always, responsibility for any errors remains our own.

One of the authors (Heung-wah Wong) would also like to express his gratitude to the National Museum of Ethnology, Osaka, Japan which provided him with a comfortable academic environment when he was on sabbatical leave from January 2016 to January 2017 and wrote up most of this manuscript there. Special thanks go to Professor Kenichi Sudo, at that time Director General of the National Museum of Ethnology, who never fails to provide personal and emotional support to Wong.

Our special thanks also go to the publishing house Routledge, in which we have been fortunate to have found a most helpful, proficient and competent publisher; particular thanks go to Peter Sowden.

Finally, we beg forgiveness of all those who have been with us over the course of the years and whose names we cannot, or have failed to, mention.

Disclaimer

Every attempt has been made to trace the copyright holders of the illustrations included in this book. We have also done our best to obtain consent forms from those whose portraits appear here. If anyone has any objection to the publication of any of the images in these pages, we ask them to contact us (hoiyanyau@ ln.edu.hk) so that we may rectify matters to their satisfaction.

Note

The authors have contributed equally to the book and their names are shown in alphabetical order.

A note on Japanese translation

In this book, we have used a modified Hepburn system, which employs macrons to indicate Japanese long vowels. Japanese personal names throughout the book have been written in Japanese order, with the family name appearing first. Japanese words, other than place and personal names, have been italicized throughout the book. However, place and period names which are familiar to English-speaking readers such as Shibuya, Shinjuku and Meiji, have been left in their English form, as have terms such as 'samurai' and 'manga' which have entered the English language and are consequently not italicized. Finally, all the translations including words and quotations are our own.

1 Introduction

One evening in May 2005, we were sitting on a comfortable sofa at one of our Taiwanese informants' home in Taipei, watching a Japanese pornographic movie clip that starred an unknown Japanese adult video actress. This clip had been given us by another Taiwanese male informant in May 2004, who had downloaded it at his university. The clip featured a role-play trope between a male ballet coach and his female student.

At the beginning of the clip, we saw that the coach who was in body stockings touched and embraced his student who was in a two-piece leotard and ballet shoes, ordering her to 'Turn your body, slowly. Please put your hands down now!' He could not refrain from forcing her back onto the sofa behind her, shouting at her, 'Sit down slowly! You got it?' He then rubbed and massaged her breasts forcefully, shouting at her again, 'You already got it right!' The female student looked at the camera, begging 'Please don't do this to me!' The coach had no intention of stopping and kept on rubbing her breasts, while preaching to her: 'If you don't do this, you won't be able to learn the genuine art! Let me see your face.' He then kissed her and pulled one of the straps of her outfit down, exposing her breasts. She pushed him backward, begging him again, 'Coach, please stop it, really!' He ignored her and instead grasped her jaw, saying to her in a very serious manner, 'You want to be successful, right? You want to debut in movies or on TV, right?' The female student looked back at him in helpless silence. The coach continued to massage her breasts, saying to her, 'Therefore, listen to what I say! Understand?!' He took her upper outfit off completely, while ordering her to 'Show me your breasts! Show me your breasts! Right, such a beautiful shape!' He then started to suck her breasts, while saying loudly, 'Oh, tasty!'

We then saw them move into a position where the female student sat on the coach's lap. He fondled her breasts from behind and was about to touch her vagina, while preaching to his student again: 'You want to succeed, right? Then listen to what I tell you! Open your legs widely!' He pushed her legs apart, telling her 'Don't be shy! It is the philosophy of art you need to learn!' He then moved one of her legs upwards; ordering her, 'Hold your leg, the ankle! Right! Right! Be brave! Don't be shy!' Now we saw the coach gently fondle her vagina, asking the female student, 'Right! This way feels good? Right....' He fondled her breasts and nipples while kissing her back. He started to murmur to himself, 'It really is a mess; make it even crazier....' We saw him continue to fondle and twist her nipples, murmuring to himself again, 'Your nipples look like eyes! You want it more, more powerfully?! Right, in this way.... I mean squeeze them [breasts] more forcefully.' He kept on fondling and caressing her nipples and asked her, 'You feel good, right? After being touched this way, you become so horny!' The coach then pressed her arms inwards and shook her body, thereby making her breasts quake, while at the same time saying to her: 'I am pushing your breasts to make a cleavage!' Then he sucked her nipples and murmured to himself again, 'They [the breasts] are shaking.... Oh, fantastic! Look at this.' The coach suddenly sucked her nipples forcefully. The female student screamed and said, 'No, no, coach!' We then saw him help her lie back on the sofa where he fondled her vagina with her outfit on, while at the same time asked her, 'You feel good, right? You cannot simply feel good but don't express it out aloud!' The coach continued to fondle her vagina and kept on asking her, 'Good feeling? No, no, you should voice your real feeling! Put your feeling into your voice!'

He made the female student bend towards the sofa, ordering her, 'Spread your legs! Very bad position!' The coach himself was there talking to the female student and rolling the lower part of her outfit to make it into a G-string. He then said to her, 'I've made this into a G-string. It gets into the crack in your buttocks; it gets into your buttocks!' We saw the coach looking at her buttocks and then massaging them, together with her vagina, while he said to her, 'Right, it's ok! Very good, very good! You're already revealing your true lasciviousness!' He moved one of her hands to hold the rolled-up part of her outfit, ordering her again, 'Hold it [the rolled-up part of her outfit] in your hand, you hold it!' He then sucked and licked her nipples. After that, the coach started to masturbate her vagina while sucking her nipples. He asked her, 'Here? It is here [her vagina], right? It's here that makes you feel good, right?' We saw the coach kissing and sucking the student's breasts while kneeling on the floor. He then moved her body quickly so that her breasts 'spanked' on his face. 'Hold your breasts, put them closer! Put them together on my face.... It's the best of the best!' the coach ordered. He then performed cunnilingus on her while she was standing and said to her, 'Look at the opposite side! Can you see it? The opposite? See it? Look at the opposite!' The female student stood while bending forward. 'Right, keep that position! Please look at this!' He said to her, while he touched and fondled her body. He then moved to massage her nipples and kissed her nipples again. 'This is the philosophy of art, have you got it?', the coach asked the female student. His hands moved to touch her vagina again. 'You feel pretty much excited, right?!', he asked her again.

The camera took us to a scene where the female student lay in the coach's lap and he moved her hands to his penis. 'Touch it [penis]! Touch it [penis]! Rub it, massage it, and make it harder! Make it [penis] feel good', the coach ordered. She massaged his penis. The coach then lay back and pulled off his body stocking from where she was about to perform fellatio. 'Touch it [penis]! Kiss it, kiss it!' She kissed his penis with his underpants still on. 'Look at it [camera].' She looked at the camera. 'Right, keep on looking at it! Please put your feelings into your eyes.' The coach encouraged her. 'Make your eyes pure! Put your feeling in it! Oh, it's [penis] got stiff!' She gently bit his penis with his underpants on. He then ordered her to take off his underpants and give him a blow job while at the same time fondling his penis. 'Right, hold it [penis] in your mouth from your heart! Hold it in your mouth tightly.... Voice your feeling! Let me hear your real feeling.' The coach then stood up from the sofa and took off his underpants, and the female student continued to suck his penis while holding it in her hands. 'Keep it [penis] in your mouth, keep it in your mouth, you can't leave it, you can't!' the coach shouted at her. At this point, we saw the female student looking into the camera while sucking his cock. The coach then took her hands off, and moved her face to the side. 'Do it only with your mouth! Only with your mouth! Right, turn your face to this side. You seem very happy! Oh you have such a horny face while doing it! You slut!' the coach yelled at her. We saw the female student kneel down beside him where he obtained pleasure by rubbing his penis against the cleavage of her breasts. While forcefully moving her breasts up and down, the coach instructed her:

> Okay, you have to work hard! Okay, human beings cannot survive on their own! Got it? You can survive simply because you've been given a lot of help by the fans and staff here! You can't forget that! Understand? So, you're now free from your inhibitions or habits? Be pure! Be pure! Tell me your real feeling now! For instance, you want me to come inside you?

The camera then turned to her face which looked desperate and painful. 'Come inside [me], penetrate [me]!' the female student begged the coach, who proceeded to move her face towards the camera, forcing her to make eye contact with it. 'Come inside me', she begged the coach eagerly. He then excitedly took off her leotard, leaving her only in her tights. 'Take these [tights] off, too', he ordered her before sitting underneath her, asking her to masturbate his penis. 'Touch it [penis]! Slowly! Touch it! Still not yet!', the coach ordered her. At that point, we saw that they were masturbating each other. 'Endure it! You are withholding your feeling, aren't you? I won't give it to you until you really want me from your heart!' As he said this, the camera stayed on her face, which appeared to be in great pain. 'Coach, come inside [me]! Penetrate [me]!' the female student screamed. He moved her hands to his penis, signifying to her that she should play with it. 'You want it, right! Show me that you want me to put it inside then! Right, here.' He then moved her legs up and took off her tights together with her knickers. 'Coach, penetrate [me]!' 'Not yet, rubbing [your vagina], enjoy it slowly...', the coach insisted. The camera moved from her face to the lower part of her body where intercourse was about to take place. The coach then pushed his cock gently inside her while holding her waist. 'Right, here right? Here? It's in? It's in? You got it? Slowly coming inside [your vagina]....' He brought her body up and kissed her breasts. He then started thrusting inside her while biting her nipples. 'Can I bite them? Bite here?' The coach continued thrusting while she held her legs wide apart, saying to her, 'let me have a full view. I want to touch the clitoris…' The camera focused on her breasts while the coach moved her hands to her vagina so that her arms put pressure on her breasts, making them even bigger.

The coach ordered the student, 'Touch here! Push your breasts closer with your arms from the side. Your breasts are shaking!' 'Coach, I can't stand your thrusting!' He then changed position to enter her from behind. 'Feel it slowly! The whole [penis]! Move like this. How do you feel now? You feel good, right?' the coach asked her. While continuing their doggy-style fucking, he brought her upper body up, kissing her back and fondling her breasts. 'Let's do it a bit harder, ok?' the coach said to her. They then swapped into the 'cowgirl' position and he fondled her nipples while they fucked. After a while, they went back to doggy-style, but with both of them standing. 'No, no, no, coach!' the female student screamed. 'You don't have to endure it [orgasm]!' he said as they returned to the sofa where he penetrated her again. 'I'm about to come!' the coach screamed. 'Coach! Coach! I'm going to come, too', the student also cried. He started to thrust into her quickly on the sofa. 'No, no, I'm coming. Coach, I want it [orgasm], I want it. It feels so good. I'm coming, I'm coming, I'm coming', the student screamed. He pulled his penis out of her vagina and moved forward to her breasts where he ejaculated. 'Breasts, push them together, push them!' the coach ordered the student. 'Look here, you should have correctly learnt what art is', he then said to her before disappearing from the screen. The lens moved closer to the student's breasts and then to her face. 'Coach. Thank you', the student said to the camera.

Salvage ideology

As we have just shown, the clip described here tells the story of how the coach wanted to teach his female student the real philosophy of art, so that she could succeed in debuting on TV or in a movie by forcing her to have sex with him. Initially, the female student did not understand the 'real' intention of her coach and resisted having sex with him. However, she finally compromised as she wished to debut on TV successfully. Later, she even realized the 'good' intentions of her coach after being forced to have sex with him. At the end of the story, she thanked the coach for teaching her 'genuine art' through sex.

This story succinctly encodes what we will call 'salvage ideology' which has been lingering on over the decades in postwar Japan and in particular in Japanese pornography. This salvage ideology consists of two mutually constituted elements. The first is men's domination over women, as we have seen from the clip above where the coach (man) taught his female student 'genuine art' by means of forced sex so that she could be successful in her performing career. It is in this sense that men are the saviour of women. The latter should feel grateful to men even though the way they save women might consist of extreme imposition, violence, or even torture, but these violent means are all forgivable because they are done to women for a good end. So good ends justify bad means. Implied in this is the second element of the salvage ideology: women cannot save themselves, but have to rely on men sexually. Men therefore are women's saviour.

The legend of men as women's saviour can also be seen in the register of sex. In the context of sex, the salvage ideology manifests itself also in two major ways. The first is women's lack of sexual agency, in the sense that it is difficult if not impossible for women to achieve orgasm by themselves. Women are often assumed to be ill-fated in their sexual life and thus are considered as nothing but problematic. They have no alternative but wait to be 'fixed' by men, because only men can salvage women from their sexual predicament through using various sexual skills to help them reach orgasm. Again, some of these skills can be very violent, if not verging on torture, but men are forgivable because they do everything for the sake of women: helping them reach orgasm and thus bringing them sexual happiness. Men, therefore, are women's saviour because only men can bring women to a climax. This leads to the second way through which the salvage ideology is expressed in sex: men's sexual domination over women, inasmuch as women's sexual pleasure is totally dependent on men. It is interesting to note that women's lack of sexual agency and men's sexual domination over women are mutually constituted and reciprocally defined. Women have to rely on men for their sexual pleasure because they are deprived of sexual agency; while men sexually dominate women because women rely on men for their sexual pleasure.

As we shall demonstrate in this book, this salvage ideology can widely be seen in most genres of Japanese adult videos. We are tempted to trace how the salvage ideology emerged in postwar Japan, and how it is made and remade in Japanese pornography – especially in adult videos (AVs) put out by the AV industry in Japan – and why. More importantly, we shall investigate in this book the role of the salvage ideology in ordering the production and consumption of AVs in Japan. In more concrete terms, we shall investigate how it serves as what Sahlins (1976a) calls a 'cultural code' that mediates the production of Japanese AVs – including an AV actress job interview, AV shooting and inspection; *as well as* the consumption of AVs in Japan. In the chapters that follow, we will show how the salvage ideology, on the one hand, specifies the needs of Japanese AV consumers *and* the ways to satisfy those needs; and how, on the other hand, it gives significance to certain properties of AVs that make certain types of videos 'useful' to certain categories of AV consumers in Japan, in the course of which certain types of AV acquire their utility from the salvage ideology. Our main concern has been to understand how the production and consumption of Japanese AVs are governed by the same cultural code in Japan. This then suggests that the dichotomy between production and consumption widely assumed by many scholars should not be exaggerated and may, indeed, be totally unnecessary.

This book therefore has two major analytical focuses. The first is the role of cultural code in shaping and ordering the production and consumption of AVs in Japan; the second is about the nature of Japanese AVs as pornographic text. These two analytical focuses further require that the production and consumption of AVs in Japan be approached from a thesis that takes into account both the determination of their 'use value' and consumer needs by a cultural code and the perspective of porn studies. In the sections that follow, therefore, we will critically review the current theories in production and consumption studies, as well as in pornography studies. In the Conclusion to this book, we will demonstrate how this study speaks to some fundamental questions concerning the relationship between cultural code and production as well as consumption, and by extension the relationship between culture and economy, the social construction of the sexual being of men and women, the objectification of women in pornography, and the relationship between pornographic representation and reality.

Production and consumption perspectives

As mentioned elsewhere (Yau and Wong 2010), production is often celebrated at the expense of consumption in traditional scholarly analyses, especially in the field of sociology. This has much to do with the way Karl Marx conceptualized commodity. According to Marxist analysis, a commodity entails two types of value: use value and exchange value. Use value is the utility of consuming a good, or the want-satisfying power of a good or service, in classical political economy. Exchange value, by contrast, is the quantified worth of one good or service expressed in terms of the worth of another. As Marx notes:

> If commodities could speak they would say this: our use value might interest men, but it does not belong to us as objects. What does belong to us as objects, however, is our [exchange] value. Our own intercourse as commodities proves it. We relate to each other merely as exchange values.... So far, no chemist has ever discovered exchange value in a pearl or a diamond. The economists who have discovered this chemical substance and who lay special claim to this acumen, nevertheless find that the use value of material objects belong to them independently of their material properties, while their [exchange] value, on the other hand, forms a part of them as objects.
> (Marx 1994: 243)

As Sahlins perceptively argues, Marx sees the commodity as having not only a double but indeed opposing nature: its value as opposed to itself, that is to say, its exchange value, as opposed to its use value. In Marx's formulation, exchange value, as we can see from the above quotation, belongs to the commodity, and it is the way commodities relate to each other in the society, hence 'an assigned function of society' (Sahlins 1976a: 150). In other words, it is relative to the society in the sense that it varies with time and context, and hence historical and social. More importantly, while exchange value, according to Marx, is the property of a commodity, it is not an *inherent* part of the commodity. Recall his argument that, 'no chemist has ever discovered exchange value either in a pearl or a diamond'. For Marx, the chemical substance called exchange value has not been found because it does not exist. In other words, exchange value is truly symbolic and thus social by nature.

While Marx rightly recognizes that exchange value is symbolic, however, he firmly believes that use value is asocial. In Marx's account, use value does not belong to the commodity; rather it is something that resides in human beings. As an attribute of man, it is thus intrinsic, innate or biological, transparently serving human needs. As Marx argues,

> What confirm them in this view is the *peculiar circumstance* that the use value of a thing is realized without exchange, i.e. in the direct relation between the thing and man, while, inversely, its [exchange] value is realized in exchange, i.e. in social process....
>
> (Marx 1994: 243; italics ours)

As Sahlins perceptively notes, the major problem of this characterization is that the use value of a commodity is rendered ahistorical, universal, and hence 'perceptually self-evident' and 'natural' (Sahlins 1976a: 150). Assuming that human desires such as eating and wearing clothes are nothing more than 'animal functions' (Marx 1963: 60), Marx would regard that the study of use value, and by extension of the consumption of commodity, is useless, thus foreclosing any discussion of the meaningful relations between men and objects.

If Marx's characterization mystifies use value, then the idea of utilitarianism takes the mystification to the next level. Utilitarianism refers to the belief that the value of a thing or an action is determined by its utility. Alternatively, it states that the best action for the general good is the one that *maximizes* utility: hence the (in)famous 'maximization of utility' that has permeated some social sciences. Utility has a long history, defined usually in terms of the well-being of human beings and other animals. Jeremy Bentham, the founder of utilitarianism, described utility as the sum of all pleasure that results from an action, minus the suffering of anyone involved in the action. Utilitarianism is a version of consequentialism, which states that the consequences of any action are the only standard of right and wrong. Indeed, Sahlins' seminal book, *Culture and Practical Reason* (1976a) offered a brilliant anthropological critique of the idea that human cultures are formulated out of practical activity and, behind that, of utilitarian interest. Here we simply wish to point out that the celebration, if not apotheosis, of practicality and usefulness once again forecloses discussion of the very nature of the pleasure (utility) derived from a certain product/action as if it were simply natural, self-evident and transparent, because all effort and attention have gone into the 'maximization' of utility. The happiness of human beings – which is indeed relative to society, as it were – is left untouched and rendered self-evident and universal.

The 'naturalness' of use value is sometimes matched by ideological depreciation. Above a minimal level of satisfying physical needs for food, clothing and shelter, the desire to consume was considered by Marx to be a pure social need induced by capitalism: the infamous commodity fetishism (Fine and Saad-Filho

2004: 25). In Marx's critique of political economy, commodity fetishism refers to the (mistaken) perception of the social relationships of labour involved in production, not as relationships among people, but as economic relationships between the money and commodities exchanged in the market (Boer 2010: 103). In other words, commodity fetishism functions to transfer inter-human relations and attributes in the context of labour – who makes what, who works for whom, the production-time for a commodity, et cetera – to relations between commodities themselves; that is, how valuable a given commodity is when compared to another commodity. As Marx puts it, this transferral is 'a mysterious thing', because

> the social character of men's labour appears to them as an objective character stamped upon the product of that labour; because the relation of the producers to the sum total of their own labour is presented to them as a social relation, existing not between themselves, but between products of their labour.
>
> (Marx, quoted in Boer 2010: 102)

The major consequence of such a transferral is the fetishization of the commodity, wherein an economic value resulting from human powers and attributes is psychologically transformed (reified) into an object, which people choose to believe has an intrinsic value, in and of itself (Boer 2010: 102). Now, a material object that does not have any value or power is seen to possess inherent value, if not supernatural power. If it is not merely that the commodity is just a material object that possesses no value or power, but that human labour is responsible for the creation of this commodity, it would not be wrong to say that the belief that the commodity has an inherent value is as much superstition and fantasy as the belief that a pretty object made out of iron or wood has supernatural power.

In line with Marx's fetishist consumption, Weber considered consumption to be nothing more than a manifestation of hedonism. This idea is elaborately discussed and expanded by Colin Campbell in *Romantic Ethics and the Spirit of Modern Consumerism* (1987). In tracing the modern hedonist consumption to Romanticism, Campbell (1987: 60) argues that modern hedonism is no longer 'a state of being' but 'a quality of experience'. In former times, pleasure was sought through the senses: food, sex, music, laughter. Thus, elites had banquets, harems, musicians and clowns while the masses had carnivals, their taste of the same. The modern economy, according to Campbell, replaced the sensory experience of the body with the 'emotional experience of the imagination' – daydreams of finer lifestyles, novel consumer goods, exotic experience, which emerge with a relocation of emotion and agency within a self both liberated from the oppressive external influences and capable of self-consciousness (Campbell 1987: 60). According to Romanticism, modern individual consumers are capable of exercising control over the meanings of the objects and experiences composing their worlds, thereby maximizing internal experiences of pleasure. The modern capacity for imagination thus becomes the source of a new kind of self-illusory hedonism (Campbell 1987: 76).

Not unlike Marx and Weber, Durkheim was also against consumption. Durkheim arguably held the most pessimistic view in that he thought that consumers' desires, once unleashed, could destroy the moral basis of social order. We will not go into this any further, but perhaps it is clear enough that all of this discussion has set the stage for prolific research on the production, rather than consumption, during the following decades (Slater 1997: 74–6). Indeed, the academic devaluation of consumption in the twentieth century has gone hand in hand with the polarization of production and consumption approaches in the social sciences, especially in sociology. One of the major advocators was Talcott Parsons, a dominant figure in the field of sociology – especially economic sociology – in the US from the 1940s to 1970s, and his 'analytical factor view' has had a profound impact on the study of economic sociology.[1] As Pratt (2004: 519) has already argued, the Parsonian legacy lies in the discrete analytical separation of the economic, social and political, and the unquestioned framing of such a division by neo-classical economic concepts and taxonomies. The result is that economic-social, or production-consumption, polarities are fixed as immutable binaries that are left to be analysed by particular disciplines and techniques.

This way of prioritizing exchange value at the expense of use value, and hence production over consumption, finds its full manifestation in the study of popular music and the coining of the term 'culture industry' by Max Horkheimer and Theodor Adorno, two major members of the Frankfurt School (Horkheimer and Adorno 1973). Presented as critical vocabulary in the chapter 'The Culture Industry: Enlightenment as Mass Deception' of the book *Dialectic of Enlightenment* (1973), they argued that popular culture is akin to a factory *producing* standardized cultural goods including films, radio programmes, magazines, that are used to manipulate mass society into passivity. The culture industry, their argument goes, claims to serve consumers' needs for entertainment, but in fact conceals the way in which it standardizes these needs, manipulating consumers to desire what the culture industry produces. In other words, popular culture not only mirrors, but also shapes, society through processes of standardization and commodification, creating objects rather than subjects (Adorno 2001[1991]: 99). The inherent danger of the culture industry is the cultivation of false psychological needs that can only be met and satisfied by the products of capitalism. Thus Adorno and Horkheimer especially perceived mass-produced culture as a danger to the more technically and intellectually difficult 'high' arts.

Central to this theory is a view of production as the prime determinant of the cultural meaning of goods, because it 'mould[s] the [masses'] consciousness by inculcating the desire for false needs.... It is so effective in doing this that the people do not realise what is going on' (Strinati 1995: 61). In short, 'products which are tailored for consumption by masses ... to a great extent determine that nature of consumption' (Adorno 2001[1991]: 98). Given the prominence of this type of production analysis, we should not be surprised that, except in the field of economics, very little was written about consumption in the humanities or social sciences from the 1950s to the 1970s (Miller 1995a: 142). Consumption studies are trivialized in such a way that 'they only capture the distribution of goods in economies via a combination of consumer choice and distribution channels' (Pratt 2004: 519).

Against this devaluation of consumption, from the 1970s, anthropologists such as Mary Douglas and Pierre Bourdieu began to shift their attention to goods and their consumers (Miller 1995a: 142). The substantial body of research that emerged in the 1980s from cultural studies fuelled the shift towards establishing consumption as an important academic topic. Scholars who undertook this research tended to focus on aspects of youth culture – especially fashion, style, popular music and fiction (Fiske 1989; Hebdige 1988, 1991; Willis 1978, 1990) – and their principal message was that consumers were not passive dupes. In consumption-oriented approaches, then, consumers are given agency and their motives can be heterogeneous and even contradictory. This shift to the analysis of audiences in media/cultural studies, and with it the notion of active viewers, has even given rise to the analysis of the 'active consumer' (e.g. Fiske 1989). Echoing this shift, Peter Saunders urged sociologists to abandon the old 'production-dominated' paradigm in favour of a new, 'consumption-oriented' one (Campbell 1995: 96). An extension of this is seen in some analyses of the materiality of cultural goods, perhaps best summed up in Miller's (1987, 1995b) term, 'material culture', in which people use material objects to express themselves and their cultures. Drawing on examples from both Western and developing societies, Miller argues that everyday life objects reflect not only personal tastes and attributes, but moral principles and social ideals. In short, the goal of recent interest in consumption has been to move beyond a singular emphasis on production in order to capture the complexity of everyday life through the study of consumption (Wurst and McGuire 1999: 191).

Transcending production-consumption opposition

However, while both sides of the argument have generated important insights into the meanings of cultural products and their relation to everyday life, we suggest that such an opposition between production and consumption is exaggerated and unnecessary, if not misleading. American anthropologist Sidney Mintz (1985) taught us long ago that the spheres of production and consumption are indeed linked. In explaining the emergence of sugar as a key consumer good in modern Britain, he showed that the need for intensive labour in sugar production caused the British to look to Africa to find cheap or free labour. In the event, sugar took slaves from Africa to the new world in America, while at the same time creating an identity for the aristocracy and later a manufactured sense of freedom among the working class in Britain. Sugar thus linked slaves on plantations in the Caribbean with the English working class, so much so that sugar increased in the British diet as a means of controlling workers at two ends of a colonial, capitalist economy.

In more recent years, du Gay *et al.* (1997) have examined the development of the Sony Walkman by situating the product in organizational practices of the firm and in young people's social practices of self-expression, individuality and sociality. They likewise show that production and consumption are connected, and more importantly, that they are not just polarized as in Mintz's study, but indeed reciprocally and mutually interact in a 'circuit of culture' with other processes: namely, representation, circulation and regulation. In other words, it is not merely that production and consumption are not opposed as is usually thought, but that they are indeed linked with other processes including circulation, regulation and so on. Similarly, Alan McKee (2004: 175) demonstrates that it is almost impossible to draw a clear line between the cultural production of fans and that of the television producers of *Doctor Who*, because many of the latter are fans and many of its fans later become producers. The difficulty in drawing a distinction between fans and producers led McKee to turn to the concept of 'canonicity' – 'the decision as to what constitutes "real" Doctor Who' – to distinguish between the cultural objects produced by different people (McKee 2004: 175).

The reason this is so difficult is that consumption cannot be determined simply from the nature of human needs or wants. As Marx taught us long ago, our wants and pleasures have their origin in society and must therefore be explained and measured from within society (Marx, quoted in Sahlins 1976a: 132). Or, put differently, '[w]ithout consumption, the object does not complete itself as a product; a house left unoccupied is no house' (Sahlins 1976a: 169). The opposite is also true. Without production of the object, the subject cannot be reproduced because '[m]en produce objects for given *social* subjects, in the course of reproducing subjects by *social* objects' (Sahlins 1976a: 168; italics in original). Marx thus argues,

> [p]roduction not only creates an object for the subject, but also a subject for the object. Thus production produces consumption (1) by creating the material for it; (2) by determining the manner of consumption; and (3) by creating the products, initially posited by it as objects, in the form of a need felt by the consumer. It thus produces the object of consumption, the manner of consumption and the motive of consumption. Consumption likewise produces the producers' inclination by beckoning to him as an aim-determining need.
>
> (Marx, quoted in Pratt 2004: 520)

Implied in this argument is that the production of the object is never absolute, but is culturally and thus socially relative. So-called biological needs (or use values) are no less arbitrary than exchange values because they are symbolically constituted by culture and thus historical.

The symbolic nature of human needs has an important implication for our current investigation. If objects are produced to satisfy not a biological need but rather a need relative to a cultural order, then production amounts to a *re*production of culturally constituted use values. Seen in this light, production, *as well as* consumption, is nothing less than a social process in which people reciprocally define objects in terms of themselves, and themselves in terms of these objects. As we shall try to demonstrate, Japanese AV makers, to rephrase Sahlins' riposte, produce Japanese AVs for Japanese sexual subjects, in the course of reproducing Japanese sexual subjects by Japanese AVs. More significantly, such a reciprocal formulation of subjects and objects renders the above opposition between production and consumption unnecessary, because they are just two manifestations of what Sahlins called 'cultural code' (1976a: 166) in governing the utility of the product and consumers' demand for the same product simultaneously. The governing power of the cultural code in both production and consumption processes bears a striking similarity to Lévi-Strauss's insightful comments on the unnecessary opposition between superstructure and infrastructure:

> Without questioning the undoubted primacy of infrastructure, I believe there is always a mediator between praxis and practices, namely the *conceptual scheme* by the operation of which matter and form, neither with any independent existence, are realized as structures, that is as entities which are both empirical and intelligible.
> (Lévi-Strauss, quoted in Sahlins, 1999: xiii; italics ours)

As we shall show in this book, the production and consumption of *tantai* (literally 'a single person', a kind of AV production that focuses on a single actress) and *kikaku* (literally 'a plan', a kind of AV production that centres on story and content) AVs constitute two major styles of Japanese adult videos that are governed by the same cultural code: that is, by the salvage ideology, which is made up of two mutually constituted elements: 'women's lack of sexual agency' and 'men's sexual domination over women'. The salvage ideology not only organizes the production system of *tantai* and *kikaku* AVs – including their narrative, genres, the way AV actresses are paid, package, marketing and clientele – but also specifies the sexual needs of certain categories of Japanese consumer as well as the means with which to satisfy those needs. The salvage ideology is the cultural reason that not only can account for what and why a *particular* style of AVs is in fact produced, but also what *specific* style of AVs certain categories of Japanese consumers would like to consume and why. In other words, this is a book about the AV industry in Japan.

Porn studies

Pornography, especially its supposed sexual violence against women, is arguably one of the most controversial and divisive issues within the feminist movement. A deep division among feminists fully manifested itself in the so-called 'porn wars' or 'sex wars' of the 1980s (Chancer 2000: 77; Duggan and Hunter 1995: 5; Rubin 1993a: 3). This phrase refers to acrimonious debates between anti-pornography feminism and anti-'anti-pornography' feminism in the late 1970s through the 1980s around the issues of feminist strategies regarding pornography, alongside other sexual issues. As numerous scholars have documented this debate (Duggan and Hunter 1995; Segal and McIntosh 1992; Wilson 1989; Wingfield and Scanlon 1992), we will not rehearse it here, but instead simply point out that the gist of this debate is whether pornography is the *cause* of women's oppression or whether it is just another *expression* thereof (Luff 2001: 80). In short, anti-pornography feminists have tended to see pornography as constitutive of women's oppression, in the sense that it is seen as the very entity that oppresses women and for this reason it should be legally banned. In contrast, anti-'anti-pornography' feminists have contended that the cause of women's oppression lies not in pornography but somewhere else. In their view, then, censoring pornography alone will not reduce discrimination against women in society, because pornography is at best another expression of such an oppression.

As a form of social and political activism, feminist scholarships, anti-pornography and anti-'anti-pornography' alike, have sought to achieve the moral high ground in their arguments. For instance, anti-pornography feminists argued that pornography should be legally forbidden *for the sake of gender equality*. As Dworkin (2003[1978]: 223) phrased it: '[a]t the heart of the female condition is pornography; it is the ideology that is the source of all the rest; it truly defines what women are in this system'.

Anti-'anti-pornography' feminists, in contrast, contended that pornography should not be banned because they were worried that the freedom of women to access pornography and to opt for non-mainstream sexual preferences would be violated. More importantly, censorship could result in increased 'stigma and persecution of pornography, prostitution and perversion', which could further 'mean police abuse and bureaucratic harassment for women and men who *have done nothing wrong* but express unfashionable [like lesbian] desires, create illicit imagery or engage in disreputable occupations' (Rubin 1993b: 39; italics ours). In view of the possible harm done to women's sexual freedom, anti-'anti-porn' feminists strongly opposed the censorship of pornography.

As we can see, both anti-pornography and anti-'anti-pornography' feminists took the stance of being morally right – one in the name of achieving gender equality and the other of protecting the freedom of speech of women, especially in minority groups – in order for their arguments, albeit completely opposed, to be seen as 'correct', and hence the truth. These arguments adopting a moral stance are typical examples of what Gerald Graff has called 'political arguments' 'mean[ing] those reasons given for or against a theory of literature or criticism which refer to the theory's alleged political motivations or consequences' (Graff 1983: 597). Here the alleged political consequences of anti-pornography and anti-'anti-pornography' arguments are used by both sides to support their positions *as if*, to paraphrase Sahlins (2000: 354), taking the proper attitude on gender equality or women's freedom of speech is sufficient to know what pornography is, or *as if* their moral high ground is the essential part of the truth of pornography. Sahlins' critique of the way anthropology in the era of late capitalism is made to serve as 'a kind of morally laudable' analysis seems point-for-point appropriate to feminist analysis of pornography: 'The problem with such an anthropology of advocacy is not simply that arguments get judged by their morality but, rather, that as a priori persuasive, *morality gets to be the argument.* The true and the good become one' (Sahlins 2000: 505–6; italics ours).

Many feminist studies are also made to serve as a kind of morally laudable analysis in the sense that concrete arguments with regard to whether pornography should (not) be banned are replaced with their moral stances: advocacy of gender equality or freedom of speech. But as Graff points out, the alleged political consequences have no logical relevance to the validity of the arguments and therefore cannot be used to support or oppose them (Graff 1983: 599).

The crucial point here is that pornography can have many different political consequences, 'but *what that consequence is* in a specific instance can't be deduced a priori from the theory itself' (Graff 1983: 603; italics in original). The political consequences of pornography in a specific context have to be determined by a thorough social analysis of how it is used in that context (Graff 1983: 605). The political arguments of both 'anti-pornography' and anti-'anti-pornography', however, work to destroy all the empirical 'facts' because of their *apriorism* whereby 'morality', as mentioned above, gets to be the argument. For the anti-pornography feminists, pornography is nothing more than a violent act against women, in which women are objectified, dehumanized and degraded for male sexual pleasure. The details concerning how, when, why, where, for what and by whom women are objectified, dehumanized and degraded are all dissolved in the acid of morality; whereas, for the anti-'anti-pornography' feminists, pornography represents a possible transgressive tool for women, but again, how, when, where and why it can bring transgressive pleasure to women remain unexplained and unclear. More importantly, such *apriorism* works to intellectually dismiss alternative points of view that are not consonant with the moral stances of anti-pornography or anti-'anti-pornography' feminists.

We suggest that the verdict on the above debate between anti-pornography feminists and anti-'anti-pornography' feminists depends on two major questions. The first is whether pornography has negative effects on users; but in order to answer this question, we need to ask what pornography really is, an important question that some anti-pornography feminists do not bother to try to find out. They tend to refuse to differentiate between different types of pornographies in different places at different times. In their theorization of pornography, some feminists seldom acknowledge the histories or cultural differences of pornography, *as if* there were only one type of pornography which never changes. This can be clearly seen in the way Dworkin and MacKinnon defined pornography as 'graphic sexually explicit pictures or words that subordinate women and also include one or more of a number of specified scenarios that typify pornography' (Dworkin and MacKinnon 1989[1988]: 138–9). These scenarios, according to them, include situations where:

> women are presented dehumanized as sexual objects, things or commodities; women are presented as sexual objects who enjoy pain or humiliation; women are presented as sexual objects tied up or cut up or mutilated or physically bruised or physically hurt; women are presented in postures of

sexual submission, servility or display; women's body parts are exhibited such that women are reduced to those parts; women are presented as whores by nature; women are presented as being penetrated by objects or animals; women are presented in scenarios of degradation, injury, torture, shown as filthy or inferior, bleeding, bruised, or hurt in a context that makes these conditions sexual.

(Dworkin and MacKinnon 1989[1988]: 801)

In this definition, we are not told what kind of pornography it is; whether it is American pornography, or a Norwegian or French, or Japanese variety. Nor are we told 'who' uses it, 'what' it is used for, and 'how', 'when, 'why' and 'where' it is used. Similarly, nothing is mentioned about the content of pornography, not to mention what kind of sexual desire it incites, what kind of ideology it imposes, or how the female characters are contextualized and why in the movie. Pornography is thus not only seen as singular and abstract, but also absolute in the sense that historical and cultural differences pertaining to different pornographies are dissolved in the generalization of pornography as 'graphic sexually explicit pictures or words' that subordinate and degrade women.

This kind of anti-pornography feminist scholarship, therefore, is a project of elimination that functions to remove the specific properties of pornography by dissolving them in generic effects. The problem, to paraphrase Sahlins (1999: 407), is that the effects that are supposed to explain the character of pornography at issue simply cannot do so. At best, they are insufficient even if correct, because they speak to the effects of pornography rather than its characteristics (i.e. its history, its style of productions, how it is produced, circulated, consumed and so on). Pornography *is accounted for* by its effects: objectifying and dehumanizing women, facilitating male aggression towards women, trivializing rape, promoting desensitization to female victims, the rape myth, hate speech, and so on. The main relationships between pornography and individual producers, and the images directors/actors/actresses entertain of the production of pornography and of themselves, are subsumed in this effect logic.

The same is also true for the pro-porn feminists: the functions of pornography to express freedom of speech are now taken as the essence of pornography. The tendency of these feminists to ignore the detail and content of pornography in favour of merely perceiving it as a form of violence against women, or a violation of their freedom of speech, unfortunately render them very close to what Sartre called 'formalists'. Beneficent and gracious as they may be, this kind of feminism becomes a project of elimination whose 'goal is total assimilation at the least possible effort. The aim is not to integrate what is different as such ... but rather to suppress it' (Sartre 1968: 48). In short, the above functional explanation of pornography is tantamount to a refusal to go into detail.

The refusal of both anti-pornography and anti-'anti-pornography' feminists to go into such details in turn explains why feminist scholars alongside others have rarely touched upon the production of pornography. In the first issue of the long awaited international journal specializing in the study of pornography, Smith and

Attwood (2014: 15) inaugurated the journal[2] by calling for a critical examination of pornography as 'industry' and hence the inclusion of production processes themselves in the study of pornography. This was because early pornography studies focused predominantly on pornographic texts with the aim of exploring how and what kinds of negative effects these texts would have on audiences, and in this way they contributed to a large body of so-called 'effects research' scholarship. As can be imagined, effects research rarely situated pornographic texts in the contexts in which they were produced or consumed, let alone the voices of producers or consumers (Boyle 2000; Ciclitira 2004; Hardy 1998; O'Toole 1999; Senn 1993). The singular focus on the pros and cons of pornography and subsequent controversy it caused prompted many scholars to move away from the 'tired binary' of pornography (Juffer 1998: 2) towards its 'contextualization' (Attwood 2002: 91).

Echoing Smith and Attwood, this book aims to fill this void by delving into the pornography industry, especially the Japanese AV industry, and retrieving the long-lost stories of AV production in order to find out why Japanese women choose to be AV actresses, how Japanese AV makers select actresses through job interviews, how AVs are shot, and inspected, in short how the whole production process is carried out according to the salvage ideology. Indeed, research into the production of Japanese AVs is badly needed not only because there are very few studies on this topic, but also because it can reveal many understudied issues pertaining to the structure and presentation of pornography in general.

Pornography reality and power politics

The second question that we need to address concerns the well-known discussion within feminist cum porn studies: is pornography just a representation of sex or its reality? This discussion has gone hand in hand with the above 'porn debate' because this split between representation and reality is precisely the issue where anti-porn and anti-'anti-pornography' feminists have been divided. There are two opposing lines of argument, which in turn intersect with the political stances of anti-pornography and anti-'anti-pornography' feminisms respectively.

The first line of argument maintains a clear distinction between the world of lived experience, and mediated representation, in the sense that the two exist in two different, or separate spheres. This argument can be commonly found among those who are anti-'anti-pornography' feminists, or among those who fear that an outright censorship on pornography will harm women's freedom in accessing various kinds of pornography that they find liberating or transgressive. As pornographic representation and reality exist in two divided spheres, anti- 'anti-pornography' feminists deemed it unnecessary, even wrong, to enforce sanctions against pornographic representation.

The second line of argument, in contrast, argues that pornography, notwithstanding its status as a form of representation, does have an impact on people – especially on women in real life – in the sense that the attitude taken toward women in pornography indoctrinates its audiences, or at least some of them, who then translate this attitude into actions that directly harm women. In other words, pornographic texts as representation *still* can have a negative impact on audiences.

In more recent years, Hardy (2008) has argued that the emergence of new kinds of pornography – including gonzo, amateur, sexblog and realcore – provides an occasion for reflection on the divide between pornographic representation and reality. One of the major characteristics of these new pornographies is their attempt to capture 'the real', thus making the distinction between the representational and the real vanish. Drawing on longstanding arguments about distinctions between pornographic representations of sex and real sex, Hardy argues that authenticity is the defining characteristic of pornography as a representational genre. The smaller the gap between pornographic representations of sexuality and real sex, the more attractive the pornographic movie is. As Hardy points out, this can be widely seen in the longstanding practices of pornographers to diminish the gap between pornographic representations of sex and real sex experiences.

From our own fieldwork experiences we happen to agree with Hardy's discovery of the collapse of the distinction between representation and reality in recent pornographies, but it is important to point out, at this juncture, that we disagree with his formulation of so-called pornographic representation and hence reality. In his formulation, since reality and representation become *one and the same*, it follows that the representation of sexual actions in pornography becomes the presentation of sexual actions. What we call pornographic representation is thus tantamount to the reality of sexual actions and hence becomes 'pornographic reality'. Although Hardy cautions that reality, in the light of postmodern thought, cannot be taken for granted, what is implied in his formulation is that there is something out there called 'real sex' or 'reality'. If sex out there is truly real, it follows that real sex is also universal, applicable to all human beings at all times and hence singular in the sense that there is only one reality.

The same is also true for pornographic reality. Of course, its actual contents might vary with different scenarios, but generally ordinary, real people making love in front of the camera for the sake of personal pleasure, rather than of a desire to make money, is what 'the real' refers to.

Our analysis in this book will show that the meaning of 'the real' or 'reality' in pornographic representation is not singular but plural. It is not just about ordinary, real people making love in front of the camera for the sake of personal pleasure. The different emphasis of *tantai* and *kikaku* AV genres leads to different representational strategies in which the former work to authenticate the actress, while the latter the storyline and the female characters in the story. These two representational strategies in turn contribute to two different kinds of 'reality' in Japanese AVs, with the first revolving around the authenticity of the actress – in the sense that she is not performing the female character, but simply acting herself in the movie – and the other emphasizing the authenticity of the story and its female character in such a way that, although the actress may just act out the female character, the story itself is real. More importantly, these two types of pornographic realism are governed by the salvage ideology that makes these pornographic realisms *specific* to Japanese AVs.

As we shall show in this book through the ethnographic case study of the shooting process of a *kikaku* AV, both the *kikaku* director and the actress made a concerted effort to authenticate the female character of the movie and thus the story, through their filming techniques and performing skills respectively, in order to make the story seem realistic. In their effort to authenticate the female character and story, we will show that the relationship between the male director and the female character is hierarchal, in the sense that the former has power over the latter. In other words, gender inequality, as 'anti-pornography' feminists assert, does exist in pornographic representation–something which cannot be ignored. But we shall go further by arguing that this male sexual domination in pornographic representation, while bearing a striking resemblance to the feminist critique of pornography as a violent act against women, is at best an expression of a more fundamental gender politics: the unique configuration of the sexual being of men and women in Japan. We shall demonstrate that the latter is itself *also* defined by the salvage ideology and is made 'real' in the production process, which is also to say that the so-called 'reality' is also discursively constructed. We will argue that the myopic focus of anti-pornography feminists on pornographic representation not only blinds us to the configuration of sexual beings of men and women in a given society, but also hides from us the very arbitrariness of such a configuration, thus making discussion or debate of this fundamental gender hierarchy virtually impossible.

Having said that, we by no means wish to suggest that the consumption process of pornography can be cast aside and ignored. Rather, our conclusion is that many heated topics within pornography research concerning the economic prowess of the industry, the degradation of women, or power politics arguably can only be better made sense of by examining the industry that produces it. Even so, although analysis of the production of pornography can provide an important window on the very nature of pornography, we need to emphasize that production and consumption are not as opposed as they are usually thought to be. As we shall show in this book, both production and consumption are indeed governed by the very same 'cultural code' and, in this sense, they are two sides of the same coin.

Methodological difficulties

In this section, we will describe various difficulties we encountered during this research; and how we successfully overcame them. While so doing, we will spell out our methodology and data-collection methods. The major reason for introducing the latter in this way is because we developed them in response not only to our research questions and the conceptual framework we used to frame our answers to these research questions, but also to the difficulties we encountered in the field.

Smith and Attwood are not alone in calling for research on the pornography industry. In a recent article titled 'Treating It as a Normal Business: Researching the Pornography Industry', Georgina Voss (2012) similarly observes that there is generally a lack of research on the industry in the study of pornography. Basing on her own research experiences, she attributes this lack of research to the stigmatized nature of the pornography industry which serves effectively to prevent scholars, especially in the field of management studies, from embarking upon industry research. She shares her experience of how she was required to attend regular meetings with a research committee which constantly checked on her research method and findings, and how she was warned that 'her work would be subject to higher standards than comparable studies on "proper" industrial sectors such as steel or automobile manufacture' (Voss 2012: 402).

Researchers as institutional being

We happen to agree with Voss's observation that the pornography industry is one of most stigmatized industries, which renders academic studies of pornography marginal, trivial and illegitimate in terms of their examination of the subject, and in turn serves very well to deter researchers from attempting any research on it. But it is important to point out at this juncture that we disagree with the simplicity of such an explanation. As Chun perceptively argues, a researcher is not only a regular social being, but

> in many cases an academic and social agent whose subjectivity is literally subject to (bound by) forces internal and external to the epistemological project that he or she is consciously engaged in. Any account of that subjectivity must incorporate those factors that define the system of practice within which scholarship is situated.
>
> (Chun 2001: 572)

Thus, one might say that a researcher chooses not to conduct research on the pornography industry not only because of potential stigmatization, but most importantly because of the specific institutional environment in which he or she is embedded. But then what kind of environment is that? What kind of system of practice is it that, as researchers, we are engaged in?

Anyone who is familiar with, or works, in the contemporary academic world will have heard of 'outcome-based' learning – an educational theory that bases each part of an educational system around its outcome. Not unlike this, the mode of assessment and evaluation of faculty performance in most academic institutions likewise places a singular focus on outcome, or more specifically on 'productivity'. While good-quality research output is celebrated, when it comes to faculty appraisal, productivity tends to take on the meaning of 'quantity', rather than 'quality' which is often relegated to a secondary consideration (Bosco 2012: 391–2). Deeply embedded in such an institutional environment, perhaps we should not be surprised that faculty members have (un)consciously oriented their research projects towards the goal of publishing more rather than better scholarly outputs.

Unfortunately, there are at least two reasons that render porn studies, especially a study of the pornography 'industry', an unattractive choice under such an evaluation or assessment system within which scholarship is situated. One of the major reasons is the huge effort required and energy invested. As Voss (2012: 401–2) observes, the stigmatized nature of the pornography industry implies that researchers need extra effort to develop trust or rapport with industry people and authenticate themselves, something which again highlights Coopersmith's observation that one major challenge in studying the pornography industry is access to sources (Coopersmith 2006: 2). In our own case, we spent many years and made a huge effort in cultivating relationships with those who became our informants before we were granted access to the field. Between October 2010 and June 2016, we made two to three visits to Tokyo on average each year in order to renew relationships with our industry contacts and conduct ethnographic fieldwork. Fieldwork itself was especially laborious and painstaking in our case as, in addition to conducting intensive interviews with the industry people, we aimed to observe how AV actresses were selected, how adult videos were shot, and regulated (inspected). Our research focused on one major and one medium-sized AV manufacturer in Tokyo. One of the authors also conducted a one-month period of fieldwork in the self-regulatory body. In total, we interviewed 41 industry people between October 2010 and June 2016 – including AV studio owners, casting directors, directors, assistant directors, actresses, actors, cameramen and managers of model companies. We likewise managed to participate in and observe four casting interviews with actresses, and two movie shootings in the summer of 2011, 2012 and 2014. We also attended one autograph campaign of a *tantai* AV actress in Tokyo, talking to the fans there. In addition, we tried to talk informally to as many people in the industry as possible. In this way, we obtained data that cannot be collected from formal interviews with informants.

One of the major difficulties we encountered in our research was the fact that it was difficult, if not totally impossible, for us to make formal requests to AV directors, actresses or actors about the possibility of conducting research on them. This was especially true for the 'Japanese' pornography industry where connections, and introductions by such connections, is of paramount importance. It follows that we needed to cultivate and maintain rapport with our key contacts, as we had to rely on them to find directors and actresses for us to talk to and observe. For example, over the past ten years, we spent much time talking to the former owner of one of the five largest AV makers in Japan. He not only introduced us to many informants working in the industry, but also told us many inside stories about the industry, from which our research benefitted a lot.

More importantly, before our departure for fieldwork, we needed to repeatedly negotiate with our contacts – as well as with actresses, actors and directors introduced by the contacts – concerning various things, including our observation schedule, who could observe, to what extent we could do so, and whether we could videotape during our observations, and so on. As we shall see later on in Chapter 7, our negotiation over observing the *genba* (the film site) was extremely laborious, to the extent that we did not even know right up to the very last minute whether we would be allowed to join the filming or not.

Indeed, the heavy reliance on key contacts might sometimes put us in a difficult, if not dangerous, position, although one should admit that anthropologists or ethnographers are destined to face this kind of risky situation in the field. As Lin (2016) reflects on anthropological fieldwork in a recent paper, the very requirement of anthropologists to temporarily suspend their own value systems and culture-based judgements in order to establish long term, productive relationships with informants with different value systems and judgements has an important implication: for this kind of fieldwork to continue, anthropologists and their informants are required to have a greater understanding of, and respect for, each other and to resolve conflicts through compromise, negotiations, and even confrontation, if necessary. As Lin notes,

> In the process of conversing with interlocutors, we are always in the process of being required to compromise with ourselves and with others, and to swap different subjectivities. Therefore, the anthropologist in the field has no choice but take up the responsibility of accepting his or her interlocutors' specific mode of social life and environment; he or she has to enter that kind of life, and to live with the likes and dislikes, jealousies, conflicts, and power struggles among the interlocutors, as well as to establish mutual trust with them, and accept all the consequences arising, both positive and negative. Equally, the interlocutors in the field have to bear the consequence of the fact that an outsider has come into their lives; the success or failure of the anthropologists in the field in turn forms part of their reputation.... There will be a cost if we have to maintain such a relationship, and most importantly, both parties have to bear the consequences.
>
> (Lin 2016: 93)[3]

Some readers might find Lin's understanding of anthropological fieldwork overstated; yet the kind of compromise, struggle and negotiation he noted was fully reflected in our own case. We came to know a casting director of Japanese adult videos through our network in 2010. He was enthusiastic about meeting us and extremely helpful in introducing us to various people in the AV industry. He was even willing to lend us his written notes and name-cards so that we could reconstruct his relationships with other people in the industry, not to mention share with us a lot of internal information. Although we somehow felt overwhelmed by his excessive enthusiasm, we deeply appreciated his kind help and effort. As he often accompanied us in our ethnographic research, we invited him to be the co-author of our book, not only to show our appreciation, but also to give him the credit he deserved. He was pleased with our invitation and even agreed to attend the launching of our Chinese book on Japanese AVs.

To our great surprise, however, he did not turn up at the book launch as planned. We tried to contact him but he refused to talk to us. As we understood it, this meant essentially that he intended to terminate his relationship with us.

Later, he appeared at another occasion, accusing us of belittling the industry and its people in the book of which he was a co-author. We were stunned, as he had been kept fully informed of its content and we had kept him posted of progress throughout the publication process. Our intention here in invoking this particular incident is not intended as an opportunity to blame our informant, as Lin reminds us that we have to bear whatever consequences the fieldwork brings to us in the field. Nor do we mean to try to explain why he behaved in this way; it would probably require another book to make sense of his actions and reactions, since, like we ourselves he is, after all, a social being embedded firmly within a specific socio-cultural context. We invoke this only to demonstrate how complex and risky this kind of anthropological fieldwork can be; and this in turn explains why not many scholars are willing to conduct research on pornography, and especially the pornography industry.

As can be seen from our own experiences, ethnographic research on the pornography industry not only requires huge effort and time, but also entails potential risk. Despite all this, this kind of research is not matched by a corresponding return, in the sense that things other than output quantity (i.e. effort and time spent and the high-risk nature of the research) may well not be recognized, let alone appreciated, in the appraisal exercise. If time-consuming difficult research only yields similar research outputs as other simpler or easier research and if the study of pornography industry invites stigmatization, then perhaps we can understand why most scholars, who are under great pressure to meet the requirement of 'quantity' in their research, lack the motivation to carry out research on pornography, and in particular on the pornography industry.

This long explanation for the lack of research on the pornography industry is intended not only to highlight the difficulties anthropologists may encounter in the field, but also to argue that such a lack of research on the pornography industry is not due to scholarly and intellectual, but rather to practical and institutional, reasons. But even if we have the courage to take up the challenge, there are still many problems to be overcome. One major problem is the lack of statistical data on the pornography industry, in particular the AV industry in Japan which has never been, and is still not, unionized. No one in the Japanese AV industry, for example, could tell us how many AV actresses are in the business, not to mention statistical data concerning their turnover rate. Neither could anyone in the industry tell us the total number of AV studios/makers in the industry. We therefore were forced to talk to as many informants as possible in order to paint an overall picture of the industry.

Another major problem is that there is no serious academic research on the Japanese AV industry. In other words, we could not find any systematic secondary material on the industry and therefore we consult what Voss (2012) calls 'grey literature': that is, materials 'from mainstream media, including news articles, and documentaries' (Voss 2012: 400). In our case, Japanese AV industry grey literature also included trade magazines published by the industry and the books written in Japanese by former or current AV directors, AV actresses and actors, and journalists who have been employed in, or reporting on, various aspects of the industry. Not unlike its counterpart in the US, the Japanese AV grey literature was uncritical and emotional; its material inaccurate, if not contradictory. We therefore had to spend much time cross checking the accuracy of the data provided with our key informants in the industry – especially when we reconstructed the history of the industry against which the production, circulation, consumption, inspection and globalization of Japanese AVs needed to be understood.

The Japanese grey literature, however, has proved to be very useful in providing contexts to our textual analyses of *tantai* and *kikaku* AVs. In this respect we should emphasize here that, while studying the production of Japanese AVs requires anthropological field research that helps contextualize the whole production process, we do not exclude text analysis of AV films since the latter is an effective way to establish meaningful connections between the narratives of *tantai* and *kikaku* AVs and the salvage ideology underpinning them (as we shall demonstrate in Chapter 4). But such textual analysis has to be contextualized in the history of the AV industry in Japan because context-free text analysis would not enable us to pay necessary attention to the contexts that encompass the text at issue.

Gendered being

Another problem facing us were the intricate, complex ethnographic situations that made a straightforward reading or interpretation impossible. As we will show later on in this book, the nature of ethnographic fieldwork implies that as researchers we were often placed in real situations, such as an 'actual' interview (described in Chapter 6), an 'actual' shooting (Chapter 7) and 'actual' inspection of AVs (Chapter 8). While these real situations allowed us to observe something which could not be otherwise seen, they also served to complicate the situation because what we observed were but tangible situations involving real people who participated in them *for their own reasons*. As we shall see in Chapter 7, the observation of the shooting was both challenging and emotionally disturbing. It was a typical *kikaku* movie that accentuated the authenticity of the story and the female character. The story revolved around how a male director brought about a seemingly infinite number of female orgasms in scenes that were highly sexist, since the actress was depicted as having no sexual agency. As the director and actress *made a concerted effort* to authenticate the story and 'the female character' in the shooting process,[4] we could not but read that she was consenting to the role she had been asked to play and that she was willing to take part in it because it was a job for her.

Yet, the different genders of the two researchers provided a unique chance for discussion and debate, which ultimately took our interpretation to a new level. It is of importance to note that the researchers, in addition to being institutional beings, are also gendered beings. This implies that they had differently 'gendered' readings with regard to the same thing. For instance, the male researcher found the above scene unproblematic in the sense that, since the actress took part in the shooting out of her free will, women's oppression was hardly an issue in this specific shooting. Or, at best, the actress was complicit in sustaining the gender inequality in pornography. Yet, the female researcher found this shooting troubling, even though the actress had consented to it, because the female character was clearly depicted as lacking any sexual agency. It is these different readings of the male and female researchers that led to further discussion and reflection on power politics, and forced us to attend to the configuration of sexual beings of men and women that indeed predicated the gender hierarchy portrayed in the movie.

The opinions of the two researchers were likewise divided when it came to observing the interview setting in Chapter 6. The female researcher, as a woman, found it rather troubling and disturbing that the actress-candidate had to be nude in front of the casting director and others. This thus led to our reflections on the 'weird' norms accepted in the casting process in the AV industry in which the participants are required to temporarily suspend social norms of politeness. In short, it is these 'internal confrontations' between the male and female researchers that help refine our arguments and perspectives in this book.

Organization of chapters

Our story begins with the brief history of Japanese pornography in general and the AV industry in particular. We will show how the two major styles of AV production, *tantai* and *kikaku*, indeed have their genesis in two different pornographic traditions: namely, *binibon* (vinyl wrapped pornographic magazines) and pink films. We will further show how *tantai* and *kikaku* AVs came to represent differential valuations of women's lack of agency and men's status as women's saviour – two major elements of the salvage ideology – with the former emphasizing women's lack of sexual agency and the latter men's skills to sexually save women, and their domination over women in sex. In other words, the consumption of these two major kinds of AVs is governed by the same salvage ideology. We will further show that the two valuations indeed have served as 'cultural code' that specifies the sexual needs of Japanese consumers, as well as the means to satisfy those needs, which in turn makes *tantai* and *kikaku* AVs 'useful' to certain groups of Japanese AV consumers.

Chapter 3 focuses on the seven 'stakeholders': namely, AV makers, model agencies, production companies, postproduction companies, regulatory bodies, dubbing and packaging companies, wholesalers, and rental or retail shops involved in the industry. We will highlight the role of each stakeholder and their power relations in the industry, showing how an adult video is stitched together by these stakeholders. We will also show in detail how the so-called Big Five AV makers formed a cartel that helped prescribe what kinds of adult videos were produced and how they were distributed or circulated in the market; and how they used the self-regulatory 'censorship' organization to exclude rivalries through the case of a newly emerged AV maker, Diamond Image, in order to show that the domination of the Big Five AV makers helped explain why the salvage ideology could linger on in the AV industry in Japan.

Chapter 4 delves into the production system of *tantai* and *kikaku* AVs, exploring how it is also organized by specific valuation of women's lack of sexual agency and men's status of women's saviour of the salvaging ideology respectively. Through a detailed analysis of *tantai* and *kikaku* AVs, we demonstrate how the narrative, number of genres, packaging, market price, circulation/acquisition methods and clientele of *tantai* and *kikaku* AVs varied with the differential valuations of women's lack of sexual agency and men's status as women's saviour.

Chapter 5 looks into one of the questions often asked by non-Japanese observers: why have more and more beautiful young Japanese women been willing to join the AV industry and why has being an AV actress come to be regarded by some as a proper, if not admirable, job since the early 2000s? We will show that the reasons for the increasing supply of young Japanese women for the AV industry lie in the socio-economic context of Japan in the 2000s, which made the career of AV actresses not just one of last resort, but arguably the best choice for making quick money as well as obtaining personal fulfilment.

Chapters 6 and 7 turn to the production processes of Japanese *kikaku* AVs – the dominant category of Japanese AV outputs since the late 1990s. The main thrust of these two chapters is to show how the cultural code discussed in Chapter 2 informs and shapes the actual production processes. In Chapter 6 we provide an ethnographic description of a job interview by which an AV maker recruits its actresses. We then ethnographically demonstrate how selection criteria are informed by the salvage ideology. Chapter 7 presents the shooting of a *kikaku* AV, analysing the complexity of the gender politics involved in the shooting process. Again, we show how the salvage ideology informs gender politics, in the course of which the formation of the sexual being of men and women embedded in the salvage ideology is naturalized as 'reality'.

Chapter 8 explores how Japanese AVs are inspected by self-regulatory bodies established by the industry. We show how these organizations attempted to position themselves as the moral guardians of Japanese society, especially in the wake of the police's crackdown on one major self-regulatory body in 2008, and how such a moral high ground not only has had bearing on the production of *tantai* and *kikaku* AVs, but has also helped sustain the salvage ideology in modern Japanese pornography.

In the Conclusion, we spell out the implications of this book for scholarly approaches to the study of production and consumption, as well for porn studies.

Notes

1 Analytical factor view refers to a view whereby economics was to study the allocation of means in the means-ends chain that constitutes human behaviour, and sociology would concentrate on the 'value factor', i.e. the 'ultimate common ends and the attitudes associated with and underlying them, considered in their various modes of expression of human social life' (quoted in Pratt 2004: 519).

2 The name of the journal is *Porn Studies*.
3 Readers are reminded that all the translations of non-English sources quoted in the text in this book are our own.
4 As we shall explain in Chapter 7, the success of this movie hinges upon the actress's collaboration. This is to say, without her collaboration and cooperation, this movie would not have been possible.

2 From pink film and *binibon* to Japanese AVs

Pornographic culture in postwar Japan

Introduction

This chapter offers an overview of the changing ways in which sex, sexuality and pornography culture have been understood and perceived in postwar Japan, and investigates how these changing sexual scenes, alongside technological advances and business competition, paved the way for the ultimate advent of Japanese AVs in the early 1980s. The first part of this chapter investigates how the policies of the American Occupation Authorities in postwar Japan, on the one hand, provided a chance for the widespread import of the notion of gender/sexual equality into Japan, but, on other hand, gave rise to an extremely flourishing publishing culture whereby the notion of such equality was ultimately reinterpreted, if not distorted, by the industry people and appeared in so-called couple-magazines or pulp (*kasutori*) magazines as pseudo pornographies.

The second part of this chapter turns to explore how these couple-magazines or *kasutori*, arguably the prototype of erotic magazines, contributed to the later pornographic, especially vinyl, cover books (*binibon*) culture. We will also examine how the pink film flourished in the 1960s as another major form of pornography in postwar Japan. Nevertheless, these two pornographic traditions lost their momentum in the late 1970s and we shall examine how this, alongside the technological advantages, gave fresh impetus to the advent of Japanese adult videos in the 1980s. Finally, we will examine how the different traditions and backgrounds of the AV makers gave rise to the two major styles of AV production: a style focusing on a single person at the expense of story (*tantai*) and a style focusing on story (*kikaku*); and how the collapse of the bubble economy has had an impact on the AV industry in Japan that finally led to the emergence of the third major category of Japanese AVs: *kikatan*. *Kikatan* is a truncated Japanese term combining *tantai* and *kikaku*. Coined in the late 1990s, it refers to *kikaku* AV in which the *kikaku* AV actresses are employed as the main and only actress.

A brief history of sexual-cum-pornographic culture in modern Japan

According to our research in Taiwan and Hong Kong (Wong and Yau 2014; Yau and Wong 2009), many women found fault with Japanese adult videos because they appeared to them to be sexist and misogynistic, making women into objects for male sexual pleasure. Some found the scenes, where male characters endlessly stimulated female characters sexually with various props, to be nothing more than an example of male-chauvinism, especially when the women appeared to be resisting amorous advances. Perhaps what was more emotionally disturbing for them was the fact that unwilling female characters would in the end feel grateful to the male characters for the way in which they treated them.

This image of Japanese porn actresses is also found among Western viewers who found scenes of feigned sexual unwillingness awkward and discomforting (Woida 2009: 3). One might infer that the typical male and female characters portrayed in Japanese adult videos amount to what we call a salvage ideology, in that women do not possess any sexual agency and have to rely on men for their sexual pleasure; or, in more concrete terms, that they count on men to help them achieve orgasm, while men have to equip themselves with various sexual skills – no matter how violent these may be – in order to fulfil their 'noble obligation' to sexually salvage their women by bringing them to orgasm (Akagawa 1999: 200). The sexual dependence of women on men, the argument implies, makes women subject to men's sexual domination.

However, we have to stress that the salvage ideology has its genesis in early twentieth century Japan. Following on from the Meiji Restoration, sexual knowledge and ideas – especially Victorian ideas about the importance of monogamy, female chastity, and purity, alongside medical and scientific knowledge about sex – were massively imported from the West by the Meiji government in order to enlighten and civilize the Japanese people as it sought to liberate them from feudal customs and bring them to a level of civilization comparable to that of modern Western nations (Kawamura and Takeda 1995: 235–6; McLelland 2012: 19). Accordingly, new laws pertaining to marriage and family were promulgated and a wide range of state-sanctioned programmes were undertaken to institutionalize the family system and discipline marriage during the Meiji era.[1] Central to all these programmes or laws was the official sanctification of monogamous marriage as the foundation of a modern nation state (Fruhstuck 2003: 75; McLelland 2012: 19). One major consequence of this was what McLelland (2012: 14) has called 'the domestication of sex and narrowing of acceptable sexual practices', as previously loose attitudes towards a wide array of sexual practices that had been practised in rural Japan began to be brought into line with official ideology. Masturbation, prostitution, homosexuality, premarital sex and concubinage – in short, everything outside monogamy – were seen as abnormal, if not totally deviant, and to be done away with (Akagawa 1999: 193–5). Inherent in this was a discourse that validated only marital sex, which arguably provided the seedbed for the new ideology concerning modern marriage and 'love'.

Despite initial confusion about the Western notion of 'love' and its applicability to the Japanese cultural context, this Western notion was gradually incorporated into Japan and found its expression in a newly coined compound of 'romance' (*renai*) (McLelland 2012: 24). This notion underwent a significant change when it conjoined with family – which was endorsed by the Meiji state as the core unit of social stability and progress – to become 'familial love' (*kazoku ai*), a kind of love and fidelity between husband and wife (McLelland 2012: 25). This immense celebration of familial love culminated in the popularization of a tripartite ideal that established a linkage between sex, love and marriage (Ueno 1990: 523). In this trio, love was seen as a prerequisite for sex, and marriage was seen as the only legitimate place for sex. Inherent in this trio were two sexual discourses. The first was that sex was *the* key to marital satisfaction; and second, that sex was only validated insofar as it occurred within marriage – as a fact which further gave cultural significance to notions of chastity, purity and monogamous marriage (Akagawa 1999: 197).

As the trio became culturally ensconced in Japan, the century-long practice of Japanese men visiting prostitutes suddenly became condemnable and came to be read as a form of 'betrayal' to their wives (Tanaka 2014: 104). There were also debates about how to re-embrace married men, who had long had the habit of visiting prostitutes. To this end, a new understanding of 'correct' marital sex gradually emerged in men's elite circles: good marital sex was not just about husbands being sexually satisfied, but also about husbands bringing sexual pleasure to their wives, where achieving orgasm was the major, if not only, indicator of women's sexual pleasure (Tanaka 2014: 104). Implied in this *native* version of 'correct sex' was the idea that women could not attain sexual pleasure through reaching orgasm by *themselves*, but had to rely on their husbands for that. Moreover, since husbands had the obligation to make their wives sexually happy, they should not ignore their sexual pleasure. This in turn meant that men should not visit prostitutes because to do so might steer their attention away from the sexual welfare of their wives. Instead, they should spend more time on learning the necessary skills to fulfil their obligation. Medical advice or sexual manuals on how to sexually please one's wives were thus developed and circulated among the local elites. However, it remained uncertain how much these ideas could spread to the ordinary Japanese people.

Although various sorts of ideas concerning Western sexualities and marriage, especially those concerning gender equality, were imported into Japan during the Meiji era, it was not until the postwar period that they were fully incorporated into Japanese society. Following the country's surrender in 1945, Japan was transformed into a 'democratic' society. Under the guidance of the American Occupation Authorities, the country's constitution, family and marriage law, and inheritance were extensively rewritten to empower women and dismantle old customs or laws that circumscribed their freedom over marriage and childbearing (McLelland 2012: 54–5). Meanwhile, science-based ideas about sexuality and gender relationships were massively imported from the West (McLelland 2012: 54). In addition, the social discourse on sex and marriage circulated in the printed media no longer just focused on the critique of men's betrayal of their wives, but more on gender equality – in particular, on the so-called equality of *sexual happiness* (Tanaka 2014: 106), whereby women had the *right* to enjoy sex in the same way that men did. Here, we can see that the American Occupation Authorities played a very important role in encouraging, if not enforcing, the import of Western notions of gender equality and monogamous marriage into Japan.

This equality in sexual happiness between husbands and wives manifested itself fully in the re-issue in 1946 of *Ars Amatoria: The Art of Love* (*Arusu Amatoria*), a sex manual that had first been published in 1930, but soon banned in pre-war Japan (Kawamura and Takeda 1995: 236). The re-publication of *Ars Amatoria* was an instant hit in early postwar Japan because, for the first time, it graphically portrayed 62 sexual postures and detailed techniques of foreplay, petting, intercourse and post-coital behaviour, teaching men (husbands) how to conduct 'good' sex and bring their women to orgasm (Kawamura and Takeda 1995: 236). However, *Ars Amatoria* was not just a manual of sex techniques but also a highly charged text in moral terms since its author also advised that men should not leave their wives and ignore their sexual happiness by visiting prostitutes. As husbands, men should strive to teach, salvage and help their wives, who were sexually inexperienced and innocent about how to attain sexual happiness, by taking them to orgasm (Tanaka 2014: 106). Interestingly, the sex manual (mis)interpreted women's right to sexual happiness by suggesting that women were sexually inexperienced and innocent *by nature*; and that men were *by obligation* required to salvage their helpless wives.

However, as Tanaka has pointed out (2014: 109), the idea of salvaging women from sexual dissatisfaction to achieve gender equality in sexual happiness, first popularized by the Japanese elites, was further reinterpreted, if not distorted, in the course of time – especially when the idea spread to the general public. This, indeed, had a lot to do with the selective censorship practices of the American Occupation Authorities in postwar Japan. As is well documented by many scholars (Abel 2012; Braw 1991; Hirano 1992; Keene 1984; Molasky 1999; Rubin 1985), although the American Occupation Authorities abolished all forms of censorship and control on freedom of speech, as enshrined by the 1947 Constitution of Japan, various forms of censorship remained a reality in the postwar era – especially in political matters deemed subversive by the American government during its occupation of Japan. In fact, not only did Occupation censorship forbid criticism of the United States or other Allied nations, but the mention of censorship itself was also forbidden. As a result, as Donald Keene observed, for some publishers in Japan

> the Occupation censorship was even more exasperating than Japanese military censorship had been because it insisted that all traces of censorship be concealed. This meant that articles had to be rewritten in full, rather than merely submitting XXs for the offending phrases.
>
> (Keene 1984: 967)

This strict censorship on anything relating to the Allied Forces, however, was in stark contrast with the lax attitude of the same American authorities towards the depiction of sex, eroticism and sexuality in the local media, where it did not intervene in the name of upholding the freedom of expression stipulated in the new Constitution (McLelland 2012: 60–1). This comparatively lax attitude allowed, encouraged even, the flourishing of local printed material, especially eroticized, couple-oriented magazines, in postwar Japan. As we shall demonstrate very shortly, it is in these erotic materials that the original meaning of gender/sexual equality was reinterpreted as they were disseminated to the general public, and in the process contributed to the advent of proto-pornography. In other words, while the American Occupation Authorities encouraged the notion of gender equality in the hope of enfranchising Japanese women, it was also the same Authorities that ultimately made different interpretations of the notion of gender equality in sex possible among the general public.

The lax attitudes of the American Occupation Authorities towards local media were first reflected in the explosion of the so-called *kasutori* – especially couple-oriented magazines – from the late 1940s. '*Kasutori*' (which literally means 'scouring the dregs') was originally a slang term used to refer to the inferior *shōchū* (a distilled liquor made from sweet potatoes, rice or buckwheat) with ill side-effects in postwar years, due to the shortage of alcohol (Matsuzawa 1995: 25). *Kasutori* magazines were thus coined to refer to hundreds of mass-oriented inexpensive magazine titles made of cheap paper published over a three-year period from 1946 to 1949, when paper was in extremely short supply (Matsuzawa 1995: 25; McLelland 2012: 6). As sociologist Yamamoto Akira (1976) has noted, *kasutori* magazines were nothing more than collections of sexual materials. Meanwhile, couple-oriented magazines that focused on eroticism, adult entertainment and the so-called hunting for bizarre (*ryōki*) between couples became extremely popular (Matsuzawa 1995: 25). Some notable examples include *Marital Life* (*Fūfu sekatsu*) and *Friends of Married Couple* (*Fūfu no Tomo*).[2] Most of these couple-oriented pulp magazines carried an extraordinarily large portion of sexual advice and material for couples, culminating in what Akagawa called the 'eroticization of sexual behaviour in marriage' (Akagawa 1999: 198). As we shall see shortly, while these magazines continued to include medical reports as evidence of their status as 'scientific' sex manuals, they gradually moved toward 'pornography' that was mainly produced for, and consumed by, men rather than couples (Hashitsume 1995; Kawamura and Takeda 1995; Tanaka 2014).

From sex manuals to proto-pornographies

Marital Life was one of the most successful magazines focusing on the sex life of married couples in early postwar Japan; its first issue in 1949 had a print run of 90,000 copies (Tanaka 2014: 109). Just like sex manuals in pre-war Japan, *Marital Life* continued to sanctify monogamous marriage and feature graphic explanations and instructions about various sexual postures and methods in the name of upholding marital satisfaction. In the *Afterword* of the first issue, the editor wrote that 'the basic unit of a nation is the family, and the core of family is the couple's relations. The magazine is honoured to be able to contribute to better marital relations in Japan' (Tanaka 2014: 110).

Nevertheless, when compared with the previous sex manuals, articles featured in *Marital Life* did not just focus on professional advice, as Tanaka argues, but carried many pornographic-like sexual stories. The first few pages of the magazine usually included portraits of nude models, followed by highly sensational stories highlighting extramarital affairs or sex between wives and burglars. Thus, even when the magazine officially claimed itself as a sex manual, it was *mainly* intended to be read as pornography. It thus seemed to readers more like softcore pornography, which made use of medical articles to camouflage its actual pornographic nature (Tanaka 2014: 112).

According to Tanaka's analysis, the core element that transformed *Marital Life* into pseudo-pornography among readers was 'men's fantasies of sexual domination' (Tanaka 2014: 116). In previous sex manuals like the *Ars Amatoria*, underpinned by the idea of gender equality in sexual happiness, it was husbands who were responsible for initiating various skills to bring their sexually inexperienced wives to orgasm. All of this, as Tanaka argues, was depicted as the male effort made for the sake of women's sexual pleasure. In *Marital Life*, as well as other couple-oriented magazines, although the salvage framework remained intact, the imperative to salvage women from sexual dissatisfaction was not only about husbands bringing sexual pleasure to wives, but also about the latter actively responding to men's sexual initiations (Tanaka 2014: 115). Women were now required to express how much they, as receivers, enjoyed the foreplay or penetration performed by men. Attention was particularly placed on women's physical reactions: how their bodies gleamed and their bodily parts contracted, how much they sweated, and how sexually ready they were, as a result of men's amorous initiations (Tanaka 2014: 115). Its central focus was, as Tanaka observes, no longer placed on how to bring about female sexual pleasure, but on how much the to-be-sexually-pleasured women enjoyed sex thanks to male stimulation. It is this changing focus that allowed these magazines to be read as a piece of pornography that indulged in the sexual fantasy of bringing sexual pleasure to women (Tanaka 2014: 115). This fantasy is based on a form of male supremacy: men sexually dominate women in the sense that it is *their* skill, not that of others, which brings forth all this (Tanaka 2014: 116). As we see it, the required 'appropriate' responses of women to men's sexual stimulation were to prove the effectiveness of the latter, confirming men's sexual supremacy and thus domination over women. Men then generated their sexual pleasure from this, in the course of which women's right to sexual pleasure was transformed into an obligation to respond to men's sexual stimulation *properly*.

More importantly, this requirement reveals in Japanese culture the *meaningful* connection between men's sexual domination over women and men's sexual pleasure. We learn from anthropologists that human sexual desires and the means to satisfy them are symbolically constituted in a way that is never the only possible one, which is also to say that they are 'stimulation-free'. They cannot be read directly from the properties of men's sexually dominant behaviour, but from the significance attached to them – something that cannot be captured by sense and thus function at the unconscious level. But such significance has to be sensible at the experiential level, which therefore requires the presence of these properties – just as in totemism natural species are required to mark the meaningful relations between human social groups (Lévi-Strauss 1963). Any empirical evidence – especially that supported by science – that 'confirms' men's sexual domination over women can stimulate men's sexual happiness. This is why, by subtly shifting the focus from the male duty to bring sexual pleasure to women to female obligation to show their appropriate responses, *Marital Life* could change from being a sex manual to proto-pornography (Tanaka 2014: 115). It is also why the magazine, despite its proto-pornographic nature, continued to identify itself as a sex manual that sanctified monogamous marriage. As Tanaka (2014: 116) perceptively points out, the dual status of the magazine as pornographic material and sex manual allowed it to hold its moral high ground while at the same time selling well in the commercial market. By presenting itself as a sex manual to salvage sexually inexperienced women, it conferred on the magazine a position that was morally superior or more scientific and thus more 'real' than those that were simply presented as pornographies. On the other hand, its polysemic nature to be read as pornography enabled it to attract a larger readership – evidenced by the fact that *Marital Life* managed to have a monthly print run of 150,000 to 200,000 copies in the second half of the 1940s and the whole of the 1950s (Tanaka 2014: 109).

This kind of subtle change could also be seen in *Friends of Married Couple*, another popular couple-oriented magazine in postwar Japan. For instance, there was a special report, in Issue 2 published in 1949, titled 'The Ten Hormones that Cause Marriage Burnout' (*Fūfu kentaiki no horumonn jūhon*) to help women who suffered marital dissatisfaction. Similarly, 1950 saw the publication of two special topics, titled 'If You Do This, Your Husband Will Fall for You!' (*Kōsureba oto ni aisareru*) and 'Ten Ways for Wives to Hold onto the Heart of their Husbands' (*Oto no kokoro wo toraeteoku tsuma no kokoroe jukkajo*) (Tanaka 2014: 117). In 1952, it had a special issue titled 'Secret Notebook for Brides' (*Hanayome no himitsu techō*). Not unlike *Marital Life*, *Friends of Married Couple* officially positioned itself as a sex manual aiming to advance female sexual pleasure, but its tone and portrayal of stories tended to perpetuate the male sexual fantasy of control (Tanaka 2014: 117).

We can now see how the emphasis on equality in sexual happiness shifted from one where women had the same right as men to enjoy sex, while men *also* had the obligation to bring sexual pleasure to their wives, to one where the focus of male sexual fantasy was on women's obligation to show 'proper' responses to men's sexual stimulations. These responses were expected to satisfy men's fantasy that they were the only source of women's sexual pleasure, and so also implied women's complete lack of sexual agency, which in turn made women sexually dependent on men. In the event, men were able to assert their domination over women and thus their sexual satisfaction because they had become women's saviours. As we shall try to argue in this book, this combination of women's lack of sexual agency and fantasy of male sexual domination, which together form the ideology of salvaging women from sexual dissatisfaction, is one of the basic narratives of modern

Japanese pornography. It is a combination which has continued to characterize most forms of Japanese pornography – in particular adult videos.

The road to Japanese adult videos

It is extremely difficult to define which publication constitutes the first modern erotic/pornographic magazine in Japan. Yet, judging from the criteria of having a nude picture as cover photo and of being printed on high quality paper, Yasuda and Amamiya (2006: 16) say that the first erotic magazine in postwar Japan was *Night of One Million People* (the *100 man nin no yoru*), which was positioned as the 'night', or erotic, version of the well-known literary monthly, *Spring and Autumn Literature* (*Bungei shunjū*) (Handa 1996: 70). Launched in 1956, the *Night of One Million People* may indeed be considered as the pioneer of the current erotic magazines in that it not only depicted sex graphically, but also framed it in a hilarious manner not found in previous *kasutori* or couple-oriented magazines (Handa 1996: 68). The title's commercial success gave fresh impetus to the development of erotic magazines and the next few years saw the publication of two similar erotic titles: *Humour Club* (*Yūmoa kurabu*) and *The Beautiful in the World* (*Sekai no utsukushii*) (Yasuda and Amamiya 2006: 19).

The discussion of erotic magazines in postwar Japan would not be complete without mention of *Average Punch* (*Heibon panchi*), the first erotic material published by a major publisher, Heibonsha, in Japan. Launched in 1964, the first issue caused a huge sensation, because it was the first time in history for a major publisher to carry colourful nude photos of female idols in its magazine. The popularity of the first issue was fully reflected in its print run: 550,000 copies (Yasuda and Amamiya 2006: 20). In view of the tremendous success of *Average Punch*, the publisher released a pocket version, *Average Punch Oh* (*Heibon Panchi Oh*), as a spinoff. Compared with the original title, *Average Punch Oh* seemed more like straight pornography targeted at a male readership. In 1971, the publisher released another pocket sized magazine titled *SM Select* (Shimokawa 1995: 55) which managed to achieve a monthly print run of 150,000 in the 1970s (Yasuda and Amamiya 2006: 20).

The next popular format of erotic magazine was the so-called 'vending machine pornography' (*jihankihon*) that garnered huge popularity in the late 1970s (Sawaki 1995: 123). As convenience stores had not yet become popular, vending machines selling drinks, snacks or instant noodles could be found all over Japan, especially in rural areas (Kawamoto 2011: 78). From the late 1970s until well into the 1980s, vending machines were used in various regions to sell pornographic photo magazines (Kawamoto 2011: 79–80). The seclusion offered by this, at the time unique, circulation method was one of the major reasons why these erotic magazines tended to be more 'sexually graphic and explicit' – a phrase we put in quotation marks because all depictions of fellatio and intercourse were simulated, but supplemented by textual material full of sexual overtones (Natsuhara 1995: 167). In addition, neither semen nor pubic hair was shown. Nevertheless, these magazines were considered during the 1970s to be rather erotic and sexually explicit. Indeed, occasionally customers were able to find illegal hardcore porn being sold in the vending machines. Coupled with the fact that consumers did not need to come into contact with anyone when making their purchases, all of this contributed to the phenomenal success of vending machine pornography in the 1970s. In 1977, for instance, there was a total of 13,000 vending machines selling erotic or pornographic photo magazines in Japan (Kawamoto 2011: 97). Some popular vending machine pornographies were *JAM*, *EVE*, and *Alice Young Girl* (*Arisu Shōjo*) (Kawamoto 2011: 91; Yasuda and Amamiya 2006: 21). However, they gradually disappeared as local governments, together with local parent-teacher associations, began to protest fiercely against the sale of pornographic material through vending machines to minors, especially in residential neighbourhoods (Kawamoto 2011: 120).

Binibon

Although vending machine pornography disappeared, it somehow survived in another pornographic format: vinyl cover books. Vinyl cover books were a kind of softcore pornographic magazine published in the mid-1970s and 1980s. Sold under sealed plastic cover, vinyl cover books typically portrayed female models in transparent panties with their legs wide open (Natsuhara 1995: 167). The pubic hair, partially visible and partially hidden under the transparent panties, was vinyl cover books' selling point and its main characteristic was its depiction of genital areas including pubic hair which, in later publications in the 1980s, could be clearly seen (Shōwa Seishiryō Kenkyū Kai and Saitō 2014: 6). Japanese obscenity (*waisetsu*) laws prohibited the depiction of the whole genitalia including pubic hair and it was only in the mid-1990s that the depiction of pubic hair was deregulated. When we recall that the vending machine pornography never portrayed pubic hair, we can imagine how sensational it was when vinyl cover books for the first time offered something prohibited in the 1980s.

Some journalists, however, have argued that vinyl cover books were indeed the successor to vending machine pornography because the way that both portrayed and represented sex was very similar (Natsuhara 1995: 167). First of all, many vinyl cover book makers were indeed former vending machine pornography publishers (Kawamoto 2011: 120), implying that they naturally produced vinyl cover books in the way they had done with vending machine pornography. Second, both vinyl cover books and vending machine pornography offered pornographic content in such a way that consumers had to make their buying decisions without seeing the content of the magazines first (Natsuhara 1995: 167). Finally, and most importantly, the girl culture first promoted in vending machine pornography found its full development in the so-called 'cute' ('*kawaii*') vinyl cover book idols.

Despite the fact that most vinyl cover book actresses in the early years were middle-aged women, young amateur girls soon took over the scene in the mid-1970s (Shōwa Seishiryō Kenkyū Kai and Saitō 2014: 6). Most of these actresses were ordinary girls scouted directly by cameramen or professional scouts and hired to perform as models in vinyl cover books. As an actress managed to garner popularity, she would soon be hired by other vinyl cover book makers, and her frequent exposure in turn made her even more popular among audiences. This gradually contributed to the emergence of 'vinyl cover book idols' (Shōwa Seishiryō Kenkyū Kai and Saitō 2014: 34) – a term implying that they were not just performers in *binibon*, they were people to be remembered by name, admired, adored and worshipped. Some famous examples of vinyl cover book idols in the 1980s were Taguchi Yukari, Ogawa Eiko and Nakamura Emi (Shōwa Seishiryō Kenkyū Kai and Saitō 2014: 33–4). Interestingly, most of these vinyl cover book idols appeared to be the typical girls-next-door who were young, pure, innocent, and most importantly cute. Ogawa Eiko, for example, caused a huge sensation when she debuted in the 1980s as she was a beautiful young girl (*bishōjo*) who looked like Yakushimaru Hiroko, a famous idol of the 1970s and 1980s (Shōwa Seishiryō Kenkyū Kai and Saitō 2014: 34). Another notable example is Nakamura Emi, who became famous for her baby face and Lolita body figure, as well as her always glorious pubic area, which allowed her to garner huge popularity among lolita complex (*rorikon*) readers (Shōwa Seishiryō Kenkyū Kai and Saitō 2014: 35). But why?

In part this had to do with the stereotypical image of Japanese pop idols. As Aoyagi (1999: 96) has argued, cuteness is the major characteristic of Japanese pop idols who 'encompass pretty looks, heart-warming verbal expressions, and singing, dancing, acting, and speaking in a sweet, meek, and adorable way' (Aoyagi 1999: 96). All these characteristics in turn explain why Japanese idols are often portrayed as the girl-next-door, cute, innocent, pure and meek (Aoyagi 1999: 7; Hoover 2011: 202; Kirsch 2014).

Another major reason is that the image of a girl-next-door who is young, pure and innocent has a strong connotation of being sexually inexperienced, a fact which further points to one legendary element of the salvage ideology mentioned above: women's lack of sexual agency. Implicated in this legendary element is women's sexual dependence on men, as only the latter can bring sexual pleasure to the former. Thus men's sexual domination over women is further reinforced – another major element of the salvage ideology. We can see that the referent of 'sexually inexperienced women' has evolved from women/wives in the *kasutori* magazines era to pure, innocent and young girls during the vinyl cover book period. Such an evolution shows how men's desire for sexual domination over women became more intensified during the vinyl cover book period in that the girls-next-door are supposed to be even less sexually experienced than women/wives.

Another major characteristic of vinyl cover books is that its narrative proceeded around the idol whom it functioned to authenticate the idol as an innocent and cute girl-next-door by means of a series of discursive strategies *as if* the girl and the character portrayed in the narrative were one and the same.

As we shall go on to show, the specific portrayal of women and the authentication of the idol arguably set the stage for the single person style of beautiful young girl (*tantai bishōjo*) AVs, one of the two major product categories of Japanese adult videos.

Pink film (pinku eiga)

Amid the phenomenal success of vinyl cover books, another major pornographic medium, pink films (*pinku eiga*), took shape in Japan from the 1960s when the precipitous decline in cinema attendance that accompanied the proliferation of television further threatened the already questionable future of cinemas in Japan. In an attempt to lure viewers back and stay afloat, film studios, especially small ones, offered an innovative genre: a low-budget kind of softcore pornography that displayed naked torsos and buttocks, and called 'pink film' (Alexander 2003: 156–7; Nikaidō 2014: 11). As Weisser and Weisser (1998: 20) remind us, it is important not to confuse pink film with hardcore pornography, for it portrayed nudity that was 'limited to breasts, leg and backside, but no full frontal nudity and no genitalia shots'. Ōkura Mitsugi, the president of Shin Tōhō and later Ōkura Eiga (Ōkura Pictures), was hailed as the pioneer of this low-budget Japanese pink film (Macias 2001: 84, 173). Upon founding his own company, he released *Flesh Market* (*Nikutai no ichiba*) [1961], which was considered to kick-start the new genre (Domenig 2014: 19–20). Our research with Ōkura Pictures[3] shows that most pink films cover a wide array of themes, are about 75 minutes long, and were almost exclusively shot on 35 mm film until the early 2000s by professional or semi-professional cast and crew. Recently, film-makers have increasingly used digital movie cameras while continuing to emphasize classical film-making techniques. Apart from Ōkura Pictures, some other influential independent pink film studios in the 1960s include Wakamitsu, Shintōhō Eiga, Million Film, Kantō (Weisser and Weisser 1998: 20). While the budget of a pink film was fairly low when compared with that of regular films, its 'erotic' gimmick managed to garner huge interest among Japanese audiences in the 1960s (Nikaidō 2014: 11).

Significantly, pink films' philosophy seems to be heavily coloured by the salvage ideology. In his autobiography, for instance, Ōkura Mitsugi detailed how deeply influenced he was by the Kinsey Report, and how disappointed he was by the fact that many Japanese women were deprived of the chance of experiencing sexual pleasure, not to mention orgasm (quoted in Fujiki and Matsui 1995: 63). Enlightened by Kinsey's discovery, he thus saw pink film as having a mission to enlighten Japanese men with better sexual skills and to help them salvage women from their sexual dissatisfaction (quoted in Fujiki and Matsui 1995: 63). As Ōkura Mitsugi explained,

> The all-mighty God is very fair. He gives women burden and pain, but He also grants women the happiness of spiritual love and bodily good fortune, which are several times more than those of men. However, a lot of women in the world cannot taste such spiritual happiness and bodily pleasure because of the ignorance of men. As a result, only men can enjoy all of this happiness.... In this world, there are many women who are over thirty and the mother of two or three children, but who have still never experienced orgasm. As I have learned from the Kinsey Report, the majority of women

in the world, due to the ignorance of men, have never experienced the happiness of orgasm in the whole of their lives, although some of them might have an inkling of that joy. They suffer from this misfortune until the very end of their lives.... Based on this consideration, I produce movies that enlighten men in sex to salvage women. Like the Christian God, I am determined to save 2.7 billion women of the world population; but unlike the Christian God, I only want to save women, not men....

(Ōkura 1998: 212–13)

The emphasis of Ōkura's pink films, therefore, was on men's status as women's saviours. As such, his argument went, they should equip themselves with the necessary and effective sexual skills by watching pink films. Again implicated in men's status as women's saviours was the latter's lack of sexual agency. In other words, the logic of pink films is the same as that of those popular couple-oriented magazines discussed above.

It goes without saying that the emphasis of pink films – especially those by Ōkura – and that of vinyl cover books are in fact two sides of the same coin. They reciprocally imply, mutually constitute, and reinforce each other, as Ōkura's pink films emphasize men's status as women's saviours, implying women's lack of sexual agency, and vinyl cover books stress women's lack of sexual agency suggesting men's status as women's saviours. Together they further strengthened the salvage ideology, of which they are two major elements. Of course, we are not going to argue that all pink films are characterized by such a 'noble' mission; it nonetheless shows that the salvage ideology did somehow find its expression in modern Japanese pornography for which it has continually set the standard.

Pink films, however, differed from vinyl cover books in that they emphasized the film's storyline at the expense of the idol, while the latter focused on the idol rather than the story. The former worked hard to authenticate the story and the female character of the story, while vinyl cover books struggled to identify the idol and the part she played as one and the same.

Because pink films shocked the audiences with 'a lowbrow mix of scares and sexploitation' (Macias 2001: 84), this genre not only lured back lost audiences to the cinema, but also attracted new audiences who considered it an interesting experience to watch pornography on the big screen. To capitalize on the pink film, many regular theatres, which had not traditionally screened pornographic movies, switched to showing pink films. This led to the explosion of the so-called 'pink film theatre' (*pinku eiga gekijō*) all over Japan, where only pink films were screened.

Roman poruno *(romantic pornography)*

As mentioned above, pink films were by and large produced by small or independent film studios. The early 1970s, however, saw a major change. Now losing their audiences to television, Japan's major film studios were also struggling for survival (Macias 2001: 168). Toei was the first to tap into this lucrative new audience and entered the sexploitation market in 1971. In films like his *Eroticgrotesque* series and *Joys of Torture* series of the late 1960s, director Teruo Ishii provided a model for Toei's sexploitation ventures by 'establishing a queasy mix of comedy and torture' (Macias 2001: 189). Producer Kanji Amao even created a set of series – sensational line (*shigeki rosen*), abnormal line (*ijōseiai rosen*) and shameless line (*harenchi rosen*) – which today are collectively referred to as Toei's 'Pinky Violence' (Macias 2001: 189). Most of Toei's films in this style used eroticism in conjunction with violent and action-filled stories (Macias 2001: 189), often depicting strong women exacting violent revenge for past injustices.

In 1971, Nikkatsu Movie Production Company (hereafter Nikkatsu), one of the oldest and most prestigious film studios in Japan, launched a variant of pink movie known as romantic pornography (*roman poruno*) to attract more viewers and stay afloat in view of the company's financial problems (Fujiki 2009: 25; Hunter 1998: 25). As a big enterprise, Nikkatsu was not only willing, but also able, to invest big money into romantic pornography projects. It also gave its romantic pornography directors, who were often radicals using the sex medium as a weapon for dissent, a great deal of artistic freedom in creating their films (Bornoff 1991: 602). Romantic pornography thus quickly diversified to fill all genres, including rape, incest, rope bondage, sadomasochism, violence, perversion, death and alternative lifestyles ranging from time-honoured courtesans to trendy wife swappers (Macias 2001: 187; Sato 1982: 229–34). Due to their high quality and large budgets, romantic pornography proved a great success, not only saving Nikkatsu from bankruptcy, but also taking the pink movie market away from the smaller, independent studios by the mid-1980s (Hunter 1998: 25).

Adult videos (AVs)

Meanwhile, Nikkatsu launched an independent production team specializing in the production of pornographic 'video', in the hope of further capitalizing on the romantic pornography boom (Fujiki 2009: 30). Many other pink film-makers followed suit. These pornographic videos were basically the video version of *roman poruno* and were largely consumed as a pastime in love hotel rooms across Japan (Fujiki 2009: 29). In January 1972, one of the pornographic videos produced by Nikkatsu was prosecuted by the police for violating the obscenity law in Tokushima prefecture, on the island of Shikoku (Fujiki 2009: 33). The original romantic pornography version was subject to the same prosecution, too, and this forced film directors to consult the Film Classification and Rating Committee (Eiga Rinri Iinkai, a.k.a. Eirin). As a result, a self-regulatory agency for adult videos modelled on Eirin was founded in 1972, and five years later was named the Nihon Ethics Video Association (the Nippon Bideo Rinri Kyōkai, a.k.a. Biderin) (Fujiki 2009: 35–6), becoming the dominant regulatory agency for adult videos during the 1980s and 1990s. While these pornographic videos were mainly products of Nikkatsu's intention to explore a new market for their romantic pornography, they were arguably the 'prototype' of Japanese adult videos, although they had not yet been so called (Fujiki 2009: 23). Nevertheless, Japanese pornographic videos were still technically unaffordable because videocassette recorders (VCRs) and videotapes were still prohibitively expensive in the late 1970s.

Pornographic 'videos' as products only became popular in Japan in the early 1980s when ownership of VCRs became widespread in Japan. This had a lot to do with the competition between SONY and JVC, the two electronic giants. In the mid-1970s, SONY and JVC released their respective formats of family-use video recorders, namely Betamax and VHS, and soon entered into the 'videotape format war' (Cusumano et al. 1992: 75). To simplify the story enormously, JVC from the beginning chose to license its VHS technology to any manufacturer who was interested. The fierce competitions for sales among the manufacturers in turn resulted in lower prices for consumers. In contrast, Sony was initially the only manufacturer of Betamax and so was not pressured to reduce prices. Only in the early 1980s did it decide to license Betamax to other manufacturers, such as Toshiba and Sanyo. But, by the time SONY made these changes to its strategy, VHS had come to dominate the market, with Betamax relegated to a niche position. Thus, JVC won the war and VHS emerged as the pre-eminent videotape format (Cusumano et al. 1992: 86).

As we can see, one of the major consequences of the 'videotape format war' was that the price of a videocassette recorder (VHS format) dropped significantly and VCRs were being purchased in large numbers by ordinary Japanese families, so that by the late 1970s VCRs had acquired their status as a standard consumer commodity, thereby paving the way for an explosion in Japanese adult videos. In addition to producing a new media form, the popularization of family-use VCR also gave rise to a new mode of pornography consumption (Inoue 2002: 16). This mode offered cheaper price, privacy and ease of mind that were otherwise impossible in public cinemas (Tōra 1998a: 28). In addition, many Japanese families by that time had at least two TV sets and VCRs, making domestic viewing of pornography on videotape more popular than viewing it in public theatres.

Meanwhile, pornographic videos could now be easily shot as a result of the availability of relatively cheap video systems (Fujiki 2009: 41).[4] In the early 1970s, video systems were prohibitively expensive – being sold at an average price of ¥1 million (US$8,800), irrespective of their manufacturer (Fujiki 2009: 56). Video systems only became available to ordinary people when JVC and Hitachi offered them at roughly half the price (Fujiki 2009: 56). *The Women of Binibon: peeping into the secrets* (*Binibon no onna: hiou nozoki*) [1981] and *The White Book of OL Buttcrack: the matured secret place* (*Wareme hakusho: juku shita hien*) [1981] are often hailed as the first Japanese adult videos in history because they were shot on video (Fujiki 2009: 16). These formally raised the curtain on Japanese adult videos. As early as 1982, AVs had attained an approximately equal share with pink films in the adult entertainment market (Weisser and Weisser 1998: 29). In 1983, the estimated sales of the entire AV industry were about ¥1 trillion (US$8.8 billion) (Suitsu 1998a: 3). More significantly, the term 'adult video' (*adaruto bideo*), or 'AV' (*ēbui*), entered the Japanese language as an idiom for sexually explicit materials and was widely acknowledged in the media (Suitsu 1998a: 3; Yau 2001: 16). At the same time, the promulgation of the new adult entertainment law (or *fūzoku*)[5] in 1995, which had stringent regulations regarding operation of adult entertainment businesses, instigated many sex workers to join the AV industry (Suitsu 1998a: 4). By the mid-1980s, AVs had almost replaced the pink film and the number of AV makers has risen to over 50 (Suitsu 1998a: 3). Nikkatsu ceased producing *roman poruno* and finally closed in 1988, after which adult videos became the dominant form of pornography in modern Japan (Alexander 2003: 159).

The two traditions of AV production: *binibon*-style and pink film-style

In the early 1980s, the production of the adult video industry was characterized by two different styles: the vinyl cover book tradition and the pink film tradition. The vinyl cover book tradition that typically depicted young, innocent beautiful girls had a profound impact on the way these former vinyl cover book publishers produced their AVs when they crossed over to the new field. Burdened with this tradition, they all tended to produce adult videos featuring young, sweet and pure women, laying the foundation for the formation of an AV style known as *tantai*. In particular, the vinyl cover book idol boom in the late 1970s gave fresh impetus to the *bishōjo* AVs, for without the 'idolization and *bishōjoization* of the *binibon* models, there would not have been AV idols or *bishōjo* AVs now' (Fujiki 2009: 87). Given that the core essence of Japanese idols was cuteness, so that *binibon* idols were almost exclusively the girl-next-door type whose images were sweet, innocent and cute, these were adopted precisely as the qualities of *tantai bishōjo* AV.

Another major characteristic of *tantai bishōjo* AVs is that they focus on sex scenes featuring young beautiful actresses at the expense of the story, although most of the sex scenes in the 1980s were simulated (Nakamura 2012: 27). More importantly, the production of *tantai bishōjo* has tended to use images or video to link different scenes – a technique which can be seen as a discursive strategy to authenticate the actress, in order to convince the audience that the actress outside the movie and the character inside the AV are one and the same.

We can now see that the characteristics of *tantai bishōjo* in fact linger on from the vinyl cover book tradition which has proved to be the model for the production of *tantai* AVs in the following decades (Tōra 1998b: 124).[6] It goes without saying that the assumption of women's lack of sexual agency emphasized by *binibon* was also carried forward to the production of *tantai bishōjo*.

On the other hand, when declining theatre revenues steered pink film studios towards producing adult videos, they substantially brought in the traditions of pink film, thereby setting the stage for what is known as *kikaku* AV. Legacies of pink film can be seen in the latter's style, use of actress, and content. For instance, Nippon Video Image's pioneering *Women of Binibon: peeping into the secrets* [1981] and *The White Book of OL Buttcrack: the matured secret place* [1981] were indeed shortened version of pink films (Natsuhara 1995: 175). Others simply followed the pink film's style and way of filming (Yoshioka 1999: 12). For instance, some AV directors retained the filming methodology of pink films (i.e. using shots as the basic unit to form the movie story) while shooting AVs; and the only difference was that a video camera, rather than still camera, was used (Fujiki 2009: 23). For instance, the *Big Joy on Tuesday* (*Kayōbi no kyōraku*) and *Wild Party* (*Wairudo Pāti*) were adult videos shot on 35mm film (Fujiki 2009: 31–3). Still others featured actresses from pink films (Suitsu 1998a: 2). For example, *The Shooting of Real Sex Act of Aizome Kyōko: libidinous rabbit* (*Aizome Kyōko no honban namadori yinyoku no usagi*) was hailed as the first adult video not only shot on camcorder, but also as the shortened version of a pink film story (Fujiki 2009: 45). In other words, it was considered as an original AV. In addition, this video hired Aizome Kyokō, the former pink film actress, as its AV actress.

More crucially, the contents of *kikaku* AVs were heavily influenced by pink films – especially by the above-mentioned Toei Pinky Violence. As these lines were about 'wild-sex, and sometimes sex-and-action', they might seem 'even a few degrees more manic and twisted than Nikkatsu's *roman porno* films' (Macias 2001: 189). Current popular themes in *kikaku* AVs – such as rape, S&M, bondage, torture, incest, violence, scatology and female aggressors – seem to linger on from the Toei Pinky Violence as well as *roman poruno* which has used sex as a vehicle to explore 'the struggle between what one thinks and what one physically demands' (Sato 1982: 233). As we shall show in Chapter 4, these themes belong to *kikaku* specializing in storyline or content (Suitsu 1998a: 4). By the early 1990s, *kikaku* AVs had exerted great influence on the AV market since makers specializing in *kikaku* already dominated it (Kajii 1998: 140–1).

Perhaps what is most significant and interesting is the obvious lingering on of the element of men's status as women's saviours from the famous salvage ideology that first took shape in the postwar couple magazines and that was retained in the genre of pink film. The earliest example of this legacy can be found in the adult videos produced and directed by Yoyogi Tadashi, the renowned pink film director who later crossed over into the adult video field. After his first adult video featuring Aizome Kyokō, he came fully into his own as a new master of documentary series (Kurata 1998: 48). His documentaries did not feature *tantai* beautiful actresses; nor did they play on fictional stories (Kurata 1998: 48). Rather, what Yoyogi endeavoured to portray was 'the bare, unadorned sexual desire of women', and 'the fiery, powerful sexual tension of men' (Kurata 1998: 48). The female characters in his documentaries were typically ordinary women (so-called 'amateurs') who, due to traumas or past experiences, failed to find pleasure in sex or experience orgasm: in short, they all suffered from some sort of sexual dysfunctions. The movies were then posed as therapies aiming to salvage them from the past and once again enjoy the pleasure of sex. The emphasis of Yoyogi's AVs, however, was placed on the various means he utilized to save those problematic women, by resorting to hypnotism, or to alternative methods such as inciting their jealousy, in helping these women regain sexual pleasure (Kurata 1998: 50) – a legacy of Ōkura's pink films, as mentioned above. Some notable examples include *The Ecstasy of Psycho Hypnosis* (*Saiko saimin ekusutashī*) [1985], *The Strict Secrecy of Sensual Technique* (*Seikan gokuhi tekunikku*) [1983] and *Channelling Fuck* (*Chaneringu fuck*) [1990] (Kurata 1998: 49; Tanaka 2007: 111, 113, 121).

The excessive use of men's status as women's saviours in the salvage ideology in *kikaku* AVs culminates in a recent genre called acme ('*akume*', literally a peak, here referring to female orgasm). As we shall elaborate in Chapter 7, acme typically features the use of alternative, if not sadistic, methods – notably the use of electric drill(s) alongside vibrators to bring about endless orgasm for the female characters. The philosophical underpinnings of this genre are that women by nature are prone to sexual dysfunctions, and it is the responsibility of men to save their women sexually. The essence of the video is thus to salvage women from sexual dysfunctions through the male use of sadistic means and as these sadistic means are employed for the sake of female sexual pleasure, they should be forgiven, celebrated even. In other words, the male sadist's act, not unlike the salvage ideology circulated in the couple magazines in the postwar years, is again posed as a form of 'noble obligation'. Again, not unlike Yoyogi's AVs, the means was the focus of acme AVs and the crucial point of *kikaku* AV is the authenticity of the story and the female character which functions to convince a male audience that men actually can save sexually problematic women, and therefore that they deserve to sexually dominate them. Here, one can see how the salvage ideology that first took shape in postwar Japan lingers on in the mindset of contemporary pornography.

The oscillation between **tantai** *and* **kikaku** *AVs*

It is no exaggeration to say that the salvage ideology is the single most important element of Japanese AVs, which can be seen by the fact that the history of Japanese AVs over the last four decades has been characterized by an oscillation between *tantai* and *kikaku* styles. The former was the main AV genre from the very start and the 1980s saw the production of a large number of commercially successful *tantai* AVs, together with their legendary idols in Japan. Following the collapse of the Japan asset price bubble, the Japanese economy as a whole entered a deep recession from the early 1990s (Okina *et al.* 2001) – something which affected the AV industry in particular, although the recession damaged *tantai* more than it did *kikaku* AV makers because of their higher production costs. At the same time, the limited number of *tantai* AV genres could not satisfy the ever-diversifying taste of AV consumers.

In 1992, the sale of AVs, especially *tantai* AV sales, dropped across the board (Suitsu 1998a: 7). Almost half the AV rental shops went out of business and many manufacturers went bankrupt or halted release of new films (Suitsu 1998a: 7; Yasuda and Amamiya 2006: 97). In the wake of this significant drop in sales, many specialist *tantai* AV makers turned to producing *kikaku* AV to try their luck (Suitsu 1998a: 7). *Kikaku* AVs appeared as a viable alternative to these AV makers because of their comparatively low production cost. By emphasizing context and storyline at the expense of the actress, manufacturers could save a large sum of money by hiring less famous or even unknown actresses (Suitsu 1998a: 2). At the same time, the *kikaku* AV market experienced another boom as many young directors joined *kikaku* production in an attempt to counter-attack the hegemony of major AV studios that by and large specialized in *tantai* AV production (Yasuda and Amamiya 2006: 97). A notable example of this trend is to be found in a Japanese adult video director, producer and entrepreneur, Company Matsuo, who rose to prominence after directing a series titled *Please Be My AV Girl!* (*Watashi wo joyu ni shite kudasai*) for V&R Planning in 1991.[7] This series portrayed how Matsuo himself met a girl through telephone club sex and filmed their encounter from the first-person perspective. Matsuo is credited with popularizing the amateur style to such an extent that he has been called 'the master of shooting pornography with amateurs' (Yasuda and Amamiya 2006: 97).

By the mid-1990s, the market share of *tantai* AVs had dropped to 30 per cent, while the remaining 70 per cent had been taken up by *kikaku* AVs (Azuma 1998: 97). Despite these initial successes, *kikaku* AVs gradually lost momentum in the second half of the 1990s, not only because many of these videos were extremely similar in content, but also because too many *kikaku* AVs were produced, thus saturating the market (Suitsu 1998a: 8). For instance, more than 500 new titles were sent to Biderin for inspection in May 1996 alone – a stunning figure when compared with the monthly average number of 250 titles inspected by Biderin in 1989 (the year before the 'bubble' burst) (Sonoda and Dai 2016: 110). This sharp increase in monthly new AV release from the mid-1990s, as Suitsu observes, can be seen as a strategy deployed by AV makers to make up for declining sales of each of their AV titles (Suitsu 1998a: 8) – a strategy which is, indeed, typical of the film industry as a whole, as well as of other music, publishing, and other 'creative industries' (Caves 2002; Thompson 2005, 2010). As the sale of each AV title dropped significantly, makers merely released more titles in the hope of covering the per title losses by means of a best seller.

The late 1990s also witnessed a new phenomenon where more and more beautiful young women were more than willing to take part in the AV industry, especially in *kikaku* AVs (Nakamura 2012: 14). This was stunning as it was almost an unspoken rule that only women with an unfortunate past history would choose to join the AV industry in Japan. However, as we shall see in Chapter 5, being an AV actress has gradually become a proper, if not admirable, choice among many young, decent Japanese women and this has a lot to do with the collapse of Japan's bubble economy which led to substantially reduced job opportunities for young people in Japan.

This change quickly caught the attention of Japanese male AV audiences. Various fan blogs and other social media forums were flooded with discussions about these *kikaku* actresses – something that had never happened before. One major reason accounting for this change has been the extremely high exposure of *kikaku* actresses when compared with that of their *tantai* counterparts. As we shall see in Chapter 4, *tantai* actresses often enter into exclusive contracts with their respective AV studios, which prevent their appearing in other studios' productions for a given period; even for their contracted studio, they have to follow an unspoken convention or norm that they cannot take part in more than one movie a month. By contrast, *kikaku* actresses are not bound by any contract and are thus free to take part in as many movies as they wish. For instance, Asakawa Ran, one of the most notable *kikaku* actresses, appeared in 516 movies in two years from 2002 to 2003.[8] Her model agency even submitted an application to the Guinness Book of World Records for making 212 adult videos in the year 2002.[9] In 2003, she outdid her previous record by appearing in 304 videos, but announced her retirement at the end of the year.[10] On average, she thus appeared in 21 movies a month for two years. This high exposure, along with her good looks and fine figure, made her one of the most popular AV actresses in 2003 – a status and popularity that were no lower than those of Oikawa Nao, a prominent *tantai* actress in the early 2000s.[11]

The popularity of these *kikaku* actresses among audiences in turn provided a fresh impetus for AV makers to hire *kikaku* actresses to start as the main character in AVs and other related adult entertainment jobs (Nakamura 2012: 132). A case in point is Nagase Ai (Nakamura 2012: 133) who debuted as a *kikaku* actress in 1998 and soon became hugely popular and famous among Japanese male audiences. Starting from 1999, a number of Japanese AV studios began hiring her to star as the main character in AVs while not signing her as an 'exclusive' actress – the first time a *kikaku* actress was hired as the main character of a Japanese AV. Other *kikaku* actresses – including Asakawa Ran and Tsutsumi Sayaka, Tachibata Niko and Akane Hotaru – had very similar offers from various AV studios (Nakamura 2012: 133). In other words, AV makers began to employ *kikaku* AV actresses who gradually gain popularity and hence come to be recognized as idols by male audiences due to their high exposure in a wide array of AV productions over a short period of time as the main and only actress in their *kikaku* AVs. This is how a new category of AVs, *kikatan* (a truncated term of *tantai* and *kikaku*, referring to the *kikaku* actresses who, not unlike *tantai* actresses, are featured as the main actresses in the movie)[12] movies, began to emerge in the early 2000s.

The new category proved very successful and *kikatan* AV actresses were also very well received and admired by audiences. In 2014, *kikatan* actress Uehara Ai was even awarded the DMM Best Actress Prize[13] of the year and, in the following year, another *kikatan* actress, Minato Riku, was awarded the same prize. But it is of interest to ask why this new kind of AV is called *kikatan* (with *tantai* subsumed under *kikaku*), rather than *tanki* (with *kikaku* subsumed under *tantai*). As will be mentioned in Chapter 4, *tantai* actresses earn the most, whereas the *kikaku* actresses earn the least per movie. *Kikatan* is after all a subdivision of *kikaku* and hence the salary for *kikatan* actress is calculated in the same way as that of *kikaku* actress. Conversely, if it were *tanki*, the actress in question would be considered as a *tantai* actress and hence paid per film with a large sum of remuneration. Thus, from the vantage of the AV makers, *kikatan* was certainly a better option which could on the one hand attract more consumers, and on the other hand be posited as a justification for paying the actresses in question less. Therefore, the emergence of the *kikatan* AVs is arguably a manipulation of categorical creation by the industry people to obtain higher-quality young AV actresses at a low cost.

Conclusion

We have outlined the history of postwar pornography in Japan, tracing how the lax attitude of the American Occupied Authorities toward erotic media allowed, if not encouraged, the advent of *kasutori* magazines in early postwar Japan, before they were replaced by *jihankihon* and *binibon* in the 1970s. We have then demonstrated how *binibon* constituted a tradition that had great impact on the production of *tantai bishōjo* AVs. At the same time, we have also shown how pink films (especially those by Ōkura Mitsugi) formed another tradition that influenced the production of *kikaku* AVs. As a result, *tantai* AVs tended to focus on the portrayal of AV actresses as the girl-next-door who is supposed to be young, pure, innocent and sexually inexperienced, while *kikaku* AVs inclined to emphasize the story rather than the beauty of its actresses.

As we will show in the following chapters, the different emphasis of *tantai* and *kikaku* AVs further leads to different discursive strategies in that the former work to authenticate the actress, while the latter the story and the female characters in that story. This in itself points to different kinds of realism. The authentication of the actress in *tantai* AVs is to emphasize that the actress is not performing the female character in the movie, but herself in reality – as someone who is young, pure, innocent and sexually inexperienced – in order to convey a message that the actress's lack of sexual agency is not staged but real. It is this realism surrounding lack of sexual agency that turns on a certain group of AV consumers. The authentication of the story and the female character in *kikaku* AVs is to convey the message that, although the actresses may just act out a particular female role, the story itself is real. The major job of *kikaku* AV actresses, therefore, is to authenticate the female character of the movie and thus the story by their performing skills in order to present the realism of a story which further sexually stimulates another male audience group.

We have to stress that *tantai bishōjo* and *kikaku* AVs are not just two major categories of contemporary AVs; they also represent a differential evaluation of women's lack of agency and men's status as women's saviors – two major elements of the so-called salvage ideology – with the former emphasizing women's lack of sexual agency and the latter men's skill at saving women, together with their sexual domination over them. That is to say, both *tantai bishōjo* AVs and *kikaku* AVs are underlined by the same salvage ideology, although each of them emphasizes its different elements. Women's lack of sexual agency and men's sexual domination over women in the salvage ideology have served what Sahlins (1976a) has called a 'cultural code' that specifies the sexual needs of Japanese consumers, as well as the means to satisfy those needs, which in turn makes *tantai bishōjo* AVs and *kikaku* AVs 'useful' to certain groups of Japanese AV consumers. This is also to say that the *meaningful* connections between women's lack of sexual agency or men's sexual domination over women of the salvage ideology and the sexual needs of certain groups of Japanese AV consumers determine the character of the 'use value' of Japanese AVs: that is, *tantai bishōjo* AVs or *kikaku* AVs. In short, the salvage ideology is the cultural reason underpinning Japanese consumers' taste for AVs.

Understood as such, the oscillation between *tantai* and *kikaku* AVs in the last four decades reveals a swaying of evaluations between women's lack of sexual agency and men's sexual domination over women among Japanese AV consumers. The emergence and popularity of *kikatan* AVs emphasizing both the beauty of AV actresses and the storyline, indicate that AV consumers in contemporary Japan can only be sexually stimulated by the simultaneous occurrence of both elements of the salvage ideology: they are sexually excited to see how a beautiful, young, pure and innocent girl is situated in a story that can best show her being sexually dominated by men. All of this should be understood in the context of the changing sexual landscape of postwar Japanese society; but that in itself is another book.

Yet the point is not just one of consumers' interest, but of the production system of *tantai* and *kikaku* AVs: of how their narratives, genres, the way AV actresses are paid, packaging, marketing and clientele are also organized by specific evaluation of women's lack of sexual agency and men's status of women's saviours respectively. Chapter 3 will be about the structure of the Japanese AV industry against which the production of *tantai* and *kikaku* AVs to be discussed in Chapter 4 can be understood.

Notes

1 For instance, the 'household system' (*ie seido*) was established as the basis for Japanese society and all family members were to be subsumed under the male head; all marriages were now required to be registered with local authorities and the bride's name be removed from her own and entered on her husband's family register (McLelland 2012: 19).
2 Other popular couple-oriented magazines in postwar Japan included *Fūfu no Tomo* (Friends of Married Couples), *Fūfu no Seiteki Seikatsu* (The Sex Life of Married Couple) *Fūfu Zasshi* (Married Couple's Magazine), *Fūfu Seikatsu* (Married Couple's Life), *Fūfu Dokubon* (Couple's Text), *Fūfu Mono* (Couple's Things), *Fūfu Kai* (Field of Married Couple), *Kekkon Zasshi* (Magazine of Marriage), *Kekkon Seikatsu* (Marriage's Life), *Atashiki Fūfu no Seikatsu* (the Life of the New Couple) and *Kanzen Naru Fūfu no Seikatsu* (Perfect Couple's Life), and so on (Tanaka 2014: 109).
3 The authors have embarked on an ethnographic fieldwork with Ōkura Pictures Ltd since May 2014.
4 Video systems refer to the set of video camera and video recorder.
5 In view of the rapid increase in youth crime and proliferation of sexual industries, the government imposed more severe sanctions in relation to the sex industries, for instance the business hours of peeping rooms and individual massage room were now designated as before 12am. Because of this, the so-called 'no pant' tea house even

disappeared from the night life in Japan. This certainly had far reaching effects on the whole sex industry, as many sex workers were forced to re-locate to places and Japanese AV turned out to be one of their options.

6 'Overview of the major AV makers', http://narrow-deep.car.coocan.jp/other/av/av_maker_list.html, accessed on 2 November 2012.
7 Founded by Aachi Kaoru in 1986, V&R Planning is a Japanese AV studio based in Tokyo, and has been described by those in the AV industry as one of its weirdest AV companies (Schoenherr 2006; Yasuda and Amamiya 2006).
8 'Profile of Asakawa Ran', http://*tantai*.net/nats/ran/, accessed on 1 October 2012.
9 'Profile of Asakwa Ran', http://*tantai*.net/nats/ran/, accessed on 1 October 2012.
10 'Profile of Asakawa Ran', http://*tantai*.net/nats/ran/, accessed on 1 October 2012.
11 Oikawa was one of the most popular and well-known AV actresses in Japan and Asia in the early 2000s. In 2003, she ranked first in the DMM list of the 100 top-ranked actresses by sales on their website. In 2004, even though she had retired in mid-year, she still ranked second, and even in 2005 she made the top 50. There have since been numerous re-issues and compilations of her earlier videos. In 2012, the major Japanese adult video distributor DMM held a poll of its customers to choose the 100 all-time best AV actresses to celebrate the 30th anniversary of adult videos in Japan. Oikawa finished in 42nd place in the voting.
12 Coined in the late 1990s, it refers to the *kikaku* AVs that star a single beautiful actress. The creation of *kikatan* was posited as a response to the increasing consumer demand to see their favourite *kikaku* actresses in AVs.
13 DMM Adult Award is an honour awarded by the DMM to recognize outstanding achievement in the Japanese adult video industry. The first DMM Adult Award ceremony was held in 2014.

3 Production, regulation and circulation of adult videos

Introduction

This chapter briefly introduces the production, regulation and circulation of AVs in Japan, and thus the industrial context against which the chapters that follow should be understood. We suggest that at least seven 'stakeholders' – namely AV maker, model agency, production company, postproduction company, regulatory association, dubbing and packaging company, and wholesalers (*tonya*) – as well as rental or retail shops are involved in the industry (Asuka 2005: 27; Inoue 2002: 26–7) (Figure 3.1).

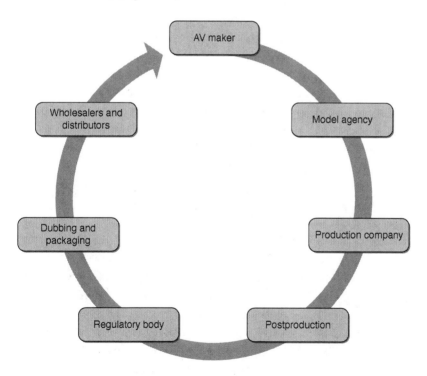

Figure 3.1 Production, circulation and regulation of AVs in Japan.

We will highlight the role of each stakeholder and their power relations in the industry, showing how an AV is stitched together by these stakeholders. In more concrete terms, we will show how production companies take subcontracted jobs from major AV makers; how model companies dispatch AV actresses to AV makers; how the regulatory body, Biderin, was used by major AV makers to establish their domination over the industry; and how and why AVs-for-sale emerged. We will also show in detail how the so-called Big Five AV makers formed a cartel that helped prescribe what kinds of adult videos were produced and how they were distributed or circulated in the market until the early 2000s; and how they used Biderin to exclude rivalries through the case of a newly emerged AV maker, Diamond Image, in order to show that the domination of the Big Five AV makers helps explain why the salvage ideology can continue to linger on in the AV industry in Japan.

AV makers

The major characteristic of the industrial structure of Japanese AVs – as, indeed, of Japanese manufacturing industries in general – is the hierarchical relationship among AV makers. On the one hand, we can find several giant AV makers that dominate the whole industry in terms of size, capital, market share and influence; and on the other there are many small and even one-man production companies that either receive subcontracting work from these giant AV makers or focus on a very narrow market niche by specializing in producing AVs in one specific genre. Giant AV makers include the so-called Big Five in the industry: Cosmo Plan, KUKI, VIP (later Altas21), Japan Home Video (JHV) and Samm Video (later h.m.p.) (Nakamura 2015: 26). Cosmo Plan, KUKI and VIP were formerly vinyl cover book publishers, whereas JHV was founded by a prominent director of the production team of Nippon Image Video (Fujiki 2009: 121). Samm Video was an AV maker that started out as a producer of S&M AVs in the early 1980s.

Founded in 1981, Cosmo Plan was the first vinyl cover book publisher to tap into the AV market. Carrying over from its vinyl cover book tradition of typically portraying sweet and innocent young girls as vinyl cover book idols (Shōwa Seishiryō Kenkyū Kai and Saitō 2014: 34), their *tantai bishōjo* AVs achieved huge commercial successes – so much so that they earned the name of 'Cosmo *Bishōjo*' within the industry (Suitsu 1998b: 156; Tōra 1998b: 119).

VIP Enterprise (later Altas21), also a former vinyl cover book publisher, chose to go a different route from Cosmo Plan. In order to compete with the latter, which had garnered huge popularity by producing *tantai* AVs (*tantai mono*), VIP made a bold decision by venturing into *kikaku* AVs (*kikaku mono*) – in particular, S&M and scatology – while producing *tantai* AVs (Ishida 1998: 206).[1] Some early famous productions include *The Nude for 48 Hours* (*48 Jikan no Ratai*) [1982] and *Torture Chamber* (*Shigyaku no Heya*) [1982] (Suitsu 1998a: 2). Meanwhile, VIP launched a new label titled *Street Hunting Empire* (*Sawagi Takuya no Nanpa Teikoku*), a *kikaku* AV that focused on men picking up girls in the street (Ishida 1998: 206). In the 1980s, the company managed to sign up many beautiful actresses and reaped huge success by returning to produce *tantai mono* such as its mega-hits *I Was About to Be Broken* (*Watashi Kowasareso*) [1986] and *Roll a Beautiful Woman Over* (*Bishōjo Korogashi*) [1986] in the late 1980s (Yoshioka 1999: 181, 183).

Not unlike VIP Enterprise, KUKI, another former vinyl cover book publisher, also went for something different from its original style. Compared with Cosmos Plan and VIP, KUKI was a latecomer in the AV market, and the fact that the *tantai* market was dominated by Cosmo Plan and Samm Video led it to venture into *kikaku* AVs.[2] Some popular titles were *Can the Adult Understand88?* (*Otona Ni Wakatte kurenai88*) and *The First Shot of Electric Shock* (*Dengeki Yipattsume*) (Sawaki 1998: 169). The former was about rape and the latter the loss of virginity. Nevertheless, after the collapse of the bubble economy in the 1990s, KUKI chose to try its luck by moving back into the more *binibon*-style (*binibon-kei*)[3] *tantai* AVs, when at the time most AV makers were producing *kikaku* AVs.[4]

Japan Home Video (JHV) is well known for its most successful label Alice Japan. As a major studio having the advantage of large amounts of capital and resources, Alice Japan is not only willing, but also able, to make a big investment in actresses. From the very beginning, Alice Japan has worked with *tantai* AVs, especially new actresses making their debut in adult video, and more often than not puts it under the genre of *bishōjo*. Over the years, Alice Japan has produced many legendary AV *bishōjo* idols including Iijima Ai, Matsushima Kaede, Yoshizawa Akiho, Mitake Ryoko, Takagi Maria, Tatsumi Yui and Komukai Minako, to name just a few. While it is no longer as dominant as it was in the 1990s, its large pool of young, comely idols continues to hold on to audiences not only in Japan but also in Asia. In fact, the declining dominance of Alice Japan is part of the result of the overall declining popularity of *tantai* AVs because the category itself has gradually lost momentum among Japanese male audiences, even though it had been the most dominant style of production throughout the 1980s and early 1990s.

As mentioned above, Samm Video started with the production of S&M AVs in 1981, but it shifted its focus to the production of *tantai* AVs from the mid-1980s – a shift that was marked by the company's launch of a new label, Miss Christine, specializing in *tantai* AVs.[5] The shift was further reinforced and perpetuated by the huge success of another new *tantai* AV label, Tiffany. Tiffany was a *bishōjo tantai* AV label that was able to gain tremendous support from consumers with the debut of a *tantai* AV actress Hoshino Hikaru in the early 1990s.[6] At the same time, Samm Video was renamed h.m.p. Seeing the decline of *tantai* AVs in the market, h.m.p. started to branch out into the production of *kikaku* AVs in the 1990s, while continuing its *bishōjo tantai* AV production. The company invited a famous pink film director, Kataoka Shuji, to help with its *kikaku* AV production.[7] Another famous *kikaku* AV director we mentioned in Chapter 2, Company Matsuo, started to take the subcontracted production of *kikaku* AVs from the company in 1996 while he was working for V & R Planning at that time (Schoenherr 2006).[8]

We can see that the former vinyl cover book publishers do not necessarily stick to the production of *tantai* AVs, which is also to say that there is no one-to-one relationship between the background of AV makers and their production style. As we have just shown, some former vinyl cover book publishers, due to practical reasons, might choose to produce *kikaku* rather than *tantai* AVs at first when entering the market, although in the end they switched back to *tantai* AVs once their financial situation allowed them to do so. Some other major AV makers shifted their production between *tantai* and *kikaku* AVs to respond to ever-changing consumer demands. Most of the time in the history of Japanese AV industry, AV makers have oscillated between the production of *tantai* and that of *kikaku* AVs – a fact which also means that these two categories have dominated the industry's production until very recently when *kikatan* AVs, as mentioned in Chapter 2, emerged in the late 1990s. We will return to this in Chapter 4.

Of course, there are also some medium sized AV makers in the industry. One typical example is Athena Image, a medium sized AV maker based in Tokyo where we conducted our fieldwork in 2011. In that year the company employed a total of 16 staff members to work in its production and business divisions. The production division employed three AV directors – including the famous Yoyogi Tadashi mentioned in Chapter 2 – two producers, two assistant directors and one production staff member. Together they produced Athena Image's own AVs rather than have their production subcontracted to small AV makers and therefore it employed three directors for its own production. The two producers were responsible for coordinating the production process, while the three directors were in charge of making AVs and the two assistant directors provided production support for them. The main duty of the production staff member was to manage the postproduction work. In the business division, there were eight staff members including two accounting staff, one marketing staff member, two administrative staff, one staff member in charge of advertising, one staff member responsible for online business, and one casting director whose job was to interview and recruit AV actresses from model agencies.

However, many makers, especially well established AV makers, have tended to subcontract their projects to professional production companies. One of the major reasons for this lies in cost reduction and risk mitigation. It is more cost effective to subcontract production to outside companies than to keep one's own production department because by so doing so AV makers do not need to finance a whole production crew during the low season when there is little or no production. There is an additional advantage for a maker to hire a subcontractor, as it can easily switch to others if the subcontractor's performance falls short of the maker's requirement. That is to say, the relationship between major AV makers and their subcontractors – unlike that found in what Michael L. Gerlach (1992: 68) called vertical *keiretsu* (enterprise groupings) in Japan – is subject *only* to the short-term calculation of profit and loss by both major AV makers and their subcontractors, which is also to say that the inter-corporate relationship between them is contingent, short-term and purely business-like.

This subcontracted strategy, however, provides business chances to many small production companies. On receiving an order from an AV maker, a production company will appoint, according to the plot given, a director, cameramen, actress/actor (if not pre-assigned), from its production team. At times, production companies may employ freelance directors or cameramen, and source actresses and actors directly from a model agency. In order to reduce costs, they may even employ directors who are not specialized in shooting pornographic movies. In some cases, the owner of a production company will serve as a film's director. Consequently, it is not surprising to find that some AV movies are cheap and nasty (Inoue 2002: 26–8). Once director, cameraman, actress and actor are decided, the production company will move on to the actual shooting (*genba*). As we shall see in Chapter 7, the shooting of a Japanese AV is short in terms of time; it usually takes one day, and not longer than two days to finish (Otsubo 2007: 99).

Shooting is largely set in the company's own studios. Small production companies which do not have their own studio might rent a studio, an apartment or a love hotel room. Some might borrow a shop or restaurant premise for filming; but often without allowing the shop owner to know what kind of film will be shot there, for fear that the owner would refuse. At other times, the director might simply film in a park or forest, on a bus or train, or in a car (Inoue 2002: 32). Clearly, the location of filming has much to do with the budget given. The common budget for an AV movie is around ¥400,000 (US$3,526), although there are big productions running up to ¥10 million (US$88,000) (Inoue 2002: 33). And it is the responsibility of the production company to make sure that production is completed within this budget (Inoue 2002: 33).

We can now see that the survival of small AV makers is to a great extent dependent on giant AV makers because the latter are the major source of the former's income. This in turn gives power to giant AV makers to impose a 'standard' across the industry, even if such a standard may favour only those giant AV makers at the expense of the small AV studios. For example, the Big Five AV makers set the maximum salary of AV actresses at around ¥200,000 (US$1,760) for one movie in the 1980s. At the same time, they also prescribed that no maker could recruit AV actresses directly but only through model agencies, to which we will return in a moment. More importantly, giant AV makers, as will be discussed below, controlled what kinds of AV could be produced and in what way AVs could be circulated in the market through their domination of regulatory bodies.

Model agencies

As mentioned above, AV makers must recruit their actresses from a so-called model agency (Suzuki 2013: 96) because the 'standard' practice imposed by the Big Five AV makers, as mentioned above, prescribes that makers should not contact AV actresses directly but go through model agencies.[9] AV makers will call upon model agencies to arrange interviews when they are looking for actress(es) to fill a particular role. These model agencies earn their income usually from the deal they make with AV makers (Suzuki 2013: 97). We need to point out at this juncture, however, that the relationship between model agencies and AV actresses in the AV industry in Japan is different from that between modelling agencies and models in the American model business. As Mears reports,

> This gross of [income] includes the agency fee of 20 percent charged to model's clients that goes directly into agency proceeds, and agencies take 20 percent of the remaining amount in commission from model's earnings. For example, I [Mears] booked a two-day catalog shoot that paid $1,600 gross to me, minus Metro's [Mears' agency] 20 percent model commission of $320, so my net pay was $1,280. Metro then charged an additional percent agency fee to the client, so the total invoice to the client was $1,920, and the agency's net profits totalled $640.
>
> (Mears 2011: 59–60)

In other words, the agency in the American modelling business functions as a broker which filters suitable models to clients while at the same time finding clients for models, and that is why it charges the model commission and her client an agency fee at the same time. The relationship between model agencies and AV actresses, especially *kikaku* AV actresses, however, is similar to the one between a staffing agency and its temporary workers (*hakenshain*) in Japan. Model agencies dispatch their AV actresses to AV makers on a per-movie basis. Once an actress is approved following a job interview, agency and AV maker formally sign a contract which is negotiated with the AV maker *not* on behalf of the *kikaku* AV actress, but between agency and AV maker. It follows that *kikaku* AV actresses are not an independent party but temporary staff employed by their model agencies; they are dispatched by model agencies to AV makers on a per-movie basis. That is why model agencies generally do not pay *kikaku* AV actresses commission, but instead pay them a portion of their income from AV makers as a salary. What *kikaku* AV actresses sell, therefore, is not their name. In fact, *kikaku* AV actresses, as will be shown in Chapter 4, are always anonymous.

It is common in the industry for model agencies to pay *kikaku* AV actresses 40 per cent or even less of the fee received from AV makers for the work they have done (Nakamura 2012: 58). As 'dispatched staff' of model agencies, *kikaku* AV actresses find it difficult to bargain with their agencies on the portion they receive from the latter. Only a small percentage of very successful AV girls have been allowed by the agencies to bargain their portion up to 50 per cent and an even smaller percentage of very successful AV actresses have been able to negotiate the portion with their own supervisors – called 'managers' ('*manējā*') in the industry (Nakamura 2012: 58).

In the 1980s and 1990s, payment was normally settled at the shooting site with cash, so that neither model agency nor the AV actress needed to pay income tax to the Japanese government. From the 2000s, when model agencies decided to formalize their business to avoid possible legal action by the authorities, the payment has been effected through bank transfers, and both AV actresses and model agencies have to pay income tax (Nakamura 2015: 33).

The size of model agencies in the Japanese AV industry varies widely, but their operation is more or less the same. They hire so-called professional scouts (*sukātoman*) to 'solicit' on the streets girls who are young, beautiful and, most importantly, sexually open – meaning that they will be willing to engage in sex related work – and then coax them into being interviewed in the agency's office (Inoue 2002). As we will discover in more detail in Chapter 5, there are increasingly more and more young Japanese women who not only feel comfortable with all kinds of adult entertainment jobs, but actually see them as 'dream jobs' because, through them, they can become *the* actress, the centre of focus and respect (Inoue 2002). In this case, women will directly approach model agencies for interviews where they often negotiate with the agency not only the nature of their job, but also their working hours and salary. According to our interviews with model agency managers in Tokyo, they generally tend to sign on whatever girls are available to them. To them, beautiful models are of course welcome, but girls with an average face are equally wanted because they can always be hired to take part in *kikaku* AVs.

After becoming an exclusive actress of a given agency, the newly signed actress will be sent to professional studios to take stills for promotional use. Meanwhile, each of the actresses will be assigned a manager (in American or European terminology, a 'booker'), who is usually a man. The manager is supposed not only to take care of her contract, jobs, filming and photographing schedules and sometimes even her private life,[10] but also find work for her by presenting her to AV makers, as well as to adult publishers, normal internet advertising agencies, and photographers. This formal presentation takes place exactly in an interview (*mensetsu*) where actresses will be interviewed and photographed, a complex process we shall go through in Chapter 6. One can see that interview is arguably the most important arena through which AV actresses come into direct contact with AV makers. It is not only an arena to 'sell' the AV actress; rather, it is a 'marketplace' where the actress is repeatedly interrogated, judged, evaluated, examined, scrutinized and checked according to a set of criteria which a casting director believes are important in the sense that they are *useful* and hence financially productive for his company. However, we have to emphasize that AV actresses do not need to be 'interviewed' every single time they go for a job, especially one offered by the same AV studio or the same director as previously. Once they pass an interview, they are put into the 'record' and are called upon when the AV studio or director needs them.

The relationship between model agencies and major AV makers is complicated. On the one hand, model agency revenue relies very much on whether major AV makers are willing to take on AV actresses who have contracts with a certain model agency. This is especially the case with *tantai* AV actresses, whose payment rate is quite substantial – of the kind that only major AV makers can afford – thus providing agencies with considerable commission. This is one reason why model agencies are always weak vis-à-vis major AV makers. But since beautiful AV actresses, as mentioned in Chapter 2, are *the* selling point of *tantai* AVs, the competition for 'high-quality' *tantai* AV actresses is always very keen among major AV makers. In the second half of the 1980s when the AV industry was experiencing a boom, one new giant AV maker even asked professional scouts to bring girls directly to them without going through model agencies (Nakamura 2015: 39–40). The AV maker would take as many girls introduced by scouts as possible – even though the AV maker suspected that some of the girls could not sell well – in order to maintain a good relationship with scouts who would then continue to introduce girls to the makers, some of whom could be of 'high quality'. This practice, of course, only increased the AV maker's production costs and offended other giant AV makers, but was welcomed by both scouts and their AV actresses because neither of them needed to share its income and profits with a model agency (Nakamura 2015: 30–40).

After the collapse of the bubble economy in the 1990s, giant AV makers could no longer afford continuing this strategy. They became more selective and cautious in signing on AV actresses, which is also to say that they tended to recruit those AV actresses introduced to them only when they believed that they would sell well. More importantly, they had become more and more dependent on model agencies in sourcing AV actresses because this recruitment method was (and is) more cost effective and efficient, inasmuch as they do not need to sign on less promising AV actresses. It is therefore crucially important that model agencies which happen to be able to source a 'high-quality' *tantai* AV actress are willing to introduce her to those AV makers which maintain a good relationship with model agencies *first*. That is why the casting director of major AV makers in many circumstances has to maintain a good relationship with model agencies to make sure that he will be the first one to get access to a high-quality *tantai* AV actress, which is also to say that major AV makers are not always in a strong position vis-à-vis model agencies.

Postproduction

On completion of shooting, the master tape is sent to the postproduction department or professional company for editing. As we shall see in Chapter 8, due to the Japanese obscenity (*waisetsu*) laws which have until recently criminalized the public representation of not only genitalia but also pubic hair (Allison 2000: 149), AV makers are legally obliged to airbrush depictions of sexual intercourse and masturbation by means of a so-called mosaic (*mozaiku*). This means that editing primarily refers to a process whereby the human phallus and vagina are mosaicked out and foul phrases are muted. In addition, of course, movies will be edited down to the required length with corrections made and special effects inserted. After these post-filming treatments, the master tape will be sent back to the respective maker for examination and then to the regulatory organization for inspection (Asuka 2005: 26). Once it has passed the latter's scrutiny, the proven master tape will then be sent to a packing factory where an elaborate and colourful jacket, alongside a cover displaying the main AV actress(es) and some core shots from the movie, are inserted (Inoue 2002: 26–34).

Regulatory body

Censorship is not new in Japan. It can be dated back to the Edo period (1603–1868) (Abel 2012) where the Tokugawa Shogunate (*bakufu*) sought tight control of the spread of information: especially over Christianity, the influx of Western ideas, and writings that were critical of the Shogun (Tokugawa Teyasu) or his family, criticism of the government and its official ideology (Neo-Confucianism) and sexual materials (Masters 1992: 85; Mitchell 1983: 2–3). After the Meiji Restoration in 1868, censorship was given legislative provisions. First of all, the Home Ministry was created in 1873 to control whatever it saw as 'dangerous to the state' (Masters 1992: 90). The term '*waisetsu*' (obscenity) and punishment of its 'public display or sale' first appeared in Article 259 of the Penal Code of 1880 (Beer 1984: 336). Article 175 of the 1907 revised Penal Code prohibited the public distribution or exhibition of 'obscene pictures and/or pictures' – a prohibition which remains today the primary legal provision concerning obscenity in Japan (Beer 1984: 336).

The Taishō period (1912–26) was often stereotyped as one of the most liberal periods in Japan. However, in view of the proliferation of new political philosophies (such as socialism, communism and anarchism) deemed subversively dangerous to the state, the government became increasingly heavy-handed in its censorship policies (Masters 1992: 92; Mitchell 1983: 190–1). In 1925, the Peace Preservation Law was stipulated to suppress individuals who provoked the above-mentioned political philosophies, religious leaders who preached religious ideas deemed threatening to the government, and intellectuals seen to challenge the regime. The Law granted the state legal power to establish a Special Higher Police Force to tackle ideological 'offences' and the court juristic power to subject ideological 'offenders' to the death penalty (Masters 1992: 92). Over the ensuing years, especially with the outbreak of the Second World War, state censorship reached its peak – to such an extent that freedom of the press was completely eliminated under the 1941 Revisions of the National Mobilization Law (Abel 2012: 33; Masters 1992: 95).

After the surrender of Japan in 1945, state power in Japan was substantially undermined. Under the guidance of the American Occupation Forces, a democratic Constitution of Japan was drafted and passed in 1947. In it freedom of speech was incorporated under Article 21 (Masters 1992: 96).[11] All forms of censorship and control previously imposed on freedom of speech were now rendered unconstitutional. From that moment on, it would be misleading, if not totally incorrect, to refer to a 'censorship law' in Japan, since censorship does not exist legally.

In accordance with the protection of freedom of speech, the American Occupation Forces stipulated that no state agency be involved in local motion picture production, but it also advised the Japanese motion picture industry to form a voluntary or advocacy group (*rinni dantai*): that is, an independent, non-governmental organization to oversee the content of motion pictures. Interestingly, Article 175 of the Penal Code, commonly known as the obscenity law, managed to survive. As perceptively pointed out by Allison (1998: 197), it was originally a measure intended to rid Japan of its stereotypical image as morally lax or primitive and to showcase to the West that Meiji Japan was as modern and civilized as the West. The survival of the code, together with the grant of freedom of speech, one way or other reveals the complex attitude of Japan towards her own image vis-à-vis the West, especially the US. On the one hand, Japan has maintained the Penal Code to showcase the fact that Japan is a modernized and civilized country, especially in terms of moral aspects (Masters 1992: 96). On the other hand, it followed the US's guidance to implement a democratic constitution – again to deliver an important message to the world that Japan is a modern state. This same fixation on the 'modern' image of Japan leads to an interesting result: the grant of freedom of speech, albeit in the face of the existence of the obscenity laws. A voluntary association, therefore, was to be founded with an aim to free the state from intervening in the local film industry while at the same time ensuring that the obscenity laws would not be violated.

As mentioned in Chapter 2, the first such association was Eirin. Founded in 1946, Eirin was modelled on the Motion Picture Association of America. Reorganized in 1956, Eirin was established to make sure that local films would not violate the obscenity laws. While Eirin lost much of its cultural sway by the 1980s due to the rise of new media such as television and VHS, it had a profound impact on Japanese society as its practices and formats continued to affect and inform other types of film censorship in Japan, including adult videos. In view of the proliferation of rental adult videos, Biderin, modelled on Eirin, was founded in 1972 to self-regulate, if not self-censor, the ever-popularizing rental adult videos (Adachi 1995: 288–9). Biderin was founded by the early participants of the AV industry who were former pink film-makers – including Toei Video, Nikkatsu Video and Toyō Recording (Adachi 1995: 288; Motohashi 2012: 122). Together with Japan Kobitte and Geneisha, their representatives were the earliest Board members of Biderin (Adachi 1995: 288), in the wake of the police's prosecution of their pornographic videos. Basically, the Board oversaw all matters within the organization, ranging from the admission of members to recruitment of inspectors. As it entered into the 1980s, the Board was taken over by the Big Five AV makers (Adachi 1995: 289).[12] Not unlike their predecessors, the Big Five continued to dominate all the decision-making processes at Biderin. In addition to the admission of members and recruitment of inspectors, they were also influential in the formulation of inspection criteria (*shinsa kijun*) and hence Biderin's interpretation of the obscenity laws. Biderin under the domination of the Big Five was notorious for imposing extremely strict inspection criteria on the AVs produced by its members throughout the 1980s and 1990s, a topic we shall return to in Chapter 8.

We have to immediately point out that Biderin inspectors were not recruited publicly but recommended by the Board. Very often, those recommended were retired employees from film related businesses or production companies who used to work for the major AV makers (Adachi 1995: 292). These arranged for retiring employees to take over the job of inspectors at Biderin – a typical practice among large Japanese companies before the long recession of the 1990s whereby it would be arranged that middle to senior managers would take up positions at one or other subsidiary of their companies or their client's companies upon retirement. But we have to add that the practice was only applicable to male employees. This recruitment method explains why the inspectors at Biderin were predominately male and their average age fairly advanced. In 1991, for instance, the oldest inspector was aged 67, whereas the youngest was 56 and the average age was 62 (Adachi 1995: 292). It also explains why the inspectors usually had close relationships with the AV makers: they came from the AV industry; in other words, they were insiders.

More importantly, many retired police officers (referred to as 'OB', or old boys, in Japanese) had occupied important positions in the Administrative Office[13] of Biderin since its inception. For instance, Uehara Tsutomu, the Head of the Administrative Office of Biderin in October 1991, was the former Commissioner of the Crime Prevention Unit of the Metropolitan Police Department, specializing in the prosecution of violations of the obscenity laws (Adachi 1995: 290). The other five general officers working in the Administrative Office in 1991 were also OBs from the police force (Adachi 1995: 290). As a matter of fact, the Administrative Office was known as 'the final destiny' for retired police officers all through the years, continuing well into the mid-2000s (Sonoda and Dai 2016: 107). This is a perfect example of *amakudari* (descent from heaven), an institutionalized practice where Japanese senior bureaucrats retire to high-profile positions in the private (sometimes public sectors) linked with or under the authority of their ministries or agencies.

Finally, the inspection environment was sloppy and procedures were neither clear nor transparent. In 1991, the Administrative Office of Biderin was located in a small office building in Nihonbashi, Tokyo (Adachi 1995: 290–1). This small office was divided into several sections, one of which was assigned as an inspection corner. This corner was then partitioned into five small spaces through the use of curtains. Each of the small spaces was lined with monitors, desks and chairs (Adachi 1995: 291). As of 1991, there were only ten inspectors, who would inspect movies in these small spaces from 1 pm to 5 pm on every weekday (Adachi 1995: 291), although by the 2000s, the number of inspectors had increased to 15 (Sonoda and Dai 2016: 110). Inspectors would work in pairs and screen each movie together. During the screening, a representative of the respective AV maker would be present as well (Sonoda and Dai 2016: 110). The official reason was efficiency because, if there were any problems, the inspectors could immediately provide instructions to the representative on how to make required revisions (Adachi 1995: 292). In other words, they could always solve matters at once. But the presence of the representative could also mean that the inspectors might have to confront the AV maker at issue *on the spot* if the latter raised objections to the judgement of the former in the inspector corner. Most inspectors would not want this to happen, especially if they knew the AV maker personally. On many occasions, the inspectors would give in and dare not ask the AV maker to revise their products.

All these characteristics of Biderin should be understood in two contexts. The first is that Biderin was not a statutory body. As a non-government organization, Biderin lacked legal authority to check whether AV makers complied with the obscenity laws or Biderin's inspection criteria. Nor did it have the authority to undertake any legal action against AV makers who, for whatever reason, did not submit their videos to Biderin for inspection or failed to pass the inspection. This is also why Biderin from the beginning invited OBs to join its Administrative Office and even appointed a former senior OB specializing in obscenity laws as head of the office to make up for the fact that it was not a statutory body. In other words, the presence of former policemen in the Administrative Office helped create within the industry an important impression that Biderin was a state-recognized, if not a governmental, association (Yasuda and Amamiya 2006: 99). This impression was further reinforced by the police's issue of the circular note concerning the operation of adult videos in 1981. The note stipulated that AV titles that did not go through inspection at Biderin might be subject to prosecution, a fact which also implied that Biderin was an agency backed up by the state. The appointment of a senior OB well versed in the prosecution of obscenity laws also implied that Biderin would have access to the most up-to-date information with regard to the perspectives of the Police Force about what constituted a violation of obscenity laws in Japan. All this led to an impression widely shared within the industry that adult videos approved by Biderin would be free of any problem: in other words, that Biderin's sticker was considered an 'indulgences' from state prosecution (Motohashi 2012: 123; Yasuda and Amamiya 2006: 98).

The quasi-state agency of Biderin also had significant impact on *what kinds of* adult videos were made and *how* they were distributed or circulated in the market (Yasuda and Amamiya 2006: 98–9). Since throughout the 1980s and 1990s, Biderin could indeed be considered a quasi-state agency, there gradually emerged a tacit understanding among industry people that adult videos not certified by Biderin were little less than illegal adult video – even though they had mosaic – and were thus subject to police prosecution (Yasuda and Amamiya 2006: 99, 103). This understanding gained more currency after the police issued the above-mentioned circular note. Frightened that they would be arrested by the police, major adult video wholesalers and rental shops chose *not* to accept adult videos uncertified by Biderin (Yasuda and Amamiya 2006: 99). To the makers, the possibility of their adult videos being denied by major wholesalers and hence rejected by major rental shops was simply too devastating, for it effectively meant that their adult videos would be unreleasable. In order to avoid this, most adult video makers, though they might not be sympathetic to Biderin's philosophy and inspection criteria, could not but join Biderin and have their videos inspected before they released them. In fact, wholesalers at that time only took AVs produced by those AV makers who were members of Biderin. That is why only AVs that complied with Biderin's inspection criteria could be on the market. Relatedly, since Biderin only dealt with rental AVs, it followed that only AVs that were designated for rental services could be on the market, even though the option of purchase became technologically feasible in the late 1980s as the unit price of videotapes dropped significantly.

The second context is that the Big Five in fact formed a cartel to dominate the industry. From the fact that Biderin prescribed what kinds of AVs could be made (content-wise) and how they were circulated, and that the organization was overwhelmingly dominated by major makers, it is quite clear that Biderin was easily manipulated by the Big Five makers to wield power and achieve their dominance in the industry. The organization's manipulation is reflected first in the inspection process. Recall that inspectors were appointed by the Board members and most importantly they used to work for the major AV makers. This recruitment method made it difficult for the inspectors to review the movies of the major makers fairly.

Using Biderin to exclude rivals

The domination of the Big Five over the industry through Biderin can be seen in the earliest and notable examples of their manipulation of censorship organization to exclude Muranishi Tōru and his company. Before rising to prominence as a result of the release of real acting AVs (*honban* AV), Muranishi was a director under Crystal Image, a minor manufacturer when compared with the Big Five. His videos under Crystal Image were by and large softcore: that is, all sex scenes were simulated. Despite the fact that Muranishi strived to become a major by producing videos comparable with Cosmo Plan and h.m.p., his initial films were of a low standard and quality (Fujiki 2009: 124). He only rose to prominence when he switched to producing real sex videos featuring S&M themes. It must be stressed that while there were some real sex AVs in the early years, and certainly many more in the underground AV industry, real sex AV shooting remained an uncommon option among the major AV makers. In 1986, Muranishi tiptoed along Biderin lines by specializing in real sex movies. A notable example is *I Like SM-ish* (*SMppoi no suki*) [1986] (Fujiki 2009: 136). This video featured real sex scenes between Kuroki Kaori and Muranishi as actor. After a short introduction and various sexy images, the movie turned to sex scenes (Fujiki 2009: 136) where Kuroki was not displayed as an innocent young girl, but as a sexually conscious and autonomous woman.

This movie caused a huge sensation in the AV industry as well as in the Japanese media as a whole. It rocked the industry not only by depicting real sex, but also by laying bare Kuroki Kaori's intense sexual desire (Fuijiki 2009: 137). Unlike previous real sex actresses who were by and large lowly educated, Kuroki Kaori was a young woman who came from a decent family and who studied at a national university. As Fujiki notes, the sexual eagerness and autonomy displayed by Kuroki was indeed threatening for many Japanese male fans, for these female images were new to them (Fujiki 2009: 137). Nevertheless, thanks to this movie, Muranishi and Kuroki found themselves in the media spotlight – being invited as guests on TV shows and programmes to discuss their views about sex, and especially about female sexuality. In the same year, Muranishi left Crystal Image and founded his own AV studio, Diamond Image (Nakamura 2015: 25).

Diamond Image leapt to fame as one of the major AV makers, leading to recognition of the so-called Big Six. In the early 1990s, Diamond Image had become a giant manufacturer specializing in producing real sex AV idols, including Matsuzaka Kimiko, Sakuragi Rui, Nosaka Natsumi, Tanaka Rōsa, Himiko, Kobata Miai and Sara Itsuki, among others (Nakamura 2015: 42). At its zenith, Diamond Image released almost 30 movies a month and took up a 35 per cent share of the total AV market with an annual revenue of ¥1 trillion (US$8.8 billion) (Fujiki 2009: 157; Nakamura 2015: 44). Nevertheless, the tendency of Diamond Image to produce real sex movies attracted the attention of the Japanese police who, in January 1988, cracked down on three major model companies which violated the Worker Dispatching Act for illegally providing young women to adult video makers (AV makers had not yet been recognized as legal clients in 1988) to work in AV filming, as well as the Employment Security Law for dispatching these women to work in real sex shooting (Nakamura 2015: 30).[14] Among these three companies, two of them had been providing models to Diamond Image which then hired them to participate in its real sex filming (Fujiki 2009: 152). In March 1988, Muranishi was arrested for hiring an underage girl to participate in real sex AV shooting under the Child Welfare Act (Fujiki 2009: 155). Again, in late September 1988, Muranishi was for the third time arrested for violating the Child Welfare Act, because the model hired in one of Diamond Image's productions, *Wind Fantasy* (*Kaze no fantajī*) [1988], was discovered to be only 16 years old (Fujiki 2009: 157). Nevertheless, the director of this movie was not in fact Muranishi, but Nosaka Shinpei (Fujiki 2009: 157).

In October 1988, the Biderin Board for the first time since its establishment issued a circular note to its members, stating, first, that those adult video studios that had hired underage (under 18) women to work in AV and subsequently been arrested by the police, would not have their adult videos accepted for inspection by Biderin for a certain period of time; and second, that member makers who by fraudulent means sold captioned videos as 'inspected' videos would be subject to punishment (Fujiki 2009: 159). Obviously enough, this circular note targeted Muranishi Tōru, for no one other than him had been arrested for employing underage young women to participate in AV shooting. As Fujiki (2009: 159) notes, this circular note was nothing more than a deportation order from the AV industry. Significantly, it essentially marked the end of Muranishi's AV career for, without the Biderin's inspection, his videos could not be stocked in any rental shop in Japan. Here one can see the cultural significance and sway of Biderin and hence the dominance of the Big Five behind Biderin in the AV industry.

Of course, that Biderin would issue this circular note had a lot to do with the prosecutions initiated by the police. The circular note could be seen as follow-up action after the police's prosecutions against Muranishi. Nevertheless, it would not be incorrect to say that this circular note was also issued to defeat Muranishi completely and take Diamond Image out of the frame. Before venturing into adult video, Muranishi had been deeply involved in real sex videos (Nakamura 2015: 12). Despised by the major AV makers as an outright outcast, Muranishi had long had an antagonistic relationship with Cosmo Plan, KUKI and VIP, the former vinyl cover book publishers (Nakamura 2015: 27). Among them, Cosmo Plan was the most unsympathetic towards Muranishi. Indeed, Cosmo Plan's anti-Muranishi attitude was well-known within the AV industry, as it had long taken the policy of prohibiting real sex shooting in its own AV productions (Fujiki 2009: 165). More importantly, however, Diamond Image was already on the verge of financial collapse even if Biderin's Board had not issued the circular note. As Muranishi had been repeatedly arrested for violating the Child Welfare Act, most rental shops became reluctant to stock any products by Diamond Image. Seen in this light, the issue of the circular note by Biderin can be re-read as evidence of how Biderin was manipulated by its Board members; it was an excuse to get rid of Muranishi completely.

This reading proves to be sound if we take into account the sudden cancellation of the deportation order issued to Muranishi in 1989 (Fujiki 2009: 165). In July 1989, there was breaking news concerning the AV industry when it was reported that Mount Promotion, a major model company, had been involved in the dispatching of an underage girl (her stage name was Ito Yumi) to work in 24 adult videos produced by five adult video studios between 1988 and 1989. Among these five makers, three of them were Cosmo Plan, KUKI and Athena Image. As a result, the president of Mount Promotion and the presidents and directors of these manufacturers were arrested for violating the Child Welfare Act in 1989 (Fujiki 2009: 162). As Fujiki pointed out, when compared with Muranishi's case, this incident was more serious both in terms of scale (a total of 24 movies were involved) and of the number of Biderin-related people arrested. In theory, the Biderin Board should have issued the same deportation order to these Biderin members including Cosmo Plan, KUKI and Athena Image, but the latter were not just Biderin's members; more importantly, they were members of its Board. In addition, these three makers had contributed substantially to the AV industry from its very beginning. Thus, in practice, it was considered difficult, if not totally impossible, to expel them from Biderin (Fujiki 2009: 164). The only way out for the Board, therefore, was to remove the deportation order issued to Muranishi (Fujiki 2009: 164–5). Here, one can see how Biderin was used by the major makers to attack other makers they did not like, or for their own benefit.

Of course, the Big Five's control of AV makers would not have been possible without the cooperation of the wholesalers and rental shops. After all, if wholesalers stocked adult video uncertified by Biderin, the whole hegemony of Biderin would fall apart. Certainly, wholesalers refusing to stock Biderin-uncertified videos, especially in the early years, had a lot to do with their fear of falling prey to prosecutions. But this fear gradually diminished – indeed, virtually disappeared – as many other self-regulatory agencies sprang up and their certified videos were fully mosaicked.[15] Nevertheless, Biderin had another trump card. The Big Five could force the wholesalers to follow their wishes; otherwise they would not supply their videos to the latter. The wholesalers could not but be complicit in Biderin's hegemony because failure to do so would mean that they might lose access to the adult videos of the major makers, who were the core members of Biderin and, more importantly, whose AV products dominated the market. This is certainly the last thing wholesalers wanted to see.

By holding Biderin as their trump card, the Big Five effectively excluded new competitors and dominated roughly 75 per cent of the adult video market share throughout the 1980s and the first half of the 1990s (Adachi 1995: 289). This long analysis is to highlight an important observation: Biderin was nothing less than a cartel deployed by the Big Five to monopolize the production and distribution of Japanese AVs and control prices. In Chapter 8, we will show that this observation is not confined to Biderin but can be applied to other self-regulatory bodies in the industry.

Wholesalers, rental and retail shops

Under the domination of the Big Five through their control of Biderin, the major circulation method of AVs in Japan in the 1980s and 1990s was through rental shops where consumers rented AVs for a fee for a certain period of time. As mentioned above, wholesalers only sourced AVs from those makers who were members of Biderin. The general practice in the Biderin era was that AV makers would send packages of their new AVs to wholesalers which then passed them to rental shops for consideration. That is to say, the operators of rental shops made their purchase based solely on the appearance of the jacket of a new AV (and not on its content). This explains why AV makers put so much emphasis on the attractiveness of the jacket by sending the proven master tape to professional packing factories. If the operators of rental shops were interested, they could place their orders through wholesalers. This was called an 'initial' order in the industry. If the AVs ordered turned out to be very popular among consumers, rental shops could then order more through wholesalers. Of course, rental shops could also order old titles of AVs, too. All these orders were referred to as 'back order' by the industrial people (Nakamura 2015: 16–17). The gross profit of wholesalers in the second half of the 1980s and the first half of the 1990s could be as high as 40 per cent of the total amount of each order (Nakamura 2015: 19). It goes without saying that if wholesalers are able to secure the supply of AVs from major makers who could always produce popular AVs, they could make substantial profit. That is also why wholesalers were willing to be complicit in Biderin's hegemony.

The circulation of AVs through rental shops, however, was challenged by a new circulation method in the 1990s: circulation through sale, which is closely related to the emergence of indie AVs in the 1980s. The term 'indie AV' refers to any video that is not submitted for inspection by Biderin (Yasuda and Amamiya 2006: 90). Thus, indie AVs can include underground (*ura*), pirated (*kaizoku*) or those AVs with thin mosaics ('*usukeshi*'). The last was particularly successful in the 1980s because the thin mosaic made the sexual organs almost transparent, which in turn meant that it was almost impossible for directors to use 'simulated' sex in their films (Fujiki 2009: 148). Some indie makers even went so far as to produce 'super see through' AVs (*chō usukeshi*), with the intention of attracting even more consumers for it is precisely the transparency of real sexual intercourse that made indie AVs sexually appealing and attractive to audiences who had longed to see the 'working parts' (Fujiki 2009: 149). However, the transparent 'see through' quality of indie AVs meant that they would not be able to pass Biderin inspection, nor be shelved in rental shops for fear of violating obscenity laws. Consequently, in the 1980s and early 1990s, indie AVs were *sold* through speciality shops at expensive prices, ranging between ¥4,000 (US$35.2)[16] and ¥6,000 (US$52.8) (Tameike 2013: 77). Hence, indie AVs were also referred to as 'AVs-for-sale', which were by and large confined to a selected few who dared and were willing, or could afford, to buy them. This meant that indie/sale AVs were in the end very marginal in the AV industry during the 1980s.

Indie AVs began to formally acquire their mainstream status in the industry when The King of Cheap Videos (*Bideo Yasuuri Ō*), a franchise enterprise specializing in the retailing of AVs, was founded in 1993 (Yasuda and Amamiya 2006: 101). The founding of the company was a landmark in the history of AVs in Japan as it made the purchase of AVs possible among ordinary AV viewers. Setting prices at between ¥1,980 (US$17.4) and ¥2,980 (US$26.2),[17] the King of Cheap Videos opened up a completely new chapter in the way Japanese AVs were consumed, circulated and made sense of among audiences in Japan (Fujiki 2009: 202). In view of the deregulation of pubic hair in magazines and customer feedback about the hassle and embarrassment involved in rental services, the King of Cheap Videos from the beginning decided to produce AVs that showed pubic hair, explored originality and offered its audiences the option of purchase (Fujiki 2009: 202). Likewise, it made a bold decision to bypass Biderin inspection as it was convinced that its new circulation method would not be approved by the association (Fujiki 2009: 203). Fully aware of the fact that dodging Biderin inspection might invite prosecution by the police, the manufacturer chose to produce videos that depicted 'simulated' rather than real sex (Yasuda and Amamiya 2006: 101). In many ways, these videos were akin to *kikaku* AVs, but in a more softcore, erotic fashion (Yasuda and Amamiya 2006: 101). As a result, a new version of AVs that showed pubic hair, and was produced for sale at a reasonable price, came into existence. One major characteristic that differentiated King of Cheap Videos' AVs-for sale from the previous indie AVs is that the former were *not* illegal in the strictest sense since, unlike indie AVs, they did not depict real sex. This specific non-illegal nature thus allowed it room to survive and expand. In just a year after its founding in 1993, the company had opened 300 chain stores all over the country (Yasuda and Amamiya 2006: 101).

Meanwhile, the King of Cheap Videos worked very hard to attract prospective franchisees. Coupled with the fact that the gap between wholesale and retail prices was huge in the 1990s,[18] the King of Cheap Video managed to experience substantial growth during its first two years of business. By 1995, the company had more than 1,000 outlets all over Japan (Fujiki 2009: 202–3). However, this prosperous situation did not last long. Many franchisees were furious at the company's mismanagement. Although the King of Cheap Videos promised to offer original videos to the franchise stores, most movies turned out to be old movies, or illegal copies of rental AVs. By the mid-1990s, therefore, many franchise stores had begun to source videos from elsewhere and the enterprise as a whole went into the doldrums before eventually going bankrupt in 1996 when one of the company's AV directors was arrested for violating local obscenity laws (Fujiki 2009: 207; Yasuda and Amamiya 2006: 102).

However, the collapse of the King of Cheap Videos in 1996 did not mean that AVs-for-sale would disappear in Japan. Quite the contrary, they had become the pre-eminent video form by the early 2000s – in large part thanks to the efforts of Takahashi Ganari, who promoted AVs-for-sale and drove the industry forward (Yasuda and Amamiya 2006: 103). Takahashi was the founder of Soft On Demand – now one of the most bankable AV makers, but at the time a small firm subcontracted by the King of Cheap Videos, and specializing in the production of 'Nude Series of Volleyball'[19] (Fujiki 2009: 208). In view of the large number of retail shops left over after the collapse of the King of Cheap Video in 1996, Takahashi sought to revolutionize the status of AVs-for-sale from marginal to mainstream (Fujiki 2009: 207). This was not, however, an easy task since Takahashi was faced with two major problems. The first was manufacturers' low profit margins. While the unit price of AVs-for-sale ranged from ¥1,980 (US$17.4) to ¥2,980 (US$26.2), most movies in the early 1990s were sold at the lower price in franchise stores, implying that wholesalers had to source AVs-for-sale from makers at an even lower price, which made manufacturers' profit margins very low. Thus, when Takahashi founded Soft On Demand, he simultaneously standardized the unit price of AVs-for-sale at ¥2,980 (US$26.2) and this substantially increased the margin of profit for AVs-for-sale.

The second problem facing Takashi was the problematic status of AVs-for-sale – something that still haunts most AV makers and industry people. The fact that AVs-for-sale were not inspected, and thus not certified, by Biderin meant that rental and other retail stores were hesitant about ordering stock for fear of being prosecuted by the police. To work around this problem, Takahashi made a bold decision by founding a new self-regulatory association in 1996: Media Rinri Kyōkai (a.k.a. Medirin, the Association of Media Ethics) (Fujiki 2009: 209). The founding of Medirin had far-reaching impact upon the whole AV industry in that, first, it revolutionized the way in which Japanese AVs were regulated and censored. Adult videos depicting pubic hair, showing the anus and using a thinner mosaic screen, could now go unchallenged – something unimaginable to both audiences and AV directors in the 1980s and the first half of the 1990s. The liberal atmosphere provided by Medirin in turn explained why AV genres experienced an explosive diversification in the 1990s.

Second, the establishment of Medirin helped establish the formal status of indie AVs within the industry itself, as well as making selling (rather than renting) AVs the normal method of distribution. Since 1997, indie AVs have primarily referred to adult videos which vow to prioritize customers' needs by ensuring creativity and authenticity in product content and by using thinner mosaic screens. AV retailers began to sell indie AVs inspected by Medirin from the mid-1990s, while they continued to rent out other forms of AV inspected by Biderin. As a result, the deviant image that had plagued indie AVs for more than a decade gradually faded away (Yasuda and Amamiya 2006: 105). From then on, Japanese AVs have been formally divided into rental AVs and AVs-for-sale in the industry.

Finally, Medirin disrupted the established hegemony formed by the major makers in the 1980s. As we have mentioned above, the establishment of Biderin for rental videos might better be seen as a strategy by the major manufacturers to establish dominance and wield power within the industry. By confining adult videos to the rental market these major AV makers forced other makers to comply with their terms, in the sense that, if the new AV makers did not subject themselves to Biderin's demands, their videos would not be certified and hence would be disallowed in rental shops. Conversely, if a rental shop did not comply with Biderin's requests to reject non-Biderin approved videos, they would lose access to the source of AVs provided by the major manufacturers. The emergence of AVs-for-sale completely disrupted Biderin's dominance, as it offered a new option whereby AVs could now be accessed through retail shops. Since then, the AV industry has been characterized by keen competition between rental AV makers (traditional AV makers) and AVs-for-sale makers (new AV makers), although most of the former began to offer the option of purchase to audiences in the wake of the emergence of AVs-for-sale. Nevertheless, they were still in many ways different from AVs-for-sale makers who not only provided sales service, but were also devoted to producing interesting AVs that took into account the diversified tastes of their audiences (Yasuda and Amamiya 2006: 106).

However, the circulation of rental AVs and AVs-for-sale was further challenged by the advent of digital technology which enabled AV makers to circulate AVs in digital files through their own websites. The cost of circulating AVs through digital files is much lower than that through video tapes or DVDs, which further enables AV makers to sell their AVs at a much cheaper price. Digital technology also enables consumers to access AVs through so-called 'streaming' (online viewing).[20] Since its inception, this acquisition method has found great favour among fans of AVs, because it allows them to access and watch purchased videos instantly, without having to wait or download them. The long-term impact of this new circulation method on the industry, however, remains to be seen.

Conclusion

This chapter has briefly outlined the overall processes by which AVs are produced, circulated and regulated in Japan and examined how major stakeholders were involved: AV makers, model agencies, production companies, postproduction companies, regulatory associations, dubbing and packaging companies, wholesalers, and rental or retail shops – all of whom interacted with one another to produce, circulate and regulate AVs in Japan. These stakeholders constitute a world of AV production in which their interactions are not necessarily in harmony with one another, since, as we have shown, they are in a struggle for power, control and ultimately profit. This world of AV production not only serves as an industrial context against which the production of *tantai* and *kikaku* AVs (Chapter 4), the job interview of AV actresses (Chapter 6), the shooting (Chapter 7) and the operation of regulatory bodies (Chapter 8) should be understood, but also helps highlight how the Big Five AV makers established their domination over the industry by acting as a cartel not only to prescribe what kinds of adult videos are produced and how they were distributed or circulated in the market, but also to exclude rivals, as we showed in the case of Muranishi's Diamond Image.

Given the fact that the production of AVs by the Big Five AV makers was heavily influenced by the *binibon*-style and pink film-style, their domination helps perpetuate the domination of *tantai* and *kikaku* AVs, which further explains why the salvage ideology – which, as we will show in Chapter 4, underlines the production of these two categories of AVs – can be sustained in the AV industry in Japan.

Finally, the structure of the AV Industry in Japan presents a kind of social organization different from the two dominant forms of inter-corporate alliance Gerlach (1992) famously identified in Japan: the intermarket *keiretsu* and vertical *keiretsu*. The intermarket *keiretsu* refers to a form of alliance that 'represents loosely structured associations of large relatively equally sized firms in diverse industries, including banking, commerce, and manufacturing' (Gerlach 1992: 67), while vertical *keiretsu* 'are *tight*, hierarchical associations centred on a single, large parent firm and containing multiple smaller satellite companies within related industries' (Gerlach 1992: 68; italics ours). The social organization of the AV industry in Japan, however, differs from the *keiretsu* in two important ways. First, the relationship between major AV makers and their subcontractors is characterized by pure business calculations: for example, there is no capital relationship between them, nor technological and management support from major AVs to their subcontractors, while the vertical *keiretsu* membership not only symbolizes the boundary of the *keiretsu* but also indicates the right to join the debt, equity, directorship and trading networks among members of the same vertical *keiretsu*. The pure transactional relationship between major AV makers and subcontractors does not guarantee that the hierarchical relationship between them can be maintained, and this includes the absolute domination of major AV makers over their subcontractors, as we have seen how Takahashi and his Soft On Demand successfully challenged the domination of the Big Five AV makers by developing a new circulation method and more importantly establishing his own regulatory body, Medirin. In the case of the vertical *keiretsu*, the single, large parent firm, however, was able to maintain its control over its member companies through multiple networks with the latter.

Second, instead of forming an alliance with equally sized firms in *diverse* industries, which in turn structures the inter-corporate exchanges among the member corporations in different industries, the Big Five AV makers tend to form a cartel *within* the industry through their control of Biderin, enabling them not only to prescribe what kinds of adult videos are produced and how they are distributed or circulated in the market, but also to exclude rivals and protect the domination of the Big Five from being challenged. This was apparent in our discussion of how Muranishi and his Diamond Image were expelled from the industry by the Big Five.

It would be interesting to explore why the social organization of the AV industry in Japan appears as it is and why it is not organized either through the intermarket or vertical-type *keiretsu*. But this in itself would require another book. The important point we would like to make here is that the famous intermarket and vertical *keiretsu* do not exhaust all the possibilities of how industries in Japan are organized. There are always many other forms of social organization, and that of the AV industry described in this chapter is one of them.

Notes

1 'Overview of the major AV makers', http://narrow-deep.car.coocan.jp/other/av/av_maker_list.html, accessed on 26 May 2015.
2 'Overview of the major AV makers', http://narrow-deep.car.coocan.jp/other/av/av_maker_list.html, accessed on 26 May 2015.
3 '*Binibon-kei*' refers to AV makers which were previously involved in *binibon* business.
4 'Overview of the major AV makers', http://narrow-deep.car.coocan.jp/other/av/av_maker_list.html, accessed on 26 May 2015.
5 'The history of h.m.p. in the 1980s', https://web.archive.org/web/20110721090105/www.hmp.jp/ordersale/column/, accessed on 1 May 2017.
6 'The history of h.m.p. in the 1990s', https://web.archive.org/web/20110721090105/www.hmp.jp/ordersale/column/, accessed on 1 May 2017.
7 'The history of h.m.p. in the 1990s', https://web.archive.org/web/20110721090105/www.hmp.jp/ordersale/column/, accessed on 1 May 2017.
8 'Famous AV directors', https://web.archive.org/web/20110721090105/www.hmp.jp/ordersale/column/, accessed on 1 May 2017.
9 While model agencies can be commonly found all over the world, they have a particular cultural salience in Japan, because model agencies in Japan have a long history in handling adult entertainment jobs and charging high commission fees. As mentioned above, there were roughly 150 model agencies in the Japanese AV industry in 2012, with a 25 per cent drop from its peak in 2005, when there were about 200 (Nakamura 2012: 16).
10 The manager is also responsible for booking the jobs, billing for the jobs and eventually paying the models for their time. By handling the details, an agency allows a model to focus on modelling work and not on the business end.

70 *Production, regulation and circulation*

11 However, press censorship remained a reality in the postwar era, especially in political matters deemed subversive by the American Force during its occupation of Japan.
12 In the mid-2000s, though the number of Board members increased to eight, the composition of the Board continued to be dominated by adult video makers (Sonoda and Dai 2016: 110).
13 The Administrative Office of a Japanese organization is the department that fulfils its central administrative or general secretary duties.
14 Model agencies were only legalized by the Japanese government in the 2000s.
15 According to our research in Japan, the 1990s saw the founding of a number of self-regulatory agencies such as Visual Software Contents Industry Coop (VSIC, 1994) and Ethics Organization of Computer Software (EOCS, 1992), to name just a few.
16 This was calculated according to the exchange rate of US$0.0088=¥1 in May 2016.
17 However, most videos ended up with a market price of ¥1,480 (US$13).
18 As of the early 1990s, the retail prices were between ¥1,980 and ¥2,980 per video, but the wholesale prices were only ¥1,000 to ¥1,500 (Fujiki 2009: 202).
19 Nude Series of Volleyball featured women playing volleyball in the nude. This was one of the most famous series subcontracted by Takahashi.
20 Streaming media is a form of multimedia that is constantly received by and presented to an end-user while being delivered by a provider. Its verb form, 'to stream', refers to the process of delivering media in this manner.

4 The production of *tantai* and *kikaku*

Introduction

We concluded in Chapter 3 that since its inception, the Japanese AV industry had been dominated by the production of *tantai* and *kikaku* AVs. This chapter therefore turns to the production of *tantai* and *kikaku* AVs, exploring how they are different and differentiated from each other. The first part of this chapter is a detailed analysis of how *tantai* AVs and *kikaku* AVs are stitched together discursively and practically by different stakeholders, including AV makers, production companies that take subcontracted jobs from major AV makers, and model agencies that represent AV actresses according to the specific valuations of women's lack of sexual agency and men's sexual domination over women respectively. We will explore how the differentiated valuations of women's lack of sexual agency and men's sexual domination over women create the corresponding differences in narrative, emphasis of storyline, number of genres, casting, packaging, promotion and clientele of *tantai* and *kikaku* AVs. We do not pretend to offer a comprehensive semiotic analysis of *tantai* and *kikaku* AVs but merely suggest that there is a cultural reason underpinning the production of Japanese AVs.

Narrative

Within the Japanese AV industry, *tantai* refers to a specific style of production starring a single actress. Known as a *tantai* actress, she is the only female performer featured throughout the whole video. As a rule, she has a name (albeit a stage name), and is thus famous and popular among audiences in Japan as an idol (Yasuda and Amamiya 2006: 129). By definition, a *tantai* actress is a beauty with a gorgeous face and fine figure for these are precisely her major selling points. Her face and figure – especially her breasts and buttocks – are overtly marketed as products to the audiences. She is also expected to have attractive, if not perfect, skin texture, complexion, body line, body proportions, buttocks contour, shape of her pubic hair and overall temperament; and most importantly she is required to have an image of a young, pure and innocent girl, all of which will be noted and verified during the job interview (Nakamura 2012: 45, 49).

72 *The production of* tantai *and* kikaku

That is the major reason why in early years the term '*tantai*' was always accompanied by '*bishōjo*' ('beautiful young girl'), the prototype of Japanese AVs, for beauty and youth are precisely the prerequisites for becoming a *tantai* actress.

Tantai AVs conventionally contain two real sex scenes alongside one simulated sex scene, though variations occur from time to time (Nakamura 2012: 39). The *tantai* AV we are going to examine in this chapter by and large follows the same pattern as it contains two real sex scenes, alongside a fellatio scene to replace simulated sex. Nowadays it has become a commonplace to have three or four real sex scenes in the wake of the keen competition.[1] Although the director is the one who oversees the organization and shooting of the whole movie, it is not uncommon for him to leave the decisions of actual flow of actions and motions to the actor. This is especially so for *tantai* AV, since the female character within the movie typically assumes a passive personality and so needs someone to guide and lead her through the sex. As we have argued elsewhere (Wong and Yau 2014; Yau and Wong 2009), women portrayed in *tantai*, especially *bishōjo*, AVs are stereotypically sexually innocent, sweet, pitiful and fragile; and their personalities presented in the AVs are, after all, simple, pure, unassuming, unsophisticated and straightforward. One can see that what *tantai* AVs sell is a pure, sweet, artless and wholesome femininity.

The cultural significance attached to the actress in *tantai* AVs and celebration of her pure femininity manifests itself in the narrative arrangement of the video. This is especially true for one genre known as 'debut'. A recent AV starring Yoshikawa Aimi is a good case in point (see Figure 4.1).

Figure 4.1 The cover of Yoshikawa Aimi's debut AV.

The production of tantai *and* kikaku   73

This AV was released by Soft On Demand in 2013. It lasts 180 minutes and is divided into three parts. The first starts with a scene that is located in a noisy classroom. Yoshikawa Aimi, the actress, is dressed in a sailor-suit, the typical Japanese school uniform. From the scene, it is apparent that she is a high school student and having a class. She is depicted listening to the teacher's class. But, all of a sudden, she looks into the camera, as if she were communicating something to the audience (see Figure 4.2).

What followed is an image scene with relaxing background music. She is depicted walking along the corridor outside the classrooms where students come and go. In the middle of walking, she again looks into the camera. Then she stops and stands still while smiling at the camera, which then switches to a seaside scene, where Aimi is seen taking a walk along the seafront and playing with water in the sea, to the background sound of relaxing music. Subtitles on the screen tell viewers that she is from Kamakura and has grown up by the sea. Shortly after, the film switches back to the classroom scene. A text again appears on the screen telling us that she is the 'High School Ideal Type' while she poses in front of the blackboard, smiling and giggling. The screen text then tell us that 'We love this kind of girl when young.' This scene ends with her drawing a heart on the blackboard (see Figure 4.3). She looks wary while looking into the camera. The screen texts then tell viewers that while she is still a child, and childish, she has an adult-like mature figure.

Then it switches to a scene where the actress is sitting on a sofa. She only wears a bra, exposing her cleavage. The screen texts read that she is a pure and innocent girl, and that she has no idea of what sex is. Then it switches back to the classroom scene. What followed is a switching between scenes of her in the

Figure 4.2 She is portrayed looking into the camera.

74 *The production of* tantai *and* kikaku

Figure 4.3 The scene where she is portrayed drawing a heart on the blackboard.

classroom and screen texts emphasizing her youthfulness (aged 18), and her breasts (H-cup). This whole scene lasts four minutes 45 seconds.

Next comes an interview with her in the classroom by the director-cum-actor who is unseen behind the camera (see Figure 4.4). This interview lasts about 13 minutes, revolving around her young age, her hometown and her sexual life – especially her sexual innocence and inexperience. What follows is a scene where she stands in the middle of the classroom and is asked to take off her sailor-suit alongside her underwear. She poses naked in front of the camera. She is then asked to sit on the desk and spread her legs. She appears nervous but duly follows the director's instructions. She is then asked to open her vagina with her hands, followed by a close-up shot of her vagina. After she puts on her underwear and sailor-suit, a male character comes into the camera shot. He is fully clothed but his erect penis is obvious. She is asked to touch the erect penis. She hesitates but in the end shyly does as she is asked. Later she performs fellatio when further asked. This scene ends when the male character ejaculates.

The second part starts with a scene where Yoshikawa is depicted sitting on a sofa in an indoor room with a big window by the side, while the screen texts advise viewers of the first massage of her H-cup breasts (see Figure 4.5). As the camera turns directly to her, the unseen director asks her if she is nervous. She nods her head. The director then announces that what will follow is breast massage. The male character comes in, walks close up to her, sitting behind her on the same sofa and starting to caress her breasts. Later he undresses her top and bra and applies oil to her breasts as he continues to massage them. This scene lasts about 20 minutes and ends with her being asked to spread her legs

The production of tantai *and* kikaku   75

Figure 4.4 The interview scene.

Figure 4.5 The beginning of the second part of the movie.

wide for the camera. She appears sexually aroused as her panties are shown to be turning wet.

The camera then turns to the next scene where she sits on a bed (Figure 4.6). Again, she is asked many times whether she is nervous or shy. The first five minutes focuses on how anxious she is after realizing what would happen next: real sexual intercourse. Then the director asks the male actor to come in. They greet each other. She looks uneasy when the male character sits right next her.

76　*The production of* tantai *and* kikaku

Figure 4.6 A new section where the actress is portrayed sitting on a bed.

The director says that he will leave the two alone. The male character asks her to look at him as he moves closer. He asks her gently if he could hold her hands. She nods her head. As he grasps her hand, he asks her to kiss him. She laughs bashfully and reluctantly. While he is asking her to kiss him again, she moves forward to do so. He then asks if they could have deeper kisses. She smiles bashfully while nodding her head. He then asks her to open her mouth. She obliges by opening her mouth and they then engage in a French kiss. Shortly after, he begins to approach her sexually, undressing her top. He kisses and caresses her breasts as he removes her bra and asks her to spread her legs while kissing her. He removes her underpants and asks if it is all right to perform cunnilingus on her. She nods her head. She murmurs and groans softly. Later on, he asks her to perform fellatio. What follows is sexual intercourse between them. They swap into several positions before the sex scene ends with the male character ejaculating on her breasts.

The final part begins with an image scene where Yoshikawa is depicted topless (but still with a sailor-suit ribbon and skirt on) in a hotel room. Once again, she looks into the camera as if she were communicating something to the audience (see Figure 4.7).

The texts on the screen: 'Having sex in her hometown', 'A hotel room that faces a sea that she loves' and 'It is the street where she often went during her high school days' (see Figure 4.8). Then the camera zooms in on her, and we hear the unseen director say 'Let's start.'

The director once again asks if she is anxious. She simply replies 'yes'. He then asks her if she is still nervous even though they are in a beautiful hotel. She again replies 'yes' and giggles. He asks if she feels nostalgic about seeing scenes

Figure 4.7 The actress is depicted looking into the camera.

Figure 4.8 A scene where she is portrayed sitting in a huge hotel room facing the sea.

similar to the ones she used to see when she was young. She nods her head. Once more, he asks if she is nervous. The director adds that she had her first sex in the studio the other day and asks her to please be relaxed and enjoy today's sex. He then asks her to place her hand on her heart and feel it to see if she is feeling better today. She says that she is after all extremely nervous. The director asks if it is all right to call in the male character. She nods her head. The male character comes in, walks towards her and immediately takes hold of her hands, asking her if she is nervous. She says, 'yes'. He then starts kissing her. She appears anxious while reacting to his sudden amorous approach. He asks her to put out her tongue. He starts to caress her body and comments on how huge her breasts are. He undresses her and asks her to relax, before starting to touch her lower part from the outside to inside of her panties which he then takes off and performs cunnilingus, making her come. Then he asks her to perform fellatio which she does shyly. Sexual intercourse then follows. Again, they swap different sexual postures and the sex scene ends when the male character ejaculates on her breasts. Lying on the bed, she looks faint and exhausted.

Three points can be identified in light of the above sketch of the AV 'narrative'. First and foremost, the above movie places singular focus on the actress to the exclusion of all else. As we have seen, concerted efforts go into portraying and aestheticizing the actress's naivety, innocent appearance, unassuming personality and wholesome character. From the beginning, she is depicted as an 18-year-old young girl. This freshness manifests itself in her extraordinarily thin makeup, which is unusual in AVs. More important, her sexual innocence is given extra attention. Not only is she depicted as having only one boyfriend so far in her life and hence scant sexual experience, but she is also made out to be extremely nervous and shy about sex. This can be seen in the undergarments which she wears in the movie. Rather than wearing sexy or sexually inviting lace bra and panties, she is filmed wearing a grey sports bra and panties typically worn by sexually immature young girls. Moreover, her sexual purity extends to her general character as well. Throughout the video, she is dressed in a sailor-suit and is constantly associated with the image of a high school girl. She is even repeatedly described as 'the perfect high school girl' or 'the kind of girl that every boy would fall for in high school'. All of this points to her naivety, freshness, innocence and purity. At the end of the introductory scene, she is even portrayed drawing a heart on the blackboard. One might say that she is the perfect girl-next-door.

Second, this specific image of the actress is repeatedly authenticated and validated through situating this image against her biographical background, upbringing, hometown, and so on. First, the movie is shot in Kamakura, the actress's hometown. As she is now residing in Tokyo, the return to Kamakura to shoot the film conjures up the popular motif of homecoming in the cultural context of Japan. Second, special attention is paid to the ocean that is endlessly romanticized as pure and nostalgic in the movie. There are several long image scenes where she is shown sitting or taking a walk by the side of the ocean. Her image of sentimentalism and purity is thus delivered to audiences through this association with the ocean. Figure 4.8 even contextualizes the sex scene directly with 'hometown' (thus sex in hometown), especially the 'street' where the actress used to hang out with friends in the past, and links her image to the fact that she loves the ocean and her sentimental ties to it. Third, her youth and scant sexual experience are also frequently invoked. As Figures 4.1, 4.5 and 4.6 show, her image of innocence, naivety, shyness and freshness is closely associated with her young age (18 years old), her scant sexual experience and hence her purity, as well as her hometown (she grew up in Kamakura which is by the seaside). The result of this association is that the AV girl is not performing, but is simply herself. The image portrayed in the AV is her 'real' self.

Finally and relatedly, if the actress is not performing or acting and hence not in a drama, it is perhaps no surprise that the movie is not underlined by a single theme or narrative. As we have seen, all three of the sex scenes depicted in the movie occur for no particular reason, when the male character all of a sudden approaches the female character amorously. Audiences are not informed about why sex takes place between them, let alone the kind of context and background against which the sexual tension between them has been built or developed.

Central to these three points is what we shall call the 'authentication of the actress', in the sense that the actress outside the movie is made to be 'identical' to the female character inside the AV *as if* she were one and the same. As we have seen, the way the actress is portrayed in the movie is to convince the audiences that she does not take on any specific role or character, in the way we usually imagine. That is to say, she is not performing or pretending that she is innocent, pure, cute or unassuming. Instead, she *truly is* innocent, pure, cute and unassuming as she just acts herself in the movie. One might say that *tantai* AVs strive to authenticate the identity and personality of an actress per se by firmly situating the female character in the movie against the biography of that same actress outside the movie to the effect that they are made to be the one and the same. The main thrust of *tantai* AV is to perform authenticity and turn on the (staged) authenticity of the actress.

Kikaku *AVs*

Kikaku AVs, by contrast, prioritize context and storyline at the expense of the beauty and fine figure of the actress (Yau 2001: 17). In other words, their main thrust is not to instantly charm audiences by means of the sexual/physical attractiveness of the actress, in the way that *tantai* AVs do. Rather, a *kikaku* AV is meant to gradually engage the audiences in the sexual fantasies or drama revolving around the *female character* and the subsequent sexual tensions arising from interactions with that character. To depict more complicated plots or storylines, it is not uncommon for *kikaku* AVs to feature more than one actress, especially in the so-called 'omnibus'[2] (Tameike 2013: 20; Yasuda and Amamiya 2006: 129). In some *kikaku* AVs, such as the *bukkake*[3] series produced by Soft On Demand (hereafter SOD),[4] there might be 100 actresses taking part in the same movie.

In order to demonstrate this, we shall offer a textual analysis of a *kikaku* movie produced by Erotica, an AV maker majoring in *kikaku* AV. This movie is a combination of two genres, mixing big breasts with blindfold play – a style which has become more and more popular in recent years. The movie is titled 'Big-boob beautiful young women and in the middle of blindfold play the guy changes from being handsome to ugly' (*kyōryū bishōjo to mekakushipurei chū ni ikemen to busamen ga kossori kōkan*). It stars two actors and one actress and lasts 139 minutes.

80 *The production of* tantai *and* kikaku

The movie begins with two men looking at comics (*manga*) while chatting in a bedroom setting. One of the men is depicted as thin, good-looking and stylish, whereas the other is plump, old-fashioned and unpolished (see Figure 4.9).

The chubby man is reading an adult manga magazine. The thin man asks him how long it's been since he had sex and he says 'three months'. The thin man who is popular with girls is shocked and decides to help his friend by finding a girl for him. He asks the fat man what kind of girls he wants. He replies that he wants a virgin. The thin man replies that that is impossible because all his female friends have had sex with him. The thin man then suggests a girl with big breasts. The fat man is pleased. The thin man then calls one of his girlfriends and asks her to come over to his house immediately. The girl agrees to arrive at his apartment in 20 minutes. Meanwhile, the thin man suggests that his female friend will not want to have sex with the fat guy because he looks ugly and disgusting. The only solution is to blindfold the woman and deceive her into believing that she is having sex with the thin guy.

Excited by his friend's idea, the fat man rushes to get an eye mask. The screen then reads '15 minutes later' as the fat man returns with an eye mask. But all of a sudden the fat man realizes that he has forgotten to buy condoms. The thin man replies that there is no need to use condoms as he never wears one. On hearing this, the fat man is extremely excited and grateful to his friend. The thin man then asks the fat man to hide himself under the bed and to appear only when he gives him a signal. The thin guy then leaves the bedroom (see Figure 4.10).

After about five minutes, the thin guy comes back to the bedroom with a young woman. She is wearing a low-cut blouse and skirt. They then sit on the bed chatting while flirting with each other. From this conversation, we know that the young woman is now attending a university and has a busy schedule meeting

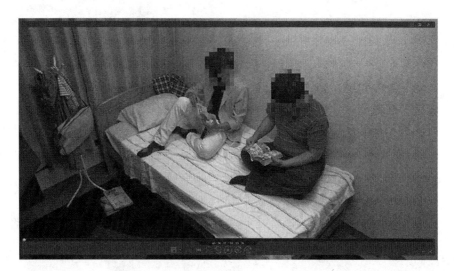

Figure 4.9 Two men are depicted reading comics in a bedroom setting.

The production of tantai *and* kikaku 81

Figure 4.10 The thin man is filmed leaving the room.

Figure 4.11 The fat man is filmed spying on them.

friends and joining recreational clubs. Meanwhile, the fat guy under the bed is portrayed spying on them (see Figure 4.11). The thin man asks the woman if she has had an affair during the period they haven't met. She says 'no' and then they start kissing. The fat man is seen sticking his head further out from under the bed in an attempt to spy more on what they are doing.

The thin man then asks the woman to undress completely. The woman asks why but nevertheless duly does as asked by taking off her outer clothing to

82 *The production of* tantai *and* kikaku

reveal a strapless bra and blossoming breasts. She then takes off her bra and skirt, leaving herself semi-nude with only her panties on. The thin man takes out the eye mask and tells the woman that they should do something special tonight. Surprised, the woman asks what. The man explains that he wants her to wear the eye mask all through their sex together and says it would be exciting for them both. A little reluctantly, the woman puts on the mask, whereupon the thin guy says loudly that everything is ready now. The fat guy under the bed then emerges. The thin guy indicates to him to come close to the woman while he himself sits on the side of the bed reading comics (see Figure 4.12).

The fat man appears awkward and does not know how to begin. The thin man signals him to kiss her. The fat man then kisses the woman. Once he starts, however, becomes very thrilled and excited; not only does he kiss the woman heartily and fervently, but he also slurps extra loudly. She finds this odd and asks the thin man what is going on. The thin man by her side, still reading a comic, just replies that he feels like doing something different that day. The fat man continues to kiss the woman eagerly. Meanwhile he begins cupping and caressing her breasts before sucking and licking them vigorously. He starts to touch her vagina outside her panties. As he does it very eagerly and somehow violently, the woman asks him please to do it slowly and gently. The thin man beside her says that he cannot help doing things this way as 'he is really horny!'.

The fat man starts to caress the woman's vagina inside her panties. She gets sexually aroused and starts groaning so he then takes off her panties and caresses her clitoris. She groans and moans. He soon penetrates her with his finger, while kissing and caressing her inner thighs which only arouses her excitement more, so he starts to loudly slurp her vagina as he performs cunnilingus in a very eager and forceful way. The woman is surprised by all this and comments that he is

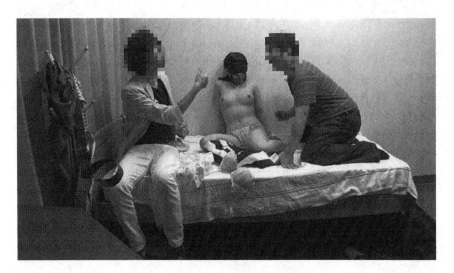

Figure 4.12 The fat man is depicted talking to the thin man.

somehow different from normal. While reading comics, the thin man replies, 'Isn't it good to have it sometimes? This makes you feel good, doesn't it? So I'll do things even more forcefully!' The woman comes as the fat man performs cunnilingus while caressing her clitoris. The fat man and thin man are depicted looking into each other's eyes. The thin man says that it shouldn't end like this and asks the woman to turn around and kneel down on the bed. The fat man then takes off his trousers and boxers while his friend says, 'Open your mouth!' Whereupon the fat man puts his penis closer to the woman's mouth and she starts to perform fellatio for him.

The woman comments that she does not know where the thin man is as his voice is far away. The thin man, sitting by her side, replies that she is getting overly concerned and orders her to take his penis deeper in her mouth (*okumade*). This she duly does and the thin man says that he is feeling good (*kimochi ii*) before ordering her to suck his testicles (*kintama*). As she sucks and licks them, the woman comments that his penis is larger than usual. The thin man counters that there is no way that it is larger than usual and accuses her of thinking that way because she has been sleeping with other men. She denies this, so the thin man then says, 'If that isn't the case, do it [fellatio] for me.'

In the course of performing fellatio for the fat man, the woman murmurs that she is tired and stops in the middle. The thin man asks irritably, 'Why are you tired?' In the meantime, the fat man turns the woman over and lays his legs over her thighs so that she is in the best position to perform breast sex for him. The woman asks, 'Do you want me to sandwich your penis between my breasts?' The thin man takes a look from behind the woman and said, 'yes'. After a few minutes, the woman asks if he's enjoying it. The thin man says yes and comments that it is a great feeling and that he's ready to come inside her now. The woman then says, 'please enter me!' while laying on her back on the bed.

The fat man looks hesitant and awkward. The thin man signals him to enter her. The thin man says that he is about to come inside her. Meanwhile, the fat man is filmed entering her from on top. Shortly after, the woman comments, while groaning with pleasure, that it is after all different. Once more she comments how strange it is, and keeps on repeating herself. She asks the thin man if it is alright to take off her mask and, as she speaks, she moves her hand to the mask, but the thin man refuses to allow her to touch it. She then says, 'The penis is somehow…' – at which point she removes the eye mask and finds herself extremely shocked. She raises her upper body and asks the fat man who is on top of her who he is. But the fat man ignores her and continues thrusting inside her. She asks the thin man who finally explains that he is his good friend. The woman keeps asking 'why?' The fat man comments that it is good. The woman, while resisting, is depicted moaning and groaning.

The woman turns to the thin man for help. However, he says, 'Don't touch me I'm playing a game now!' The woman is portrayed as somehow enjoying the physical sex while trying to resist. She finally reaches an orgasm in the midst of the fat's man thrusting. The thin guy then says that it was good and vehement (*hageshii*) and the fat man agrees with him. The thin man takes out his smart phone and takes a picture of the two of them coupling from the side. The woman resists and cannot help stopping, whereas the fat man appears very excited. The thin man even shows the picture to the fat man who turns the woman over and enters her from behind. She is shown groaning and moaning. The fat man wants to kiss her while entering her from the back, but at first she rejects him. The thin man, though, orders her to kiss with the fat man and she does so, so that she is portrayed somehow as submitting to an amorous attack. She groans and moans loudly as he continues to thrust inside her from behind, from time to time kissing her. She murmurs, 'no!' ('*iya!*') but still submits to it. She climaxes again, her body trembling involuntarily before the couple shifts back to the missionary position. The fat man cups her breasts and kisses her from time to time. The woman does not resist but groans. The thin man comments that it is disgusting that she likes kissing the fat man who asks if it is OK to ejaculate inside her vagina. The woman objects: 'No, no, stop!' ('*Iya da iya da! Dame!*') But the thin man tells the fat man that it is fine to ejaculate inside her, so the fat man carries on thrusting until he finally ejaculates inside her.

What follows is a close-up shot of the woman's vagina, from which the fat man's semen is dripping out. The fat man then sits up on the bed while the woman lies on the bed murmuring, 'awful!' ('*hidoi!*'). She then sits up and uses a pillow to hide her body from them. The thin man suggests that the two might become boyfriend and girlfriend instead. She murmurs, 'This is too awful!' ('*Hidoi yo!*) and goes on to ask the thin man whether they are not a couple. The thin man replies, 'We, a couple? I have never intended to be with you!'. The woman again murmurs, 'awful!'. Then all are silent. Finally, the thin man breaks the silence by asking the woman to leave as sex is over. He picks up her clothes and undergarments from the floor and throws them to her. This part ends when the woman starts putting her underclothes back on.

The narrative of this *kikaku* AV displays three characteristics that contrast with those found in the *tantai* AV described earlier. First, the actress who appears in this *kikaku* AV, from the beginning, is understood to be performing or taking up a specific character in this movie: the role of a university student who has had a colourful school life. But it is more than this. She is also depicted as having a colourful sex life, alongside various sex partners. In addition, she is also posed as a woman with 'huge breasts'. Second, the sole focus of the *kikaku* AV is the story that develops from, or revolves around, the female character. The story flows when the female character is called upon by the thin male character who actually sets her up for forced sex with the fat male character. As she is painted as being sexually active and one of the sex partners of the thin male character, she goes to his flat accordingly. The sexual tension and pleasure of this movie lies in the secret swapping of the thin male character with that of the fat one and the dawning suspicion of the female character over the identity of her current sex partner. The whole movie climaxes when the blindfolded female character takes off her eye mask and realizes that the man with whom she has been having sex is not the thin man she knows, but the fat male character. Notwithstanding her attempts to resist the setup-cum-forced sex, she in the end succumbs to it as evidenced by the immense physical pleasure she experiences during intercourse. As we can see, the whole movie develops from or revolves around the role/character the actress is assigned to play in this specific *kikaku* movie: the character of being sexually promiscuous, desiring and open and indiscriminate in her choice of sexual partners, yet still willing to subject herself to the domination of her boyfriend.

In light of these two points, one is tempted to say that a *kikaku* actress is more like a movie actress than a *tantai* actress, inasmuch as a *kikaku* actress, not unlike a movie actress, is acting or performing a specific role in the movie, whereas the *tantai* actress is simply seen as being herself. As the *kikaku* actress is performing a specific role and apparently will switch to another role in the next movie, the image she has performed in this movie will not be considered or seen as her own 'real' or 'authentic' self. In other words, the image is understood to be different from her real self and hence faked. Put differently, the real nature or persona of the actress is completely ruled out of consideration in *kikaku* movies. What is relevant here is the character/role she plays in each of the stories. We are arguing for a realism that is different from that of *tantai* AVs: authentication of the story, the gist of which is that all the elements of the story – in particular, the image as well as the act of all *kikaku* AV actresses – have to help authenticate the story, which is also to say that *kikaku* AV actresses should make the female characters inside the movie look 'real': the authentication of the female characters. One might conclude that, in contrast to *tantai* AVs that strive to present (staged) authenticity of the actress, *kikaku* AVs work to authenticate the story including the female characters inside the movies. In other words, while both *tantai* and *kikaku* AVs turn on authenticity, the former revolve around the authenticity of the actress per se, whereas the latter focus on the authenticity of the story and the female character.

Finally, what the *kikaku* AV in our case was selling is the story in which the female character is sexually promiscuous, desiring, open and indiscriminate in her choice of sexual partners. Yet, despite her unwillingness, she finally succumbs to the domination of her boyfriend because such a story can best reveal men's sexual domination over women. The crucial tension of the story lies in the unwillingness of the female character to have sex with her boyfriend's friend inasmuch as her unwillingness can make her boyfriend's domination over her stand out. In other words, the *kikaku* AV emphasizes men's sexual domination over women rather than women's lack of sexual agency. In the case of the *tantai* AV described earlier, the image of the actress as an innocent, pure, cute or inexperienced girl-next-door attracts male audiences. In other words, the *tantai* AV is selling women's lack of sexual agency. But we have to hastily point out that men's sexual domination and women's lack of sexual agency are two major elements of the salvage ideology: the former being generally emphasized in the pink film tradition, while the latter is the focus of the *binibon* tradition. Now we can see how the pink film tradition and the *binibon* tradition have influenced the narrative of *kikaku* AVs and *tantai* AVs respectively in the contemporary Japanese AV industry.

AV genres

As *tantai* AV has a singular focus on the actress, in particular on her pure, unassuming femininity at the expense of content or story, it is not surprising to find out that *tantai* AVs have far fewer genres than their *kikaku* counterparts do. Apart from *bishōjo*, there are only a few genres associated with it: 'debut', 'young girl', 'high school girl', 'sister' and 'actress'. Among these, '*bishōjo*' is the most popular one, followed by 'debut', 'high school girls', and the others. When compared with other genres under *tantai*, the genre of 'actress' might appear odd in the sense that participants are themselves actresses. This genre was a product of the specific cable TV regulations that came into force in Japan when, in 1997, pornography was for the first time broadcast nonstop on SKY PerfecTV!'s 24 hour programming (Suitsu 1998a: 8). Obviously enough, AV makers were eager to tap into the cable businesses by broadcasting their videos there. However, SKY PerfecTV! imposed strict regulations on content, stipulating that only the genre of 'actress' be allowed to be broadcast on it. All other genres – including '*bishōjo*', 'debut' and 'school girl', not to mention 'S&M' or 'rape' – were excluded. As a result, all AV makers made a concerted effort to develop the 'actress' genre from the late 1990s (Suitsu 1998a: 8). Since then, 'actress' AV has become one of the major genres specialized in by Japanese AV makers. We can see that the circulation channels of the AV industry in Japan can have a substantial influence on forms of AV production.

As mentioned above, *kikaku* AVs work precisely to ignore the actress in favour of the *character* or the *role* she takes in a movie. Apparently, the character will vary depending on the stories or genres. But there are simply too many stories or 'genres' within *kikaku* to list here. For in fact, anything other than '*bishojō*', 'debut', 'young girl', 'actress' and 'school girl' can be lumped together under the *kikaku* category. Some common *kikaku* genres turn on the social identity of the female characters concerned. For instance, 'amateur' ('*shirōto*'), 'mature woman' ('*jukujo*'), 'wife' ('*hitotsuma*'), 'widow' ('*mibojin*'), 'female groper' ('*chijo*'), 'pregnant woman' ('*ninpu*'), 'mother-in-law' or 'stepmother' ('*gibo*'), 'daughter-in-law' ('*yome*'), 'wife-to-be' ('*hanayome*'), 'priestess' ('*miko*'), 'gal' or 'girl' ('*gyaru*')[5] or 'new half' ('*ryūhāfu*').

Others emphasize the body fragments of the female characters namely 'big breasts' ('*kyonyū*'), '"super" breasts' ('*chōnyū*'), 'beautiful breasts' ('*binyū*'), 'small breasts' ('*hinnyū*'/'*binyū*'), 'big buttocks' ('*kyojiri*'), 'chubby women' ('*pocchari*'), 'slender women' ('*surendā*'), 'petite' ('*kogara*'), 'sun burned' ('*hiyake*') and so on. Still others emphasize the occupation of the female characters, such as office lady (OL), maid, secretary, teacher, nurse, policewoman, waitress, private tutor, schoolgirl, sex entertainment girl (*fūzoku*) or race queen. Relatedly, some focus on costume including race queen, bunny girl, swimsuit, mini-skirt, sailor-suit, kimono, and so on. Still others revolve around set-ups such as nurse-doctor, student-master, student-private tutor or son-mother or the so-called like 'kiss' ('*kisu*'), 'threesome' ('3P'), 'vibrator' ('*rōtā*'), 'lotion' ('*rōshun*'), 'facial ejaculation' ('*gansha*'), 'enema' ('*kanchō*'), 'fellatio' ('*ferachio*'), 'breast-sex' ('*paizuri*'), and so on. Of course, there are also popular genres such as 'male groper' ('*chikan*'), 'seduction' or 'scouting' ('*nanpa*'), 'sadomasochism', 'rape', 'bondage', 'threesome', 'group sex', 'sex with Afro-American men', and so on where the female characters are variously depicted as victims, or femme fatales. As the aforementioned *kikaku* movie produced by Erotica shows, a combination of two genres is now a commonplace, for instance, 'seduction' or 'wife scouting' ('*hitozuma-nanpa*'), or 'OLs kissing' ('*OL no kisu*'). One can see the sexual attraction of *kikaku* AVs does not come from the authenticity of the actress herself, but from the authenticity of the character/role the actress plays in the movie.

This characteristic of *kikaku* movie apparently implies that all *kikaku* movies are presented as fictions. As we have seen, *kikaku* AV is renowned for its extremely colourful, fictional presentation predicated on the idea that sex is play (*asobi*) (Buruma 1984; Matsuzawa 1998: 24). Even in woodblock pornography (*shunga*), sex is often portrayed as a form of imaginative play. For instance, a princess is engaged in coitus with her loveable dog and an octopus is portrayed masturbating a girl (Matsuzawa 1998: 24). Equally playful is the peeping (*nozoki*) theme in *shunga* (spring pictures).[6] For instance, there are scenes in which pubescent boys experience their first sexual awakening via peeping at a female naked body or children happen to peep through a chink in a wooden building in which a couple is copulating (Screech 1999: 217). This fictional nature of *kikaku* actresses is likewise reflected in the marketing strategies of the *kikaku* AVs. Unlike *tantai* AVs whose release is usually accompanied by a series of elaborate marketing campaigns, *kikaku* AVs do not. More often than not, they will be lumped together with similar genres and marketed as a new release of that genre – precisely because what *kikaku* AVs sell is not the actress herself but stories revolving around the female character.

Production system

Tantai AVs are usually produced by big studios because only they can afford to hire *tantai* AV actresses whose pay, as will be mentioned below, is far higher than that of *kikaku* actresses. Indeed, the overall production costs of *tantai* AVs are also very high. According to our data, the cost of producing an average *kikaku* AV movie in 2013 was around one to 1.5 million yen (US$13,200), excluding actress fees (Tameike 2013: 23). Yet the production cost might increase substantially in the case of a *tantai* AV because still photographs, props, costumes, underwear and filming locations for *tantai* AVs, unlike those for *kikaku* AVs, have to be of a certain quality. According to Tameike who is a Japanese AV director, the production cost of a *tantai* AV in the late 1990s to early 2000s could run up to three million yen (US$26,400) excluding the actress's pay (Tameike 2013: 23). Assuming that the actress's fee was two million yen (US$17,600), the total production cost would be as high as five million yen (US$44,000). Obviously enough, only big studios can afford to invest in producing *tantai* AVs.

As mentioned in Chapter 3, most AV studios do not have their in-house production team. Japanese AV makers, especially established ones, have tended to subcontract their projects to professional production companies because subcontracting can save production costs. Professional production companies also have to make sure that the movie is completed within the budget because any overbudgeted cost will fall on them (Inoue 2002: 33). That is why they always try their best to finish the shooting process as soon as possible.

In contrast to *tantai* AVs, *kikaku* AVs are by and large manufactured by small AV studios and even one-man studios. Unlike the Big Five majors, small studios cannot afford to make big-budget productions, let alone sign up exclusive actresses. Thus *tantai mono*, especially *bishōjo*, will not be their trump card in expanding their fan base or securing market share. This financial constraint has in turn explained why small capital AV studios have usually opted for *kikaku mono*. A case in point is *hamedori*, which is similar to what is known as gonzo pornography in the West where the camera is placed right into the action. In Japanese *hamedori*, the director-cum-actor will wear his camcorder on his forehead, both filming and performing sexual acts, without the usual separation between camera and performers seen in conventional porn and cinema (Fujiki 1998: 198). The same is also true for *bukkake*, a genre where a large number of men take turns in ejaculating onto the face and body of a single girl. Despite the fame they have gained in Japan as well as overseas, *bukkake* were originally created, according to some of our informants, because of a lack of financial resources. It is precisely the financial constraint that made small studios – especially one-man studios – focus on low-budget *kikaku* movies requiring just a single actress (something we will return to in Chapter 7).

Like *tantai* AV manufacturers, major makers of *kikaku* AVs have chosen to subcontract their projects to production companies in order to save costs. But many extremely small studios or one-man studios, according to our research, cannot afford to do this. The only solution for them is to shoot the films by themselves, regardless of how unprofessional they are. In the process, they tend to hire a freelance director and cameraman, and source both actress and actor through personal networks to minimize costs. To further lower their budget, it is not uncommon, as mentioned in Chapter 3, for production companies to hire amateur directors who are not specialized in shooting pornographic movies; alternatively, they randomly assign one of their ordinary staff members to stand in for the director (Inoue 2002: 26–8).

Not unlike *tantai* AV, *kikaku* tend to have two real sex scenes and one simulated one. But if, for any reason, the original filming schedule cannot proceed as planned, it is always possible to shorten the movie or to integrate other clips to form a new video. This flexibility is made possible by two things. First, while most *kikaku* AVs do have detailed plots or stories, they tend to consist of several short stories that are usually not directly related. Therefore, even if one of the stories changes, it will not create problems for other stories. Second, *kikaku* AVs, as mentioned above, have tended to hire a number of actresses who are unnamed and unidentified in a movie. This in turn suggests that it will not create any problem even when the story or plot changes. For instance, in the famous series Smutty King Game (*ecchi na ōsama gēmu*) produced by SOD where a few actresses alongside a few actors are hired to participate in the movie, since most of them are unnamed or unidentified participants, a change in the role they play – for instance, from students to office ladies – or even change in sexual content does not create any specific problem.

The anonymous nature of *kikaku* AVs in turn provides Japanese women who desire to appear in AVs, but who, for whatever kind of reason, wish to hide their identities, with an alternative. As mentioned above, *kikaku* AV focuses on storyline rather than actresses. Accordingly, actresses are often unnamed, or and portrayed as just one of a large crowd. At times, *kikaku* actresses might not even show their faces which are either pixelated or excluded from the camera. This is why *kikaku* actresses are also nicknamed 'women without names' (*namae no nai onna tachi*) within the industry (Nakamura 2009: 2; 2012: 36). This nature of *kikaku* AV thus provides those Japanese women who are concerned about privacy with an opportunity to make quick money by appearing in an AV without being identified by friends, colleagues, lovers/partners or family members.

Model agencies

It must be emphasized that the threshold for entering a career as a *tantai* AV actress is extremely high and complicated. Potential candidates have to get hired by a model agency, which is the major means through which they can find employment with the AV makers. As mentioned in Chapter 3, Japanese AV makers will call upon model agencies to arrange interviews when they are looking for one or more actresses to fill a particular role in a movie. But what is more common is that AV makers or studios will regularly have interviews with the new faces to make sure that they have a constant source of new actresses and earlier access to high-quality actresses than other competitors do, which are apparently the key to their success. Indeed, the availability of *tantai* AV actresses hinges upon good business networking with the model agency. According to our interview with the casting director of a major AV maker in Tokyo, he has been nurturing and maintaining good relationships with various model agencies, in the hope that the latter will bring beautiful, high-quality actresses to his company, rather than to other AV makers. We followed him for several days when we conducted our fieldwork in Tokyo and observed that one of his major tasks was to introduce job opportunities to the AV actresses supervised by the manager of model agencies he knew well – actresses who he thought could perform as models for printed or electronic media such as magazines or TV. This example confirms what we said in Chapter 3 that, while major AV makers appear to have the upper hand over the model agencies, they are indeed mutually dependent for their survival and existence.

In the wake of the continuous recession, it has become increasingly difficult for young women who are interested in the AV industry to start as a *tantai* actress (Nakamura 2012: 39). According to the casting director mentioned above, his company used to carry a large number of *tantai* actresses in the 1990s but now since the recession just a few. This meant that only extremely beautiful women would be given a *tantai* actress contract. The reason for this change is fairly simple: the cost of hiring a *tantai* actress is extremely high, something we will come back in a moment.

Like *tantai* actresses, Japanese women aspiring to a *kikaku* career have to sign up with a model agency. As the central focus of *kikaku* AVs is not on the actress's face or body, the threshold for *kikaku* actresses entering the industry is considerably lower. *Kikaku* AV production is open to women of any age, background, style, weight, figure and colour, so long as they are willing to join the AV production (Tameike 2013: 36). This relatively easy entry into *kikaku* AV production is made possible by the availability of a large number of job opportunities for *kikaku* actresses. *Kikaku* roles have traditionally made up more than 70 per cent of all the available AV actress jobs because genres requiring a *kikaku* actress are far more than those (i.e. debut, *bishōjo*, actress and school girl) requiring a *tantai* actress (Tameike 2013: 36). Model agencies have thus tended to take on as many *kikaku* actresses as are available to them. According to recent data, the category of *kikaku* actress has made up about 75 per cent of all AV girls in a majority of model agencies in Japan (Nakamura 2012: 48). They have a higher chance of being employed than *tantai* actresses because the latter, as will be mentioned below, cannot appear in more than one movie per month. That is to say, even though a *tantai* actress earns much more than a *kikaku* actress per movie, there is no guarantee that she can earn the most every month (Tameike 2013: 21). From the perspective of the model agency, it is better to get hold of more *kikaku* actresses because they have more chance of being employed and therefore can generate more income for the model agency. For instance, among the 2,000 actresses on model agency books in 2013, 90 per cent of them were *kikaku* actresses (Tameike 2013: 20). However, this does not mean that model agencies should not take on any *tantai* actresses, not just because their income per movie can be very high, but also because having a *tantai* actress in its stable can bring prestige to the agency and thus enhance the overall social status of the model agency in the industry. The ideal ratio between *tantai* and *kikaku* actresses for a model agency, according to our research in Japan, is for 10 to 20 per cent to be *tantai* actresses, and the rest *kikaku* actresses.

Employment system for AV actresses

An exclusive contract system (*senzoku*) is by no means unique to the Japanese AV industry, since it is found in one form or another in entertainment industries all over the world with the artist and respective agency/company entering into a deal which usually requires exclusivity for a fixed period of time, whereby the artist agrees not to sign up or work with any other companies during the period of the contract.

In the Japanese AV industry, only the *tantai* actress will enter into such an exclusive contract with an AV maker. As mentioned before, a *tantai* actress by definition has to possess a gorgeous face and a fine figure, for what *tantai* AV

The production of tantai *and* kikaku   91

sells is precisely the physical beauty and sexual appeal of the actress concerned. To fully capture the potential profit of the actress, it is therefore common, if not beneficial, for an AV studio to enter into an exclusive contract. Overwhelmed by the 'freshness' imperative, only beautiful young girls who have not yet debuted in the AV or sex-related industry will be hired as *tantai* actresses. For, no matter how gorgeous her appearance is, if she has previously debuted in films produced by other big AV studios, her sexual freshness as a product will be substantially discounted – though celebrities who have already achieved moderate fame in the mainstream entertainment industry are an exception. However, freshness has another meaning in the Japanese AV industry. It refers not to the zero experience in AV shooting, but to a refreshed attraction made possible by an actress's intermittent appearances. This can be clearly seen in a tacit agreement in the AV industry that *tantai* actress cannot appear in more than one movie per month. The logic is that too frequent appearance in AV productions will wear out her sexual freshness for the male audiences. By restricting the movie appearance of *tantai* actresses to once per month, the AV companies aim to extend the sheen of the actress's sexual freshness as long as possible.

The importance of refreshed attraction is also expressed in the 'unit' by which the work of a *tantai* actress is measured and thus how she is employed. In the Japanese AV industry, the exclusivity contract is not based on the length of time she is contracted (i.e. one or two years), but on the number of movies she is hired to take part in. It is common for AV studios to sign a three- or four-film contract with *tantai* actresses to see if, as a product, she can sell (Nakamura 2012). If she is still popular among audiences after appearing in several AVs and hence has the refreshed attraction required for continued success, she might be invited to enter into a new contract.

The salary for *tantai* actress in the Japanese AV industry ranges roughly between one million (US$8,800) and 2.5 million yen (US$22,000) per movie in 2012 (Nakamura 2012: 39). Although most *tantai* actresses will start at the lower rate due to the recession since the late 1990s (Nakamura 2012: 39), it is important to point out that they still remain the top-earning actresses *per movie* in the AV industry. For instance, Minako Komukai, a former celebrity in Japan, debuted as an exclusive *tantai* actress for Alice Japan with the video *AV Actress Minako Komukai* in October 2011. Her AV debut film was a huge commercial success, selling over 200,000 copies, when a sale of 10,000 copies already constitutes a hit in the industry. It was rumoured that she was paid ¥100 million (US$880,000) for a five-film contract (Nakamura 2012: 74).

The ultimate reason that AV studios are willing to hire exclusive *tantai* actresses at such a high price is the significance of the cultural code of women's lack of sexual agency attached to *tantai* actresses. As we have seen, the AV makers have encoded *tantai* AV actresses with images of purity, cuteness, innocence, freshness and wholesome personality because these images can best indicate their lack of sexual agency in Japanese culture. This in turn gives *tantai* actresses special cultural significance and status within the AV industry. Indeed, they are referred to, and celebrated as, AV idols (Nakamura 2012: 34). Like mainstream idols, an AV idol is a personality marketed as someone to be admired, fantasized and consumed, for her adorability, sexual innocence and immaculacy, which provides 'use value' to certain groups of Japanese AV consumers whose sexual desire is governed by the same cultural code that gives significance to women who lack sexual agency. The 'use value' of *tantai* actresses is then converted into exchange value; and that is why their perfect appearance and innocent character are seen as a guarantee of huge profits in the AV industry. That is also why most *tantai* actresses, despite their fundamental nature as porn actresses, will comport themselves as cute, sexually innocent, inexperienced or as pure as they can on screen. More interestingly, the significance given to *tantai* actresses is meaningfully connected to the *senzoku* system, high pay, emphasis on freshness, and so on. We can see that they are not only produced *materially*, but also *symbolically* and thus *culturally* according to the cultural code that gives significance to women's lack of sexual agency.

The high financial and cultural expectation the industry people invest in *tantai* actresses means that the access threshold to a *tantai* actress is exceptionally high. This is especially true in recent years when the AV market has fallen into a deep recession (Nakamura 2012: 40). Some big Japanese AV studios will arrange a special position called 'casting director', who is responsible for selecting a certain type of actress for a particular role or part in an AV script. In Chapter 6, we shall ethnographically examine the interview process by a casting director. In the interviewee auditions for a *tantai* role, the casting process is very serious and complex. The very few winners to emerge from the screening process can count themselves as lucky twice: once for being able to enter the contest, and second for winning it. AV girls take long odds against the clock of ageing. On average, most *tantai* AV actresses work for fewer than five years.

The understanding of *tantai* actresses as idols is also expressed in how they are marketed to audiences. Each actress must be identified by showing her 'face', alongside her name, just like an ordinary celebrity, to the public (Nakamura 2012: 34). She cannot hide her identity from the general public and media. Before her actual debut, the respective AV studio will put a great deal of effort into arranging a series of advertisements using various marketing tools to promote her to a target audience. Advertisements bearing her face and name, not unlike mainstream celebrities, will appear in all kinds of media – including television, radio, the Internet, magazines, comics, direct mail and billboards. As the sole actress in a *tantai* AV, she is also required to participate in all kinds of promotional strategies, including autograph events, meeting the public, shaking hands, having their photograph taken, and so on. In addition to her movie appearance, she is also required to take part in many other promotional activities. All of this once again speaks volumes to the meaningful connection between women's lack of sexual agency and marketing of *tantai* AV actresses as idols.

In contrast, the salary of *kikaku* actress is calculated on a daily basis, since they are temporary workers dispatched to the AV studios by their model agencies. As temporary workers, it is rare for them to enter into long-term contracts, let alone exclusive contracts, with AV studios. Thus, they are free to work for as many studios as they wish, so long as shooting schedules allow. As *kikaku* actresses work for a lot more studios than the *tantai* actresses do, it follows that they are subject to a lot more job interviews as their agents arrange 'castings' for them to meet prospective employees. As we shall see again in Chapter 6, AV actresses especially *kikaku* actresses have to audition for jobs especially those offered by AV companies with which they have never worked before.

Data inform us that the daily salary of *kikaku* actress ranged between ¥150,000 (US$1,320) and ¥250,000 (US$2,200) in 2012 (Nakamura 2012: 40). As a *kikaku* AV accentuates storyline, its actresses are often required to perform far more complicated contents, role-plays and sexual acts. During the negotiation with model agencies, it is typical for a *kikaku* actress to ask for detailed job description including whether there is one sex scene or more, whether there is facial ejaculation, sex with African actors, hardcore rape, gang rape, special sex acts such as S&M or scatology, and whether all the sex scenes are real or some of them simulated.

In one sense, the temporary employment nature of *kikaku* actresses explains why their job content is more flexible and negotiable than that of a *tantai* actress. And so is their pay. In the AV industry, the standard daily salary for a *kikaku* actress with two real sex and one simulated sex scenes is ¥200,000 (US$1,760) (Nakamura 2012: 39). If the actress, for any reason, only wishes to participate in one sex scene, she can negotiate with the director and will likely receive ¥100,000 (US$880) as a result of the reduction of one sex scene. Alternatively, she can share her job with another actress, with the result that two actresses take part in the same AV. In this case, they might be asked for a discount, say of 10 per cent, for the change of actress and each of them will receive ¥90,000 (US$792) (Nakamura 2012: 40).

Still, *kikaku* actresses have some measure of flexibility over their job content, even though they are also the ones who bear the brunt of the shrinking of the AV industry. First, their remuneration has remained more or less the same over the past 20 years, even though *kikaku* AV has become the mainstream since the 1990s (Nakamura 2012: 41). Yet, *kikaku* actresses are increasingly asked to perform 'harder', if not abnormal, sex acts in the AV. As a second-tier actress, they are generally required to perform *even* harder, grosser and darker sex, and they have little choice but to accept such terms because they cannot compete with A-list actresses (Nakamura 2012: 41). However, some of them with beautiful faces can become as popular as, or even more popular than, *tantai* actresses because AV makers started to produce hybrid *kikatan* AVs from the late 1990s where they hired good-looking *kikaku* actresses as the only actress in the AV to perform 'kinky' sex acts, in the hope that their appearance can prevent the AV market from further shrinking in the face of recession.

The workload of AV actresses especially *kikaku* actresses has also increased as a result of technological advances. The advent of DVD and Blu-ray has substantially lengthened the running time of an AV movie from 90 minutes to four hours or even eight hours. It follows that actresses have to perform longer hours of physical sex even though their salary remains the same. One can imagine then

94 *The production of* tantai *and* kikaku

how heavy is the physical labour that goes into taking part in an AV movie for a *kikaku* actress.

Cover design

As mentioned above, *tantai* AVs are pornographic videos that revolve around one single beautiful actress and are marketed to male audiences as idols. As idols, *tantai* actresses have names that are visibly printed on the cover – as can be seen in Figure 4.13: a typical *tantai* AV cover jacket manufactured by Alice Japan. The name of the actress is clearly printed at the top and when it comes to displaying AVs in rental or retail shops, especially famous actresses will be shelved according to the names rather than AV genre. As mentioned earlier, AV studios often arrange autograph and hand-shaking campaigns to market the *tantai* actresses as idols to audiences.

In contrast, *kikaku* AVs are pornographic videos that sell male audiences a 'story' via the use of a number (sometimes a large number) of actresses. *Kikaku* AVs thus tend to depict a wide range of themes, genres or scenarios, such as S&M, rape, bondage, humiliation, wife, amateur, mature women and so on. As storyline is the key, the quality of these actresses is usually not important and very often their names are not printed on the cover of an AV (see Figure 4.14).

Starting from the mid-2000s, most Japanese AVs, both *tantai* and *kikaku*, have taken the format of DVD or sometimes Blu-ray discs with a plastic

Figure 4.13 A *tantai* AV featuring Tokunaga Shiori released by Alice Japan in February 2016.

The production of tantai *and* kikaku 95

Figure 4.14 A *kikaku* AV featuring sexual pranks on women who are asleep by Japan Home Video.

transparent case. Yet, as we can see from Figure 4.13, the printed-paper sleeve of *tantai* AV is obviously more eye-catching, decorative and sophisticated with a central focus on the actress, so that AV studios tend to hire professional photograph crews to take stills and photographs for *tantai* AV products. These stills are close-up shots, of good quality with high resolution, as they are intended to be used for a jacket cover or other advertising and marketing materials. As mentioned in Chapter 3, since rental shops in Japan have tended to make their purchasing decisions based only on the jacket of a new AV, these elaborate, beautiful jackets and covers are absolutely essential. In the 1980s when the AV industry was dominated by the genre of *tantai bishōjo*, the package itself received extra attention, to such an extent that it was considered more important than the AV's content. That is to say, a mere beautiful paper sleeve could sell, whereas the content did not matter (Nakamura 2012: 41; Tameike 2013: 29). The cultural significance invested in packaging was reflected in the shooting schedule in the 1980s: one full day out of the three days of shooting was allocated to taking stills and photographs (Tameike 2013: 29).

On top of this, the *tantai* actress depicted on the cover is beautifully made-up, adorned and bejewelled. Typically, she is scantily clad or nude (i.e. Figure 4.13), but there are also cases where she is fully clothed (i.e. Figure 4.15). But no matter whether she is nude or fully clothed, she usually looks into the camera as if she were talking to the audience. On the back cover, there are usually shots of

96 The production of tantai and kikaku

Figure 4.15 A *tantai* AV featuring Uehara Ai.

sex scenes alongside descriptions of the actress. For instance, the top of the back cover displayed in Figure 4.15 reads that 'Uehara Ai is an eternal *bishōjo* descending from the heaven' ('*chijo ni maiorita eien no bishōjo* Uehara Ai'). Similarly, it says that 'the purifying smile just falls into insult and degradation' ('*tenshin ranmanna egao ga ryōjoku ni ochiru*') at the bottom of the cover.

In some cases, even the back cover of a *tantai* AV displays beautifully captured stills, rather than just shots of sex scenes. As we can see in Figure 4.16, in addition to the close-up shot of the *tantai* actress Itoh Beni on the front cover, the back cover likewise depicts her stills alongside shots of sex scenes. As we can see, the front cover reads 'Itoh Beni's debut AV' and this is one of the major reasons why her beautifully captured stills are also used in the back cover.

In contrast, *kikaku* AV covers seem less sophisticated or decorative. Like the one shown in Figure 4.14, the front cover of a *kikaku* AV is made up of shots of sex scenes rather than stills or photographs of an actress. In a way, the front cover and back cover of *kikaku* AVs are the same because both simply display shots of sex scenes. It is rare for AV studios or the production companies to hire a professional team to take care of the stills due to limited production budget. To work around this, it is not uncommon for directors or cameramen to take photographs while shooting the movie and simply use the photographs as cover pictures.

The production of tantai *and* kikaku   97

Figure 4.16 A *tantai* AV featuring Itoh Beni by Alice Japan.

Market price

These packaging differences are in turn reflected in their sales prices. The *tantai* AVs are usually set at a higher retail price, ranging from ¥2,650 (US$23.32) to ¥3,980 (US$35). According to our research, the standard sales price of *tantai* AVs offered by Alice Japan and SOD is ¥2,980 (US$26.22) (tax exclusive), whereas that of *tantai* AVs offered by Silk Labo is ¥3,980 (US$35) (see Table 4.1). On the other hand, the sales price of *kikaku* AVs is considerably lower. For instance, the standard market price of *kikaku* AVs by Alice Japan is ¥1,980 (US$17.42), whereas those by S1 No are as low as ¥1,650 (US$14.52). More importantly, while the retail price of *tantai* AVs has remained more or less the

Table 4.1 Comparison of the market prices of *tantai* and *kikaku* AVs

AV makers	*Standard price for* tantai *AV(¥)*	*Standard price for* kikaku *AVs(¥)*
Alice Japan	2,980	1,980
SOD	2,980	1,780
Silk Labo	3,980	N/A
S1 No. 1	2,980	1,680
Momotarō	2,980	1,995
h.m.p	2,980	2,415

same over time, that of *kikaku* AVs can substantially deteriorate during the same period. It is not difficult to find many outdated *kikaku* AVs being retailed as cheaply as ¥400 (US$3.52).

Circulation/acquisition methods

So far as acquisition is concerned, most *tantai* AVs can be acquired as DVDs from rental and retail shops all over Japan. Of course, they can also be accessed as digital files from the makers' own websites alongside other websites. As mentioned in Chapter 3, the selling of Japanese AVs as digital files (downloading and streaming) has become the major circulation mode in the contemporary AV industry as it offers convenience and ease of mind to the audiences. Some major AV studios, for instance Alice Japan and Silk Labo, also offer pre-sale orders at a discounted rate on their websites. Nevertheless, we have to emphasize that audiences of *tantai* AVs usually perceive *tantai* actresses as 'idols'. As a result, many of them prefer to 'collect' DVDs with a proper cover jacket and jelly box. According to our interview with a group of *tantai* actress fans, during a fieldtrip to her autograph campaign held in Tokyo in March 2010, many of them preferred to buy DVDs of the actress concerned, Tatsumi Yui, rather than downloading the digital versions because they could bring the DVDs to campaigns and have them autographed by Yui, a precious chance to meet their idol in person.

Kikaku AVs, by contrast, tend to be accessed via the Internet as digital files, although they are also available at rental as well as retail shops. One reason is that online websites especially DMM[7] offer discount rates that rental and retail shops cannot do. This explains why some *kikaku* AVs can be sold at a price as cheap as ¥400 (US$3.52) on the DMM website. Figure 4.17 is a capture of a *kikaku* AV titled 'A complex toward the huge breasts since childhood: A complete emancipation of much-hated 100 cm H-cup breasts (*"kotomo no goro kara zutto ōkina basuto ga konpurekkusu deshita" daikirai datta 100 cm H kappu opai wo zenryoku kaihō*') on DMM.

As we can see on the right hand side of the webpage, this *kikaku* movie is on sale and only costs ¥380 (US$3.34) to download. Users preferring higher quality or resolution might instead opt for the HD (high definition) version costing ¥680 (US$5.98). Apart from the option of downloading, a purchaser might also opt for 'streaming' (online viewing). According to our research, DMM alongside other websites increasingly offers its videos, especially *kikaku* AVs, via streaming media at a very cheap price. As in our example, the streaming of the video for seven days costs only ¥200 (US$1.76). As *kikaku* AVs portray unidentified and unnamed actresses, it is very rare for audiences to watch the very same videos for a second time, not to mention collect them, and thus purchasing them does not in fact make much financial sense to users. Seen in this light, the offering of streaming media and limited period of viewership offers them a perfect alternative to watching *kikaku* AVs once-and-for-all at a cheap cost.

The production of tantai *and* kikaku 99

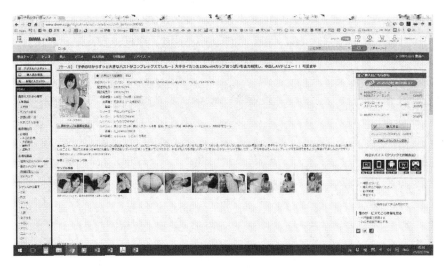

Figure 4.17 A *kikaku* AV on sale on DMM, captured on 21 February 2016.

Clientele

In terms of target audiences, *tantai* AVs are oriented towards audiences who have a strong attachment to AV actresses as idols. Like the fans of Tatsumi Yui mentioned above, most *tantai* AV consumers tend not to treat *tantai* actresses as just porn actresses, but love, adore and admire them as 'idols'. They thus devotedly and excessively love and worship them. From the vantage point of the AV makers, this attachment to actresses is of paramount importance because it engages the fans and makes them willing to follow and support them by purchasing their new AVs and to pay higher prices for their videos. The autograph campaign of the *tantai* AV actress Tatsumi Yui held in Tokyo in March 2010 illustrates this point.

We arrived at the video rental shop, the venue of Yui's autograph campaign rather early so we chose to have a look at the AVs displayed inside the video rental shop. We saw some customers browsing around different corners of the shop searching for AVs they liked. At the same time, we saw the staff of the AV maker that had an exclusive contract with Yui busy preparing the venue for her autograph campaign. Just as we finished browsing around the shop, we were caught by the announcement that the autograph event was about to start. We saw a group of middle-aged men lining up and waiting to meet Yui. All of them had her new AV with them; some of them had prepared gifts to present to her; and some even had Yui's posters with them so that she could sign them later. Each of them took turns to meet the actress who was sitting on a chair, in front of which there was a table on which we saw some small gifts prepared by Yui's company to be given to fans. Each of them came forward to Yui for her signature. We were surprised to discover that she knew all of them and chatted with them over fairly trivial matters whenever she met them. Yui's fans also asked her some personal questions such as whether she was busy these days or commented on how they liked her new AVs. One of the fans even showed his concern about her health because he saw Yui appear in several new AVs over a short period of time. The staff standing beside Yui would push her to autograph the AV or the posters brought by each fan, while at the same time urging the fan to move on so that the next one could meet the actress. Some fans were reluctant to stop talking to her and move on so Yui would push the fan to do the lucky draw to see what small gift on the table he could get from her. Usually, the fan would not move on until she had agreed to have her picture taken with them. In short, we can see that the interaction between Yui and her fans was like that between idols and their fans.

We learned that this group of fans knew one another too. They gathered after the autograph event at the entrance of the shop. We thought it a very good chance to talk to them while they were waiting for the last fan who was still meeting Yui inside the shop and, as we talked, we learnt that they all knew the schedule of Yui's various autograph events. They told us that they would try their best to attend all of them so that they could meet her in person again and show her their support. Some of them even took the bullet train from Kansai area to Tokyo to meet Yui. We also heard that they knew every detail of how the actress dressed up, what food she liked most, and a lot of other information about her. As we listened to them talking about Yui, we got the feeling that they were talking about her as if she was one of their family members. Of course, they kept all of Yui's AVs. She was undoubtedly their goddess.

Kikaku AVs, on the other hand, are catered to audiences who are tired of the single pattern of *tantai* AVs, especially *bishōjo* featuring just beautiful actresses in uncontextualized sex and who prefer to watch videos with stories. *Kikaku* AVs are highly diversified and compartmentalized, catering to a wide array of genres or scenes ranging from sadomasochism, through rape, fetish, to scatology, or mania. As *kikaku* AV buyers are not bound by strong attachment to any specific actresses, *kikaku* AV manufacturers have to keep on creating new genres to attract the audiences.

Conclusion

In this chapter, we have offered an analysis of the production of *tantai* and *kikaku* AVs, focusing on their differences in narrative, emphasis of storyline, casting and production costs. *Tantai* AVs tend to emphasize women's lack of sexual agency, while *kikaku* AVs are inclined to stress men's sexual domination over women. This differential emphasis of *tantai* and *kikaku* AVs derives from the difference between the *binibon* and pink film traditions we mentioned in Chapter 2. We further contended that *tantai* and *kikaku* AVs in fact share the same salvage ideology because women's lack of sexual agency and men's sexual domination are two major components of that ideology. We also pointed out some of the meaningful connections in the categorical distinctions of *tantai* and *kikaku* AVs among package, sales price, circulation/acquisition method and clientele.

Implied in this analysis is a cultural economy in which the production of *tantai* and *kikaku* AVs is organized by specific valuations of women with and without sexual agency, and men with and without sexual domination over women respectively. These are not the only valuations possible and thus cannot be justified by any biological reason. We can see how the narrative, number of genres, package, retail price, circulation/acquisition method, clientele of *tantai* AVs and *kikaku* AVs correspondingly depend on the differential valuations of women's lack of sexual agency and men's status as women's saviours. In the case of *tantai* AVs, women's lack of sexual agency is attached a specific significance and thus appears to have 'utility' to a certain category of men in Japan; which this further dictates not only the way a typical *tantai* AV is narrated, packaged, marketed and circulated but also how AV actresses are valued and thus paid. As we can see from the history of postwar Japanese pornography, the empirical referents of women's lack of agency changed from sexually unsatisfied wives to young, pure and innocent girls, in the course of which the typical image of a *tantai* AV actress as a young, pure and innocent girl acquires a specific valuation: an idol who participates in the everyday life of Japanese men as a 'real' *subject*. She is 'real' because she is a girl-next-door or a young girl who comes from her hometown to attend school in Tokyo; she is a 'subject' as she has a name. Taken together, they dictate that the story of *tantai* AVs is narrated around the *tantai* AV actress and that, most importantly, she is depicted as identical to the female character in the sense that the actress and the female character are one and the same: the authentication of the actress in *tantai* AVs. The centrality of *tantai* AVs as idol in turn determines how many genres of *tantai* AVs can exist. As the variants of the images of *tantai* AVs actresses as young, pure and innocent are limited, the genres of *tantai* AVs thus cannot be too many. The supremacy of *tantai* AV actresses as idols also prescribes how the cover of *tantai* AVs is designed, how the product itself is promoted and sold at what price, and more importantly how many movies a *tantai* AV actress can appear in over a certain period of time and how she should be paid – her pay being inversely related to her image as a young, pure, innocent and beautiful girl, which in turn specifies her motivation in getting a job as *tantai* AV actress in the industry.

All of these factors could change if Japanese men stop preferring women's lack of sexual agency – as we can see in the case of *kikaku* AVs in which AV actresses are no longer the focus. They participate in *kikaku* AVs as objects: they are always anonymous, acting in *kikaku* AVs according to the character assigned to them, neither directly relating to audiences nor to their imagined existence in everyday life. What matters in *kikaku* AVs is how well the story can reveal men's sexual domination over women; hence the extra importance paid to the authenticity of the story, as well as to the female character, in contrast to *tantai* AVs which stress the authenticity of the actress, which in turn determines the number of genres. Since there are so many stories that can perform this function, the number of *kikaku* AV genres could extend beyond human imagination. This allows as many different actresses appearing in *kikaku* AVs as possible, so long as they match the requirement of the character concerned. This results in a demand-side market in which supply is always overwhelming as *kikaku* AV actresses, employed as temporary staff of model agencies, can be easily substituted because it is never difficult to find a replacement in the market. *Kikaku* AVs actresses' pay per movie thus tends to be much lower than that of *tantai* AV actresses, which further reinforces the latter's high standing in the industry. But since the emphasis is placed on the story rather than on the actresses, *kikaku* AV actresses are allowed to appear in as many AVs as their physical condition permits them. The total income of a *kikaku* AV actress could be more than her counterpart in *tantai* AVs over a certain period of time, which further structures the job choice of AV actresses in the industry.

As we mentioned in Chapter 2, the consumption of *tantai* and *kikaku* AVs was governed by the cultural codes of women's lack of sexual agency and the men's sexual domination over women respectively – which are not the only codes possible – by determining the sexual desire of certain groups of Japanese AV consumers, as well as the means to satisfy their sexual needs. In this chapter, we have shown that the production of *tantai* and *kikaku* follows the same cultural codes. That is to say, both the production and consumption of Japanese AVs are governed by the same cultural code, which then has theoretical implications to the debate between the production and consumption perspectives – something to which we will return in our Conclusion. But here we are tempted to ask: why are there so many beautiful Japanese women wanting to join the AV industry? Indeed, why are they willing to become AV actresses in the first place? In the next chapter, we will show that becoming an AV actress has gradually become a proper, if not admired, career choice among many young, decent Japanese women and this has a lot to do with larger social environments that have effectively blocked Japanese women from climbing the social ladder.

Notes

1. For instance, Alice Japan has recently released a *tantai* AV starring Tokunaga Shiori with four sex scenes – as is made clear in the title: *Tokunaga Shiori Four Sex Scenes Debut* [2016].
2. Literally, omnibus means a collection or anthology. Here it refers to the *kikaku* AV where there is a collection of AVs starring different actresses.
3. *Bukkake* is a kind of fetish AV genre, the hallmark of which is multiple men ejaculating onto the face and body of a single girl.
4. Soft On Demand is now one of the largest AV makers in Japan. Together with Hokuto Corporation, they are known as sale-style AV studios.
5. *Gyaru* fashion is a type of Japanese street fashion that originated in the 1970s (Kinsella 2014: 60–3). Its popularity peaked in the 1990s and early 2000s. *Gyaru* fashion is typically characterized by having heavily bleached or dyed hair (mostly shades from dark brown to blonde), highly decorated nails and dramatic makeup. The makeup typically consists of dark eyeliner and fake eyelashes used in ways intended to make the eyes appear larger, as well as contouring of the face for a slimming effect.

6 *Shunga* is the traditional Japanese term for erotic paintings and prints. They are also called *makura-e*, 'pillow pictures'.
7 Founded in 1990, DMM, formally Hokuto Corporation, is a Japanese joint stock company involved in the distribution of adult videos and adult toys. By late 2008, DMM was handling products from more than 150 different adult video studios, making it one of the largest AV distributors in Japan.

5 Who wants to be an AV girl?

Introduction

This chapter takes the reader inside the mysterious, convoluted world of actresses, the major protagonists in Japanese adult videos. It is widely reported that hundreds of thousands of new AV actresses are entering the adult video industry in Japan every month (Nakamura 2012) so much so that the term AV actress does hold sociological sway in modern Japan. To better comprehend 'AV actresses', we shall begin with an exploration of *who* the AV girls are by examining a set of data we collected from a major adult video studio in Japan in the early 2010s. These data centre on the background of a group of AV actresses, including their age, marital status, family background, educational background, birthplace, occupation, life goal, age at first sexual experience, number of sexual partners, dreams and aspirations and so on. Relatedly, we shall look into *why* they aspired to be AV actresses, amid a wide range of job choices. The major aim of this exercise is to spell out some of the common characteristics of these AV actresses, with an eye to finding out how such characteristics are related to socio-cultural and economic contexts of contemporary Japan and ultimately how these have shaped and informed their choice of becoming an AV actress.

AV actresses

It is widely reported that there are hundreds of thousands of AV actresses working in the AV industry in Japan (Inoue 2002; Yasuda and Amaniya 2006), but it is difficult to know the exact number of their total population because there is hardly any serious survey of the issue. However, we can still do some estimation based on the number of model agencies that sign on AV actresses in the AV industry. If we can work out the figure of the total number of model agencies and how many AV actresses each of them signs on, we can roughly estimate the total number of AV actresses in the industry. Based on his research with a major AV maker, Nakamura (2012: 16) estimated that there were roughly 150 model agencies in the Japanese AV industry in 2012 and that the average number of AV actresses signed to each of these agencies was 60 in the same year. That is to say, there were 9,000 AV actresses in the industry in 2012. Nakamura further observed that about two-thirds of these 9,000 AV actresses retired from their jobs within a year and that the same number of women was required to fill their vacancies. That is to say, there were 6,000 newly recruited AV actresses in 2012 (Nakamura 2012: 16).

Obviously, the turnover rate of AV actresses is very high. One possible reason, among others, is that some Japanese women consider a short stay in the AV industry as an AV actress as a sort of moratorium before becoming a mother and wife – just like going abroad for an adventure.[1] Another reason is that 'youth' is at a premium in the AV industry. One of the common metaphors used among the industry people to describe the actress is 'raw produce' ('*genryō*'): actresses are akin to raw produce whose freshness will deteriorate in the course of time (Nakamura 2012: 37). That is to say, the life cycle of the AV actress is characteristically short. As a matter of fact, many of those in our data set below are extremely young.

The high turnover rate naturally leads to high demand for new AV actresses, as we have just seen from Nakamura's research. But this high demand is also closely related to the economic downturn in Japan in the 1990s. As mentioned in Chapter 2, the economic recession caused by the collapse of Japan's bubble economy hit the AV industry very hard. *Tantai* AV makers suffered most at the beginning of the 1990s, and many of them were forced to turn to the production of *kikaku* AVs. In the mid-1990s, the sale of *kikaku* AVs also started to decline, to which AV makers responded by further increasing production in the hope of covering the per title losses by means of a best seller, which also explains why the demand for new AV actresses was also very high. One question, however, remains unanswered: why do so many Japanese women want to join the industry as AV actresses?

Who are the AV girls?

To better make sense of why Japanese women would dare to pursue a career in the AV industry, we need to turn to a key question: who are they? In what follows, we are going to analyse a set of profile data, part of the interview sheet that Japanese AV girls are required to fill in when they attend a job interview with an adult video studio. We collected this set of data from the casting director for a famous adult video studio in Japan in the early 2000s. In total, there were 588 interviews, taking place from September 2007 to October 2010.

The interview sheet designed by the studio was comprised of three parts, namely a profile card, questionnaire and publicity preference. In what follows, we shall focus mainly on the first part of the interview sheet – that is, the profile card – in order to find out who these girls are and leave the analysis of the questionnaire and publicity preference to the next chapter where we analyse their job interviews.

The profile card (see Table 5.1) can be roughly separated into four parts. The first part focuses on personal information including the actress's name, stage name, birthday, horoscope, blood type, height, weight, vital statistics, body type, the model company she belongs to and previous working experience.

Table 5.1 The profile card of the interview sheet

The Profile Card

1. Name:		20. Pocket Money:			Yen/month
2. Stage Name:		21. Favorite Type of Man and Talent:			
3. Date of Birth (Profile Use)	Y M D Age:	22. Least Favorite Type of Man and Talent:			
4. Date of Birth (Real)	Y M D Age:	23. Personality:			
5. Horoscope: 6. Blood Type:		24. The Most Important Thing in life:			
7. Company Name: 8. School Name:		25. Which part of your body you like the most?			
9. Current Home Address:		26. Which part of your body you like the least?			
10. Hometown:		27. Your Dream:			
		28. Family Structure			
11. Three Sizes	Height: cm Weight: kg B: cm W: cm H: cm Bra: cup	Name	Relationship	Age	Occupation
13. Working Experiences:					
14. Hobbies, skills, sports:					
15. Favorite Color:		29. Motivation in AV performance:			
16. Favorite Music:		30. The First Time Watching AV:			
17. Favorite Food		31. Interviewer:			
18. Least Favorite Food		32. Interviewing Date:	Y	M	D
19. Favorite Books or Magazines		33. Publicity:			

The second part likewise revolves around personal information, but with the purpose of authenticating her identity by seeking information on the name of the schools she attended or graduated from, her home address and the name of companies where she has worked previously. The name of the school the AV actress attended or graduated from can sometimes be very important, especially when it comes to the question of how to market the AV actress concerned. If she is a student or a graduate of a famous national university, it can often be used as a gimmick to make her 'stand out' from other actresses when marketing her to the audiences.

The third part centres on trivial questions such as hobbies, interests, favourite colours, favourite food, least favourite food, favourite book, favourite type of male celebrity, least favourite male celebrity, and so on. The main purpose of these questions is to make the AV girls relax, and prepare her for the upcoming private questions.

The fourth part is concerned with the actress's motivations for becoming an AV actress. To the adult video company or studio, this question is extremely important, for her motivation will directly inform and shape her attitude and aspiration as an AV actress.

Characteristics of AV girls

Out of the 588 samples we have, 472 of the actresses filled in the age column, whereas 116 of them did not. The average age of these 472 actresses was 24. Among them, almost 15 per cent of them were aged between 16 and 19, which was the second largest age group of the sample. This means that many of them were high school students or graduates if they had already quit school. The largest age group in our data set was the one between 20 and 25, which accounted for 60 per cent of the total respondents. Meanwhile, 19 per cent of them were aged between 26 and 35, with 57 actresses aged between 26 and 30 and 34 actresses aged between 31 and 35. Actresses aged above 35 constituted 7 per cent of the total respondents, with only 12 (3 per cent) of them being above 41. Thus, one might say that young AV actresses are the majority in the AV industry (see Figure 5.1).

In terms of birthplace, 513 out of 588 actresses filled in this column whereas 75 did not. If we divide these 513 samples according to the eight regions of Japan, and working from north to south, we have 40 from Hokkaidō, 46 from Tōhoku, 273 from Kantō (which includes Tokyo), 71 from Chūbu (which includes Nagoya), 35 from the Kansai or Kinki region (including Osaka, Kobe and Kyoto), seven from Chūgoku (including Hiroshima), seven from Shikoku and 30 from Kyūshū (see Figure 5.2).

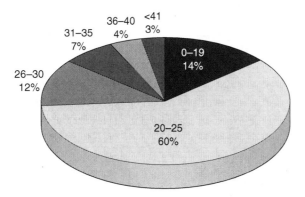

Figure 5.1 Age distribution of the actresses.

108 *Who wants to be an AV girl?*

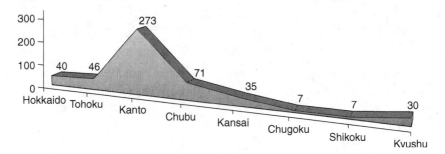

Figure 5.2 Birthplace distribution.

If we look at the data in more detail, it is surprising to see that only 127 and 13 out of the 513 actresses who filled in this column were from the cities of Tokyo and Osaka respectively, which is to say that more than three-quarters of these actresses came from the so-called *chihō* (regional or local) areas or urban peripheries (Figure 5.3). *Chihō* refers to areas outside the major cities of Tokyo, Osaka and Nagoya. Culturally speaking, the mentioning of one's coming from regional areas also automatically implies a relatively low cultural status when compared with people born and raised in major cities.

In terms of working experience, out of the 588 actresses, 556 of them filled in the occupation column and the remaining 32 did not. It is of interest to note that among these 556 actresses, 144 of them had worked in the sex-related entertainment industry before or did so at the time of attending the interview. The higher proportion of actresses previously engaged in the adult entertainment is in some way understandable as model companies have recently started to solicit actresses from the adult entertainment industries (see Figure 5.4).

In terms of their dream, 393 of the actresses answered this question whereas 195 did not. Of those 393 actresses, 98 of them – accounting for almost 25 per cent of the total number of respondents – suggested that they had one overarching goal in life, which was to get married and start a family of their own. Many of them even stated clearly that they wished to get married or have a family before a certain age, for instance 25 or 30. The next most popular dream among these actresses was 'career' development, which accounted for 18.3 per cent of the 393 actresses. Relatedly, starting a small business like a flower shop or fashion boutique was another common dream among these actresses (15.3 per cent; 60 actresses). Meanwhile 14.5 per cent stated that gaining 'fame' was their dream (57 actresses). Living overseas or travelling around the world ranked fifth (12.2 per cent; 48 actresses). Another 8.1 per cent of them stated that becoming rich was their life goal (32 actresses). Buying a house/apartment ranked eighth (3.6 per cent; 14 actresses). The remaining 3.1 per cent opted for the category 'other' (12 actresses) (see Figure 5.5).

Regarding why they aspired to be an AV girl, out of the 588 actresses, 545 answered this question, of whom 230 (42 per cent) stated candidly that they

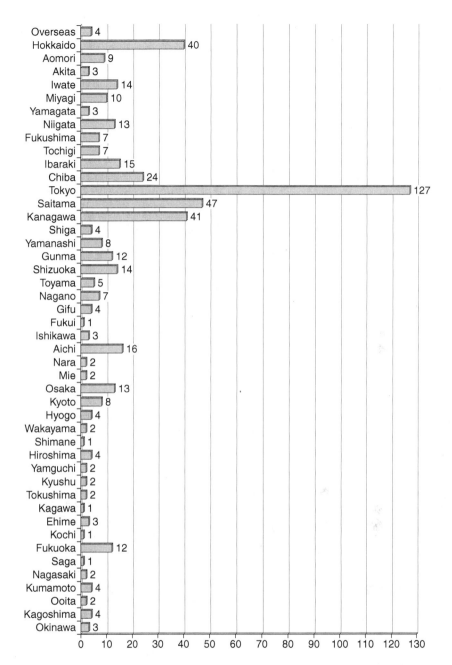

Figure 5.3 Birthplace distribution.

110 *Who wants to be an AV girl?*

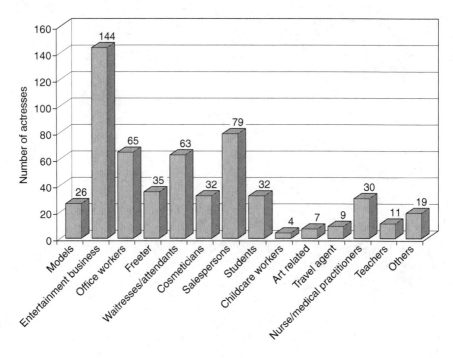

Figure 5.4 Occupation distribution.

Note
'Freeter' is a Japanese expression for people who lack full-time employment or are unemployed, excluding housewives.

went into the AV industry simply to 'make a fast buck'. Many of them believed that debuting in an adult video could bring them a quick and reasonably good income. Meanwhile, 53 actresses (9.7 per cent) claimed that gaining fame was the reason why they chose to enter the AV industry. In contrast, 186 of them suggested that they entered the AV industry as performers simply out of interest. In other words, they thought that performing in AV as actresses was an interesting and fascinating job. Twenty-eight of them even reported that they became AV actresses simply because they loved having sex. Put differently, they found it great that they could do something they liked for money. Six of them also suggested that they became AV girls because they wanted to improve their sexual skills and sex life. Another 13 reported that they decided to join the AV industry because they wanted to make a change before marriage or become more beautiful. In other words, they all joined the AV industry of their own accord. On the other hand, 16 of them reported that they joined the AV industry simply because they were scouted. Meanwhile, another 13 entered the AV industry for a wide array of different reasons (see Figure 5.6).

Figure 5.5 Actresses' dreams.

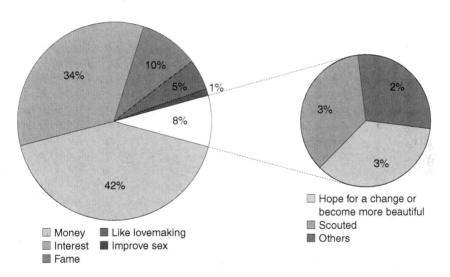

Figure 5.6 Reasons for becoming an AV girl.

Concerning how the Japanese women were recruited into the AV industry, 498 out of the 588 sample actresses filled in this column. Of these, 248 were scouted which accounted for almost 50 per cent of total respondents. The next most common recruitment method was 'introduction through network', accounting for 24.2 per cent. Network here refers mainly to friends or colleagues who introduce them to the AV industry. Surprisingly, the Internet only ranked third, accounting for 18.3 per cent of total respondents. The remaining method was through magazines which often carried a wide range of job advertisements especially for the adult entertainment industry. This accounted for 7.7 per cent of total respondents (see Figure 5.7).

In terms of when the actresses had had sex for the first time, 506 actresses filled in this column, with 82 for unknown reasons leaving this empty. The average age of first sexual encounter among these 506 actresses was 16. It is important to note that almost 84 per cent of them had had sex for the first time between the ages of 13 and 18, with 207 actresses having sex for the first time between 13 and 15, and 216 actresses between 16 and 18. Meanwhile, there were 71 actresses having their first sexual intercourse between the age of 19 and 24. We can see that most of these actresses (98 per cent) had their first sexual experience between the ages of 13 and 24. Eleven of them even reported that they had had their first sexual intercourse between the ages of nine and 12 (see Figure 5.8). Under the Japanese Penal Law regarding rape, the age of consent for sexual activity is 13, which is also to say that anyone having sex with a girl or a boy under 13 is committing a criminal offence. Considering the age of consent in Hong Kong (16), China (14), Taiwan (16), UK (16), the US (16 to 18) and Australia (16–18), Japan has the lowest age of consent. However, we have to add immediately that many prefectural governments in Japan, such as Tokyo Metropolitan government, have their own local law stipulating that sexual relationships among young people under 18 are illegal.[2]

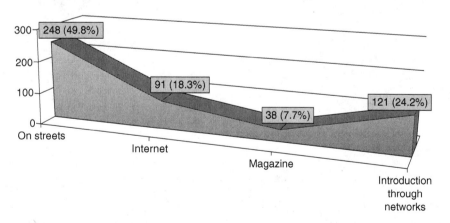

Figure 5.7 Recruitment methods of AV girls.

While it is not easy to find data that are comparable to our data set, we still can find some surveys carried out in so-called Greater China and Britain that enable us to better understand our AV actresses comparatively. According to an online survey conducted by the Chinese Association of Social Workers in 2015 about sex, dating and marriage of young people who were born in the 1990s (15 to 25) in mainland China, the average age of first sex among the young people was 21.78 years old. The same survey also had figures for Hong Kong, Macau and Taiwan, according to which the average age of first sex among the young people in these areas was 19.24 years. Another survey in Britain – in which 6,293 men and 8,869 women between 16 and 74 years of age were interviewed – reported that the median age for first sex for men and women of all age groups was 17, while that for the age group of 16 to 24 was 16 (Mercer *et al.* 2013: 1785). We are fully aware of the danger of trying to reach a definite conclusion drawn from all these surveys because the comparability of the data collected in them still needs to be verified. But we can generally say that the Japanese AV actresses in our data set tend to have their first sex at the same age as the participants in the above-mentioned survey in Britain, while they tend to have their first sex earlier than participants from Hong Kong, Macau, Taiwan and Mainland China in the online survey.

With regard to the number of sexual partners, out of the 588 samples, 504 actresses answered this question, 195 (39 per cent) reporting that the number of their sexual partners ranged between two and ten people. The next common number of sexual partners was between 11 and 20, which accounted for 26 per cent of the total number of respondents (131 actresses). Surprisingly perhaps, the

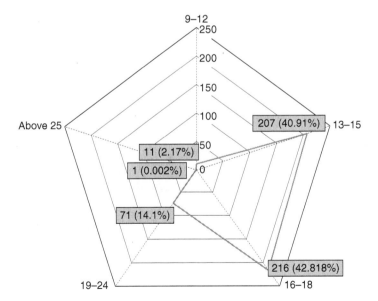

Figure 5.8 The average age of actresses at first sexual intercourse.

114 *Who wants to be an AV girl?*

range between 50 and 100 partners ranked third, accounting for 11.9 per cent of respondents (60 actresses). Meanwhile, 49 actresses (9.7 per cent) reported that the number of their sexual partners ranged between 21 and 30. Likewise, 48 actresses (9.5 per cent) reported that they had had between 31 and 50 sexual partners. On the other hand, there were seven actresses who reported that they had had only one sexual partner so far. Perhaps what is more surprising is that two actresses reported that they had never had sexual intercourse before. In other words, they were still virgins at the time of their interview (see Figure 5.9).

The above-mentioned survey in Britain reported that the average number of sexual partners over respondents' lifetime was 7.1 for all age groups, while that for the age group of 16 to 24 was 5.2. We cannot find similar data about Hong Kong and Mainland China but one survey conducted in Taiwan in 2010 reported that 6.5 per cent of male participants and 2.2 per cent of female participants in the survey had had more than two sexual partners in the year before the survey, while 12.3 per cent and 5.4 per cent of male and female participants in the 19 to 21 age group reported that they had had more than two sexual partners in the year before the survey (Hwang *et al.* 2010: 8).

Again, while we have to be cautious when we make a comparison here, it is still safe to say that the Japanese AV actresses in our data set generally have had more sexual partners than female participants in the surveys in both Britain and Taiwan.

Regarding the 'most important things in life', out of the 588 sample actresses, 466 of them filled in this column, with 141 of them reporting that the most important thing in their lives was family. More than half of this number stated specifically that their future family and children were as important as their own lives. Ninety-eight of them reported that their most important thing in life was

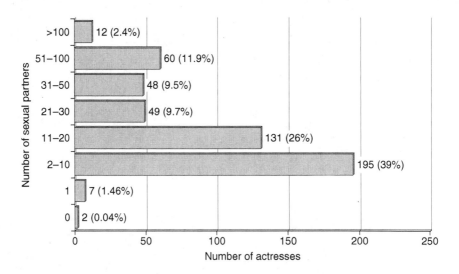

Figure 5.9 The sexual experiences of the actresses.

something they received from family, boyfriends, lovers or close friends. Surprisingly, 'pets' ranked third, accounting for 20 per cent of the total respondents (92 actresses), which was even higher than 'friends' (15 per cent: 69 actresses). Both 'money' and 'lovers' accounted for 4 per cent of respondents' answers (17 actresses each). In contrast, only 15 of them stated that the most important thing in their lives was 'themselves'. Answers from the remaining 17 actresses were put under the category of 'Other' which included 'heart', 'time', 'romance', 'smile', 'dream', and so on (see Figure 5.10).

Concerning the 'the happiest thing about being an actress', 37 per cent of the 254 actresses who responded to this question stated that the shooting process itself was the most joyous and rewarding experience of being an actress (94 actresses). More than half of these 37 per cent said precisely that they enjoyed the 'friendly and humorous atmosphere' of the shooting process during which some said that they felt respected and loved. Similarly, 26 per cent of them said that the happiest thing for them was to chat with different staff and crew members on site (66 actresses). Nine per cent did not mention directly anything about chatting with staff, but they did suggest that crew members were extremely friendly and funny (23 actresses). In contrast, only 5.1 per cent of them found interaction or communication with fans the most joyous and rewarding experience of being an actress (13 actresses). Meanwhile 5.5 per cent said that they were happy to be photographed and filmed onsite (14 actresses). Another 6.3 per cent said specifically that they enjoyed being beautified by makeup artists

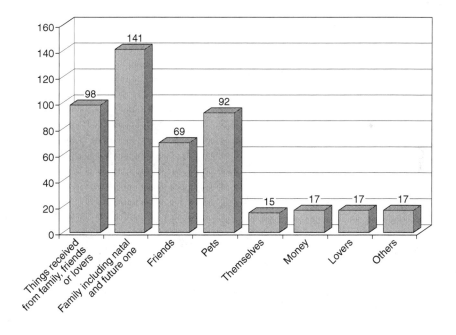

Figure 5.10 The most important things in life.

116 *Who wants to be an AV girl?*

(16 actresses). Another 11.1 per cent suggested that the most exciting thing was to meet many new friends and people on site (28 actresses) (see Figure 5.11).

From the above statistical data, it seems safe to say that the typical Japanese AV actress is a single woman, aged between 20 and 25, coming from a regional or local area. She had her first sexual experience when she was between the age of 13 and 24 and the number of her sexual partners is up to ten persons. She used to work, or is currently working, in the sex-related entertainment business. She was recruited by a scout, or joined the AV industry through her personal network – the major reason for her doing so being that she wants to earn a lot of money quickly, or that she finds performing in AV as an actress interesting and fascinating. She enjoys the AV shooting process very much. Her life goal is to get married and have children and she considers her family, especially her future family and children, to be extremely important.

Several observations

In reviewing the above profile data, several interesting observations can be made. The first is about the motivation. Almost half of the actresses reported that they entered the AV industry simply because of monetary reward. As we have seen, out of 545 actresses who filled in their motivation for becoming AV actresses, 42 per cent of them stated clearly that they did so simply for the money, although another 33 per cent of them claimed that they joined out of interest.

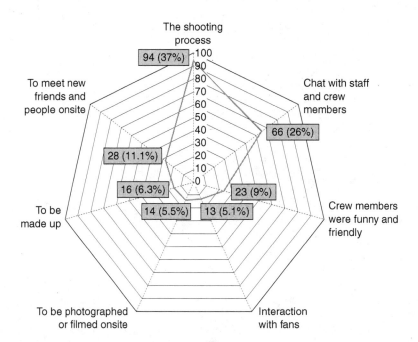

Figure 5.11 The happiest thing about being an actress.

Who wants to be an AV girl? 117

The fact that money was the major motivation for joining the AV industry is perhaps straightforward. One might even say that it is totally understandable. Yet, even though actresses are all hired for similar sexual performances before the camera, they are paid rather differently according to a specific pay system. As mentioned in Chapter 4, this system differentiates actresses according to the type of AVs in which they act, with *senzoku* (exclusive) *tantai* actresses earning the most, *kikatan* earning slightly less than the *tantai*, and *kikaku* actress earning the least per movie (Table 5.2).

Table 5.2 The differentiating pricing system of *tantai*, *kikatan* and *kikaku* actresses

Type	Salary per movie	Description
Tantai	¥1 million (US$8,800) to ¥2.5 million (US$22,000)	A-list *tantai* actresses who have never debuted under major studios.
Kikatan Super A+	¥800,000 (US$7,040)	Mostly A-list *tantai* actresses who debuted under major studios a few months ago and have just finished their contract. Their names and faces are still fresh in the minds of their audiences.
Kikatan Super A	¥700,000 (US$6,160)	*Tantai* actresses who debuted under famous studios a few months ago and have just finished their contract.
Kikatan A+	¥600,000 (US$5,280)	Those who did not formally debut but took part in several movies produced by big makers and who achieved some fame and tended to have fans.
Kikatan A	¥500,000 (US$4,400)	Those who took part in several movies and had some fame.
Kikatan B	¥400,000 (US$3,520)	Those who would like to start as *kikatan* actresses will start from this pay grade. About 40 per cent of the *kikatan* belong to it.
Kikatan C	¥300,000 (US$2,640)	Above *kikaku* and below *kikatan*. While the outlook is not perfect, they often have special characteristics, like strong sexual desire, sexual deviance or good acting skills, and so on. Again, about 40 per cent of the *kikatan* belong to this pay grade.
Kikaku Super A	¥250,000 (US$2,200)	Above *kikaku* but below *kikatan*.
Kikaku A	¥200,000 (US$1,760)	Within *kikaku* hierarchy, this refers to those actresses who have some special appearances, body figure or characteristics, which can in turn become a selling point.
Kikaku B	¥150,000 (US$1,320)	Ordinary women in their 20s, older women, and so on.

Source: Nakamura (2012: 39, 43–4).

Four observations can be made in light of the above table. First, AV actresses are generally differentiated along the lines of physical beauty and sexual freshness. The more beautiful they are, the higher the pay. Second, the same is also true for their sexual freshness: the fresher they are to consumers, the higher the pay. Third, from the category of *kikatan* C and below, actresses are further differentiated according to their sexual and biographical particulars. Taking all these together, AV actresses are classified by their freshness, facial, physical, biographical and sexual particulars and paid accordingly, although different categories of AVs may place different emphasis on these particulars (Table 5.3). We will return to this in Chapter 6.

Finally, actresses who debuted as *tantai* actresses from the beginning of their careers seem to have an advantage over *kikatan*, not to mention *kikaku*, actresses because they have more options: they can act as *kikatan* actresses if they want. In fact, *kikatan* actresses can take part in as many AV shoots with different studios as she likes, so long as her schedule allows. This earns her more money than remaining as a *tantai* actress. The opposite, however, is not possible: that is to say, *kikatan* and *kikaku* AV actresses cannot perform in *tantai* AVs. This is parallel to fashion modelling where there is a divide between models who specialize in editorial work and those who model in commercial jobs. The former, however, can move to take up a commercial job – specifically an advertising campaign – if they want, although the opposite is less likely (Mears 2011: 40). Models who specialize in editorial work are usually paid the least, but have high symbolic value that might help them to get an editorial jackpot campaign in the future that might bring them a fortune at the end, while those who model in commercial jobs earn most in the short term but have less symbolic value. As Mears summarizes the situation:

> Models working at the far end of the Economic Capital axis earn high rates in catalogs, showroom, and commercial advertising but are essentially 'stuck' there, in the land of 'cheesy' catalog jobs, unable to move up into editorial work. Models working at the far end of the symbolic Capital axis earn less money in magazines and catwalk jobs, but their prestige can translate into higher rates in commercial jobs as they move along the Economic Capital axis, and they can, so they hope, hit the jackpot by booking lucrative campaigns.
>
> (Mears 2011: 40–1)

As we have just mentioned, *kikatan* actresses, not unlike *kikaku* actresses, can act in as many AV shootings with different studios as they like because, unlike *tantai* actresses, they are not required to enter into an exclusive contract with the studio. As a result, it is now a known fact that although the pay for *tantai* actress *per movie* is the highest, it is the *kikatan* actress who earns the most *per month*. As we can see from Table 5.3, a *kikatan* actress can earn up to ¥3 million (US$26,400) per month if she works slightly harder than the average white collar worker working an average of 20 days a month. Indeed, this reality leads to a

Table 5.3 Comparison among *tantai*, *kikaku* and *kikatan* actresses

Themes	Tantai AV focusing on actress	Kikaku AV focusing on story	Kikatan focusing on both the actress and story
Facial	***	*	***
Physical	***	**	***
Biographical	*	***	**
Sexual	*	***	**
Pay per movie	Highest	Lowest	Mid-range
Exclusive contract restricting movie appearance	Yes	No	No
Average earnings per month	¥920,000 10 working days (US$8,096)	¥296,000 7 working days (US$2,604)	¥3,120,000 25 working days (US$27,456)

Source: Nakamura (2012: 60–2).

Notes
*** most significant;
** slightly significant;
* least significant.

new phenomenon in contemporary Japan where more and more young women are willing to take part in the AV industry and among them most aim to become *kikatan* rather than *tantai* actresses, because it is the former, not the latter, that earns the most.

The above pay difference among *tantai*, *kikatan* and *kikaku* AV actresses shapes the job choice of AV actresses, which further gives rise to a unique actress composition in the AV industry: 5 per cent for *senzoku tantai* actress; 20 per cent for *kikatan*; and 75 per cent for *kikaku* actress (Nakamura 2012: 48).

Monetary reward seems to be more important to the many girls coming from regional areas of Japan. While they travel to Tokyo in search of better employment opportunities and livelihoods, they are in many ways less competitive than those born and/or raised there, in the sense that they are less familiar with the systems, rules and norms of the capital. This is especially true of corporate culture in Tokyo which tends to have a whole set of unstated norms. This in turn suggests that it would be extremely difficult for women coming from regional areas to be admitted to major corporations in Tokyo. Although we do not have data on the educational background of the AV actresses in our data set,[3] one might infer from other data that they were perhaps lowly educated and this has prevented them from being hired in other more 'proper' professions. This can be testified by the relatively young age of these actresses in general. As we have seen, about 15 per cent of these actresses are aged 19 or below. Unless they were studying in universities at the time of interview, one might say that most of them did not go to university. As we have seen, almost one-third of the actresses have been engaged in the sex trade or in some minor jobs. In the cultural context of Japan, as in other Asian cultures, working in sex-related jobs is often seen as a last resort for women. It means that they are already marginalized on the fringe of society, leaving them with not many options for future career development. Even if they have been working in other service sectors such as office work, catering, sales or cosmetics, their salaries will still have been relatively low, with less job security and fewer prospects for career development (Okano 2009: 154). Seen in this light, it is not incorrect to say that 'AV actress' appears to be one of the highest paying jobs in the eyes of these women.

While monetary reward is certainly an important motivation for those who are economically disadvantaged to join the AV industry, how about those who were born and raised in Tokyo and those who are not as disadvantaged as those from regional areas? Obviously, money is not a sufficient condition for these women to become AV actresses, for many of them joined the industry for other reasons such as exploring their sexuality.

Exploration of sex

The willingness to explore sex is another observation we can make from the data. As we have seen, the average age for respondents' first sexual encounter was 16. More importantly, 2.17 per cent of them had their first sexual encounter between the ages of nine and 12, even though the legal age for having intercourse in Japan is 13 (see Figure 5.8). Meanwhile, 40.9 per cent of them had sex for the first time between 13 and 15, and another 42.6 per cent between the ages of 16 and 18. In other words, 84 per cent of the (would be) actresses had their first sexual experience at 18 or before – considerably younger than their counterparts in Hong Kong or Taiwan (Yip *et al.* 2013: 5).

Similarly, their willingness to explore sex is reflected in the number of sex partners they have had so far. As we have seen from the above figures, 39 per cent of 504 respondents said that they had had from two to ten partners, and another 26 per cent between 11 and 20 sex partners. Respectively, 9.7 per cent and 9.5 per cent reported that the number of their sex partners ranged between 21 and 30 and between 31 and 50, while a further 11.9 per cent claimed to have had between 51 and 100. Even more surprisingly, 2.4 per cent (12 actresses) actually claimed that they had made love to more than 100 men (or women) so far (see Figure 5.9). In fact, one even claimed that she had had sex with more than 900 men. Of course, some of these actresses might have been blowing smoke and we need to bear in mind that these data were provided by women who were applying to become porn actresses, so that they might have been prone to exaggeration on the assumption that having a large number of sex partners would increase the possibility of their being hired. On the other hand, we need to accept the fact that, in comparison with the data reported in the above-mentioned surveys in Britain and Taiwan, the Japanese AV actresses in our data set have been generally liberal toward sex and more willing to engage in sex and explore sexuality.

Success and upward mobility

Another observation about Japanese AV actresses from the data we collected is their strong motivation for success or upward mobility. This can first be seen in where they come from. As we have seen, only 27 per cent of them were from Tokyo and Osaka, whereas the remaining 73 per cent were from regional areas. Traditionally, major cities – especially Tokyo – are seen as the social and financial centres where young people from regional areas go in search of better jobs, more satisfying challenges, and better living standards (Tachibanaki and Urakawa 2012: 188). This is so because the GDP per capita of Tokyo has been characteristically higher than other prefectures. According to the data provided by the Cabinet Office, the GDP per capita for Tokyo City and Osaka Prefecture in 2013 was ¥4.5 million (US$39,600) and ¥3 million (US$26,400) respectively – considerably higher than for most other prefectures which was below ¥2.9 million (US$25,520) (Cabinet Office, Government of Japan 2016). Thus, it can be suggested that many of these AV girls were young women from the provinces who had left their hometowns and gone to Tokyo alone, in the hope of finding better jobs and livelihoods in Tokyo. If these women dared to leave their hometowns to live alone in a new city, it can also be suggested that they were far more ambitious and aggressive than those who chose to stay in the provinces for they had the willpower and determination to leave for a better life in Tokyo.

Their motivation for success or upward mobility can also be seen in the fact that 18 per cent of the 393 actresses who responded to the question of 'their dreams' reported that their dream was career development. This figure is mildly astonishing in the cultural context of modern Japan. Notwithstanding that the 'dream' of getting married or forming a family still ranked first, accounting for almost 25 per cent of the total number of respondents, it suggests that more and more young women in Japan increasingly aspire to pursue a career, rather than just stay at home and serve as a 'good wife and wise mother'. This change can also be captured in a change in unemployment figures from the late 1990s. In 1996, men's unemployment rate (3.4 per cent) was higher than that of women (3.3 per cent) (Osawa 2005: 100). In 2003, the male unemployment rate rose to 5.5 per cent while that of women stood at 4.9 per cent (Osawa 2005: 101). Declining job opportunities resulting from the big recession was perhaps one of the reasons, but it obviously speaks volumes for the increasing ambition of young women in contemporary Japan.

Of course, on top of monetary reward or wealth, success is also expressed in fame acquired. For instance, 14.5 per cent of 393 actresses stated that their dream was to achieve fame in their lives. Equally, almost 10 per cent of the 545 actresses who responded to the question of 'their reasons for becoming AV girls' suggested that they entered the AV industry because of 'potential fame'. In other words, many Japanese actresses regarded debuting in AVs as one of the major ways of getting fame.

These data all speak volumes to one important point: these women strived very hard to achieve fame or success in the cultural context of Japan where upward mobility and career opportunities for women are still relatively difficult, an important topic to which we will later return.

Attention and personal satisfaction

Attention and personal satisfaction also appear to have equally cultural importance to the actresses concerned. As we have seen above, among the 254 actresses who responded to the question of 'the happiest thing about being an actress', about 37 per cent of them stated that the very shooting process was the most joyous and rewarding experience of being an AV actress, which seems to contradict the claims of some feminist scholars (Dines 2008; MacKinnon 1983) that pornography functions to exploit and subordinate women. As mentioned in Chapter 4, the shooting process of most Japanese AVs lasts only one to two days. But still, as actresses, these women found the shooting the most joyful and emotionally rewarding experience of being an actress. This can be seen in the fact that half of these 37 per cent reported that they revelled in the 'enjoyable, friendly and humorous atmosphere' of the shooting process. Some even thought that they felt respected and loved in the shooting process. More importantly, about 35 per cent of them suggested that the happiest thing about being an actress was to chat onsite with different staff and crew members who were extremely kind and funny. Equally, another 11.1 per cent reported that they were delighted to meet many new friends and people on site.

If their most joyous experience of being an actress all revolved around the pleasant and friendly atmosphere of the shooting site, the rewarding and enjoyable experience of the shooting process, the kindness and friendliness of crew members, and the staff and people on site, it is not incorrect to say that what these actresses enjoyed was the immense attention and personal satisfaction they received during the shooting process. That is to say, they felt that they were the centre of attention from the minute the film crew and staff laid eyes on them. It is especially true if we take into account the fact that 11.5 per cent reported that they took great pleasure in being photographed, filmed, made-up and beautified by staff or crew members on site. We can see that what they revelled in is the fact that they were the very centre of the attention and well taken care of by the surrounding people.

Marriage as the destiny

Another interesting observation from the data we collected is that while these prospective AV actresses were willing to take part in the AV industry, many of them still perceived 'marriage' or 'establishing a family' as their life goal. As we have seen, 24.9 per cent of the respondents reported that their overriding dream was to get married or establish a family before a certain age, usually before 25 or 26. There is an old Japanese saying that women who remain unmarried after the age of 25 are sometimes scornfully referred to as Christmas cakes on Boxing Day (even though not many women in fact get married at that age). Not unlike the way Christmas cakes remain unsold on Boxing Day, women after their 25th birthday are no longer of any cultural value. While the saying has become passé as many Japanese women remain single after 25 without being stigmatized, marriage is still considered the destiny for women.

As we have seen, notwithstanding the fact that 'having a career', 'gaining fame' or 'opening a shop' were also important dreams among these actresses, it is of crucial importance to note that one-quarter of these women still regarded marriage or family as their overriding goal. This figure is stunning when juxtaposed with the fact that Japan is now one of the latest marrying societies in the world with the mean age at first marriage reaching 27.6 for women and 29.4 for men in 2003 (Raymo and Iwasawa 2005: 801). There might be many reasons for these contradictory figures, but one is certain: that the privilege to have late marriage is by and large confined to those who are born in big cities and are highly educated (cf. Raymo 2003). Those who come from regional areas and do not receive higher education might not have either the financial or cultural capital to defer, not to mention resist, marriage.

Japanese corporate system (*kaisha* system)

In this section, we will situate the above observations concerning the AV girls in our data set in the socio-cultural contexts of Japan, of which the Japanese corporate system (*kaisha* system) is an important one. Since one of the authors

(Wong 1999: 31–50) has offered a comprehensive analysis of the Japanese concept of *kaisha*, we are going to be very brief here.

Employees of the *kaisha* are always divided into regular employees (*seishain*) and non-regular employees (*hiseishain*): the latter include any contingent form of employment. Regular employees are those who have passed the company's entrance examination (*nyūsha shiken*) and have completed a probation period. They are expected to stay in the same company until mandatory retirement. In contrast, non-regular employees are hired individually at any time during the year and, most importantly, they cannot assume that a company will employ them until they reach retirement age (Wong 1999: 48–9).

The differences between regular and non-regular employees are reflected in the differential rights to choose job classifications. In the *kaisha* system, jobs are classified into generalist (*sōgō shoku*) and clerical staff (*jimu shoku*). Employees belonging to the generalist job classification can have subordinates; their job assignments are very flexible; and they could be asked to do any job which conforms to their career paths. Clerical staff are required to stick to their specific job as defined by the company. Regular employees enjoy the most freedom to choose among the available job classifications, while non-regular employees usually are asked to take up clerical work (Wong 1999: 48–9).

More importantly, the division of generalist and clerical staff among regular employees is always gendered. The *kaisha* tends to recruit women for clerical work and men as generalists. This gender-biased practice has always been justified by the two major pillars of the so-called Japanese style of management: the lifetime employment system and seniority-based promotions (Abegglen 1960[1958], 1985; Clark 1979; Dore 1973). In Japan, the common recruitment pattern is bulk hiring which usually occurs at entry level positions. When hiring regular employees for entry level positions Japanese corporations typically target recent graduates, both high school and university. These employees will eventually become the pillar of the corporation as they advance systematically within the company's internal structure according to their age and length of service, both of which in turn determine their status and wages (Miller 2003: 165).

This requirement for uninterrupted service poses a unique disadvantage for Japanese women workers. In the event that a woman opts to suspend work upon marriage or childbirth and subsequently decides to re-enter the labour force, she must start as a part-timer or a temporary worker, and is biased toward job types in the '4Cs' (Caring, Cleaning, Cooking, Cashier) (Zhou 2015: 120). In other words, she must sacrifice her previous work experience (Miller 2003: 165–6).

The fact that women workers cannot provide uninterrupted service for the corporations in turn becomes a justification for their assigning women only to secretarial but not managerial positions, regardless of their educational levels and abilities. This situation did change to some extent when the Equal Employment Opportunity Law was passed in 1985 (Miller 2003: 167; Roberts 1994: 173). Yet, most Japanese corporations opened management-track positions to a select few. As a result, most Japanese women workers remained confined to the so-called pink-collar world of clerical positions (Miller 2003: 168), giving rise to a woefully underutilized talent pool of 'OL' ('office ladies') in the domestic labour market even in the twenty-first century's Japan (cf. Koh 2011). This is confirmed by Brinton's survey conducted in the 1980s, according to which '60 percent of the women who entered a large firm when they left school entered as clerical workers' (Brinton 1989: 559).

The result is the famous cultural model of Japanese women workers, according to which women are not only transient but also supporting members of the labour force. Most of them will begin work in a *kaisha* upon graduation from school, resign from their *kaisha* when they get married or after they become a mother, and re-join the labour force as part-time workers when their children grow up and no longer need intensive maternal care. This is why women are considered to be transient members of the labour force; it is assumed they will take supporting roles because, almost invariably, they are not assigned to positions with managerial responsibility. The most prominent example is what we mentioned above: 'OL', who are young, white-collar female employees who are just helpers in the office and usually without managerial responsibility. In other words, women workers can never become the centre of attention in the workplace.

The *kaisha* system, however, has encountered a more severe challenge since the 1990s when the Japanese economy entered into a big and long-lasting recession, the impact of which was so far reaching and profound that the 1990s were described as 'the lost decade' – an appellation that seems to have extended into the 2000s (Dasgupta 2009: 79). Brinton (2011) effectively demonstrated in a recent monograph that Japanese employers addressed the long economic recession by substantially reducing the number of both regular employees and clerical employees in favour of part-time and temporary workers in their yearly recruitment plan (Miller 2003: 173). As she points out:

> Middle-aged male workers were largely protected while the youngest and oldest male workers, along with women, suffered the brunt of the negative impact. Even in the conditions of economic downturn most Japanese employers exerted great efforts to maintain the commitments they had made to make workers hired during Japan's high economic-growth years.
> (Brinton 2011: 25–6)

That is to say, young workers, including men and women, have been sacrificed since the 1990s. As noted of a survey conducted by the Ministry of Economy, Trade and Industry of Japan on how Japanese firms have addressed the long economic recession since the 1990s through different adjustment methods:

> Looking at those firms cutting 10% [of their employees] or more, the most common methods were a freeze in hiring new graduates (61%), voluntary early retirement (49%), transfers to other firms (37%), and internal

reallocation (36%).... A very similar patterns applies to firms cutting more than 25% of their employees. Thus, Japanese firms have aimed to preserve their core workforce largely by reducing intake and giving incentives for exit to older employees.

(Jackson 2007: 289)

As a result, young graduates have found it difficult to get full-time jobs upon graduation since the 1990s. As a result, they have been forced to accept temporary, part-time or any contingent employment, or remain unemployed. The unemployment rate of young people in 2003 was three times higher than it was in 1975 (Brinton 2011: 24). More importantly, the possibility of taking contingent employment only among young Japanese men is very popular in the lost decade and now. Brinton comments on how this is comparable to the situation of married women taking part-time jobs in the 1980s:

> The current probability that a young man is in irregular work is nearly equivalent to the probability that a married woman in 1980 would have worked part-time. Part-time work for Japanese married women became widespread during the era of the modern postwar family, and has remained a common way for women to balance work and family during their prime childrearing years. But part-time work among young single men? This brings into sharp relief the economic peripheralization of young men – what we might call the de-gendering of irregular employment in postindustrial Japan.

(Brinton 2011: 30)

Certainly, those elite young men who graduate from prestigious universities might still be able to find a full-time job; but many young men graduating from ordinary universities have difficulty in getting a full-time job, and many of them are forced to take up part-time or temporary jobs; some of them even remain unemployed upon graduation.

Women graduating from non-elite universities have suffered even more than their male counterparts from the substantial cuts in employment. Since the 2000s, Japanese female graduates have increasingly found themselves unable to find clerical track not to mention managerial track positions. They have had no alternative but to take up temporary positions as their first jobs (Miller 2003: 173). Data indicate that the percentage of Japanese women being hired as temporary workers has increased from 41.9 per cent in 1995 to 55 per cent in 2006 (Miura 2008: 166). This employment situation certainly suggests that Japanese women, regardless of how smart and hardworking they are, will never be recognized, not to be mention valued, by their employers. That is why women workers are always the first to be sacrificed by their *kaisha* whenever necessary. During the rapid economic growth in the 1980s, the female labour force was still largely utilized by Japanese employers to cut costs and increase flexibility. As Miller concludes, female labourers can be hired and fired in accordance with economic conditions, women constitute a group of temporary employees that function as a safety valve that affords firms flexibility during economic downturns, thereby protecting men's permanent employment status.

(Miller 2003: 166–7)

The situation of women workers, however, became even worse during the lost decade. As Brinton quotes Wakaisaka:

part-time and other nonregular employees are not being used to adjust employment levels nor as a buffer, but as substitutes for regular employees; that is, enterprises are beginning to replace the former kind of workers with the latter.

(Brinton 2005: 432–3)

Many Japanese women have thus ended up being *permanent* part-time or temporary workers during the recession.

The *kaisha* system helps shed light on the above-mentioned characteristics of the young women in our data set. First, about 73 per cent of young girls in our data set came from regional areas. They were strongly motivated to succeed or become upwardly mobile as they were unwilling to stay at home and assume traditional housekeeping roles, but chose to leave their hometowns for Tokyo for a better job there. The situation of women workers described above therefore appeared to be particularly frustrating to them because most of these girls did not have the necessary social or cultural capital; and even worse, not many of them possessed high educational qualifications. Among those jobs that were available to these girls, being an AV actress or working in adult entertainment industry appeared to be one of the best ways for them to make quick, if not big, money. In fact, 25.8 per cent of the young girls in our data set, as mentioned above, ended up working in the adult entertainment industry.

Yet, money was at best just one of the reasons for their participation in the AV industry. Attention and personal satisfaction was another important reason. As we have just seen, Japanese women have not been, and can never be, the centre of attention in the men-dominated *kaisha*, not to mention given positions with great responsibility or decision-making power. Even when female graduates are given managerial positions during labour shortage, they might be sacked or put in temporary positions when the economy slows (Miller 2003: 172). For those who are lucky enough to stay in professional or managerial positions, it is still not a rewarding experience. Umeda *et al.* (2015) have shown that Japanese women in professional or managerial occupations in modern Japan are more vulnerable to poor psychological health due to high levels of effort-reward imbalance (Umeda *et al.* 2015: 14). It follows that in order to receive rewards comparable with those of their male counterparts, Japanese career women have to work a great deal harder and contribute a great deal more.

Seen in this light, perhaps we are in a better position to appreciate why the actresses in our data set would be willing to join and stay in the AV industry, not to mention the fact that many of them indeed found the job of being an AV actress rewarding and emotionally fulfilling. For it is being an actress during the shooting that these Japanese women for the first time felt that they were fully valued and recognized by the crew members and staff. They were no longer clerical or temporary staff. They were not required to assume a supporting role as they would have been in regular Japanese corporations, preparing tea for meetings or making photocopies for their male colleagues (cf. Fujimoto 1994: 39–40). Instead, they were actresses – the most important role during the whole shooting. They were surrounded by a whole crew of members who treated them with extra care and respect.

Third, this unfavourable female labour market in modern Japan also implies that marriage is after all the destiny for most Japanese women, especially for those who do not possess financial or cultural capital. Yet, marriage in Japan, as in other cultures, has entailed a whole set of responsibilities, norms and taboos for women. Once a wife and mother, a Japanese woman will not be as physically, mentally and emotionally free as she used to be. It is for this reason that many of the actresses in our data set suggested that they entered the adult video industry precisely to try out something that they could not do in the future – after they enter marriage and motherhood, which contributes to the above-mentioned high turnover rate of AV actresses.

Women's right in selling their bodies

The lack of decent job opportunity, however, is just one of the social contexts against which the phenomenon of many Japanese young women joining the AV industry as actresses can be understood, because having no alternative job opportunity does not necessarily motivate them to join the industry. Their relatively sexual permissiveness could also be one major reason, for there is a women's sexual culture that expresses – indeed encourages – women's sexual desires, as we can see from the rich publication of ladies' comics in Japan.[4] In fact, there has been a whole range of literature on the sexual openness of Japanese young women, especially their earlier sexual initiation and engagement in a wide range of sexual activities like 'compensated dating' (*enjokōsai*) (Hashimoto 2000; Kelsky 2001a, 2001b; Kinsella 2011, 2014; Leheny 2006; Rosenberger 2001; Ueno 2003). However, we would like to add here that the so-called 'original theory of self-determination of sex' ('*sei no jiko kettei kenron*') advocated by some public intellectuals (Miyada *et al*. 1998) in Japan in the late 1990s has been playing an important role in raising the awareness of young women's right to determine their own sexual bodies. This theory itself is akin to C. B. Macpherson's political theory of possessive individualism that advocates a conception of the individual as quoted by Sahlins:

> A conception of the individual as essentially the proprietor of his own person or capacities, owing nothing to society for them. The individual was

seen neither as a moral whole, nor as part of a larger social whole, but as owner of himself. The relation of ownership, having become for more and more men the critically important relation in determining their actual freedom and actual prospect of realizing their full potentialities, was read back into the nature of the individual.... Society becomes a lot of free individuals related to each other as proprietors of their own capacities and of what they have acquired by their exercise. Society consists of relations of exchange between proprietors.

(Sahlins 1976b: 98)

We can recognize in the above description the 'original theory of self-determination of sex' in contemporary Japan that individual Japanese women 'own their own body; the use of which they have both the freedom and necessity to sell to those who control their own capital' (Sahlins 1976b: 97). That is to say, Japanese women owe nothing to Japanese society and, therefore, society has no right to stop them from exercising the ownership of their bodies. They have the right to exchange their bodies with, or provide sex service for, any man who is willing to pay. Inspired by Sahlins (1976b), we suggest that the 'original theory of self-determination of sex' is not only the self-consciousness of Japanese society as a highly capitalist society, but it also serves as the ideological base for Japanese women to engage in a wide range of sex trades, including being an AV actress.

All of this provides the important social contexts against which more and more Japanese young women are willing to participate in the adult industry – especially the AV industry – in the 2000s should be understood. Back in the 1980s and 1990s, it was widely recognized that only women from low-class or low-educational backgrounds or in exceptional financial situations would make the daring decision to join the AV industry (Nakamura 2012: 15). As is the case in the West, 'porn actress' as a job is marginalized on the fringe of the society and is considered as the last resort for some unfortunate women. However, the 2000s have witnessed two important changes in Japan. First, more and more 'normal', if not 'decent', young Japanese women are willing to take part in AV productions. Indeed, many young Japanese women are increasingly seeing 'AV actress' as a proper occupation or even a good career (Nakamura 2012: 15–16). In contrast to the situation in the 1990s, it is reported that there are now many Japanese women who have debuted in the AV industry with the support of their lovers, friends and even family members (Nakamura 2012: 16). Thus, the nagging fear about being identified or uncovered by friends or relatives is simply out of context for them.

This change can also be confirmed by our field research in Tokyo. According to the casting director of an AV manufacturer, many girls consider being selected for the interview something to be proud of, because only one or two at the most out of ten applicants get selected. An experienced AV director also echoes the casting director when he said that he was surprised by the enthusiasm displayed by many young women in their AV actress interviews; it was *as if* they were casting for a movie actress post.

Second, many young Japanese 'good-looking' women are willing to take on 'hardcore' or 'kinky' roles that were traditionally only accepted by women who were of relatively 'low quality' (Nakamura 2012: 78). In the 1990s, genres like S&M, imprisonment or scatology by and large starred so-called 'low quality' women – a term which largely refers to below-average-looking young women or average-looking women in their 30s and 40s. But since the 2000s, many regular, and indeed above average, attractive young women are more than comfortable in accepting such roles. Of course, the fact that only young, above-average women will be given a job opportunity, as a result of the emergence of the category of *kikatan* AVs in the industry, is one of the major reasons why beautiful women are willing to become AV actresses.

Conclusion

The aim of this chapter has been fairly simple. We wished to spell out the socio-cultural contexts against which the fact that so many Japanese young – especially good-looking – women aspire to be adult video actresses should be understood. To do this, we first looked into who these actresses were by exploring the profile data of a group of actresses including their age, marital status, family background, educational background, birthplace, occupation, life goal, age at first sex, number of sexual partners, dream, aspiration, and so on. We discovered that the 588 actresses in our sample were by and large young, fairly sexually open, ambitious, success-oriented, coming from rural areas, involving in sex-related businesses, and so on.

From this data set, we were also able to make several observations. First, almost half of the actresses reported that they entered the AV industry simply because of monetary reward. Their willingness to explore sex is another observation we can make from the data. The third observation about the Japanese AV actresses is their strong motivation for success or upward mobility. Attention and personal satisfaction also appear to have equal cultural importance for the actresses concerned. The final observation is that our AV actresses perceived 'marriage' or 'establishing a family' as their life goal.

All these observations point to one fundamental socio-cultural reality in modern Japan: women's labour, both in the reproductive private sphere and in the formal labour market of the public sphere, is used extensively, yet women are not given sufficient recognition and representation in real terms, in spite of their increasing educational qualifications and the implementation of Equal Labour Law. Women are characteristically considered as assuming a supporting role in the labour market. This situation has become worse since the lost decade of the 1990s because Japanese employers chose to sacrifice young people for the benefit of the older generation. They substantially reduced the yearly intake of new regular and clerical employees, forcing many young people to take up part-time or temporary jobs or even remain unemployed upon graduation. However, this substantial reduction affected women more than men. Those women who come from *chihō* areas with low education, like the young girls in our data set, are the worst among the worst. They would get into the AV industry because the job of AV actresses can precisely offer them things that they would never be able to get in a normal career path in contemporary Japan – money, attention, job satisfaction, upward mobility, sense of success, and so on.

The lack of decent job opportunities, however, cannot exclusively explain why our young Japanese women are willing to join the industry as AV actresses. We suggest that the so-called 'original theory of self-determination of sex' in Japan in the late 1990s has been serving as an ideological base for Japanese women to engage in a wide range of sex trades, including being an AV actress. It is against this that the fact that more and more Japanese young women are willing to participate in the AV industry in the 2000s should be understood.

Notes

1 The authors would like to express their gratitude to Professor Ben-Ari for pointing out this interesting observation.
2 'Age of consent in Japan', www.ageofconsent.net/world/japan, accessed on 21 April 2017.
3 For some unknown reasons, most of the actresses did not fill in this column. As a result, we did not have data on this.
4 The authors would like to express their gratitude to Professor Mark McLelland for pointing out this interesting observation.

6 AV girl job interview
An inventive production process

Introduction

This chapter focuses on the job interview, a mundane activity for AV (especially *kikaku*) actresses, and explores how actresses are evaluated, examined, judged and selected by the (so-called) casting director. We shall first examine the interview sheet that every interviewee is required to fill in, and identify some of the major characteristics of the questions and their underlying logic. Then we will ethnographically examine the interview process between a casting director and a *kikaku* actress, with an eye to exploring how he approaches and interviews her; and how she responds to, and interacts with, the casting director. We will then move on to the final part of the interview where the actress is required to pose for photographs and videos, paying particular attention to how she responds to the casting director's requests. The data of our examination in this chapter are extensively drawn from observations of four job interviews conducted in Tokyo in the early 2010s. Due to the limitation of space, we will mainly focus our ethnography on one job interview, and from time to time, complement our discussion with observations from the other three interviews.

The major point of this chapter is that AV job interviews intended to recruit AV girls who can bring financial success to the company – not unlike those selection interviews in reality shows (Grindstaff 2002) or fashion modelling (Mears 2011) – are a very important practice because they reveal some of the major logics and concerns of AV production. We identify 13 themes from the interview process and further show that they point to a set of qualities that are, from the vantage of the casting director, useful and hence financially productive to the AV company.

We will show, too, that the interview process can also reveal the complexity of the interactive process among casting or AV directors, AV actresses as text, and the classificatory system of genres and categories in the Japanese AV industry, as a result of which a woman is transformed into a certain kind of AV actress. The AV job interview therefore is a production process which is also governed by the cultural code of the salvage ideology. In short, it is the very arena where the logics and rationale of AV production are revealed.

AV girl interview: meeting the actress[1]

On an afternoon in early autumn in 2011, Wakaranai is chatting with us in a conference room in his main office in Tokyo. We are waiting for a young actress who will come for an interview. Wakaranai, as the casting director, is responsible for holding the interview. We are a bit nervous as it is the first time we have joined in an AV girl interview. To fill in a little waiting time, we hurry to the restroom. When we return, the actress and her manager are already seated in another conference room. As we enter, we see a young woman in the middle of filling in a set of forms. Wearing a trendy straight-across fringe and light makeup, the actress has sharp facial features. While she might not potentially qualify as a top actress, she is certainly a good-looking young woman. She is slender, with big breasts that even her black pullover cannot cover.

When our eyes meet, her manager rises from his chair and exchanges business cards with us whereas the actress gives us a smile and soon returns to her form. Then, an uncomfortable silence fills the room. A few minutes later, Wakaranai enters. Once again, the manager immediately rises from his chair, bows and exchanges business cards with Wakaranai, while not forgetting to introduce his AV actress to him. Meanwhile, we feel a bit awkward since we are about to witness the start of a seesaw battle between a buyer and a seller: the seller-cum-manager doing his utmost to sell his girl to Wakaranai and Wakaranai, as the buyer, not hesitating to *scrutinize* the commodity, and the commodity today is precisely the young actress. The only difference is that she can *market* and *speak for* herself.

The first thing Wakaranai does is to photocopy the actress's passport, since if the AV actress has not reached 18 years of age, it will be a great problem for the AV studio. According to current laws in Japan, employing young girls below the age of 18 in the entertainment business is a criminal offence and is subject to government prosecution. Therefore, confirming the age of the actress is one of the most important jobs of any casting director.

Interview sheet

After making the photocopy, Wakaranai returns the passport to the actress. He meanwhile collects the interview sheets she has filled in and will use her data as the basis for interviewing the AV girl. As mentioned in Chapter 5, these interview sheets contain three pages. The first page is a 'Profile Card', a curriculum vitae of the actress that takes the form of a table (please refer back to Table 5.1). Figure 6.1 displays the image of the original Japanese form filled in by the actress we observed during our fieldwork (please refer to Figure 6.2 for the translated version of the form filled in by the actress).

The second page is a questionnaire (see Figure 6.3). Although Wakaranai skips some of the questions on page one, it is of importance to note that he does not skip any questions on page two. We might then infer that the second page is far more important than the first in the whole interview process. This questionnaire

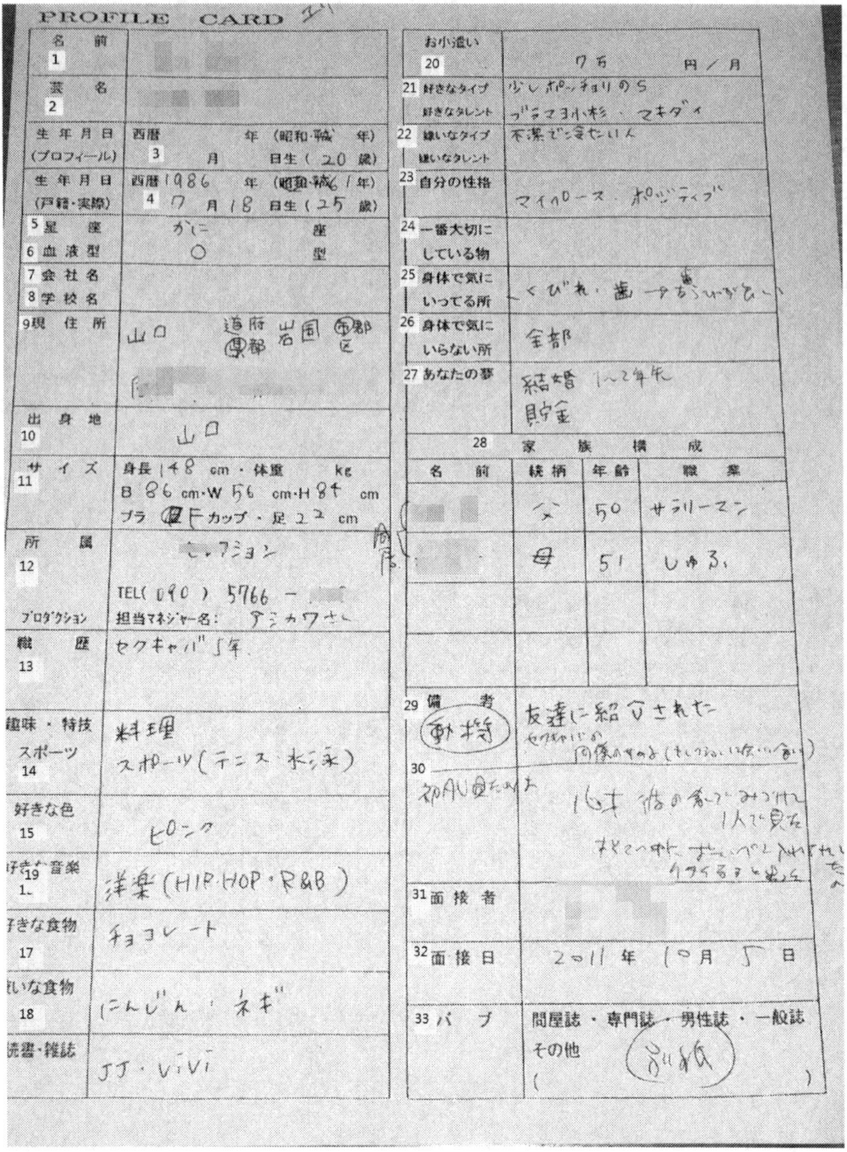

134 *AV girl job interview*

Figure 6.1 Original Japanese profile card filled in by the actress.

has 30 questions in total, divided into three parts. The first part is about how and why the actress joined the AV industry in the first place and her experiences as an AV actress, with an aim to better understand her attitude toward the AV industry and her understanding about having a career in the industry as an AV actress.

AV girl job interview 135

The Filled in Profile Card

1. Name:	Disguised	20. Pocket Money:	70,000 Yen/month
2. Stage Name:	Disguised	21. Favorite Type of Man and Talent:	A 'S' (sadist) with a bit chubby Kosugi Nyūichi, DJ Makidai
3. Date of Birth (Profile Use)	Y M D Age: 20	22. Least Favorite Type of Man and Talent:	Dirty,
4. Date of Birth (Real)	1986 Y 7 M 18 D Age: 25	23. Personality:	My pace, and positive
5. Horoscope:	Cancer	24. The Most Important Thing in life:	Empty
6. Blood Type:	O positive		
7. Company Name:	Empty	25. Which part of your body you like the most?	Waistline, Teeth
8. School Name:			
9. Current Home Address:	Yamaguchi Prefecture	26. Which part of your body you like the least?	All
10. Hometown:	Yamaguchi	27 Your Dream:	Marriage (in 1 to 2 years) Save money

		28. Family Structure			
11. Three Sizes	Height: 148cm Weight: Empty kg	Name	Relationship	Age	Occupation
	B: 86 cm W: 56cm H: 84 cm		Father	50	Salaryman
	Bra: F cup Feet size: 22cm				
12. The modelling agency that represents you	Tel: 090-5766-disguised Your manager:		Mother	51	Housewife
13. Working Experiences:	Sex Cabaret				
14. Hobbies, skills, sports:	Cooking, sports (tennis, and swimming)				
15. Favorite Color:	Pink	29. Motivation in AV performance:	Introduced by friends		
16. Favorite Music:	Western music (Hip Hop, R&B)	30. The First Time Watching AV:	16 years old, at boyfriend's place		
17. Favorite Food	Chocolate	31. Interviewer:			
18. Least Favorite Food	Carrot and Welsh onion	32. Interviewing Date:	2011 Y 10 M 5 D		
19. Favorite Books or Magazines	JJ, Vivi	33. Publicity:	In another sheet		

Figure 6.2 Translated profile card filled in by the actress.

The second part turns to her sexual life. The questions here involve her sex life such as 'Are you in the habit of masturbating?', 'How is your sex life now?', 'When was your most recent sexual experience?', 'Have you ever experienced an orgasm?', 'Do you moan while having sex?' and 'Is your body sexually

The Questionnaire on the Second Page of the *Mensetsu* Sheet

1. Name(Stage Name)_____
2. How you became a model? Please circle the relevant ones:
   a) Scoutman   b) Ad in Magazines   c) Internet   d) Friends   e) Others
3. About your modeling job experiences
   a) What is the most pleasant or delightful job so far?
   b) What is the most painful or tough job so far? _____
4. About your first sex: a) When and age: b) Where   c) With Whom?
   d) Age of your partner_____   d) feeling_____
5. Do you think you are erotic?   a) Yes   b) No   c) Don't know
6. Love and money, which you think is more important?   a) Love   b) Money   c) Both
7. What is your favorite sexual position?   a) Missionary   b) On top   c) Doggy-style   d) Others
8. Where is your most sensitive body part?   a) Clitoris   b) Vagina   c) Nipples   d) Ears   e) Neck   f) Others
9. The number of sexual partners you have had so far? _____ Among them, how many did you date with ?
10. The highest record of sex per night? _____
11. Do you have a boyfriend now?   a) Yes (_____ year old, how long: _____)   b) No (How long? _____)
12. For your sexual experiences with men till now:
    a) The oldest one?   Partner: _____ years old   Yourself: _____ years old
    b) The youngest one?   Partner: _____ years old   Yourself: _____ years old
13. The longest dating relationship so far? _____ years _____ months
14. Your menstruation: a) Normal (roughly _____ days a cycle)   b) Abnormal (problems: _____)
    Have you ever had sex during menstruation?:   a) Yes   b) No.
15. About contraception: a) Definitely do (i. Condom   ii. External ejaculation   iii. Pill   iv. Others)
    b) Depends on mood   c) No
16. Have you ever masturbated?   a) Yes   b) No
17. For masturbation, will you still do it now?
    a) Yes (frequency: per day;   per week;   per month)
    b) No.
18. Your current sexual life?   a) _____ per week   b) _____ per month
19. When was the most recent sexual experience?   a) This week (early, mid, late)   b) This month (early, mid, late)
    c) Last month (early, mid, late)   d) Others
20. About experiences of orgasm: a) Yes   b) Almost fake   c) Never come   d) Only come when masturbating
21. Your moan during sex: a) Loud   b) Normal   c) Quiet   (easy to get wet, normal, difficult)
22. Experiences of fellatio: a) Yes   b) No   (Like   Normal   Dislike)
23. Experiences of anal sex: a) Yes (with whom _____)   b) No   (Like   Normal   Dislike)
24. Experiences of lesbian sex: a) Yes (with whom _____)   b) No   (Like   Normal   Dislike)
25. Experiences of SM: a) Yes (with whom _____)   b) No   (Like   Normal   Dislike)
26. Experiences of Mouth Ejaculation: a) Yes (Swallow   Not Swallow)   b) No   (Like   Normal   Dislike)
27. Did you have any abnormal sexual experiences? _____
28. What kind of sex or play you want to try? _____
29. NG Things or NG actors:
30. About Releases: the Debut movie: when _____   Maker: _____

Figure 6.3 English version of the questionnaire.

sensitive?' We might infer that the aim of these questions is to understand her sexual particulars so that the company can arrange plots that are suitable for her.

The third part touches on her experiences in non-mainstream sexual behaviour such as anal sex, homosexual sex and S&M, as well as her least favourite plots, genres and actors, to determine what kind of plots or genres she can take part in her upcoming AVs and what should be avoided. Finally, Wakaranai asks her how many adult movies she has so far participated in. If she has released a number of films under the names of other AV makers, Wakaranai's company would be unlikely to sign her up because she has already lost her fresh attraction, and thus would not bring in large profits to the company (please refer to Figure 6.4 for the original Japanese form filled in by the actress and Figure 6.5 for the translated version of the form filled in by the actress).

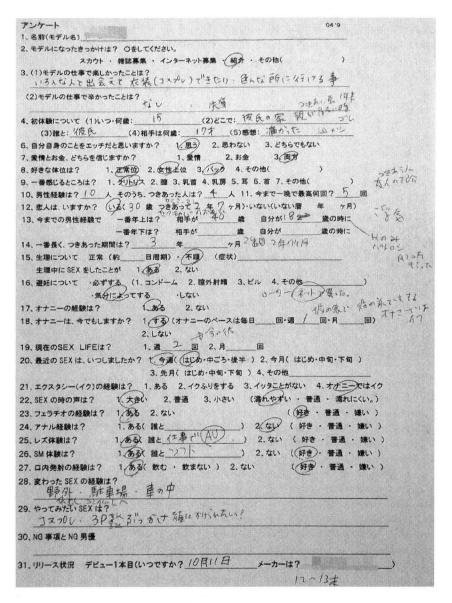

Figure 6.4 Original questionnaire part filled in by the actress.

The Questionnaire on the Second Page of the *Mensetsu* Sheet

1. Name(Stage Name)____Disguised_____
2. How you became a model? Please circle the relevant ones:
       a) Scoutman   b) Ad in Magazines   c) Internet   **(d) Friends**   e) Others
3. About your modeling job experiences
       a) What is the most pleasant or delightful job so far? __Can meet many different people, trying on different costumes and can go to many different places_____
       b) What is the most painful or tough job so far? __No_____Her senior
4. About your first sex: a) When and age: _15_   b) Where: Boyfriend's place   c) With Whom? __Boyfriend_
       d) Age of your partner: __17____   d) Feeling: __Painful_____
5. Do you think you are erotic? **(a) Yes**   b) No   c) Don't know
6. Love and money, which you think is more important?   a) Love   b) Money   **(c) Both**
7. What is your favorite sexual position? **(a) Missionary**   **(b) On top**   **(c) Doggy style**   d) Others
8. Where is your most sensitive body part? **(a) Clitoris**   b) Vagina   c) Nipples   d) Ears   e) Neck   f) Others
9. The number of sexual partners you have had so far?   10   Among them, how many did you date with?   4
10. The highest record of sex per night?   5   Those she had dated before were introduced by friends
11. Do you have a boyfriend now? **(a) Yes**   30 year old, how long: 2 years 7 months)   b. No (How long?   )
12. For your sexual experiences with men till now:
        a) The oldest one?   Partner: 40   years old   Yourself: 18   years old
        b) The youngest one?   Partner: years old   Yourself: years old
13. The longest dating relationship so far?   3 years   months
14. Your menstruation: a) Normal (roughly   days a cycle)   **(b) Abnormal** problems:)
    Have you ever had sex during menstruation?: **(a) Yes**   b) No.
15. About contraception: a) Definitely do (i. Condom   ii. External ejaculation   iii. Pill   iv. Others)
        (b) Depends on mood   c) No
16. Have you ever masturbated?   **(a) Yes**   b) No
17. For masturbation, will you still do it now? Bought the vibrator from internent
        (a) Yes (frequency: per day; 1 per week;   per month)   Masturbated in front of her boyfriend
        b) No.   With the current boyfriend
18. Your current sexual life? **a)**   2 per week   b)   per month
19. When was the most recent sexual experience? **(a) This week (early,** mid, late)   b) This month (early, mid, late)
        c) Last month (early, mid, late)   d) Others
20. About experiences of orgasm: a) Yes   b) Almost fake   c) Never come   **(d) Only come when masturbating**
21. Your moan during sex **a) Loud**   b) Normal   c) Quiet   **(easy to get wet** normal, difficult)
22. Experiences of fellatio: **(a) Yes**   b) No   **(Like)**   Normal   Dislike)
23. Experiences of anal sex: a) Yes (with whom   )   **(b) No**   (Like   Normal   Dislike)
24. Experiences of lesbian sex: **(a) Yes** with whom Job)AV   b) No   (Like   Normal   Dislike)
25. Experiences of SM: **(a) Yes** with whom   Soft)   b) No   **(Like)**   Normal   Dislike)
26. Experiences of Mouth Ejaculation: **(a) Yes** (Swallow   Not Swallow) b) No   **(Like)**   Normal   Dislike)
27. Did you have any abnormal sexual experiences?   Outdoors, carpark, and inside the car
28. What kind of sex or play you want to try?   Cosplay, 3P, Bukkake   Want to experience facial ejaculation
29. NG Things or NG actors:
30. About Releases: the Debut movie: when   11 Oct   Maker: Disguised

Figure 6.5 Translated questionnaire part filled in by the actress.

AV girl job interview 139

The last page of the interview sheet is a checklist where the actress decides which magazines and journals should show advertisements featuring her AVs. AV makers will advertise their products in adult and general comic books, sports magazines, AV specialty magazines, and so on. Many AV actresses take part in the AV industry without letting their parents, family and friends know so that where their AV advertisements appear is an important issue for them. This page is usually filled in by the manager, who by definition is the one who should know best where her advertisements could appear. As this part is related to the actress's preference and company policy, Wakaranai does not ask anything connected with information provided on this page (see Figure 6.6).

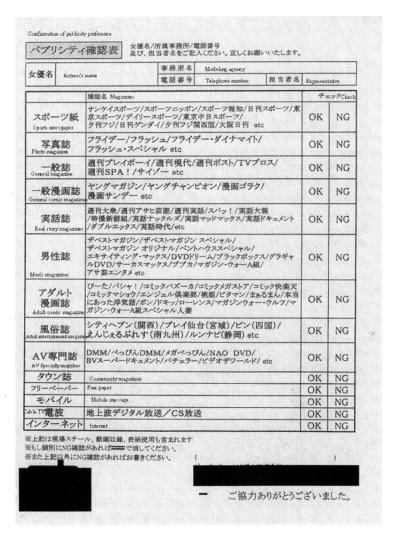

Figure 6.6 Publicity checklist.

Interview process

After all the bureaucratic hassle, the interview starts and continues for about 20 minutes. In what follows, we will organize our discussion by closely following Wakaranai's flow of questions.

About the actress's job as a hostess

The very first thing that catches the attention of the casting director is the actress's job. She has worked as a club girl in a 'sex cabaret' in Tokyo for more than five years. When Wakaranai realizes from the questionnaire that she has been a sex cabaret girl, he raises a series of detailed questions.

'What is the exact nature of your job in the sex cabaret?' Wakaranai asks curiously.

'*Oppabu.*'[2] The actress answers in a sharp and simple way.

Wakaranai appears to be surprised by the fact that she has been involved in this kind of sex business, as he continues to ask:

'I see. Can the customers kiss the club girls?'

'Yes, they can!' The actress answers serenely. On hearing this, Wakaranai raises his eyebrows and wonders aloud how come there could be good things like this. The actress's answers have obviously fuelled his interest because he continues to ask her questions relating to her *oppabu* job.

'Are the customers allowed to touch the lower body of the club girls?' Wakaranai asked excitedly.

'No ... I'm afraid not.' The actress replies clearly.

'Do the club girls wear panties?'

'Yes, most of them do, or else stockings at work. They don't go in for 'no pants'.[3] Wakaranai seems a bit disappointed to hear this.

'Basically, customers are allowed to fondle or grope the girls' breasts, but they aren't allowed to do more than that', the actress explains.

Wakaranai then asks her how long she has been working in the sex cabaret. The actress replies that she has worked there for five years. 'That's great!', he says, as he tries to get her to let her inner guard down and feel comfortable talking about her experiences of sex and AV jobs.

In view of the fact that she is working in the sex cabaret, Wakaranai asks the actress whether she lives with her parents. 'Yes', she replies. This confuses Wakaranai who asks: 'If you're living with your parents, don't they say anything about your work schedule? You know, about why you're free during the daytime and so busy at night?'

'Ummm ... my parents don't intervene in my life', she replies.

Wakaranai still cannot understand why, arguing that her parents would have actually known about it, but she counters that she works during weekends and for most of the time she stays at her boyfriend's place in Tokyo when she works. Moreover, her family lives in another city, so her parents have not found out that she has been working at the sex cabaret.

About the actress's favourite male celebrity

Wakaranai shifts to her favourite male celebrity. Contrary to our expectation, the actress does not fantasize over young Japanese male idols such as Arashi or Kattun, but Kosugi Nyūichi, a 40-something average Joe. Kosugi is a member of the Black Mayonnaise – a famous comedy duo from Osaka with a large following in Western Japan. When Wakaranai sees Kosugi's name on the interview sheet, he is surprised because Kosugi is not particularly handsome. But he is even more surprised by her reason for identifying with Kosugi.

'So you're attracted to Kosugi's talent or special personality?'

'Not really!', she replies directly.

'So what, then?' Wakaranai cannot help but ask.

'I don't think he is handsome, but I like his clumsiness, being a bit lumbering or bumbling … I think he's cute!', she explains in a cheerful way.

'Do you think Kosugi is good at making love?', Wakaranai asks suddenly.

The actress is silent for a while. Then she replies laughing:

> My impression is that 'his' [penis] is really small! Hahaha…. Although I also wrote that DJ Makidai is one of my favourite male artists. But when it comes to appearance, I would say that Kosugi is my cup of tea.

DJ Makidai is an active member of EXILE, a famous Japanese male band with a worldwide following. He is known for his handsome and cool looks, and hence represents a totally different image from Kosugi.

'If Kosugi wanted to make love to you, would you do it?' In view of what the actress has said about her fondness of Kosugi, a strange idea has sprung into Wakaranai's mind.

'Absolutely! Absolutely! It would be my great pleasure!', the actress answers immediately without a second thought while nodding her head forcefully.

'Even though you think "his" [penis] is really tiny?', Wakaranai asks.

'That's right! He's really cute', the actress replies in a very confident way.

'What an amazing story!', Wakaranai simply replies.

About the actress's like and dislike of herself

Wakaranai is somehow confused as he reads from the interview sheet that the actress is 'most' satisfied with her teeth.

'Teeth?', asks Wakaranai.

'My teeth are straight naturally and are always praised by my friends', answers the actress. She tells us that she herself also is proud of her teeth.

Wakaranai is equally confused to find out that the actress writes that the body part she is least satisfied with is 'all'. He asks the actress curiously: 'What do you mean by "all" here?'

The actress pauses a while with a bitter smile on her face. All of us are confused. Her appearance is no doubt above average, although she might not be considered to be A-list when it came to looks. Meanwhile, Wakaranai asks her manager to show him her advertising stills. He hands over a professional still where the actress appears half naked, standing, with arms raised, clearly exposing her breasts.

'Wow … that's great, isn't it? It's something you should be very proud of yourself, isn't it?' Wakaranai seems mesmerized as he stares at the photograph, while exclaiming at her body curves and sexual attractiveness. The interesting thing is that the actress does not feel the way we do for she says unenthusiastically:

'Even though many people praise me about this, I don't feel very happy.'

'Oh really? You're really "negative" about your breasts, aren't you?', Wakaranai comments.

'Right, perhaps they're big and therefore I don't really like them!', the actress replies rather unexcitedly.

'However, with a figure like that you must get lauded by lots of men!', Wakaranai says, with a puzzled look on his face.

'Yes, that's true, but the problem is that I don't feel happy about them!', the actress replies with a bitter smiling face.

About the actress's first sex

After all this casual conversation, Wakaranai jumps to questions about her first sex. Here he goes into an extensive and elaborate set of questions. After learning from the interview sheet that the actress had her first sex at 15 and that the partner was her boyfriend who was at the time 17 years old, Wakaranai asks how she came to know him. The actress replies that he was her senior at school. In other words, they were a so-called perfect match in terms of the male-senior and female-junior.

'Did he look like Kosugi?', Wakaranai asks.

'No … completely different. He once dated our school's Princess Charming', the actress laughs.

'So, was he a handsome guy?'

'Yes, he was …', she answers extremely cheerfully.

'So you loved him and he responded to your love … that sort of pattern?'

'Well, it was pretty much like that!'

As Wakaranai further learns that their first sex took place in the boyfriend's home, Wakaranai could not help but ask: 'Didn't you worry that his parents would find out?' However, the actress explains that they simply made use of the daytime when his parents were out.

'So, it was a "planned crime", was it?', Wakaranai asks in a funny way. He continues to ask some very private questions.

'Did you guys have a condom ready [in the first sex]?', he goes on to ask.

'Yes, he did!', she answers very calmly.

'So you guys did use one, right?'

'Right …', she replies.

'Was there any blood during the first sex?'

'No ... there wasn't any blood', she answers plainly.
'So how long you were with him?'
'About one and half a years!'

We are so impressed by the calmness the actress displays when replying to Wakaranai's extremely private questions. This also reminds us of what Mears refers to as 'weird' casting arrangement in the fashion model business where social norms of politeness are always violated and fashion models 'must suspend such ordinary social norms and accept, at least for the duration of the casting, that they are display objects for sale in a silent auction' (Mears 2011: 81–2). In our context, the casting is even more 'weird' because some *very* private questions would be put directly to the candidate as we have seen in above conversation between Wakaranai and the actress. Similar occasions happened all the time during the interview.

About the actress's affairs

Wakaranai goes on to ask about her other sexual relationships. He asks her how she came to know the men with whom she had sex before. The actress pauses a while. She suggests that those who she had been together with were basically introduced by friends and that others were mostly through *nanpa*[4] (accosting) or customers from her cabaret work.

'Would you date two men at the same time, like Mr. A and Mr. B concurrently?', Wakaranai asks all of a sudden.

'Yes. *Futamata* [meaning dating with two persons at the same time]. Like my current boyfriend, too, between him and the previous boyfriend, there were roughly two months when my relationships with them overlapped', the actress explains seriously.

'Right, a question, then. When you were dating someone, have you ever had an affair with someone else?', Wakaranai asks, again, directly.

'Yes!', the actress answers energetically.

'Wasn't it easily exposed or discovered by your boyfriend?', Wakaranai asks curiously.

'No! I haven't been found out. I don't think it'd be that easy to do so either. Anyway, in my case nobody found out', the actress answers in a rather high tone.

'I see. So was there any reason for having an affair? Was it because your boyfriend had an affair, and you wanted revenge by having one of your own?'

'No no ... I simply wanted to have sex', she answers and soon burst into laughter as if she has said something inappropriate.

'Your poor boyfriend ... wouldn't he check your smart phone?', Wakaranai asks while laughing.

'Yes ... he would', she replies somehow reluctantly.

'It's dangerous then, isn't it?'

'Yes ... even with my current boyfriend. But he hasn't said anything to me.'

'Really?' Wakaranai raises his eyebrow.

'Well, now I don't have many [affairs].'
'So you're in a serious relationship?'
'Yes, right!', she murmurs.
'I see. How long do your affairs usually last?', Wakaranai continues this topic.
'Once an affair starts the passion usually goes out of it gradually after about three months...'
'Three months?'
'Yes, three months ... roughly', she replies.
'Really?' Wakaranai says it somehow in a curious tone.
'About...', the actress says it again.
'OK. I sort of understand.'
On reading from the interview sheet that her oldest boyfriend was 40 years old, Wakaranai couldn't help but ask probingly:
'What was your relationship with him?'
To our great surprise, the actress brashly answers: 'We only had sex, not love!'
Since her sex partner was 40 years old, Wakaranai infers that he should have had a wife and children. However, the actress shows no concern for this at all, as if she were talking about someone else. As she notes somewhat matter-of-factly:
'Right, right, he perhaps has [a wife and children]. But we didn't talk about this ... normally.'
'So why were you with him?'
'Because of money!' The actress says it in a very straightforward and candid tone. We are all silent as we are all stunned by the candidness of her intentions.
'Was it that he asked you "I'll give you money, so be with me?"', Wakaranai makes fun by asking her.
'Yes...', the actress replies dispassionately.
'So how much did he give you each month?' Wakaranai cannot refrain from pursuing this topic.
'Right, ¥200,000 (US$2,500)[5] per month, excluding clothes and accessories I bought. Just pocket money', she says. 'I had a good life.'
'Wow, he must be very rich[6] then!'
The actress just nods her head, indicating that her previous sex partner was rather rich. Wakaranai comments, a bit ironically, that she must have had a good time.

About the actress's current boyfriend

Realizing from the interview sheet that the longest dating relationship she had been in so far was three years, and that her relationship with her current boyfriend was two years and seven months, Wakaranai speaks in a laudatory term as if he wants to make her feel respected so that she can talk more freely about herself: 'So you are going to break the record!'
'How did you meet your current boyfriend?', he then asks.

'Ummm ... I met him in my work place ...', the actress answers reluctantly. On hearing this, Wakaranai immediately raises his eyebrow. The actress pauses for a while. She continues to clarify the matter, though somewhat embarrassedly:

'We met in the sex cabaret ...'

'So he was your customer there!', Wakaranai exclaims as he comes to realize what it meant.

'Yes, he was *originally* my customer', the actress says in a defensive tone, as if she wants to emphasize that he is no longer her customer but boyfriend.

'So your boyfriend must have known that you are working in the sex entertainment industry! In normal situations, I guess he'd ask you to quit, right?'

'Yes, he didn't like it! So I quit the job [sex cabaret] once and worked in a normal cabaret[7] [which does not allow body touching] for three months, instead. However, I came back [to the sex cabaret] later on', the actress explains.

'So your boyfriend knows about that?', Wakaranai asks curiously.

'Ummm ... this time he doesn't ... hahaha', the actress can't help laughing and Wakaranai joins in.

'Isn't it strange for your boyfriend to be dating you now, given that he used to be your customer!', he goes on to ask curiously.

A bitter smile twists her face, and most importantly what she answers is not what she has been asked:

> My boyfriend usually came with his colleagues. Although he'd request that I come to sit at his table, he only chatted with me and never touched my body. That kind of customer is almost extinct these days. So I think he is really special and that's why I fell in love with him!

Wakaranai then asks her how she celebrated her birthday this year. The actress pauses a while:

'He didn't give me any present this year!'

'What's his job?'

'He's a normal salaryman ... I've asked him to write letters to me, but he always says that he's busy ...'

About the actress's masturbation and unusual experiences

Learning that the actress masturbates by herself, Wakaranai asks how she usually does so:

'I use a vibrator', the actress replies instantly.

'So where did you buy your vibrator?'

'On the Internet.'

Wakaranai is a bit surprised on hearing that the actress bought the vibrator by herself. He continues: 'So when do you use it? During sex?'

'No', the actress replies quietly.

'So you use it at home then?'

'No, at my boyfriend's house.'

'So he knows about it?', Wakaranai asks curiously.

'Yes, he knows about me using the vibrator, because I masturbate in front of him', she replies again very plainly.

Upon hearing that, Wakaranai raises his eyebrows as if something unbelievable has happened. He continues asking: 'Oh ... so is it used before or after sex?'

'Um ... mostly before sex, because I'm not the kind of person who can easily come, so I'll use the vibrator to stimulate myself, so that I can come [before sex].'

'How often do you have sex now?'

'Umm ... about twice a week, I guess.'

'With your boyfriend? Or with other partners?'

'With my boyfriend.'

Realizing that the actress once had a same-sex experience at an AV shooting, Wakaranai asks her if it was because she was acting in an AV.

'Yes!'

'During the same-sex play, were you the active or the passive one?'

> In the beginning, I prepared to play the role of the passive one as I used to [in other heterosexual themes]. But when it came to the actual filming, I started to play an active part. I mean I started to 'attack the actress' for some reason. I was rather surprised I could change to an active role

the actress replies enthusiastically.

Her surprise is somehow understandable as she identifies herself in the interview sheet as a heterosexual 'M', meaning that she has been the passive masochist or receiver in sex. She reasons that she could act like an active attacker in that movie because the actress was simply too cute. She even suggests that she would not mind being made love to by a girl.

Realizing that the actress has had S&M experiences, Wakaranai asks her whether she likes it or not.

She thinks for a while and says: 'If it's mild S&M, I quite like it...'

On reading in the interview sheet that the actress had had an outdoor sexual experience, he asks her for details: 'How did this come about?'

'Once I had sex with some "pillow friends" in the car, or in the car park, or on the stairs...'

'So did your male friends wear a condom?'

'No...'

'So where did they ejaculate, then?'

'Outside ... I think', she answers.

'Where exactly outside?'

'Perhaps on the concrete wall in the car park or some other place...'

'So did he clean it up?'

'No ... he ... did not!', she replies while laughing.

'Oh! No! That's really disgusting!!!!'. All of us laugh at that moment.

About her AV career

Then, Wakaranai asks her how many adult videos in total she has taken part in.
'About 12 to 13.' The actress pauses a while.
'You wrote that you want to try *bukkake*? Right?'
'Yes ... I want to try having my face splashed with semen.'
'I see.' Wakaranai nods his head in a surprised manner.
'Have you watched your own videos?'
'Never ever ...'. She shakes her head while answering.
'Oh really!', he replies surprised.

On reading from the sheet that she is willing to try a threesome, Wakaranai asks: 'By threesome, you are referring to two men or two women?'
'I'm fine with both types!', she just replies as if a threesome were nothing out of the ordinary.

Then, Wakaranai asks her about her use of AVs:
'Do you still remember when you first watched AVs?'

> The first time I watched AVs was when I was 16 years old. I was in my boyfriend's place. He just went out to buy something. I was alone in his place, and started to look in his drawers. I found some Japanese AVs, and so I watched one and finished watching it by myself

she explains quite casually.
'How did you feel after watching it?'
'The movie featured a woman whose vagina had many different things thrust into it, so the overall feeling I had about it was that it was just so-so.'

Then Wakaranai asks her how she got into this industry:

> Because of my friend Miss B, who was originally working in the sex cabaret. She knew an AV director who was looking for actresses at that time, and who said I could give it a try if I was interested

the actress replies.
'I see ...'
'My thinking at that time was that I'd just have a peek, but then I discovered that the AV industry wasn't the way people tended to think. In reality, the AV industry is very clean, professional, and not as horrible as we imagine.'

Realizing that her dream is to get married and save money, Wakaranai suddenly changes course:
'When do you think you'll get married?'
'Um ... In fact, I want to get married now, but I'm just worried about the work I'm doing now, so I won't get married right away. Maybe in one or two years' time!'

At this point Wakaranai slowly rises from his chair and faces the actress: 'Today's interview will finish here. We'll follow with photograph and video taking session.'

At which point, he walks out from the conference room.

Taking photographs and videos

A few minutes later, we see Wakaranai come back with a camera in one hand and a camcorder in the other. He immediately locks the door, and asks the actress to stand in the corner and take off her clothes. She asks him back whether she needs to take off her shorts as well. He nods his head and keeps talking to her while she is taking off her clothes. As she removes her black pullover, our eyes are met by a large pair of breasts which somehow are made to look even bigger by her fuchsia bra with black stripes. She removes her shorts, to reveal a G-string with the same design. She then takes off her brassiere, revealing firm, large breasts. We feel rather surprised but at the same time admire her for being able to accept being naked in front of so many unknown people. Wakaranai asks the actress to pose.

'When did you enter puberty?', Wakaranai asks as he starts to press the shutter button.

'Um ... roughly from Primary Four. At that time my breasts were about B cup in size, but then they started growing bigger and bigger, and now they're F-cup.'

'Can you turn your face to the side? Oh, which side you prefer? The left or the right?', Wakaranai asks seriously.

However, before the actress can reply, Wakaranai steps towards her and from close-up checks which side of her face looks better. Again, this is another typical example of what Mears (2011: 81) calls a violation of the social norms of politeness in casting arrangement because it is rude to do this to a woman. We have to reiterate that things like this happened throughout the photo and video taking session.

Wakaranai then adjusts the angle of her head by slightly pushing it downward, before starting to take photographs and a video of her from the right side.

Wakaranai then shifts the topic to her hair.

'Is the length of your hair now the longest it's been so far?'

'Yes, perhaps it's the longest it's ever been, soon it'll reach down to my waist!'

Wakaranai instructs her to hold her hair with her hand and face the camera; he then takes more photographs as well as a video. Then he moves closer to the actress and takes photographs once again.

Instructing her to remain in the same position, he moves to film her from another side.

'What kind of role in AVs do you most prefer?'

'Right ... perhaps the female high school student...'

'I think that sort of role suits you very well...'

Wakaranai asks her whether she have taken her own snapshots of herself like this. 'Never!', she replies.

'Why not? Are you really concerned about your body?'

The actress smiles bitterly.

Wakaranai makes fun by asking her: 'If God gave you a chance, and allowed you to "fix" your body, which part you would like to change?'

'I'm really concerned about the lower part of my body, especially my buttocks ... I really hate them ...' She says it seriously. The actress appears to be somehow embarrassed as she uses her hands to cover her breasts.

Then, Wakaranai once again asks her to hold her hair up and smile at the camera, for another round of photographs. He then instructs her to face the camera and use her arms to press the sides of her breasts, so that they appear even bigger. Perhaps the pose she adopts falls short of Wakaranai's expectations, for he simply moves closer to her and directly adjusts her body once again. First, he slightly opens up her chest and reminds her to straighten her shoulders. Then he slightly lifts her two forearms and pushes them towards her breasts from the side, thereby producing an appearance of larger breasts. We are surprised that the actress remains not only passive but also calm, allowing herself to be completely 'managed' by Wakaranai. She even gives us a duck face. This is another example that shows the actress's ability to accept the weird treatment by Wakaranai who then asks her to smile at the camera for another round of photographs and video. He then tells her to remain in the same positions, but turn to another side for another round of photographs and pictures.

Wakaranai then asks her to bend her body forward and do a half squat.

'Did you join any extracurricular clubs at school?', he asks while taking pictures.

'Yes, I joined the chess club', the actress replies while swinging her arms as if she were really uncomfortable. Wakaranai instructs her to slightly nod her head downward, and smile at the camera. At this point, she appears exceptionally uneasy, placing her hands over her stomach. It seems that the actress's acceptance of all of these weird arrangements has reached a limit. Wakaranai continues to chat with her about her hobbies, sports and so on. The actress replies that she did not join any sports club at school, but that she had practised swimming in her private life ever since primary school.

Wakaranai instructs the actress to turn her back to the camera, while moving toward the actress to adjust her shoulder. Although she is not very tall, the sway of her body curves from her back is nothing short of perfection. As he focuses on another round of picture and video, Wakaranai advises her that he is going to take close-up pictures of her buttocks. He then squats on the floor.

'I guess many men fell for your buttocks, right!', he comments, as he continues to press the camera shutter.

'Um ... well ...', the actress falters, indicating that she does not think so or has no confidence in her buttocks at all.

'How come! Your curves are just great ...'

Clearly, Wakaranai cannot agree with how the actress talks about herself and believes that she is too harsh on herself. He again instructs her to look into the camera lens, bend her upper body forward and place her hands on her waist. He then takes pictures of her contours from her bottom upwards.

Instructing her to turn her upper body a bit more to the front, Wakaranai yet again moves forward to adjust and correct her posture, adjusting the position of her shoulders and arms, and arranging her hair so that it spreads onto her shoulders.

He then takes another round of pictures and video. He asks her whether she has been on a diet before and issues related to the control of weight. He also asks her how many meals she has a day. The actress replies: 'I have two meals a day.'

Wakaranai instructs her to remain in the same position, but just to turn to another side. He likewise moves forward to rearrange her hair and asks her to look downward.

Then he asks her quite casually whether she ever has any fights with her boyfriend.

'Sometimes.'
'What about your boyfriend do you dislike the most?'
'Perhaps when he really likes to lecture me.'
'What do you spend most of your money on?'
'Cosmetics.'

He tells her to face the camera and suggests that he is going to take a longer video so he asks her to do a self-introduction (*jikoshōkai*), introducing herself by her stage name, and including her vital statistics and some personal information for the camera.

'By the way, what is your stage name?'
'Shiritakunai.' The actress looks into the camera while saying her name.
'And when is your birthday?'
'1st September, I'm 25 years old', she replies with a smile.
'Your body height is ...'
'148 cm.'
'And your weight is ...?'
'42 kg.'
'And your vital statistics are ...?'
'86 cm, 56 cm and 84 cm ...', she replies cheerfully.

At this point, Wakaranai asks her to slowly turn her body in front of the camera. She duly does what he asks and slowly turns her body and ends up smiling at the camera.

We are somehow shocked by this part of videotaping. Basically, all this information could be found in her 'Profile Card' and there was no need for repetition here. However, Wakaranai makes a real fuss of asking the actress to introduce herself again. This suggests that all this information has an extraordinary significance in the AV industry, especially in view of the fact that this video is taken specifically for the AV directors who do not attend the interview on that day.

Meanwhile, Wakaranai instructs the actress to hold up her hair again and turn to another side for another round of photos and video. He tells her to face the camera.

'Do you go out drinking?'
'Yes ...'
'Who do you drink with? Boys or girls?'
'Both, but I tend to drink with girls!'

What follows is Wakaranai's long conversation with the 'half-naked' actress standing in the corner while continuing to videotape her. Most of the questions he asks are, in our eyes, trivial, if not useless, and thus can be labelled as 'chat' rather than part of an interview as such. We speculate that this part is meant to allow the AV director(s) to experience the real feeling of how the actress responds and talks.

'Have you ever drunk so much that you lost consciousness?'

'Yes...', she answers excitedly.

'When?'

'Most recently early this year...'

'So where were you when you woke up?', he asks curiously.

'Already home.'

'How did you manage to go home then?'

'I guess my friends all brought me home together.' She pauses a while.

At this point, Wakaranai thanks the actress, whereupon she waves to the camera and says goodbye. We assume that the video filming part has finished. However, Wakaranai again picks up the camera on the table and instructs her to smile at it for yet another round of photos. After taking some close-up pictures, he stands back and takes a picture of her whole body from a distance. Then, he takes close-up pictures of her breasts and face. We are filled with a powerful sense of strangeness, partly because Wakaranai has taken a lot of pictures, and partly because her body is being evaluated, checked and viewed over and over again. But this also confirms what Mears (2011: 82) says about casting arrangements in the fashion model business where models are treated as merchandise to be traded in an auction.

Suddenly, Wakaranai asks the actress to pose coquettishly and invitingly in front of the camera.

'Please pose invitingly, look into the camera coquettishly with lips slightly parted, eyes partially closed...', Wakaranai instructs her in minute detail.

'*Eee* ... I'm not very good at this...',[8] she replies and laughs hesitatingly while using her hands to cover her face.

However, in less than a minute, she stops laughing, and starts to pose seriously in front of the camera, looking straight into the lens of the camera; her eyes quite dramatic, with a great deal of coquettishness; her lips slightly apart, her eyes partially closed, and her head thrown back. Then, Wakaranai instructs her to bend forward again, using her arms to put pressure on her breasts to make them seem larger.

He then asks her to put her brassiere back on, and continues to take photos of her from the front, before instructing her to turn her back on the camera. The interesting thing at this point is that Wakaranai cannot refrain from commenting in some amazement.

'I cannot understand why you are so dissatisfied with your buttocks.'

The actress again smiles bitterly.

'I really don't understand it. Men will definitely go crazy over your buttocks', Wakaranai murmurs while taking photos.

He then instructs her to hold the same pose, turn her upper body to the front, place her hand on her waist, and smile at the camera.

We think that the photographing is about to finish because Wakaranai asks her to put all her clothes back on. But, to our great surprise, he continues to take pictures of her after she has done so. After taking pictures of her from the front, he instructs her to bend forward. The pullover she is wearing is scoop-necked. As she bends forward, what come into view is a deep cleavage and a pair of blossomy breasts. Wakaranai instructs her to look straight into the camera again before, after several rounds of photos, he finally puts his camera down on the table and thanks the actress for coming to the company today. The actress thanks him back in reply. The whole filming process has finished.

We have to add immediately here that the data collected in the interview, the photos and videos taken in the photograph and video taking session, were for the AV director(s) who had not joined the interview on that day but would be the one to make the final decision about whether the company would like to sign on this actress. According to our fieldwork investigation, AV directors usually make their decisions based on the looks, figure and biographical and sexual particulars of an AV actress. It is to these that we now turn.

Analysis

So, what was going on during the interview and photo shoot? First, while Wakaranai largely followed the questions listed in the interview sheet when conducting the interview, he by no means asked all the questions listed in the questionnaire. When we compare the interview sheet with what we have ethnographically observed, we can see that questions in Figure 6.1, nos. 14, 15, 16, 18, 19, 20 and 22 and in Figures 6.2, nos. 3b, 5, 6, 7, 8, 14, 15, 19, 20, 21, 22 and 23 all remained untouched. For example, questions relating to hobbies, sports, favourite music and favourite colour listed in Figure 6.1 were all skipped. Likewise, questions relating to personality, sensitive body part and anal sex in Figure 6.2 were skipped.

Second and more importantly, while Wakaranai skipped some questions on the interview sheet, he nonetheless paid more heed to some other questions or themes. For instance, he seemed particularly interested in the actress's affairs. Questions on this theme were the longest and the most elaborate as he asked in great detail about her affairs following two lines of questions. The first centred on her sexual relationship with a man (or men) while having a stable boyfriend. The second focused on her illicit relationship (as a mistress) with a married man who financially supported her. Equal attention was given to her dating history and pattern. Wakaranai asked her in detail how a customer at the sex cabaret became her current boyfriend and how her boyfriend accepted her as a girlfriend in his private life. Some questions Wakaranai asked in this part were not only private but also offensive in the eyes of Japanese people, but he took pains nevertheless to ask the actress about such topics.

Similarly, he also asked her extensively about her sexual practices – especially about her first experience of sex and her masturbation pattern. Questions about her first sex experience probed into her use of a condom, where sex had taken place, how she felt during intercourse, and so on. The same is true for her masturbation pattern, when Wakaranai asked at some length about her usage of sex toys, including questions about frequency, feeling and location.

The questions he focused on allow us to reconstruct the following 13 themes (Table 6.1). If we take a deeper look at these themes, especially from the vantage of the casting director who took great pains to look for AV actresses whose videos could sell, it is not incorrect to say that these 13 themes that repeatedly appeared in the interview reveal some core characteristics of an AV actress that the casting director believed were crucial in bringing big sales to his company. It follows that a thorough analysis of these characteristics can help us identify the criteria used by the casting director to select his AV actresses.

For analysis sake, we have further categorized the 13 themes into three different qualities, namely the 'uniqueness of the AV actress' (which is further divided into 'biographical particulars' and 'sexual particulars'), 'degree of freshness' and 'determination of success' (Table 6.2). Themes including 'her affairs', 'her views towards her own self', 'her favourite male celebrity', 'her first sex', 'her job in sex cabaret', 'the way she came to know her sexual partners' and 'how her customer at the cabaret became her current boyfriend' all point to her biographical particulars. Themes such as '*bukkake*', 'masturbation', 'same sex', 'threesome', 'S&M' and 'outdoor sex' instead point toward her sexual particulars. Like her biographical particulars, this part of the questions is designed to understand her as a unique sexual being with her own dating and romantic history.

In contrast, 'the number of AVs she had taken part in' points to the degree of her freshness as a product. In a similar way, 'how she came across the Japanese AV industry' and 'her dream' indicate her determination to succeed in the AV industry.

Of course, the next crucial question we need to ask is why all of these qualities would be considered 'useful' and hence important to AV production in Wakaranai's eyes. However, for the moment, we will first move onto another

Table 6.1 13 themes that repeatedly appeared in the interview

Theme	Figure	Question number
1 Same sex, threesome, S&M, outdoor sex	6.5	24, 25, 27
2 Her views towards her own self	6.2	25, 26
3 Her favourite male celebrity	6.2	21
4 Her first sex	6.5	4a, 4b, 4c, 4d, 4e
5 Her job	6.2	13
6 The way she came to know her sexual partners	6.5	9
7 How her customer at the cabaret became her current boyfriend	6.5	11
8 *Bukkake*	6.5	28
9 Masturbation	6.5	16
10 Her affairs	6.5	11
11 How she came across the Japanese AV industry	6.2	29
12 The number of AVs she had taken part in	6.5	30
13 Her dream	6.2	27

154 AV girl job interview

Table 6.2 Rationale and logics of AV production I

Quality that might have use values		Theme
Uniqueness	Biographical particulars	Her affairs
		Her views towards her own self
		Her favourite male celebrity
		Her first sex
		Her job in sex cabaret
		The way she came to know her sexual partners
		How her customer at the cabaret became her current boyfriend
	Sexual particulars	*Bukkake*
		Masturbation
		Same sex, threesome, S&M, outdoor sex
Degree of freshness		The number of AVs she had taken part in
Determination of success		How she came across the Japanese AV industry
		Her dream

major theme buried in the photographing and filming session: the facial and physical uniqueness of the AV actress.

As we can see from our ethnographic description of the photographing and video session above, Wakaranai's central focus was on the AV actress's body curves, especially her big breasts and shapely buttocks. Recall that the actress was endlessly asked and instructed to pose in specific postures to 'accentuate' and 'enlarge' her huge breasts during the session. For instance, she was asked to lift her arms up to hold her hair so that the shape of her breasts could be clearly seen. Alternatively, she was asked to cross her arms and press on her breasts so that they appeared bigger. The side view of her breasts was also crucial as Wakaranai requested her to turn to the side, left and right alike, to take close-up photos of her breasts. In a sense, the breasts appeared to be the most important part of her body to the effect that they came to equal her whole physical appearance. The significance of this can be seen in how she was *still* asked to pose for several specific positions that exposed or attenuated the size of her breasts, even when she had put her brassiere or clothes back on.

Attention was also given to her shapely buttocks. She was instructed to turn her back to the camera. Very often, Wakaranai squatted on the floor to take close-up photos of her buttocks. She was even instructed to fold up her panties to reveal her 'apple bottom'. In a similar way, the side view of her buttocks, both left and right, was the focus of his attention. He repeatedly instructed the actress to turn to her side, left and right alike, to capture the side views of her buttocks.

Facial contour was another quality to which Wakaranai devoted himself during the session. For instance, he would instruct the actress to look straight into the camera. More importantly, he would take two versions of the same pose, one smiling and the other unsmiling. However, when compared with her breasts and buttocks, we have to emphasize that her facial contour was considerably less emphasized during the whole photographing and videotaping session.

We can now see that the breasts, buttocks and facial contour of an AV actress are the major elements of 'bodily capital' in the AV industry (Mears 2011: 6).

Readers might wonder if what took place was a purely professional photographing and videotaping session, as Wakaranai did ask the actress a lot of private questions. In view of the singular focus on the body curves of the actress, it is not too much to say that the whole conversation or discussion that took place during this session was trivial, if not totally meaningless. Indeed, Wakaranai also confirmed to us after the interview that most of the questions he asked during this session were meant to make the actress more relaxed and comfortable as she was naked. That is to say, these questions were not important or useful in helping him evaluate the actress.

In light of the photographing and videotaping sessions, we should add the bodily and facial uniqueness of AV actresses to the category of 'uniqueness' (Table 6.3) that now consists of biographical, sexual and bodily and facial particulars. In other words, what Mears called 'the model's look' (Mears 2011: 5) in the case of AV actresses refers to a whole package including the biographical, sexual and bodily and facial qualities of an AV actress as 'raw material' which, as will be seen in a moment, can be converted into personality, sexual and bodily capital that make an AV actress's look sellable. But why would these qualities be considered 'useful' or 'significant' and hence 'important' to Wakaranai as a casting director of his company?

Table 6.3 Rationale and logics of AV production II

Quality that might have use values		Theme
Uniqueness	Biographical particulars	Her affairs
		Her views towards her own self
		Her favourite male celebrity
		Her first sex
		Her job in sex cabaret
		The way she came to know her sexual partners
		How her customer at the cabaret became her current boyfriend
	Sexual particulars	*Bukkake*
		Masturbation
		Same sex, threesome, S&M, outdoor sex
	Bodily and facial particulars	
Degree of freshness		The number of AVs she had taken part in
Determination of success		How she came across the Japanese AV industry
		Her dream

Determination for success in the AV industry

Let us start with the 'determination for success'. This quality would matter to AV makers because if an actress is determined to succeed in the industry, it is assumed that she will be prepared to stay on for a certain length of time. From the viewpoint of AV makers, an actress with such mental preparation is considered more financially viable than one who is not determined to succeed and hence might leave anytime. In other words, Wakaranai wanted to ensure that the effort and time invested in this specific actress would not be wasted. This is especially important in view of the high turnover rate of the Japanese AV industry. As mentioned at the beginning of Chapter 5, it was estimated that two-thirds of the actresses retired from the industry in 2012. More importantly, an uncommitted AV actress could suddenly fail to show up at the shooting location without giving the director notice, or even completely disappear from the industry – something, we were told by the industry people, happens very frequently. The sudden absence of an AV actress, not to mention her evaporation into thin air, can prove to be very costly because it is very difficult to find a replacement in such a short time and the director then has no alternative but to cancel the shooting.

Degree of freshness

For the degree of freshness, the reason is perhaps very simple: the fresher the actress is to the audience, the better the AV studio can sell her and hence earn more. But this simple reason speaks volumes to a complicated interpretation of 'freshness' within the AV industry. As we have pointed out in Chapter 4, freshness does not necessarily refer to the zero experience of the actress in AV shooting (though it might be true in the case of a *tantai* actress); more often than not it refers to her intermittent appearance in AV productions, which duly reminds audiences of who she is, but yet does not exhaust their interest in her and hence satiate them. To maintain the freshness of an actress for audiences and hence extract the highest possible profit from her, AV manufacturers often regulate her appearance in AV productions. The logic is that overexposure will reduce her sexual attractiveness to the audiences.

'Satiation theory', which suggests that satisfaction deriving from consumption tends to fade with repetition (Roy 2012: 45), helps make the point. Many scholars explain 'satiation' through a psychological phenomenon called 'sensory-specific satiety' on food. This refers to a decrease in sensory pleasure derived from consumption of a specific food or drink (Rolls *et al.* 1981: 141). Furthermore, this decrease in sensory pleasure will extend to other foods with similar colour, flavour or shape (Rolls *et al.* 1982: 409). Likewise, AV users enjoy a given AV actress less when they continue watching her – they become satiated, especially over a period of time. Thus, one might argue that AV users experience a reduction in sensory pleasure from repeatedly viewing a specific actress's AVs and, more importantly, this reduction can extend to actresses with similar styles and roles. As we have seen from the above analysis, the Japanese AV industry has attempted to reduce satiation by limiting the exposure of a given actress to the audience. As we have pointed out in Chapter 4, this is especially true for *tantai* actresses, whose appearance in AV production is restricted to one film a month. But even for *kikaku* AV, the satiation theory also holds, even though the restriction on exposure is less strict. That is to say, AV makers also try to lengthen the interval time between various AV productions of a given *kikaku* actress, in the hope that the audience will not become satiated by her.

Uniqueness of the actress

We can also see from the above analysis that the uniqueness of AVs actresses was given most emphasis. Wakaranai was shown to pay special attention to discovering the personal, sexual, bodily and factual uniqueness of the actress who attended the interview. For example, he tried to dig out details about the incident when the actress once had sex in a car park where her sexual partner did not wear a condom and ejaculated on the wall of the car park. Wakaranai was also interested in another incident where the actress often masturbated in front of her boyfriend with a vibrator. Likewise, we observed Wakaranai's interview with another actress, Miss A, one year before the interview we have described here, in which it was revealed that she had had sex in a graveyard before. Again, Wakaranai made a considerable fuss over the details of what happened.

The same is also true for personal particulars. As we have mentioned in Chapter 4, the major characteristic of *kikaku* AV is to contextualize and situate the actress against the story. The personal particulars – including first sex, affairs, job nature and experience and preference for male celebrity – enabled the casting director, and later the director, to contextualize this actress firmly against a particular story. In this regard, the example of the above-mentioned Miss A is also illustrative. She claimed in her interview with Wakaranai that she used to be a ritual mortician (*nōkanshi*), which is obviously an exceptional job for a young Japanese girl like her. Wakaranai spent much time on digging out as much detail about her job as possible during the interview.

Physical uniqueness also attracted Wakaranai's attention. For instance, the actress we have examined here had large breasts, a tiny waist and shapely buttocks. For that reason, Wakaranai spent a lot of time on her body curves, and especially on her breasts. Here we would like to draw the reader's attention to the fact that, although Wakaranai stressed the AV actress's facial contour less than her physical uniqueness, he did show concern about the former.

The major reason for paying particular attention to the uniqueness of AV actresses is that such uniqueness helps AV directors work out which genre a certain actress particularly matches. This contemplation process is in fact akin to the process of how human experience is symbolically constituted. As Sahlins notes, in citing the long philosophical tradition from Kant, through Saussure and Whorf, to Boas and Lévi-Strauss:

the experience of human subjects, especially as communicated in discourse, involves an appropriation of events in the terms of a priori concepts. Reference to the world is an act of classification, in the course of which realities are indexed to concepts in a relation of empirical tokens to cultural types.

(Sahlins 1985: 146)

Sahlins further explains formal classification by what Walker Percy said about the nature of conscious perception:

Every conscious perception is of the nature of a recognition, a pairing, which is to say that the object is recognized as being what it is ... it is not enough to say that one is conscious of something; one is conscious of something as *being something.*

(Sahlins 1985: 146; italics in original)

Likewise, what AV directors do is to pair the AV actress at issue with a series of AV genres to see whether the former can be inserted into a certain genre. In the course of this process the AV actress acquires her significance from the structure of genres and categories of Japanese AVs, none of which is the only one possible. The significance she acquires from the classificatory scheme is her use value – '[f]or "utility"', as Sahlins (1976a: 169) has effectively argued, 'is not a quality of the object but a significance of the objective qualities' – which is a 'must' for the creation of exchange value of the AV actress in the market – 'because (1) in order to be exchanged for something else (money), the goods produced must (2) contrast in one or another original property with all other goods of the same general kind' (Sahlins 1976a: 215). It follows that the major function of the interview is to 'discover' and list the 'objective' qualities a certain AV actress presents in the interview so that AV directors can do the pairing later. It is through this pairing that the AV actress at issue acquires her use value. That is to say, the selection process at interviews involves recognition of a certain girl as an empirical token of a genre, '[b]ut then recognition is a kind of *re-cognition*: the event is inserted in a pre-existing category, and history is present in current action' (Sahlins 1985: 146; italics ours). The process thus can be seen as a production process through which the girl is transformed into a certain *kind* of AV actress, in the course of which the genre and the classificatory scheme of AVs is reproduced. For example, the sexual particulars of the AV actress who took part in the interview included the facts that she once had sex in a car park where her sexual partner did not wear a condom and ejaculated on the wall of the car park, and that the actress liked to masturbate in front of her boyfriend with a vibrator. These can be picked up and used to represent her as an open, sexually aggressive and wild girl with endless sexual desires, who will do whatever she can to satisfy them – including having sex outdoors with a man who does not wear a condom. This resulting image can be rendered as a typical token of the genre of 'outdoor sex AV' ('*roshutsu*'). Likewise, the above-mentioned sexual and personal particulars of Miss A can also be used to create an image of her as a totally abnormal (*hentai*) woman with abnormal sexual desires who would thus best fit the genre of '*hentai* sex AV'.

But an AV actress is always more particular and more general than the genre used to represent her. She is more particular because the genre is an arbitrary division of a continuum in a way pertinent to a particular classificatory scheme. Very different AV actresses can be included in the same genre provided that they do not become confused with their counterparts in other genres. This is also to say that their differences are non-functional within the structure of genres and categories of Japanese AVs in the sense that these differences are not used to distinguish between two genres, for the identity of the AV actresses of the same genre is relational. Saussure's definition of the identity of linguistic units helps make this point, as it is framed as an analogy to a train timetable:

> We are willing to grant that in an important sense the 8:25 Geneva-to-Paris Express is the same train each day, even though the coaches, locomotive, and personnel change from one day to the next. What gives the train its identity is its place in the system of trains, as indicated by the timetable. And note that this relational identity is indeed the determining factor: the train remains the same train even if it leaves a half-hour late. In fact, it might always leave late without ceasing to be the 8:25 Geneva-to-Paris Express. What is important is that it be distinguished from, say, the 10:25 Geneva-to-Paris Express, the 8:40 Geneva-to-Dijon Local, and so on.
> (Culler 1986[1976]: 37)

In other words, the difference among the AV actresses of the same genre is 'quantitative' not 'qualitative'. This must also mean that AV actresses with very different biographical, sexual and bodily and facial particulars can be selected to act in AVs of the same genre without confusing consumers' stereotypical expectations of AV actresses imposed by the identity of the genre. More importantly, we can always find a certain AV actress whose image is more 'typical' and thus looks more 'real' than others from the consumer's point of view, in the sense that either the AV actress and the character she is going to perform is one and the same in the case of *tantai* AVs, or that one AV actress is better able to authenticate a female character in the case of a *kikaku* AV than do other AV actresses in the same genre. This is why an interview with AV actresses is necessary for AV makers to locate 'typical' AV actresses for certain genres.

An AV actress is also more general than the genre used to designate her. She is more general because the properties she presents to AV directors are always more than those selectively picked up and valued by the genre, which can be manipulated to create another 'use value'. AV makers are eager to turn non-functional differences into functional ones, or quantitative differences into qualitative ones, with the intention of creating 'exchange value' for them by bestowing significance on these non-functional differences. These then function to demarcate a new genre, so that a particular type of AV appears significant to a certain category of AV consumers. In fact, the AV industry people, especially directors, have long thrived to subcategorize actresses into 'specific body aspects' (long legs, big breasts, flat breasts, tiny waist or shapely buttocks), 'specific types of woman' (wife, hostess, prostitute, mother, pregnant woman, school girl or female mortician), and 'specific plays' (S&M, lesbian, anal sex, fellatio, outdoor sex or threesome). By doing so, according to Redden (2008: 624), who argues that consumers satiate less if they categorize consumption episodes at lower levels, AV users will pay more attention to the aspects (for instance, legs, breasts, waist or buttocks) that differentiate a set of generally similar AVs. The increased salience of unique, rather than common, qualities makes AVs seem less similar to each other. For instance, an AV in which a young woman is portrayed as a hostess will be entirely different, in the eyes of users, from an AV in which the young woman is portrayed as a high school teacher, for their specific roles override their commonness as women. Likewise, sex in the graveyard will never be the same as sex in the car park in the eyes of audiences, whose attention will be drawn to distinctive qualities that are deemed culturally significant rather than to their commonality as, for instance, instances of outdoor sex. As subcategorization like this causes fewer AVs to be placed in the same category, this results in the perception by consumers of less repetition over the course of many AVs. Understood as such, the selection process is also an inventive production process.

All of these operations depend on two major kinds of decisions made by AV directors. The first is that of a quantitative difference among AV actresses of the same genre. As we have shown, within the same genre there are always more typical AV girls who thus look more 'real' than others, and the job interview of AV actresses is designed to select the more typical among particular AV actresses. The second is the decision to create utility by converting quantitative into qualitative differences, or by rendering non-functional differences functional and thus meaningful, through which 'use value' is produced in order to create 'exchange value'. It goes without saying that these two major decisions by AV directors are further dependent on the 'discovery' of the uniqueness of AV actresses by casting directors through their job interviews.

In short, the recruitment process is a productive process. First, subsuming a woman in a particular AV genre according to a scheme of genres and categories – itself organized by specific valuations of women with and without sexual agency in the case of *tantai* AVs, and men with and without sexual domination over women in the case of *kikaku* AVs, neither of which is the only one possible – is to select some of her properties valued by the genre to represent the woman, in the course of which she is transformed into a certain *kind* of AV actress. The selection of AV actresses is thus like the production of AV actresses according to a particular cultural code.

Second, the conversion of non-functional into functional differences or quantitative into qualitative differences in a woman creates her as a kind of AV actress pertinent to a new genre, the invention of which necessarily involves a change in the classificatory scheme because the relationships among genres are altered. Understood as such, the selection process amounts to an inventive production process. But we have to add immediately that the invention of a new genre as an event has to take place in terms of the original classificatory scheme, which is governed by the cultural code of salvage ideology. For the new genre can be understood as new only when it is in contrast to the original classificatory scheme. That is to say, the inventive production process is also governed by the same cultural code of salvage ideology.

Conclusion

In this chapter, we have described and analysed the recruitment process in which the AV casting director of an AV manufacturer in Tokyo interviewed, photographed and videotaped a *kikaku* AV actress. This analysis allows us to identify three crucial qualities of AV actresses that AV makers are most concerned with: the uniqueness of every actress through their personal, sexual, bodily and factual peculiarities, degree of freshness and determination for success in the AV industry. The uniqueness of actresses, no matter whether it is manifested in the biographical and sexual particulars or the bodily and factual peculiarities, helps AV directors either to transform the woman-applicant into a token of a certain genre of AV actress, or to invent a new genre of AVs in the course of which the actress is recreated as a new kind of AV actress. The former amounts to a production process in which a woman is produced as a certain *kind* of AV actress, in the course of which the genre at issue is reproduced. The latter can be seen as an *inventive* production process through which a new genre is invented by creating a *new kind* of AV actress. Both of these processes are organized by the same cultural code we mentioned in Chapters 2 and 4 which gives significance to either women's lack of sexual agency in *tantai* AVs, or to men's sexual domination over women in *kikaku* AVs. In addition, the freshness of AV actresses can also help prevent AV users from being totally satiated. Finally, the quality of the determination for success in the AV industry is designed to tackle the high turnover rate of AV actresses.

According to our interview, Wakaranai normally informs an actress of the result of an interview within two weeks. If she is selected, she will soon enter into a contract with Wakaranai's company through her agent. Once this is done, the next thing the AV maker has to do is to contextualize her against the storyline in any possible upcoming *kikaku* AV production. As mentioned above, these lucky winners are actresses who possess qualities that might be 'useful' and hence financially productive for the AV studio. By contextualizing her against a particular story, the AV studio has to place an actress in the most suitable 'genre' out of many different genres, so that her use value can be fully converted into market (exchange) value. After a suitable actress is recruited, the next step is to shoot the AV. Let us now make a radical jump in ethnographic setting from the interview room to shooting site to see how an adult video is actually filmed.

Notes

1 Parts of the chapter have been used elsewhere in different contexts and for different purposes (Yau and Kobori 2012a).
2 *Oppabu* refers to a kind of sex service in Japan where young women's breasts can be groped and caressed by the male customers.
3 In Japan, 'pants' do not refer to trousers but underpants. Thus, no pants means not wearing underpants.
4 *Nanpa* is a type of flirting and seduction popular among teenagers and young adults in Japan.
5 This was calculated according to the exchange rate ¥1=US$0.0125 in May 2016.
6 It must be emphasized that the average salary of a normal *sararīman* (salaryman or salaried men) in Japan is about ¥250,000 to ¥300,000 (US$3,125 to 3,750) a month. If her sex partner could give her monthly pocket money of ¥200,000 (US$2,500) excluding other expenses, it meant that he had to earn at least ¥1,500,000 (US$18,750) monthly, otherwise he could not afford to take care of the actress financially.
7 By the normal cabaret, it refers to the club hostesses who only pour drinks for customers but do not provide body contact services.
8 This is a very common colloquial expression in Japan. In this particular context, it indicates that she did not believe what she was asked to do by Wakaranai.

7 The reel thing

A lecture on infinite female orgasm

Introduction

This chapter turns to the ethnographic examination of the shooting of a *kikaku* movie titled '*Shiranai's* [the pseudonym of a Japanese director] *Lecture on Portio* [an inner part of a woman's uterus]'.[1] As the title suggests, the movie is not a story but a lecture which revolves around the director-cum-actor, Shiranai,[2] who appears as a sexologist, teaching his audience how to bring about infinite female ecstasy through a demonstration of his unique sexual skill in stimulating the uterus of the female character.[3] This specific *kikaku* movie serves as a good example to demonstrate how a *kikaku* AV is actually made. We have argued in Chapter 4 that the gist of *kikaku* AVs is to authenticate the story and female character by contextualizing the sex scene firmly within a story. In this chapter, we shall explore how the sex scene of this *kikaku* movie is contextualized through the specific portrayal of the director-cum-actor as a sexologist who possesses unique skills in bringing about infinite female orgasm; and the portrayal of the whole shooting process as 'real' where female orgasm is depicted as predictable and controllable.

We further suggest that such pornographic realism can be seen as a discursive practice that not only produces but also naturalizes the salvage ideology as the only one possible, in the course of which the specific definition of the sexual being of man and woman – woman is equivalent to lack of sexual agency and man to woman's sexual saviour – is authenticated. This salvage ideology in turn serves as *the* reality through which the production of acme AVs is organized. It is the dialectics between the pornographic realism and the salvage ideology that helps sustain the latter in the production and consumption of acme AVs.

The methodological implication of this chapter is that the shooting process to be described here can be seen as what Sherry Ortner has called 'key scenarios' that 'are culturally valued in that they formulate the culture's basic means-ends relationships in actable forms' (Ortner 1973: 1341), inasmuch as from the shooting process we can understand not only how men's sexual domination of women is defined as an appropriate goal, but also how the cultural strategies to achieve the goal are formulated in Japanese culture. In the event, we can see how culture is linked to actable form.[4]

Pre-filming negotiations[5]

One morning in early 2011, we meet Wakaranai at the Hachikō Park in Shibuya, a fashionable district in Tokyo. We are very nervous because we are not sure whether we will be allowed to observe the shooting of an adult video as planned because Wakaranai called us the day before the shooting, informing us that the director, Shiranai, is worried by the fact that a female researcher, in addition to the male researcher, is going to 'observe' his shooting. After several phone exchanges between us, Wakaranai suggests that we would be better off negotiating directly with Shiranai.

After an exchange of greetings, Wakaranai walks us to the place where Shiranai lives. His apartment is located in central Shibuya. He is in his mid-40s, wears black-framed glasses and a headscarf. He has white skin, small eyes and a huge nose. The black T-shirt and a pair of black trousers he is wearing makes him look even whiter.

Four of us then gather around a small Japanese-style low table in the living room. Shiranai brings out snacks and soft drinks that he has prepared for us. He starts to brief us on his background. He joined the AV industry after quitting college, but he only made his presence felt when he developed the 'acme' ('*akume*') or 'bringing one to orgasm' ('*ikase*') style of AV. As the name implies, this style is mainly about sending the female characters into sexual ecstasy. From the debut of his first acme style AV, Shiranai has been majoring in the production of the so-called acme style.

As Wakaranai had warned us before, Shiranai directly expresses his concern that the actress might be sexually distracted and inhibited by the presence of a 'female' researcher. We are confused, as we do not understand why the actress would be distracted or inhibited by the presence of a woman rather than by the three men there. Shiranai explains to us in an authoritative tone that the male researcher, Wakaranai and himself are all male and hence the target audience with whom the actress can sexually identify and from whom she can receive sexual gratification. In contrast, the female researcher cannot offer her any sexual gratification because she is not her target audience. More problematically, the presence of the female researcher, according to Shiranai, would inhibit the actress's sexual tension as she could become nervous about being naked in front of someone of the same sex. Shiranai is very firm in his argument, even though we remain unconvinced by his logic. Finally, we come up with a solution: the female researcher should wait downstairs and only come back to Shiranai's place if the actress consents to her presence. However, Shiranai warns us immediately that since the actress today is not the one whom he has originally arranged to shoot and knows well, but one who has been urgently called up to replace the original actress who had suddenly become sick before the shooting, he has no confidence that she will agree to our presence.

Accompanied by the male researcher, the female researcher courteously follows Shiranai's instruction to wait in a coffee shop nearby. At around 8:30am, we get a call from him, informing us that the female researcher can go upstairs as the actress has consented to her participation. Upon returning to Shiranai's apartment, and walking into the room, we immediately meet the actress who is sitting quietly in one corner. She has long brown hair and is wearing a black one-piece. She is fairly tall, at least 168 cm, and tells us that she has also been modelling for several fashion magazines in Tokyo. We duly introduce ourselves and thank her for her generosity in allowing us to observe her AV acting. To our surprise, the actress displays not even slightest hesitation or embarrassment in the presence of the female researcher.

The fact that Shiranai bothers to make such a fuss about her being there seems rather trivial if not strange, but, in this case, it is important because it indirectly fleshes out Shiranai's eagerness and effort to convey a message to, if not convince, us that everything – especially the actress's reaction in the shooting process that follows – will be 'real'. For, if the movie were just a staged performance as we usually imagine, then it would have made no difference if the observer were male or female. But precisely because the movie and the actress's sexual actions are truly 'real', then the very presence of the female researcher, according to Shiranai's argument, would pose a problem for the actress.

The 'authenticity' of the upcoming shoot is further reinforced by Shiranai's authoritative tone, widely heard in pre-filming negotiations, because such a commanding tone speaks volumes to his concerted effort to appear as a 'professional' on sex: a sexologist. As a sexologist, Shiranai knows everything about the female sex – from sexuality, through physiology, to sexual pleasure – and thus knows more about these than the female researcher herself would. He therefore always expresses his views in an authoritative manner. The same is true when he shares with us his filming philosophy.

Like all other Japanese AV directors, Shiranai grounds his AV films in a range of 'philosophical ideas'. He tells us that the major thrust of his filming today is to make the actress experience deep and multiple orgasms so that she can have a taste of what is meant by a 'real' orgasm – the kind of orgasm, he promises, the actress has never experienced before. He even claims that the female researcher-observer might also be *astonished* by the upcoming scene. He tells us that, in order for women to experience orgasm and pleasure in sex, their male partners cannot merely rely on skills or techniques. Shiranai continues to preach to us, *as if* he were a professional sexologist, that the most important thing lies in the ability to establish 'spiritual communications' with the woman. He earnestly points out that many women do not even experience a single orgasm in their whole life, let alone multiple orgasms. The reason for their inability to experience an orgasm is precisely because of the failure of their male partners to achieve with them a spiritual and loving communication. He argues that the male partner relies on the use of 'sweet talk' such as 'I like you!', 'You are gorgeous!' or 'You are sexy!' to melt his woman's heart, thereby sexually warming her up. Shiranai is obviously proud of himself as an AV director and claims that, as a result of his spiritual skills, he is the only director in the Japanese AV industry who can give actresses 100 orgasms in an hour!

Shiranai's so-called 'spiritual skills' in bringing forth female ecstasy turn out to be what the AV industry people in Japan called '*kotoba-zeme*'. '*Kotoba-zeme*' is a combined Japanese word of '*kotoba*' ('language') and '*seme*' ('attack'), referring to a specific way of play in sadomasochism (S&M) where the sadist 'attacks' or abuses the masochist, not by means of whip or candle but through words (Ozawa 2009: 12). '*Kotoba-zeme*' however is not Shiranai's invention. By the 1970s, the term had made its inroads into Japanese popular culture and soon became ensconced in the local language used by Japanese young adults (Ozawa 2009: 12). But it was Shiranai who renders '*kotoba-zeme*' as a central and recurring technique in his adult movies, especially his acme style movies. According to what he elaborates on his online blog, *kotoba-zeme* is a whole made up of nine elements: 'to deliver love', 'to verbalize her attraction', 'to induce her shame', 'to see through her mind,' 'to despise her', 'to tell her what is the next step', 'to confuse her', 'to command her' and 'to make her imagine'. Shiranai even provides some examples for each of these nine elements in his blog:

One can see that seven out of the nine elements in *kotoba-zeme* are highly morally charged acts, attempting to inflict pain or humiliation upon others by making commands, causing confusion, imposing contempt and inducing shame. Moreover, while communication is generally understood as mutual, *kotoba-zeme* is not. It is about men taking the initiative to communicate to women, but not the other way around. This can be clearly seen from the 'pronoun' Shiranai uses in Table 7.1 – it is always 'her' but not 'him'. However, despite its sadistic content and highly sexist connotation, the term is used in the cultural context of Japan to refer to 'communication tactics' in heterosexual sex to enhance pleasure for both participants. Recall, too, that Shiranai always speaks of communication, especially spiritual communication, arguing that communication is *the* way men can spiritually connect with women, thereby sending the latter into sexual ecstasy. In many Japanese popular magazines alongside grey materials, this term is even celebrated as a solution to the problem of sexual dissatisfaction among couples.

Table 7.1 The content of *kotoba-zeme* by Shiranai

Elements	Examples given by the director
A To deliver love	I really like you!
B To verbalize her attraction	You are really cute, or sweet.
C To induce her shame	You are so cute ... but how come you become so wet? [implying that she is lewd]
D To see through her mind	You cannot stand anymore right?
E To insult her	You are really a bitch or a lewd woman ('*sukebe*!')
F To tell her what is the next step	So, I am gonna put [penis] inside you!
G To confuse her	I think I better stop [doing it anymore] here!
H To command her	You better make me feel good! Otherwise, I won't put [penis] inside you.
I To make her imagine	It is good feeling if [penis is] put inside you!

Inherent in it is an important logic that, although the means (i.e. *kotoba-zeme*) is bad in the sense it is sadist and even sexist, it is acceptable if it is done with good intentions (to bring women to orgasm). For good intentions justify bad means. In sum, a spiritual connection is seen as the prerequisite for sexual ecstasy and a sadistic form of *kotoba-zeme* is one of the very means to achieve such a spiritual connection. ozawa Maria, a famous Japanese adult video actress who recently published a Japanese book we just quoted, even likens *kotoba-zeme* to verbal foreplay (Ozawa 2009: 12) designed to sexually stimulate a partner. We can see how, for his part, Shiranai uses *kotoba-zeme* as a 'spiritual' means to stimulate the actress in the shooting, and it is to this that we now turn.

Shooting

At about 9 am, Shiranai signals the actress to take a shower and takes out a few sets of white bikinis from a drawer and places them all on a table for the actress to choose from. She picks one out and then goes straight to the bathroom. Meanwhile, Shiranai prepares the shooting in one of the rooms. He sets up the video camera on a tripod, before unfolding a sofa bed and putting a white flat sheet on it. By the side of the sofa bed, there is a small table on which he proceeds to line up a set of props he is going to use in the upcoming shooting. Among these props are massage oil, towels, love eggs, vibrators and an anal hook. What really grabs our attention, though, is a huge 'electric dildo' modified from an electric saw, a prop that Shiranai makes a real fuss of introducing to us. He claims that he is the first person in the Japanese AV industry to introduce the use of a modified electric dildo in shooting film shoot, although the use of electric dildos, as far as we know, has been commonplace in Japanese AVs for a long time. Basically, it consists of removing the metal saw attached to the front part and attaching a silicon dildo to it. Shiranai criticizes many people in the AV industry for making similar electric dildos without paying attention to their safety, as a result of which a number of AV actresses have been injured. Shiranai claims that, for his part, he makes a concerted effort to ensure the safety of his electric dildo. More than this, he claims that his modified electric dildo can bring an actress to orgasm an infinite number of times. From the way he talks about this, we can sense that he is very proud of his self-made dildo.

About 15 minutes later, the actress emerges from the bathroom wearing a shower robe. The atmosphere becomes all the more tense as the real filming is about to kick off. Watching an AV being filmed is totally different from watching AVs as finished products. It is no doubt a huge challenge to us as we have to witness how the actress is going to be sexually stimulated and penetrated by different props, especially the electric dildo. Shiranai turns on the video camera and adjusts the angle. The filming is about to start!

Sensuous and uterus massage

The female character takes off her shower robe and walks towards the sofa bed. Surprisingly, Shiranai starts to put on a white mask and a white coat typically worn by medical doctors or laboratory researchers. Together with the plain setting and small table with all kinds of props, it strikes us that what he is going to do is not shoot an adult video, so much as perform an operation or surgery. First he blindfolds the female character and instructs her to lie down on her stomach on the sofa bed, as he is going to start by giving her a body massage with oil that he picks up from the table and pours onto the female character's back from high up in the air, while explaining to us that the massage oil is mixed with an aroma designed to make the female character relaxed and feel good. This scene nonetheless reminds us of the 'wax play' commonly found in sadomasochistic pornography, both Western and Japanese. As the female character cannot see her back, she screams as the 'cold' oil falls onto her back. However, her screaming not only fails to stop Shiranai from continuing what he is doing, but in fact 'encourages' him to pour more oil onto her back, making her scream even more loudly (E1). In order to facilitate the massage, Shiranai unfastens the string of the female character's bikini top. He then rubs and kneads her shoulders gently. He works softly down her back and along her spine, smoothing the oil over her entire upper body in sweeping, broad strokes with the flat part of his palm. He does not knead her body as yet.

Next, he pours the oil onto her legs, again from high up. As the cold oil falls onto her buttocks, she screams again and shouts: 'it's cold!' Shiranai slowly works up from her feet to thighs in a circular movement. After a while, he stops and announces that he will give her a sensuous massage (*seikan massāji*) (F1). He starts with her buttocks, touching them lightly with his fingertips. He works up her spine to her shoulders in the same fashion. At times, he gently taps her back in a circular movement. The female character is certainly very sensitive to this kind of 'light' touching as she screams every single time he taps her like this. He asks her if his touching her this way is too much and she replies that it is. He continues to work along her back, especially the side of her spinal cord, with his fingertips. He uses upward strokes laterally along the spine until reaching her tailbone, after which, suddenly, he forcefully works his way up from the spine to her shoulders. Such a sudden, forceful move brings the female character to exclaim aloud. Shiranai continues to work her back with his fingertips. He once again suddenly applies a forceful upward touch to her back and as a result, the female character yells out. He then moves downward to her buttocks where he starts to give her a light massage in a circular movement with his two index fingers. The female character appears to be unable to bear this kind of kneading as her body just shivers and shakes.

Shiranai continues to knead her buttocks in a circular movement for another three to four minutes while talking to the female character. Suddenly, he spanks her buttocks, which surprises her because of its unexpectedness. Interestingly, he asks her whether she likes 'spanking' and she replies that she does. Meanwhile, he slips his fingers into cleavage between her buttocks. While we could not see it clearly, it seems that he is massaging her vagina. This becomes more obvious as he starts to use his middle finger to move upward and downward along her buttock crack and the female character groans and moans. He continues to caress her vagina while touching her back sensuously. Shiranai then opens her legs wide and moves his hand to her vagina. The female character cannot avoid exclaiming how 'unpleasant' ('*iya*') it is. Surprisingly, the director shouts: '*Iya ja nai*', meaning that it is not that you don't like what is going on (H1). Meanwhile, he makes fun of the way she pronounces *iya* as '*iyan*' (a girlish and sweetie way to pronounce *iya* which is common among young girls) while continuing to knead her (C1) and sensuously touch her vagina. His hands then return back to her buttocks and again he gives her a soft fingertip massage. His fingers move slowly and gently to her inner thighs, before moving back to the upper half of her body. He works downward from the shoulders to the spine in very slow motion. She responds by uttering '*ahaha...*'. He then uses his two index fingers to lightly move along her back, giving her a forceful upward touch from her buttocks to her shoulders. She utters a sound like '*ahahahahaha*'. He then uses his index fingers to touch the sides of her torso before finally giving her a proper massage.

Shiranai then instructs the female character to lie on her back. He removes her bikini top completely, thus revealing her breasts. He pours the massage oil onto her stomach in the same way as before, while praising her skin for being as soft and silky as a baby's (B1). As observers we find ourselves in full agreement with what Shiranai has said. He asks the female character if her boyfriend ever comments about how good it is to make love to her (B2) and she replies 'yes'. He gives a circular massage around her breasts. The female character responds by uttering '*ahahah*'. Then he again touches her body with his fingertips, with the result that the female character starts shivering. After touching her body with his fingertips for a while, he uses them to tap the sides of her breasts. Her body trembles and shivers again. He asks her whether she feels it [sexual pleasure] (D1). She replies that she does. Meanwhile, her two forearms rise, as a kind of instinctive response to his external teasing, but Shiranai stops her by pushing her arms down (H2). He continues to knead her breasts and she can't stop herself from moaning and groaning with pleasure. On hearing her continued moaning, Shiranai reminds her that all of us are listening to her, hinting that she should feel embarrassed about being excited (C2, H3). Her hands rise again and again he stops her by pushing her forearms down (H4). He massages her breasts in a circular movement and asks if her nipples are sexually sensitive or not. She murmurs that she can come even if only her nipples are stimulated. Shiranai then tells her that he is going to focus on caressing her nipples to make her come, but the next moment orders her not to come but to wait for a minute (G1). He murmurs that he has to 'explore' her uterus and that he is going to give her a uterus massage (*shikyū massāji*) (F2). He then moves to massage her belly and she moans and groans. Her body, too, starts to tremble. He suggests that this is what is meant by the phrase 'good feeling' (*kimochi ii*) (I1). She groans while she is shivering, murmuring '*kimochi ii*'. However, Shiranai suddenly moves sharply back from her, and so stops massaging her, as he asks her whether she doesn't feel ashamed of herself (*hazukashii*) because her uterus can make her so sexually excited (C3).

Love eggs

Shiranai resumes by fingering her breasts and hitting her uterus with the side of his hand while caressing her nipples. The female character then comes. Interestingly, he once again immediately steps back from her side. He says to the camera that she can come even with her panties still on (C4). He continues to caress her nipples and she comes again. He again comments on how she reaches orgasm even when she is still wearing panties (C5). He repeats this comment several times (C6) before saying that he is about to caress the organ that is supposed to lead directly to orgasm (F3). At this point, he pulls off her bikini bottom, brings a 'love egg' (a vibrator in the shape of an egg) from the table nearby, and suggests that it is what the female character loves the most, although we have never heard her say so (I2). He uses the love egg to stimulate her nipples, causing her to scream and moan loudly. He explains that although he knows how pleasurable it is to be stimulated by the love egg, he had not expected her to become so sensually excited (C7). Surprisingly, he then picks up another love egg and invites Wakaranai to stimulate the female character with him together. What is equally surprising is that Wakaranai accepts Shiranai's invitation to take part in the shooting. She groans and moans with great pleasure in accordance to the rhythm of the vibrating love eggs. Shiranai cups her breasts with his bare hands, massages her breasts in a circular movement, and finally focuses on her nipples. We are both surprised that the forceful pressure he exerts, along with his caresses, are sufficient to bring her to an orgasm!

Shiranai then uses both love eggs to caress her nipples. Her body trembles and she groans and moans, saying how good she feels and how she wants to be stimulated more. He moves the two love eggs to her vagina and she seems even more sexually excited. As he stimulates her clitoris with the love eggs, she cries out that she cannot bear it anymore. When he asks why and how (I3). She tells him that she is going to come soon. However, he tells her: 'It isn't yet the time for that, is it?' (G2), as he moves the love eggs up to her breasts and then back to her vagina (G3) where he caresses her clitoris. He orders her to tell him first before she comes (H5) and then asks her if she has not come yet. She replies: 'Not yet. I need some more stimulation.' He caresses her clitoris with the love eggs again and warns her that he will take them away before she comes (G4). He also tells her she is a *sukebe* because she groans in such a lustful way (E2). He again caresses her clitoris until she is clearly about to come. But then all of a sudden he stops and says: '*uso*' (a 'joke'), meaning that he is not going to do what she was expecting (G5). She murmurs '*mō*' (meaning she cannot believe that he would stop when she is about to come). Shiranai then carries on caressing her clitoris. She cries out that she cannot bear it anymore and then comes. He tells the female character that she has already come three times and now the fourth time is about to happen (C8) as he continues to caress her clitoris. She says that she feels good and that she is about to come. Whereupon she comes in great ecstasy and he again steps back from the female character.

A lecture on infinite female orgasm 171

Vibrator

Next Shiranai switches to using a vibrator to stimulate her vagina. She groans and moans while her body quivers. He then strokes her uterus with the side of his hand. She groans and mutters that she is going to come again soon. However, he orders her not to do so (H6). Surprisingly, the more she expresses her desire for orgasm by groaning, the more Shiranai seems to want to stop her from reaching an orgasm (H7). He repeats the same order six times (H8) and even suggests that he would be angry if she comes without his permission (H9). He then comments on the fact that her nipples are hard and asks her whether she wants to come (C9). She says yes and, a little surprisingly perhaps, he tells her that if she wants to come, she should say so before she does so (I4). When she murmurs: 'I want to come', he proceeds to lecture her on how she cannot do so without saying 'please' (H10). She then says 'please', but Shiranai is still not satisfied and orders her to say 'please allow me to come!' (H11). The female character repeats what he has said and he proudly points out that she is in fact 'made' to come by him (H12). He even orders her to come (H13) and she finally does so with a lot of loud moaning. Once again, he immediately steps away from the female character who is groaning and moaning in ecstasy. As she pants, he caresses her nipples before suddenly forcefully caressing her breasts. Her hands rise as a reflexive response, but once again he pushes them down (H14). He then performs a body massage, ordering her not to come now (H15) as he massages her body and then caresses her nipples. The female character groans loudly, expressing her bodily pleasure and seems to be about to reach orgasm again, but Shiranai commands her not to (H16).

Bare hands

Next we see Shiranai put his fingers into her vagina. The female character murmurs that she is sexually excited. He suggests that she will come soon as she is groaning (D2) and, as he repeats himself (D3), she comes. He suggests that the next thing to go for is the G-spot (F4) which he stimulates with one hand while stroking her uterus with the other. He says proudly: 'See, you're about to come!' (D4). She keeps on groaning and he asks her whether she is coming as he raises her legs in the air (D5). She keeps groaning and he tells her that it is alright for her to come now (I5). She then groans loudly and comes.

He puts his middle finger into her vagina. She screams and comes again. He says that he is going to caress the opposite side of her vagina (F5). She replies that she is about to come. He again says that it is okay to come now (H17) so she comes again. He then says that the next step is to sexually stimulate the lower part of her vagina (F6) and he asks if she feels anything special (I6). She replies that it is a strange feeling, to which he responds that it might feel strange now, but her body will soon recognize the feeling (I7) and that the strangeness will change to good feeling (I8). He says to her: 'Right now you getting to realize the good feeling, right?' (I9). She says that she is about to come and does so in the midst of her groaning. Once again, he steps swiftly back from her. He then says that the next step is the uterus and that he is about to start now (F7). She murmurs that it is exciting and she keeps groaning for a long time.

Shiranai continues to use his fingers to caress her vagina. She screams and her body twitches. He comments on how hard her nipples are (C10) and asks her why (C11) before ordering her to touch them herself (C12). Rather than waiting for her to reply, he suggests that it might be because she has come too many times in a very short time (C13).

But, then, all of a sudden, he announces that she is going to come in 20 seconds (I10) and that he asks her to count the time (H18). She then counts: 'One, two, three, four, five …' Meanwhile, he strokes her uterus with the side of his hand and orders her not to come yet (H19). She continues to count and only comes on the 20th second.

Shiranai suggests that now she is already in the 'right' mood and that just by clapping his hands near her ears can make her reach orgasm. He then claps hands close to the female character's ears and murmurs proudly: 'See, you start to feel good, right … you like having your uterus stroked' (D6). To our great surprise, she comes and this scene ends with the female character screaming loudly.

Shiranai starts to put three of his fingers into her vagina. He suggests that he will make her come in three seconds (I11). He starts to count: 'One, two and three …'. She then comes, as he says again that it took only three seconds (I12) and suggests that they do it once more (I13). As he counts, she comes again in three seconds. He once again announces that she will come in one second (I14) and the female character then comes in ecstatic pleasure. He says that he will make her come in a different and perhaps difficult way (I15). She screams loudly and he bounces away from her.

As she pants, he takes off her eye mask and asks whether she feels ashamed (C14). He points out how she sobs and weeps, indicating that she is now being sent into ecstasy (C15). Meanwhile he strokes her uterus and she moans loudly. He teases her about how strange it is that stroking her belly can make her sexually excited (C16, E4). The female character cries out again that she is about to come, but he even suggests that she is perverted because stroking her belly can make her come (C17, E4). He starts to stroke her uterus forcefully and she comes.

He then caresses her vagina and says: 'Using fingers like this makes you so excited, it's weird … see, you're about to come. But you can't come that quick…' (C18, H20). As his hands move from her breasts to her vagina, he says: 'you want to be touched right … but no…' (G6). She moans. As his hands move back to her vagina, he says: 'They [his hands] are back, you want to be touched, right? Although you want to be touched, I won't give it to you!' (G7). He then lectures her on how her breasts also want to be touched right and that she should not keep silent if she wants to be touched (H21). She says: 'I want to be touched!' He asks if she really wants to be touched and even comments that she is such a *sukebe* (E5). He puts two fingers into her vagina while caressing her nipples. She moans loudly and comes. He says that he will make her come again in ten seconds (I16). As she moans, he counts: 'One, two, three, four and five...'. She comes again. The scene ends with the female character shivering and panting.

Modified electric dildo

After a short break, the shooting resumes. This time the scene consists of the female character lying on the bed with her arms and legs tied to it with bondage cuffs. Shiranai puts his fingers into her vagina. She moans. He asks her whether she wants it (D7), then thrusts and later strokes her vagina with his fingers. He continues to thrust into her vagina while caressing her nipples. He comments that her nipples are hard as she screams (C19). He goes on to say that although she has not come yet, she is getting more excited, and this makes her nipples hard (D8, I17). He asks her whether she wants to come but emphasizes that she is not allowed to do so immediately (G8). He then says: '30 seconds from now, you'll come!' (I18). She counts: 'One, two, three and four...'. She then comes, and pants. He steps quickly back from her again.

Shiranai then picks up a curved shaped sex toy which has two ends: one to stimulate the vagina and the other end to the anus. He puts the toy into her vagina and starts to thrust. She moans and comes. He starts to thrust to the other side. She groans loudly and comes again. He takes the toy out of her orifices and she appears faint.

Shiranai then speaks directly to the camera and says that today's climax is about to come. It will give her a sexually pleasurable feeling that she has never experienced before (F8). Whereupon he takes out the electric silicon dildo which he uses first to caress her vagina. After a while, he puts the silicon dildo into her vagina and rubs her clitoris. She screams loudly. He then turns the electric silicon dildo on and off. He shouts that her vagina is about to collapse (I19). She screams that she is about to come (G9) and he orders her to do so (H22). She then comes. He comments that it is good feeling (I20) as he once more stimulates her with the dildo, and she moans. Meanwhile he strokes her uterus, to which she responds by moaning loudly. He points out how she sobs and weeps, indicating that she is extremely excited (C20). He asks her to come again (H23) and she groans loudly. He says: 'Please send me to orgasm' (H24). She duly repeats what he has said to her. She comes in loud moans and he steps quickly away from her again.

She lies exhausted on the bed breathing deeply. Shiranai then comes close to her asking her softly and gently whether she has felt any pain (A1). She replies: 'no'. He strokes her forehead and gently asks her whether she has felt good (A2). She replies: 'yes'. Then, he grasps her nipples again and she screams. Then he once again strokes her belly with the side of his hands. She screams again. He says: 'Isn't it strange that you get sexually excited when your belly is being stroked and that you keep having orgasms during the last hour' (C21, E6). He keeps stroking while shouting 'uterus'. The female character reaches orgasm again. Again, he bounces away from her. He then touches her nipples again and says that she has become erotic (*eroppoi kei*) (C22, E7). He keeps saying this while shaking the two sides of her buttocks (C23, E8). She groans loudly. He intentionally leaves his hands off her buttocks and her groaning stops. He returns to shake her buttock again and she groans again, indicating his ability to bring her to orgasm as he pleases.

Then, he unfastens the buckles of the cuffs on her ankles. He puts her legs up and strokes her buttocks against his thighs. The female character groans loudly and comes again. He then gently spanks her buttocks while holding her two legs up in the air. She screams and comes again and once more her body shivers.

He unfastens the buckles on her wrists, placing her hands on her belly and pressing them from the top. She groans loudly. He comments that it is really *hazukashii*, the way pressing the belly can make her so sexually excited (C24). She screams that she is coming. He suggests increasing the pressure (F9). The female character comes again with loud moans and he takes his hands off her again before once again putting his fingers into her vagina and thrusting forcefully to make her moan and groan. Her body shivers and reaches orgasm once again. Interestingly, he gently strokes her forehead and suggests that there are two more orgasms to come (A3). He says that what she is going to have next is a jet-coaster-like orgasm (I21), a pleasant feeling she has never imagined or felt before (I22). Meanwhile, he keeps asking her whether she is alright and whether she feels good (A4). She replies: 'yes'. He comments on how she has kept on reaching orgasm until now (C25) as he strokes her uterus, making her come again. Then he moves both her legs upwards and strokes her buttocks with his legs, and she comes again but this time with maximum intensity. Shiranai again suddenly moves away from her.

It takes at least three to five minutes for the female character to calm down. We see her lying down on the sofa bed, completely exhausted like a dead fish on a chef's table. We are astonished to discover that she is in tears. Shiranai then announces that the shooting is over.

Authentication of the story and the 'female character' in the AV

The above ethnographic description of Shiranai's shooting reveals his major strategy to authenticate the story and the female character in the AV. First, the director-cum-actor consistently comports and depicts himself as a professional, or more correctly a sexologist, who is knowledgeable about female sexual physiology and anatomy in the shooting process, just as he did in the pre-filming negotiations. Shiranai's comportment can be seen clearly in terms of what we can call a 'medical-cum-scientific front' that he adopted in the filming process (Goffman 1958). This 'medical-cum-scientific front' is first manifested in the development of his unique method in bringing on infinite female orgasm: the uterus massage. Shiranai told us after the shooting that the uterus, in addition to the clitoris and G-spot, constitutes another important part of the vagina that is capable of producing an extremely intense orgasm when stimulated properly. He has thus developed a unique way of *massaging* the uterus. When accompanied by the use of modified electric dildo and various props, the uterus massage, Shiranai claimed, could bring forth infinite female orgasms.

Shiranai's 'medical-cum-scientific' front was also expressed in some mundane ways, like his dress code. As mentioned above, instead of a normal outfit, he wore a white coat and surgical mask during the filming precisely to denote his professionalism, dexterity and scientism in relation to female sexuality. His front was likewise reflected clearly in his filming room that differed tremendously from a typical AV filming room that is at least decorated, or presented as a comfortable bedroom. As we have seen above, Shiranai's filming room was extremely simple, actually like an 'operating room', highlighted by the sofa bed covered with the white flat sheet placed in the middle of the room and the small table where all the props were laid out for his use during the shooting. We argue that all these were manipulated by Shiranai to deliver a significant image of himself to the audience: he is not an ordinary AV director but one who is well trained in sexology, especially in female sexuality. A related and equally important message was likewise conveyed to audiences: what he was doing was not filming a movie but conducting a *scientific demonstration* and that is why he names this AV *Shiranai's Lecture on Portio*.

Shiranai's 'scientific' demonstration as a whole proceeded like this: it started with preliminary stimulation – that is, sensuous and uterus massages – followed by further stimulation using love eggs, vibrator, bare hands, anal hook and modified electric dildo. As a result of these, the female character was shown to reach a number of orgasms with an increasing degree of intensity. What Shiranai intended to demonstrate was the positive correlation between the force and form of stimulation and the intensity of the female character's orgasms. We can see how the intensity of her orgasms accelerated with the increasing force and different forms of stimulation. When Shiranai stepped up the stimulation by replacing sensuous and uterus massages with love eggs, vibrator, bare hands, anal hook and modified electric dildo respectively, the female character went from *kimochi ii*, via the increasing number and intensity of orgasms, to a situation where the timing of each orgasm could be controlled, before finally reaching the so-called jet-coaster-like orgasm.

The relation between the force and form of stimulation and the intensity of the female character's orgasms is not just a positive correlation but a *causal* relation. Remember how Shiranai usually stepped briskly away from the female character whenever she climaxed. Our argument is that he intended to impose what political scientists, who adopt the behaviourist approach to power, call counterfactual – used to show what the female character would have done without his stimulation (Dyrberg 1997: 23). Behaviourists' idea of power, according to Dyrberg, 'express[es] an asymmetrical view of power as "power over"' (Dyrberg 1997: 22), defined as

> A gets B to do something B would not otherwise have done: 'that A gets B to do something' is the event (which is most visible in cases of clashing

interests), and 'otherwise' indicates; (1) conflict; and (2) a hypothetical claim about what B would 'have done' in the absence of A, which is thus the imposition of a contrary-to-fact conditional that cannot, by definition, be observable.

(Dyrberg 1997: 23)

The major functions of the above hypothetical claim, according to Dyrberg, are two-fold. The first is to show that A's power can have significant effect over B. Second, it helps capture the nature of such power that it happens only when A applies his or her power to B (Dyrberg 1997: 23). More importantly, the behaviourist idea is an asymmetrical view of power in which A is the cause of B's changes in his or her own behaviour, which further implies that A has power over B.

Likewise, the fact that Sharanai stepped swiftly away from the female character whenever she reached orgasm serves as a counterfactual, which functions to prove that his stimulation was the ultimate cause of her orgasm. But if the behaviourists are theorists, Shiranai's shooting is theory in practice where he is able to turn the unobservable counterfactual into the observable by showing how the female character would have looked without his stimulation, proving that the relation between the force and form of stimulation and the intensity of the female character's orgasm is a *causal* one, which is also to say that there should be a biological and thus natural law that explains this causal relation.

It follows that if the relation between the force and form of stimulation and the intensity of the female character's orgasm is law-governed, the response of women to the force and form of simulation can be predicted and controlled. As we have just seen, Shiranai could predict and control the number as well as timing of the female character's orgasms. When he said that there would be another orgasm, the female character did experience another orgasm accordingly. Likewise, when he predicted that she would come in ten seconds, she duly did so in the tenth second. More importantly, he could even predict what kind of sexual feeling the female character was going to experience as we watched him predict that she would be going to experience something extremely special like the jet-coaster-like orgasm. In other words, all the responses of the female character to the stimulations by Shiranai were predictable; and because they were predictable, they were also controllable. If the responses of the female character are predictable and controllable, it must also mean that they are governed by a natural law, and thus must be universal and hence real because they are the outcomes of that natural law. That is also to say, what was portrayed in the movie was not a staged performance but a truly authentic human sexual reaction according to a natural law. Just as Shiranai made a real fuss about convincing us in the pre-filming negotiations that what we were going to see were real female reactions to sexual stimulation rather than a performance, a lot of effort went into authenticating the female sexual responses during the shooting.

To say that the responses of the female character were law-governed is also to imply that if audiences closely follow the procedures and duly apply all the necessary conditions demonstrated by Shiranai, they would also yield very similar, if not the same, results as Shiranai did. Recall that he invited Wakaranai to use the love eggs to sexually stimulate the female character's vagina during the shooting. In our opinion, this invitation is better seen as another strategy employed by Shiranai to convince the audience that what they were seeing was real. Inasmuch as Wakaranai, and by implication any other lay member of the audience could equally well bring about the same effect: immense sexual pleasure for the female character.

By showing that the relationship between the force and form of stimulation and the intensity of the female character's orgasm is 'law-governed', the director authenticated her responses to his sexual stimulation. In other words, Shiranai intended to show that the AV is not a representation of reality; it *is* reality. We can now see how the *kikaku* AV as representation is authenticated as 'reality'. In the event, the gap between representation and reality is filled. More importantly, our intent in invoking the behaviourist conception of power as causation here is not just to argue that Shiranai's intention was to show that his stimulation was the ultimate cause for the female character's orgasm, but more importantly to pick up the behaviourists' conclusion that Shiranai and the female character were in an asymmetrical power relation in which the former had power over the latter.

Pornographic realism as a discourse

In spite of all this, we cannot agree with the behaviourists' argument that 'power only exists when exercised' (Dyrberg 1997: 23). Certainly, Shiranai's shooting demonstrated that he had power over the female character; there can be no doubt about that. But it is important to point out here that power exists *prior* to filming, in that Shiranai is a *particular* kind of man and the female character a *particular* kind of woman. By this, we mean that power lies in Shiranai's shooting as a discursive process that helps impose an arbitrarily defined male and female sexual being on the audience. There is general agreement among anthropologists, sociologists, political scientists and even ordinary people on the street that human phenomena are meaningful and take place in terms of that meaning, which is never the only one possible. As we learn from some good anthropologists, such a meaningful scheme has a Saussurean structure of signs in which '[t]he sense of a sign (the Saussurean "value") is determined by its contrastive relations to other signs in the system' (Sahlins 1985: ix). The value of a sign, say in our context 'women', is defined by its differences from other signs, again in our context 'men', and *not* directly from the worldly objects of men and women. Instead of being an *objective* representation of men and women, the signs of men and women are a function of the internal differences among the categories of 'men' and 'women' within a meaningful scheme that is not the only one possible. To paraphrase Sahlins (1985: 147) who quoted Culler in saying,

> The contrast in French between the terms *fleuve* and *riviere* entails a different segmentation of fluvial objects from the usual English glosses 'river'

and 'stream', inasmuch as the French terms do not turn on relative size as the English do [*sic*], but on whether or not the water flows into the ocean (cf. Culler 1977).... There is no necessary starting point for any such cultural scheme in 'reality',...

Sahlins then concluded,

> ...the particular culture scheme constitutes the possibilities of worldly reference for the people of a given society, even as this scheme is constituted on principled distinctions between signs which, in relation to objects, are never the only one possible distinction.
>
> (Sahlins 1985: 147)

That is to say, the definition of any sign is 'stimuli free'; it is a culturally intended selection in which a certain set of differences is assigned significance while the other sets are deemed irrelevant to the definition of the sign at issue. Any cultural sign, therefore, can never exhaust the representation of an object. This is also to say that any definition of 'men' and 'women' is *political* because in the event there have to be some differences that are suppressed; and there must be some other differences that are selected to stand out. All of this is done arbitrarily as the definition of 'men' and 'women' in any culture does not follow directly the absolute existence of men and women, that is, as biological beings. However, the politics lies not just in the arbitrary selection of differences, but more importantly in hiding the arbitrariness of such a selection of differences through naturalizing the *specific* definition of men and women. This is done, for example in Shiranai's shooting, by means of pretending to be scientific, in the course of which the arbitrarily defined sexual being of men and women is made biologically true. By pretending to be biologically true, this naturalized sexual being of men and women suppresses other equally possible definitions of their sexual being, as a result of which the specific definition of sexual being is *presumed* to be the only possible one and thus must be accepted as real (Deetz 1992: 136). In other words, Shiranai's pornographic realism – that is, the authentication of the story and the female character mentioned in Chapter 4 – not only articulates but also authenticates a specific definition of a woman embedded in the AV as a 'real' woman. But what kind of 'real' woman is she?

Woman as Hobbesian man

We argue that this 'real' woman is no different from Hobbesian man. According to Hobbes (1981), human beings are nothing more than sophisticated machines, all of whose functions and behaviours can be described and explained in purely mechanistic terms. Even a thought can be understood as an instance of the physical operation of the human body. The same is also true for sensations – including sexual pleasure, for example – which involve a series of mechanical processes operating within the human nervous system, by means of which the sensible features of material things produce ideas in the brains of the human beings who perceive them.

Not unlike Hobbesian man, this 'real' woman in the AV was simply a sensory machine because all her sexual pleasure and responses can be defined and explained in terms of mechanics. In the shooting, female orgasm was depicted as involving a series of mechanical processes: massaging the uterus with a set of props – from love eggs, through hands and anal hook, to electric dildo. Precisely because a woman's orgasm was seen as mechanical, not only this particular woman but also any other ordinary woman could achieve an infinite series of orgasms, provided that mechanical stimulation was applied correctly. That is the reason Shiranai argued that the uterus massage could invariably produce intense sexual pleasure in every single woman. Just like Hobbes, whose aim was to develop a geometrical account of the motion of bodies which would reveal the genuine basis of their causal interactions and the regularity of the natural world, Shiranai in the shooting process aimed to develop a mechanical account of female sexuality, which would reveal the genuine basis of (infinite) female orgasm. In the end, the female character was dehumanized to the extent that she possessed no symbolic capacity – an essential species-specific quality of *homo sapiens*. She was rendered 'mechanical' in the sense that she was incapable of doing anything at will with regard to her sexuality since all she could do was simply respond to Shiranai's stimulation. More importantly, this total deprival of female sexual agency indeed implies the sexual domination of men over women, because only men can give orgasm to women – as we can see from the above description of the shooting where the female character's sexual pleasure was completely dependent on what Shiranai did, or did not, do to her.

We cannot forget that Hobbesian man is situated in a State of Nature. Our intent in drawing the parallel between the female character in the AV and Hobbesian man, therefore, is to point out that women and Hobbesian man alike are authenticated by being situated in a State of Nature: that is, in the authentication of the female character in the AVs.

Woman as animal

Such sexual domination of men over women was further reinforced by the obvious use of *kotoba-zeme* in the shooting, in the sense that not only the physical, but also the emotional/mental, part of a woman could be controlled. As we can see from the above ethnographic descriptions of the shooting process, all the nine elements of the *kotoba-zeme* outlined by Shiranai on his personal blog were clearly found in the movie. Among them, Element C (to induce her shame), Element H (to command her) and Element I (to make her imagine) appeared more than 20 times in the movie. Meanwhile, Element D (to see through her), Element E (to insult her), Element F (to tell her what is coming next) and Element G (to confuse her) also had about six to nine instances. In some cases, the dialogues that appeared in the shooting are exactly the same as the examples given by Shiranai on his blog. For instance, the example of Element E given by

180 *A lecture on infinite female orgasm*

Table 7.2 The ideology of *kotoba-zeme*

Elements	Numbers of instances appearing in the movie
A To deliver love	A1–A4
B To verbalize her attraction	B1–B2
C To induce her shame	C1–C25
D To see through her	D1–D8
E To insult her	E1–E8
F To tell her what the next step is	F1–F9
G To confuse her	G1–G9
H To command her	H1–H22
I To make her imagine	I1–I22

Shiranai is: 'You are really a *sukebe!*' which also appeared in the shooting. Although Shiranai did not even mention a single word with regard to the logic of the filming, it is very clear that he was alluding to the ideology of *kotoba-zeme* when framing and shooting this specific *kikaku* film.

As mentioned above, *kotoba-zeme* is inherently contradictory in the sense that while its contents are sadistic and sexist, it is considered to be a major 'communication' tactic to enhance pleasure in heterosexual sex in modern Japan. This contradictory nature of *kotoba-zeme* is akin to what Boyle calls the 'pornographic double-speak' (Boyle 2010: 7) which she explains this way:

> industry insiders describe how dirty, filthy, disgusting women are degraded, abused, humiliated and hurt in their films – but they call it sex. This pornographic double-speak makes critiques of the industry extremely difficult as there is no language that has not been colonized and rebranded as sex.
>
> (Boyle 2010: 7–8)

One can see that *kotoba-zeme* is a perfect instance of this pornographic doublespeak where Shiranai described how shameful and disgusting the female character was as she was humiliated, commanded, confused and teased in the shooting of the film, but he *called* this a means to bring about female sexual pleasure. The double-speak here takes the form of not just making the truth less unpleasant, but actually of reversing the truth. Dominating and degrading as it might be, *kotoba-zeme* is elevated to the form of a moral act: done for the sake of female sexual pleasure.

Thus, not unlike the whole series of sexual techniques performed by Shiranai to physically control the female character, we can see that *kotoba-zeme* was likewise employed by him to control her *spiritually* and *psychologically*. As we have seen, 'to induce her shame', 'to insult her', 'to confuse her' and 'to command her' constituted the core discursive elements of the shooting of the AV. If *kotoba-zeme* aimed to induce a woman's shame, to insult her, to confuse her and to command her, it is not incorrect to say that what it aims at is to dehumanize the woman portrayed in the AV. Setting aside how *kotoba-zeme* might be received by actual audiences, it clearly aims, at least within the AV, to deprive the female character of such human qualities as her individuality, personality, dignity, emotionality and so on. In the event, she is rendered mechanical, nothing more than an animal.

Men as women's saviours

We have argued that woman is discursively defined as a sex machine, as well as an animal, in Shiranai's shooting process. But if women are a sex machine, then men should be the engineers who operate that machine. Recall that Shiranai pretended to be the sexologist who knew everything about sex in the shooting. In fact, the whole shooting was designed to teach (mainly male) audiences how to fix those 'problematic' women who either don't have good orgasms or have no orgasms at all. The AV's audience was taught two things in the film. The first was about how to use various tools – including sensuous and uterus massage, love eggs, bare hands, anal hook and electric dildo – to stimulate a woman's body and ultimately bring a problematic woman to orgasm in the same way as a skilful engineer uses different effective tools to fix a machine.

Second, if, as we have argued, *kotoba-zeme* is a technique employed by men in Japan to reduce women to animals, it can also be seen as a technique through which women as 'problematic' animals can be tamed. 'Problematic' animals here refer to those women who, for one reason or another, are deprived of an ability to achieve orgasm. As we have noted, Shiranai saw *kotoba-zeme* as consisting of nine elements: 'to deliver love', 'to verbalize her attraction', 'to see through her mind', 'to insult her', 'to tell her what is the next step', 'to confuse her', 'to command her' and 'to make her imagine'. The first two elements can be seen as a carrot, while the elements of 'to insult her', 'to induce her shame' and 'to command her' can be treated as a stick; and through carrot and stick, men can reward women when they behave correctly and punish them when they do not. The element of 'to see through her mind' is to tell those 'problematic' women that men know them well and therefore they should never try to trick men. 'To tell her what the next step is' and 'to make her imagine' function to convey a clear message that men are in firm control over women. We can see that *kotoba-zeme* provides the necessary tricks for men to tame women. So if women are animals, men then are animal tamers.

Regardless of whether women are either a machine or an animal, men are superior to women because they fix their problems, either as an engineer or as an animal tamer: men are able to give women an orgasm. From this comes our final point: men are women's saviours. Behind this point are several assumptions. The first major one is that women have no sexual agency in the sense that they can neither define their sexual pleasures nor achieve orgasm by themselves. Second, only men can define women's sexual pleasure: that is, orgasm, *as well as* how to bring women to orgasm. In other words, only men can give women orgasms. Accordingly, women have to rely on men to achieve orgasm and thus sexual pleasure. Finally, those women who have never experienced orgasm are considered by men to be 'problematic', if not sick, and they need men to fix their problems or cure their 'disease'. In these respects, men become women's saviours. As such, they have the responsibility of giving women orgasm and thus sexual pleasure. We can now see how men's sexual domination over women and women's lack of sexual agency reciprocally define each other to form the famous salvage ideology.

Understood as such, Shiranai's shooting can be seen as a discursive practice that helps produce the salvage ideology – a particular way of defining the sexual being of man and woman – which functions to provide an identity for a woman or man as subject (that is, man is woman's saviour and woman is a machine or animal) and certain rights and characteristics for a woman or man as an object (that is, man is to save woman and woman is to be saved because she does not have sexual agency). But this perspective is only one possible way to define the sexual being of man and woman. The politics here lies in the formation of experience in which the salvage ideology is naturalized as the only possible one by the pornographic realism in the AV, as we have just demonstrated. It follows that the effectiveness of the salvage ideology as cultural code – including all these discourses of woman as Hobbesian man, as sexual machine, as animal, and man as woman's saviour in this *kikaku* AV – lies in the pornographic realism in which the discursive, and thus arbitrary, 'reality' as the effect of all these discourses is naturalized as a biological and thus universal truth by the authentication of the story and the female character in the AV which functions to make the salvage ideology look 'real' and thus 'true'. In this regard, some instances of *kotoba-zeme* in Shiranai's shooting are remarkably illustrative.

The elements of 'to tell her what the next step is' and 'to make her imagine', for example, emerged out of practical reasons in the production process. For instance, when Shiranai said that the female character would come in ten seconds, it was of course to warn her of what was to come next (Element I), but from the perspective of Shiranai as a producer, it was also an important means to signal her that she *had to* come in ten seconds' time. Likewise, when Shiranai said: 'See, you are about to come', it is certainly one of the examples of 'seeing through her' (Element D), but it also serves as an important hint to the female character that she *had to* come soon. Similarly, Shiranai commented: 'It was really *hazukashii*, pressing your belly can make you so sexually excited.' Again, it can be seen as an instance of 'inducing her shame' (Element C); nevertheless it was also a clue to the female character that she *had to* act sexually excited. It is particularly necessary in this shooting as Shiranai did not know the actress well because, as we mentioned above, she was called in at very short notice to replace the original one with whom Shiranai was very familiar. It would have been difficult if not impossible for the actress to follow Shiranai's flow of acts if she did not receive hints in advance; and if the actress were not able to follow his flow of actions, the shooting would not have gone smoothly. It was also especially important in the shooting of an acme AV because, if filming were interrupted, Shiranai's portrayal of the actress's responses as 'real' during the shooting process would have been futile. We can see here that *kotoba-zeme* is primarily informed by Shiranai's need to pursue pornographic realism in the acme AV, in the course of which the sexual being of men and women defined by the salvage ideology is made 'real'. That is to say, while Shiranai pursued pornographic realism in the AV, he in fact helped naturalize the salvage ideology that dehumanizes woman as a machine or an animal.

More interestingly, once the salvage ideology is naturalized, people tend to accept it as self-evident, which is also to say that people – perhaps including even Shiranai – may not necessarily be aware of the arbitrariness of the ideology, but take it as natural and thus real at the experiential level. If that is so, it follows that Shiranai and perhaps other directors simply follow the salvage ideology when producing other acme AVs. The salvage ideology then serves as a pornographic reality which further dictates the production of other acme AVs in which the same ideology as a cultural code of men's domination over women and women's lack of sexual agency organizes their production and determines the character of the use value of the AV. This accounts for the utility of the AV to a certain group of Japanese AV consumers, as the cultural code itself is materially reproduced and visually authenticated. To paraphrase Sahlins (1976a: 168), the acme AV is produced for men who sexually dominate women and women who do not have sexual agency, in the course of reproducing these particular *kinds* of men and women by their consumption of the acme AV. The dialectics between the pornographic realism and the salvage ideology help sustain the latter.

Conclusion

This chapter started with the shooting process of a *kikaku* AV, inviting readers to experience with us the real, disturbing and complex dynamics involved in the shooting of a specific *kikaku* genre: acme. During the shooting, Shiranai, the director, tried to demonstrate how to bring the female character to sexual ecstasy by using sensuous and uterus massage, love eggs, vibrator, bare hands and modified electric dildo, and as a result, the female character was shown to reach multiple orgasms with an increasing degree of intensity. We also saw how the shooting was underlined by *kotoba-zeme*, a male-oriented, if not sexist, and sadist ideology that was made up of nine elements. As a double-speak, this ideology on the one hand takes pleasure in imposing command and contempt upon women, and causing them confusion, while on the other hand pretending that all these sadist acts are done for the sake of a woman's sexual pleasure.

Adopting the behaviourist approach to power, we demonstrated that the fact that the director was the ultimate cause for the female character's orgasm shows that the former has power over the latter. But there is a more deep-rooted politics that lies in the discursive construction of the sexual being of men and women. Shiranai's shooting implied a series of pre-existing assumptions about the sexual being of men and women. These include: (1) orgasm as the only possible sexual pleasure for women and those women who do not reach orgasm are therefore considered to be nothing but problematic; (2) women are not capable of achieving orgasm and only men can give them one; (3) problematic women are therefore animals or machines waiting to be tamed or fixed by men; and (4) men are women's saviours because only men can bring women to orgasm. This series of assumptions further speaks to two mutually constituted, implied and reinforced elements of the salvage ideology: women's lack of sexual agency and men's sexual domination of women.

This series of assumptions is obviously arbitrary, which is also to say that it is not the only one possible. The politics here lies in Shiranai's scientific pretension that functions to make these assumptions unspoken and thus silent, and therefore cannot be challenged. In the event, the arbitrary definition of the sexual being of men and women was made *the* reality. Once the salvage ideology is authenticated, it becomes *the* reality by which the production and consumption of acme AVs are organized. In another line of development, this is interlaced with Geertz's idea of 'model for/model of' (1973: 93), in the sense that the salvage ideology, once authenticated as real, provides people with both a sexual worldview (a world as it is) and a sexual ethos (a world as it should be). The point is that one's sexual ethos is always seen against a sense of one's worldview and vice versa. How people think their sexual world should look is affected by how sex appears to them; and how sex appears to them is in turn reinforced by the so-called 'proper' sexual ethos. It is the dialectics between the pornographic realism and the salvage ideology that makes the salvage ideology sustainable. This is how the salvage ideology is produced and reproduced in the production and consumption of acme AVs.

Indeed, this ideology is akin to what Sahlins calls a 'single consistent system of relationships' which is 'deployed or mapped onto various planes of social action' in Japan (Sahlins 1976a: 6). One common plane of such influence is popular culture, a notable example of which is a television drama called *Great Teacher Onizuka* (*GTO*). This drama features a young male ex-biker teacher Onizuka whose ambition is to become a great teacher. As a low-class ex-gang member, Onizuka adopts a completely different teaching philosophy. By inflicting physical and psychological pain on his students, he in fact wholeheartedly aims to enlighten them through a journey of self-discovery. The same is also true for a more recent Japanese drama called *The Queen of the Classroom* which portrays a female teacher who attempts to help her students by inflicting psychological pain on them. Central to these dramas is the salvage ideology that while the means adopted by the teachers is bad, in the sense that it inflicts pains upon the students, since all of this is done for the sake of the students and for their good, the teachers should not only be forgiven but indeed thanked for saving their students. Hence the good end justifies the bad means.

More importantly, such salvage ideology is also mapped onto other domains of social life, such as the workplace where female workers are assumed to have no managerial competence and thus should be assigned a supporting role in Japanese companies (as we showed in Chapter 5), in the course of which the salvage ideology is reproduced and reinforced. Consequently, the salvage ideology is carried by what Deetz calls 'the interrelated web of support and dependence that makes the single change difficult' (Deetz 1992: 126). We are not going to further elaborate here on 'the structural interrelation of institutional forces' (Deetz 1992: 126) that helps sustain the salvage ideology in Japanese society in general because that would require another book. We just want to point out here that, by focusing on the AV filming process, we not only come to understand how the salvage ideology is produced, reproduced and sustained by the interrelated web of support and dependence in society as a whole, but also how that ideology can be linked to the actual shooting; and how culture is realized in action.

An important implication for the feminist critique of pornography is that we have to address the politics deeply rooted in the formation of the sexual being of men and women in which a *specific* sexual being of men and women is generalized as universally true and naturalized as biologically real, thereby preventing the gender inequality embedded in the definition from being challenged and criticized. It follows that any effective feminist critique should not focus *only* on the pornographic depiction of how men oppress women in and/or through sex; nor should it simply embark on the 'feminist pornography' that seeks to revise sexual subjectivity by 'creating its own iconography and is committed to depicting diversity in gender, race, ethnicity, nationality, sexuality, class, body size, ability and age' (Taormino 2013: 262). Certainly, the feminist pornography that has grown out of a third-wave, sex-positive feminist ideology in recent years provides mediated spaces that attempt to challenge the mythologies of the mainstream pornography industry. Notable directors of feminist pornography – including Tristan Taormino, Joanna Angel, Courtney Trouble, Madison Young and Shine Louise Houston – have recently opened up a whole new way of looking at female sexuality and pornography (Liberman 2013). But while feminist pornography might offer a unique 'heterotopia' for a particular population of females – that is, feminist-identified consumers – to actively explore sexual practices and develop sexuality subjectivity (Liberman 2015: 186), we argue that such a feminist attempt is at best a partial remedy as it fails to address the fundamental issue by denaturalizing the specific sexual being of men and women in a given society. We will return to this in the Conclusion to this book.

Notes

1. The vaginal portion of the cervix projects free into the anterior wall of the vagina between the anterior and posterior *fornices vaginae*.
2. Shiranai is a pseudonym to disguise the identity of one of our important informants in the adult video industry.
3. In other words, the movie features only two persons and the director himself is simultaneously the actor.
4. The authors would like to express their gratitude to Professor Ben-Ari for pointing out this interesting observation.
5. Parts of the chapter have been used elsewhere in different contexts and for different purposes (Yau and Kobori 2012b).

8 The 'censorship' of Japanese adult videos

Introduction

This chapter turns to the so-called 'censorship' of adult videos, the process that every Japanese adult video title must go through before it can be on the market. But we have to point out immediately that it is misleading, if not totally incorrect, to call it 'censorship' as such. The organization involved is merely a self-regulatory association voluntarily founded by adult video makers for the matter of ensuring adherence to the local obscenity laws in order to prevent the government from doing it for them. Thus, while the industry people do not hesitate to use the English word 'censorship' to refer to their job, what it has been doing is nothing more than the screening of adult videos. Founded in 1977, Biderin[1] was the first such self-regulatory body to handle adult videos, followed by Medirin[2] established in 1996 and Eizōrin[3] in 2010. As we mentioned in Chapter 3, Biderin was formed by the early participants of the adult video industry and was later taken over by the Big Five. Endorsed by the active participation of former police officers, Biderin was rendered a quasi-state agency manipulated by the Big Five to dominate the market and exclude new competitors, so much so that it functioned more like a cartel. While Medirin also functioned like another cartel founded by indie makers to resist the dominance of Biderin, it was by and large seen as inferior to Biderin and hence illegal. Eizōrin is distinctly different. Frightened by the police's crackdown on Biderin in 2007, Eizōrin has from the beginning been haunted by the nightmare of being prosecuted. As we shall see in a moment, its whole mission has been to address this nightmare by promoting itself as a neutral, fair and socially reflective organization that represents the views of the wider society on sexual morality by devising various measures and taking a moral high ground on the inspection of AVs. In the final part of this chapter, we will analyse some problematic cases in order to delineate the general logic of the AV inspection done by Eizōrin and spell out its consequences for the production of AVs.

Resistance against Biderin

The above-mentioned development of the regulatory system of the Japanese AV industry, we suggest, can be understood as an example of what Victor Turner

(1974: 23–59) called a social drama. Every social drama is supposed to go through four phases: breach, crisis, redressive action and reintegration. As mentioned in Chapter 3, Biderin had been notorious for enforcing a very strict interpretation of the obscenity laws from its inception (Adachi 1995: 288; Motohashi 2012: 123). Over the years, it required AV makers to have airbrushed the whole genital region including pubic hair, such that the lower parts of the characters in some adult videos of the 1980s were completely blurred. From the mid-1990s, adult video makers alongside AV directors became increasingly dissatisfied with the outdated criteria imposed by, and the uncompromising manner of, Biderin (Motohashi 2012: 123; Yasuda and Amamiya 2006: 100). While the portrayal of pubic hair in magazines was deregulated in 1996, Biderin still refused to loosen its grip and continued to require its members to airbrush pubic hair.

A group of so-called indie AV makers headed by Soft On Demand made a bold decision by withdrawing from Biderin and creating a new screening body called Medirin in 1996 (Yasuda and Amamiya 2006: 104–5). As a voluntary, non-governmental body, Biderin could not stop others from founding a new body to handle the screening of AVs if such a body managed to gather support from many adult video makers. Since most AV makers were frustrated with Biderin's outdated interpretations of the obscenity laws and its uncompromising manner, they were therefore more than willing to support Medirin, which vowed to deregulate the prohibition of pubic hair and give emphasis to individuality as well as creativity. Considering that adult video wholesalers dared not accept videos deprived of Biderin's approval, Medirin found a way out by providing a screening service for AVs-for-sale, instead.

At the same time, many more self-regulatory agencies sprang up in Japan during the late 1990s and the 2000s (Fujiki 2009: 210).[4] To compensate for the fact that they were far less famous compared to Biderin and Medirin, these new agencies tended to be far more lenient in terms of inspection criteria (by allowing the use of thinner and smaller mosaic) and charged less to attract AV makers to join their agencies. As can be imagined, videos certified by these agencies were far more sexually explicit and graphic, and thus well received among audiences (Sonoda and Dai 2016: 105). Meanwhile, AV makers who chose not to join any self-regulatory agency gradually emerged and produced whatever kind of sexually explicit videos they felt like. All of this dealt a serious threat to videos certified by Biderin, since they could offer audiences something that Biderin-associated makers could not – something which further challenged the legitimacy of Biderin as the sole 'censoring' body in the adult video industry (Fujiki 2009; Nakamura 2015; Yasuda and Amamiya 2006: 105).

What had been happening so far was akin to what Victor Turner called the first phase of a social drama: that is, a

> breach of regular, norm-governed social relations occurred between persons or groups within the same system of social relations, be it a village, chiefdom,

office, factory, political party or ward, church, university department, or any other perduring system or set or field of social interaction.

(Turner: 1974: 38)

As we have just seen, the emergence of Medirin and other regulatory bodies not only challenged the legitimacy of Biderin and the domination of the Big Five AV manufacturers over small AV makers, wholesalers and retailers; it also had profound and far-reaching consequences for the whole AV industry in that it not only revolutionized the 'norm' about how Japanese AVs should be circulated and regulated in Japan, but also opened up a new way of how to consume and make sense of adult videos, since viewers did not need to return the videos by a given time, but could re-watch them at their own pace and comfort. We therefore suggest that the emergence of Medirin and other regulatory bodies can be seen as indicating that the regulatory system of the Japanese AV industry was going through a phase of breaching the standard practice established by Biderin.

Medirin getting recognition

At the beginning, Medirin was fully aware of its inferior status vis-à-vis Biderin, as it had emerged out of its resistance against the dominance of Biderin in the industry. Medirin was plagued by this inferiority and hence the possibility of being arrested. According to our interview with one of the important figures in the formation of Medirin, he was on tenterhooks everyday about whether the police would come to arrest them (Interview with Omoiatanarai 2014). To cope with this inferiority, Medirin made a concerted effort to acquire formal recognition from the Japanese government. In August 2005, Medirin received an award in recognition of its positive efforts to tackle the widespread violations of intellectual property rights in the adult movie industry from both the Ministry of Education, Culture, Sports, Science and Technology, and the Kanto Bureau of Economy, Trade and Industry, which is a regional branch organization of METI (Ministry of Economy, Trade and Industry) (personal communications with Omoiatanarai). From the early 2000s, these two ministries had started to provide financial funding to corporations that aimed to improve the business environment in Japan and to offer certification of appreciation to corporations that made efforts contributing to the development of the Japanese economy. Although this recognition had nothing to do with obscenity laws, it marked the new status of Medirin and further dealt a severe blow to the dominance, as well as legitimacy, of Biderin, which had not been recognized in the same way. Upon recognition, Medirin was renamed Contents Soft Association (CSA) in 2005. Thereafter, screening services were passed to its subsidiary organization, the Medirin Committee.

Apart from obtaining government recognition, Medirin also got rid of its isolation through building a thriving and healthy relationship with adult video makers, as well as collaborative relationships with other 'censoring' bodies. In contrast to Biderin which acted rather dominantly, Medirin from the outset was more attentive to manufacturers' problems, needs and comments. As advised by the Kanto Bureau of Economy, Trade and Industry, CSA, Biderin and other self-regulatory associations for the first time in September 2006 reached an agreement on inspection criteria and formed a limited liability intermediary body called the Inspection Centre (*Shinsa sentā*) which was a restructuring of the Medirin Committee. From then on, all screenings of adult videos previously operated by the Medirin Committee were transferred to the Inspection Centre. CSA was no longer as isolated as it had been previously.

Facing tremendous pressures both from outside and inside, the Board of Biderin finally eased its restrictions. From August 2006 onwards, it deregulated the portrayal of pubic hair and anuses in AVs, which it had prohibited since the early 1980s, and most importantly allowed the use of a thinner mosaic (Sonoda and Dai 2016: 106). However, Biderin's relaxation of its inspection criteria shocked and surprised the whole industry. Perhaps a metaphor from the industry people can best capture how Biderin's change in policy surprised them. Biderin was not unlike 'a stubborn father who had long set a curfew for his daughter at 6 pm, but all of a sudden, said that midnight would be fine' (Motohashi 2012: 123). It is precisely Biderin's radical step that led to an irreversible mistake.

Biderin's consent to reach an agreement with Medirin on inspection criteria and its subsequent relaxation thereof marked the arrival of the second phase of a social drama: crisis. For the consent and the relaxation themselves had to mean that Medirin had begun to assume a similar, if not the same, status as Biderin as the latter was forced to follow the former's inspection criteria. This further testified publicly that indie AV makers headed by Takahashi and his Soft On Demand had the same, if not more influences, on the industry as Biderin did, which is also to say that the dominant cleavage between the Big Five AV makers and those indie AV makers headed by Takahashi and his Soft On Demand was formed and reinforced. The power structure of the whole industry, therefore, changed from the singular domination by the Big Five AV makers to the sharing of power between the Big Five AV makers and those indie makers headed by Takahashi and his Soft On Demand. The Japanese AV industry was indeed deeply divided.

Arrest of Biderin members in 2008

On 23 August 2007, the Tokyo Metropolitan Police raided Biderin in Tokyo and several adult video production studios, confiscating thousands of videos as part of an investigation into video producers and distributors suspected of having produced and/or sold videos containing obscene depictions of sexual organs, and of Biderin allowing these materials to go on sale due to an insufficient screening process (Japan News Review, 23 August 2007). The raid caused a huge sensation not only within the adult video industry but also the whole of Japanese society, as no one would have expected it. On 1 March 2008, five people associated with Biderin – including the head of its inspection division and one of its Board member who was also head of a production company – were arrested for the sale, distribution and abetting of indecent materials (Mainichi Shimbun, 1 March 2008). Upon their arrest, Biderin ceased all its screening services and in April 2008 announced that it would form a new organization to provide reforms and uniform screening practices for adult videos.

The government crackdown on Biderin in 2007 was unprecedented in the history of the adult video industry in Japan, not only because its division head and Board members were arrested, but also because the videos that were approved and certified by Biderin were still targeted by the Japanese Police. The crackdown thus constituted a serious challenge to the very authority and legitimacy of Biderin. This was especially true if we take into account the fact that there were many more sexually explicit adult videos, even underground videos, out there, but the Japanese Police did not target them; just those certified by Biderin.

When the case was brought to the Tokyo Supreme Court in 2011, it was clear from the indictment that what was problematic in the eyes of the police was the sudden, radical change of Biderin's inspection criteria and most importantly the reasons for such a change (Sonoda and Dai 2016: 105). As we have mentioned above, the emergence of Medirin and other regulatory bodies enabled some AV makers to offer audiences something that Biderin-associated makers could not. From the 2000s onwards, there were increasing voices of dissatisfaction among Biderin maker-members, who lobbied for the alleviation and relaxation of the rigid inspection criteria so that their videos could be as competitive as those certified by other bodies or even uncertified videos (Sonoda and Dai 2016: 106). In addition to this internal pressure, Biderin likewise suffered a serious legitimacy crisis because other self-regulatory agencies such as CSA had gradually acquired government recognition. Taken together, they explained why the number of Biderin maker-members dropped to a record low, with only 98 in 2006, in contrast to 170 in 1997 (Motohashi 2012: 123; Sonoda and Dai 2016: 106).

All of this, from the police's vantage, was the major reason leading to Biderin's sudden and radical relaxation of its inspection criteria in 2006. In view of its declining domination and decreasing revenue due to ever shrinking membership, Biderin, *for the first time*, listened to the requests of its members and responded to them by considerably relaxing its inspection criteria. In other words, Biderin's decision to substantially relax its inspection criteria was coloured by its organizational interests; it chose to side with its members in order to protect their commercial interests, and ultimately its own interests. In short, Biderin's interest in its members corrupted its status as moral gatekeeper.

In response to this accusation, Biderin's defence was that it was not being lenient to its members; rather, it had slackened its criteria in view of changing societal attitude toward pornography (*tsūnen*) (Sonoda and Dai 2016: 108). As social values and standards concerning sex and sexuality had indeed witnessed considerable change, what would have once been considered as '*waisetsu*' should change too, so that Biderin's defence shifted the emphasis to current sexual mores in Japanese society. In other words, Biderin was still fulfilling its role as the neutral, moral gatekeeper to ensure that obscenity laws were complied with.

As we can see here, the two different versions of 'reality' presented above represent two different readings of Biderin's relaxation of inspection criteria. The major difference between the two readings lies in their motivation: the police argued that Biderin simply sided with the maker-members to advance its members' commercial, and ultimately its own, interests, a typical prosecution strategy adopted in postwar Japanese censorship trials (Cather 2004: 167); while Biderin defended itself on the grounds that it fulfilled its role as a moral gatekeeper of obscenity laws by relaxing its criteria simply to reflect changing societal attitudes toward pornography. In other words, the latter pointed to the neutrality of Biderin, whereas the former focused precisely on Biderin's favouritism towards its members, thus corrupting its motivation as a self-regulatory organization formed to protect obscenity laws.

Nevertheless, the judges at the Tokyo Supreme Court sided with the prosecution, adopting the reading provided by the police and convicted the five defendants. The judges believed that Biderin, as a respectable self-regulatory body in the field of adult video for 30 years, had failed to fulfil its role as a moral gatekeeper. This understanding can be clearly seen in the ruling given by the Tokyo Supreme Court in 2010:

> Biderin accepted the demands from its maker-members, and subsequently relaxed the inspection criteria; regardless of actual inspection, or the results thereof, it chose to side with the demands of the makers with whom it had a conflict of interests; in terms of the mosaic level, when compared with the past, there was substantial relaxation both in terms of the criteria and application ... taking into consideration the actual context when the inspection was carried out, it is not true that it took into consideration the *tsūnen*.
> (Sonoda and Dai 2016: 111–12)

In 2014, the case was brought to the Tokyo Court of Appeals as the defendant – including Biderin's head of division, division members and Board members – appealed against conviction and/or sentence by the Tokyo Supreme Court (Motohashi 2012: 128). Nevertheless, the Tokyo Court of Appeals upheld the original verdicts, finding the five defendants guilty, and each of them had to pay a penalty of ¥500,000 (US$4,400) (Sonoda and Dai 2016: 103).

The intervention of the police force, we suggest, represents what Victor Turner called redressive action that 'limit[s] the spread of crisis' (Turner 1974: 39) by taking Biderin to court. Conviction by the Tokyo Supreme Court, upheld subsequently by the Tokyo Court of Appeals, defeated Biderin totally and more importantly ended the dominant cleavage, if not antagonism, between the Big Five AV manufacturers and Soft On Demand and its followers.

The new 'censoring' body: Eizōrin

The sudden collapse of Biderin, however, ushered pure chaos into the Japanese AV industry. To bring order out of chaos, former adult video makers-cum-members of

Biderin founded a new association called the Nihon Eizō Rinri Shinsa Kikō (a.k.a. Nichieishin, Japan Image Ethics Association) in June 2008 to manage the screening of their adult videos. In July 2008, Nichieishin made a formal announcement that it would transfer its screening service to the above-mentioned Inspection Centre co-founded by CSA, Biderin and other self-regulatory associations in 2006, following the advice of the Kanto Bureau of Economy, Trade and Industry. In December 2010, Nichieishin formally merged with CSA to form a new association called Eizōrin, and all future screening services of adult videos was to be provided by the new inspection centre, now integrated under Eizōrin.

This is akin to the final phase of a social drama: reintegration. Turner explained the phase of reintegration in the context of Ndembu, a tribe in Africa where he conducted his famous fieldwork:

> The final phase I distinguished consists either of the reintegration of the disturbed social group or of the social recognition and legitimation of irreparable schism between the contesting parties – in the case of the Ndembu this often meant the secession of one section of a village from the rest. It frequently happened then after an interval of several years, one of the villages so formed would sponsor a major ritual to which member of the other would be expressly invited, thus registering reconciliation at a different level of political integration.
>
> (Turner 1974: 41)

In the context of the regulatory practices of the Japanese AV industry, the phase of reintegration is expressed by Nichieishin (the former Biderin) being integrated into Eizōrin, a new regulatory body formed by both the Big Five AV makers and the indie AV makers headed by Soft On Demand.

Following Turner's suggestion (1974: 42) that '[f]rom the point of view of the scientific observer the fourth phase – that of temporary climax, solution, or outcome – is an opportunity for taking stock', we can now analyse what has been changed and more importantly what has not been changed following this social drama. The first major change is obviously the power structure of the industry. As mentioned in Chapter 3, the Big Five AV manufacturers had been dominating the production, circulation and regulation of AVs in Japan since the 1980s by imposing a set of 'standard' practices on other AV makers, model agencies, wholesalers and rental shops; they also interfered with the content of AVs and excluded rivalries through their control of Biderin. After the social drama, the Big Five could no longer maintain their domination over the industry, which further triggered many other changes in the production, circulation and regulation of AVs in Japan. This brings us to the second major change: the circulation method. As mentioned in Chapter 3, the traditional way of circulating AVs was through rental shops. The establishment of Medirin, however, made AVs-for sale possible, and this has since become one of the major circulation methods in the market.

Third, the emergence of AVs-for-sale gave fresh impetus to those who had been interested in AV production, but hesitated to get involved due to the dominance of Biderin and the strict regulations imposed by that organization (Nakamura 2012: 133). When the display of pubic hair and anuses, and the use of a thinner mosaic screen were allowed in 1997, many AV makers specializing in maniac tastes or bizarre desires sprang up in Tokyo (Nakamura 2012: 133). Such specializations by these AV makers obviously had an important bearing on the adult videos they produced. The AVs-for-sale resulting from the makers' specialization in maniac taste can be in many ways seen as an expansion of *kikaku* AVs. This further contributed to the dominant position of *kikaku* AVs in the industry. Fourth, the Big Five AV makers could no longer levy their influence on the industry through their control of Biderin once Nichieishin (the former Biderin) was absorbed into the new Eizōrin.

The final major change is how the new Eizōrin operates, itself fundamentally related to the nature of Eizōrin as a self-regulatory body. Recall that Eizōrin, while appearing to be rather new since it was founded in 2010, was actually restructured from CSA (Medirin) first founded in 1996. As mentioned in Chapter 3, Biderin was eager to position itself as *the* 'censoring' body. Although CSA was wary of being prosecuted due to its inferior status vis-à-vis Biderin, nothing really happened after its founding in 1996. Nevertheless, the legal prosecutions encountered by Biderin in 2007 greatly alarmed CSA of the possibility of being arrested, and most importantly laid bare its status of permanent liminality.

As famously formulated by Victor Turner (1967: 47; 1969: 94–5), liminality refers to the quality of ambiguity or disorientation that occurs in the middle stages of rituals. Eizōrin as a self-regulatory 'censoring' body bears a striking similarity to ritual in the sense that it underwent a transition characterized first by a separation (from other self-regulatory bodies in the AV industry), then by a phase of ambiguity and disorientation which was neither this nor that, and finally by an aggregation. More importantly, as Szakolczai reminds us, in many real-world liminal situations, the liminality is not merely a temporary condition but rendered permanent (Szakolczai 2000: 211). This happens when any of the three phases 'becomes frozen, as if a film stopped at a particular frame' (Szakolczai 2000: 212). Eizōrin here has faced a similar dilemma. In the aftermath of the police's raid on Biderin in 2007, the whole adult video industry was enveloped in the darkness of uncertainty and despair. Restructured from Medirin and founded in 2010 to take over all the screening of adult videos provided by Biderin, Eizōrin has been preoccupied with a singular aim: how to stay afloat without being arrested by the police. To do so, it was no surprise that it strived for legitimacy by becoming a state-recognized agency, as we can see from its concerted effort to gain an METI award for its contribution to the protection of IPRs (mentioned above). Nevertheless, in the process of attempting to transform itself into a state-recognized body through various means, it gradually found itself stuck in the middle phase, without being able to arrive at the final phase of aggregation: that is to say, by becoming a truly state-recognized organization.

This failure can be accounted for by a number of factors, the most obvious of which is that the Japanese government does not recognize Eizōrin as a state-run regulatory agency, lest it violates the freedom of speech incorporated in the Japanese constitution in 1947. As a result, Eizōrin has been left in a situation of liminality, regardless of what kind of governmental recognition or qualification it has acquired. The formal arrest of even the quasi state body of Biderin in 2007 was the final wake-up call for CSA since it became clear that CSA could not exempt itself from such a fate. Having said that, it does not necessarily mean that it is totally impossible for Eizōrin to get rid of this liminality.

In developing the concept of liminality into a proper conceptual tool, Szakolczai argues that the final phase of liminality should be rephrased from an 'aggregation' to a search for a new order. As he remarks,

> In the case of real world liminality, the previously taken-for-granted order of things has actually collapsed. It cannot therefore simply be restored. This means that the central task in a real-world large-scale liminal situation is an actual search for order, with all the existential anxiety this entails.
> (Szakolczai 2000: 210)

One can see that what follows the phase of ambiguity and disorientation can never be a restoration of the previous, but a search for a new, order. The following quote is from Mr Omoiatanarai,[5] a senior member of CSA as well as of the current Eizōrin, who clearly indicated his intention to achieve a new order: 'The current inspection of Japanese adult videos is chaotic. There are lots of things we need to change, change, change and change.... Otherwise, we cannot move on.' To impose a new order is indeed to achieve an authority of another kind. But how?

> I always feel that, since we are a self-regulating organization, therefore we need to have higher standards than legal regulations with regard to *morality* and *ethics*. Given this, I believe that I have to run the Centre according to an even higher level of moral and ethical standards.
> (Interview with Omoiatanarai; italics ours)

In unpublished material written by Omoiatanarai, he further explains what he means by moral and ethics within the industry:

> The central foundation that supports the capitalist economy is ethics, and our mission is to establish an ethics and enlighten people within the industry. When Ogura Masao, the founder of Yamato Transport, made a speech, he quoted from Max Weber's *The Protestant Ethic and the Spirit of Capitalism*, 'The interactional relationship between demand and supply is certainly the principle of capitalism, but what is more important is the ethics that lays the very foundation for everything ... I believe that it is of paramount importance to have ethics in industry.' In addition, he said, 'Of

course the balance between demand and supply is something that we usually cannot ignore under the great influence of the capitalist economy, but the most important thing is still ethics. At the centre of society or industry, there should lie ethics…'. From this we can see that he believed that ethics is of extra importance to every single industry, and an industry that ignores ethics will soon be excluded. It is especially true in our industry circle, and it will be really difficult for us to move on if we are not conscious of ethics. Therefore, we believe that Eizōrin has to play a very important role in establishing a set of ethical ideas and in enlightening the people within the industry.

(Omoiatanarai n.d.)

As we can see, Eizōrin under Omoiatanarai has attempted to build a new order by taking the moral high ground over the regulation of adult videos. This moral high ground refers to the status of being respected for remaining moral, and adhering to and upholding a universally recognized standard of justice and goodness. Since 2010, Omoiatanarai has pursued the ethicization through a series of reform that, as we shall see, speak to several key notions: namely, neutrality, fairness and social reflectivity/representativeness.

Neutrality

One of the major reforms was to emphasize neutrality, the so-called 'third person status'[6] of the body. The third person status was reflected in a number of ways. First of all, the current Eizōrin's Board of Directors was no longer made up of major adult video makers but outsiders. Eizōrin had from the outset strived to maintain its neutral status by forbidding its members to sit on the Board, so that its policies would not be coloured or affected by them. To heighten its neutrality, Eizōrin recruited its Board members from outside – scholars, professionals and experts from a wide range of fields[7] across the country – to create the impression that Eizōrin is a neutral-cum-professional screening body that does not have any direct relation with AV makers or the Japanese government.

The third person status can also be seen in the fact that Eizōrin ceased the practice of taking in OBs from the police force. As mentioned in Chapter 3, Biderin had a long history of hiring retired police officers to work in its Administrative Office. While the presence of former police might provide certain conveniences and advantages, Eizōrin refused to do so, not only because it blurred the relationship between the Japanese Police and itself, but also because it put itself at great risk, as Eizōrin might be accused of receiving favours from the police.

Neutrality has also been secured by revising the recruitment method of inspectors. In contrast to Biderin whose inspectors were recommended by, and hence were close to, the Board members and their companies, Eizōrin has chosen to openly recruit its inspectors. According to our research, all inspectors are required to declare no conflict of interest with any AV makers before taking up the job. All of this is to convey a message to both makers and participants in the

AV world that Eizōrin, unlike Biderin, is not an instrument for profit making, or a body to be manoeuvred by AV makers or police, but a neutral and professional body aiming to uphold *waisetsu* laws.

Fairness

Closely related to neutrality is the significance placed on fairness, equality and transparency of the body. There are at least two major measures designed to uphold fairness. First, Eizōrin set up an Advisory Board, inviting a number of external Japanese scholars, experts and practitioners from the fields of law, Japanese constitution, art, film and feminism to sit on its Advisory Board, in order to provide professional advice, comments and suggestions at critical moments. There are also regular meetings and discussion forums between the Advisory Members and the Board to review current inspection criteria and procedures to ensure the fair and effective operation of the body.

In view of the fact that Biderin was accused of being partial to its core members, Eizōrin has for the first time introduced a systematic and transparent inspection procedure. It gives all its members a manual laying out clearly how the inspection process proceeds and how fairness and equality are ensured in the process. In contrast to Biderin's practice, every adult movie is to be reviewed by two randomly appointed inspectors *separately*. More importantly, no representative from an AV maker is allowed to be present at the inspection. Together with a better environment, including individual headsets, inspectors at Eizōrin are now given more privacy and space in reviewing the movie without any pressure from a co-inspector or maker-representative. After the review, their reports are passed to a third inspector to further ensure fairness. The latter crosschecks their reports and serves as the final arbitrator if the inspection reports of the first two inspectors contradict each other.

If a contradiction cannot be settled by the third inspector, it will be passed to the monthly Meeting of Inspection Verification (Shinsa Kenshō Kaigi) attended by a group of inspectors who discuss the issues concerned. If, in any case, the issue of contradiction remains unresolved, then it is further passed to the Committee of Third Person Inspection Verification (Shinsa Kenshō Daisansha Iinkai) where an *external* inspection officer will attend and serve as an arbitrator of unsolved issues (see Figure 8.1). Unlike the Shinsa Kenshō Kaigi, this committee does not hold regular meetings. Meetings are only called for when extraordinarily important or knotty issues arise.

Representativeness of inspectors

Another important area to which Eizōrin has paid extra attention is whether its team of inspectors can accurately represent the social attitudes of people in the wider society. As mentioned above, Eizōrin has chosen to openly recruit its inspectors rather than allow the Board to appoint them. However, the neutrality of the inspectors is not enough. Eizōrin has aimed for something higher: that is,

The 'censorship' of Japanese adult videos 197

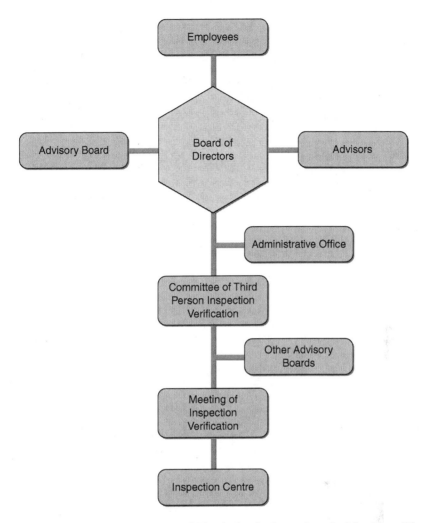

Figure 8.1 The internal structure of Eizōrin for the inspection of adult videos (Eizōrin 2011: 1).

whether the member profile of its inspectors is large and diverse enough to represent the different views and attitudes held in the larger society. To this end, Eizōrin has first substantially increased the number of its inspectors from just ten to 15 in the 1990s, to 35 in 2012, and further to 60 in 2015 (personal communication with Omoiatanarai). More importantly, Eizōrin emphasizes that their inspectors should include both sexes of all ages, and come from all walks of life, in order to better represent society at large.

According to our own research in 2012 and 2015, among the 35 inspectors in 2012, surprisingly more than half of them were indeed female. Many of these women were fairly young, aged between 24 and 35. Most were single, and the rest were wives or mothers. Many women in the latter group made use of their spare times in the afternoon to work as part-time inspectors. They had all worked in diverse fields before joining Eizōrin. Some had joined simply out of curiosity, while others just thought that it was a job. Indeed, this represents a big step forward as Biderin had never thought of hiring a female to be an adult video inspector. This can be clearly seen in the interview between Uehara, the Head of Administrative Office and Adachi in 1991. In the interview, Adachi asked if Uehara would hire women as inspectors. Uehara was quoted as saying:

> It is impossible, isn't it? I don't think women can tolerate the current situation [referring to all the men's environment and the fact that the office was always filled with women's groans and moans as headphones were unavailable in those days, thus sound would be played out from the speakers directly]. This might happen many years from now. But I think that as we are dealing with the adult market; it is fine to provide some 'hardcore' things to consumers ... it is the trend all over the world [so I don't think women can accept it].
>
> (Adachi 1995: 293)

One can see that Eizōrin's decision to hire women as inspectors was a breakthrough in the history of adult video inspection in Japan because for the first time it was willing to incorporate the views of 'women' (both single and married), a group making up half the population of Japan, in its inspection process. As a whole, the substantial increase in the number of inspectors and emphasis on their diverse backgrounds are clearly meant to turn Eizōrin into an organization that is the epitome of the larger Japanese society.

Eizōrin has also had a policy of making decisions based on consensus among inspectors to ensure that the final decision is not dictated by one single opinion backed up by a simple majority vote, because there are many occasions in which the simple majority could just be a bare one. According to our research at Eizōrin, in most decision-making processes, relevant members will be summoned to engage in a dialogue, during which they can express and exchange views on the issues with an aim to reach a consensus among themselves about what the conclusion should be. One important implication of this mode of consensus building is that minority rights and opinions are heard and served, although the process might take a much longer time than the majority rule. As the majority cannot dominate and because minority ideas are respected, this mode of decision-making is meant to better reflect the general attitude toward pornography of the wider Japanese society. We argue that the actual implementation of the above-mentioned reforms is perhaps best seen in an ethnographic context. At this point, we shall make a radical jump in setting to Eizōrin's office where the AV inspection is carried out.

One day in Eizōrin's office

In the early morning in the summer 2012, we arrive at Eizōrin's office in central Tokyo. We are there to undertake a two-week-long internship as part of our ethnographic research.[8] The office is spacious, with approximately 150 square metres. As of 2012, it had 36 staff members and of whom 32 were hired as inspectors (*shinsain*). In our last visit in 2015, the number of its inspectors had reached 60.

Soon after we arrive, we are given a brief office tour. The office is partitioned into three different areas: a huge meeting room, an Administrative Office and an area exclusively devoted to inspection. The whole office has three entrances: one directly leads to the meeting room, while the other two lead to the Administrative Office. These two entrances are equipped with a security card system and hence only staff members with a valid staff card can have access. The inspection area, which is located at the farthest end, does not have a separate entrance as it is linked directly to the Administrative Office.

The inspection area itself is further divided into two parts, alongside two conference rooms. One is for the inspection of adult videos, and the other for video games. Thirty booths separated by partitions are lined up for the inspection of adult videos. At each booth, an office chair faces a desk with headphones, controls and a PC. Each of the inspectors reviews the sample videos there.

At 9:30 am, we are all seated in one of the conference rooms. On the one side of the conference desk are the interns, with senior members sitting on the other side. The director greets us with a brief instruction. We are then led to the Administrative Office to be introduced to all the staff. Soon after, we return to the conference room. A staff member, our instructor on that day, then comes in. He is here to brief us on the office environment, work culture and job nature of inspectors and the procedure of how to do video screening. We are told that office hours are from 10 am to 6 pm during which each of the inspectors will have to screen (hence watch) 360 minutes of sample video. Calculated according to the current format of adult videos, 360 minutes of sample video are equal to three whole adult videos. According to our instructor, the reason for this arrangement is that 360 minutes is considered the maximum length of time that can be tolerated by a person's physical body and concentration. We are repeatedly reminded that the main duty of each inspector is to ensure that no genital area, alongside other forbidden items, is shown in the videos. Thus, what inspectors have to do during the screening is to focus on the genital parts, especially during the middle of sexual intercourse, and ensure that the mosaics placed are 'thick' and 'big' enough to cover the genital parts properly. We are told to pay careful attention to the genital areas, especially the working parts, and mark everything that is problematic. For instance, if the mosaic is too thin, we can mark it as *mo usui* (*mo* meaning 'mosaic' and *usui* meaning 'thin'); if the mosaic is not properly covering the genital areas, we can put down *mo hazure* (meaning 'out of place') or *mo more* (meaning 'leaking out') and so on.

Actual Shinsa processes

After all the briefing, we are then led to an individual booth to start our own screening of adult videos. We are given a mobile hard drive which contains the data of the movie (Figure 8.2) and are told to screen it in as much detail as we can. Before we start to screen the movie, we have to fill in the following inspection form including the name of the inspector, the inspector's number, the title of the video being inspected, the media format of the video, the length of the video being inspected, booth number, inspection time, and so on (Figure 8.3).

Figure 8.2 The PC, screen, headphone and mobile hard drive for screening.

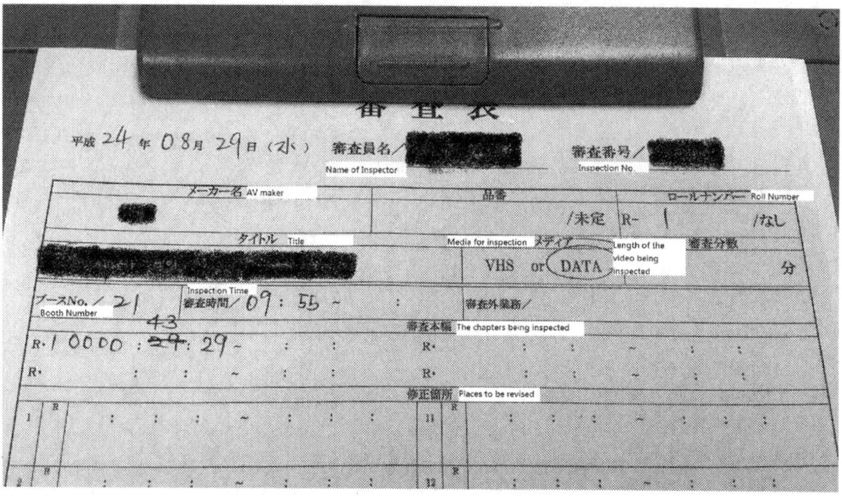

Figure 8.3 The inspection form.

As we are all amateurs, we cannot but go back and forth to check if the genitalia are properly covered or airbrushed as required. We have to stress that this exercise is extremely physically demanding and time-consuming, in the sense that the image is all over in a moment. It therefore requires intense concentration and focus. By lunch time, we have barely managed to finish screening the movie and submit our reports to the instructor. After lunch, we re-watch the video together to see if we have managed to spot all the problems and hence what kind of problems we have missed out in our screening.

In this meeting, what surprises us is that not only are our reports different from one another, but our reports *greatly* differ from the official, or so-called 'correct', report. Certainly, as amateurs, we have unavoidably overlooked problematic places such as *mo more* or *mo hazure*. We are also not sensitive enough to spot places that might be considered evidence of illegally using images of certain brands. On the other hand, there are a few cases where we mark certain places as problematic (for instance, the mosaic was too thin, or too small) when they are instead considered to be 'fine' and hence 'acceptable' in the official report. Together with the other participants, we find it extremely difficult, if not totally impossible, to draw the line between what is considered acceptable and what not.

This difficulty is especially acute when it comes to the screening of the DVD inserts. It is of crucial importance to note that, apart from the movie content, the movie title, telop (superimposition)[9] and DVD inserts have to be inspected, too. This inspection is usually carried out by a different group of inspectors so as to avoid the possibility of lack of impartiality in judgement resulting from the same set of inspectors. That afternoon, therefore, we are scheduled to receive training in screening DVD inserts and movie titles. We are given a set of DVD inserts and asked to examine the titles and the pictures printed on both the front and back of the inserts. This task is no less easy as the pictures printed on the inserts, especially on the back of them, are typically small (Figure 8.4). As soon as we finish marking all the 'problems', the instructor reveals the 'correct' answers. Once again, while we overlook some problems, we mark other pictures as 'problematic', when in fact they are considered 'fine' and hence 'acceptable'. We are particularly confused as to why what seems like an extremely similar treatment of mosaic is considered 'fine' in one case but not in the other. We are still perplexed, even though the instructor provides explanations, if not justifications, for each of the cases – about why it is acceptable in one case and not acceptable in another – because their treatment of the mosaic appears to be, at least in our eyes, *not* so different from each other.

In view of our confusion, frustration even, the instructor attempts to comfort us, suggesting that it is not impossible for us to acquire the screening skills and that the more we watch the videos and discuss them with other colleagues, the better we will become and hence the more similar judgements we can achieve when compared with other inspectors.

Two important implications can be drawn here. First, although the line between something acceptable and unacceptable is 'subjective' and seems to

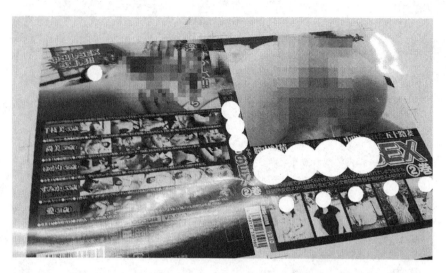

Figure 8.4 One of the DVD inserts distributed to us for examination.

lack clearly defined parameters, there *is* such a fine line and hence difference, which is repeatedly emphasized by the instructor, as well as by other inspectors. Indeed, the ambiguity of this line bears a striking similarity to pornography, which, as famously described by Justice Potter Stewart, is something which 'I know it when I see it'. Second, it implies that consensus in the field of self-regulation of adult video at Eizōrin is of paramount importance and that consensus, as a collective judgement, can be achieved through intensive discussion about, if not debate over, the issue among inspectors.

Consensus building and ad hoc decision-making

The consensus-based decision-making process is all the more difficult and time-consuming, especially when all relevant inspectors are usually asked to participate in it. As we have seen from our ethnographic fieldwork, each of the interns did have different judgements, which were also different from those of the official report. Thus one major problem facing the inspectors at Eizōrin is how to achieve, or indeed build, consensus. As we have seen in the above ethnographic account, consensus within the agency was by and large built through intensive discussion among inspectors. Typically, inspectors in Eizōrin had to participate in a wide range of meetings as part of their daily routine. But these meetings also provided a perfect occasion for them to discuss issues among themselves. According to our ethnographic research, participants in these meetings were usually invited to express their own ideas or comments first. Then, a senior member-cum-inspector would intervene and frame his or her comments in line with Eizōrin's ethics and ideologies. Very often, these comments would develop into lectures about the importance of ethics and morality within the adult video industry. We were not in a position to judge how effective these lectures were among the participants, not all of whom were easily and immediately convinced. Nevertheless, these lectures were likely supported by the veteran staff who would repeatedly rehearse them in other meetings, which were the very routine of their office work. Seen in this light, it is not incorrect to say that these meetings were the perfect platform for the inspectors to discuss all the controversies about a certain AV among themselves, thereby paving the way for an ultimate complete consensus.

Perhaps what is more significant here is that the consensus or collective decision over a given scene or sex act is after all based on an ad hoc, if not totally arbitrary, interpretation of such a scene or sex act; and if it is just one possible reading of a given scene or sex act, it is, to paraphrase Sahlins' wording, an interpretation which is never the only one possible. Extra effort, therefore, is required to convince the maker concerned, in the course of which a number of additional criteria with regard to the inspection of adult videos is created and subsequently legitimized as *the* 'rules', after being repeatedly applied to other AVs. These in turn have a profound impact on how Japanese adult videos are produced. In this regard, the minutes (*gijiroku*) of the Meetings of Inspection Verification held at Eizōrin to deal with problematic cases[10] are very illustrative.

The problematic cases

The minutes we collected here dated from November 2009 to June 2012, totalling 84 controversial cases. Studying them, one can see that the so-called problematic cases can be divided into four major categories: namely, the violation of social/moral norms, the portrayal of violence, the portrayal of underage/real characters and the portrayal of male/female sex organs.

The first thing that would alarm Eizōrin is certainly the portrayal of male/female sex organs, which has 20 instances out of the total 84 cases. An interesting case in point is a *kikaku* movie from a small AV maker in which the use of a vagina-shaped sex toy was depicted. At the initial screening, both the inspectors raised the issue that the sex toy was too genuine to the extent that it looked like a 'real' female vagina. The third inspector also agreed on the 'realness' of the sex toy, but he was not sure whether it was acceptable or not. The issue was thus brought to the monthly Inspection Verification meeting. The minutes stated that since the shape of vagina appeared to be *more* obscene than that of a penis, the depiction of a vagina-shaped sex toy would be more susceptible to prosecution for disregard of obscenity laws than that of the penis-shaped sex toy. In view of this, Eizōrin required the AV maker to modify the sex toy so that it would *not* look like a real vagina and stipulated that, if the sex toy was to be placed near the lower part of the female character, it had to be pixelated to avoid violating the obscenity laws. To further support the committee's judgement, the minutes concluded that Eizōrin had a long tradition of being stringent with regard to the representation of female sex organs, as there was a similar case where a fake vagina made up of vegetables was portrayed in the past and Eizōrin did not pass it on account of its perceived obscenity.

Eizōrin's concern is not only about upholding obscenity laws but also preserving social morality. This was reflected in the category of the 'violation of social/moral norm', with 24 instances out of the total of 84 cases. In this regard, the following case is very illustrative. An adult video of a small AV maker containing scenes where the background characters were shown using drugs was sent to Eizōrin for screening. During the screening, these scenes were highlighted by the two inspectors as 'problematic', although one of the inspectors appeared to be more lax, suggesting that it was only the background characters using drugs. After some discussion and meetings, the third arbitrator concluded without any hesitation that these scenes were 'problematic' – even though it was the background rather than the main characters who were portrayed using drugs – because drug use was clearly portrayed in the movie. According to the minutes, the portrayal of drugs and/or the use of drugs were strictly forbidden by Eizōrin. The reason given in the minutes was that use of drugs was illegal in Japan; it followed that the portrayal of the use of drugs in adult videos was therefore illegal. Eizōrin then sent a formal report, requesting that the AV maker erase those scenes in order to pass the inspection.

Another related case was about an adult video portraying the use of a syringe. After screening the film, Eizōrin informed the AV maker that revisions were required before the video could be given certification. According to the minutes, while the use of a syringe itself was not illegal, the portrayal of this was disallowed by Eizōrin because in Japan only licensed nurses could operate one. Ordinary people without relevant training were not allowed to carry out injections using a syringe.

The third category concerns 'the portrayal of violence' in the movie, which constituted 21 instances out of the 84 cases. A video featuring S&M produced by a major AV maker is illustrative of this issue. This adult video raised exceptional concern because all three inspectors agreed that the beating and spanking of the female character featured in the video was not acting and that the bruises and cuts all over her buttocks and back were real. Eizōrin called for a special meeting with the Advisory Board to decide whether the bruises were real and how far these scenes had to be revised. After the meeting, the Board concluded that the S&M role-play portrayed in the movie had crossed the line and it finally informed the maker that the scenes featuring the beating and spanking had to be removed in order to pass Eizōrin's screening.

Eizōrin's final major concern lies in the portrayal of underage/real characters. A case in point is an ordinary DVD insert in a Japanese adult video featuring sexual molesters on a train. While ordinary as it might be, the insert raised a heated debate among the inspectors in Eizōrin because it portrayed three male characters wearing yellow student caps commonly worn by Japanese elementary school students. Notwithstanding the fact that the male characters were obviously adults rather than elementary school students, the use of the yellow student cap was still thought to be highly 'problematic': a yellow cap conjured up an image, or gave audiences the wrong impression that these male characters were underage children. Eizōrin thus requested that the maker revise the movie. However, the latter insisted in response that the use of the yellow cap was just a trope, as readers would immediately realize from the faces of the male characters. In the end, Eizōrin explained to the maker concerned that the use of the yellow cap on the adult video cover might arouse resentment from the PTA, causing them to react against adult videos as a whole. In the end, the maker withdrew its complaint and revised the cover.

Another interesting case is about a DVD insert featuring the high school girl theme that was sent to Eizōrin for screening. As usual, the actress portrayed on the cover jacket was young, cute, sweet and innocent. While the two inspectors passed it, the third inspector considered this 'problematic' because a large character print of '138 cm' was put right behind her on the DVD insert cover to indicate that the height of the actress was only 138 cm. The previous two inspectors passed it because a note was put at the bottom of the insert suggesting that the actress was over 18 years old. However, the third inspector argued that the phrase of '138 cm' might mislead readers into thinking that she was a *real* high school girl and therefore underage. This issue was brought to the Third Person Board of Inspection Verification. After some consideration, the Board concluded that the cover was problematic as it might lead to a misunderstanding that a real high school girl was performing in an adult video, which was and is illegal. Eizōrin then requested the AV maker to remove the phrase '138 cm'.

A similar case concerns the title of a *tantai* movie that clearly indicated that the actress was a former idol with her stage name printed. As the reports of the two initial inspectors contradicted each other, this case was bought to the third inspector and finally to the Inspection Verification meeting. According to the minutes, Eizōrin concluded that it was inappropriate to reveal the true identity of the actress, especially in view of the fact that the AV maker had not received permission to do so from the model company to which the actress previously belonged. Eizōrin thus required the AV maker to remove her stage name from the cover and insisted that certain pixilation had to be applied to her face in the cover.

We can see from the above cases that the inspection conducted by Eizōrin is not just about whether an AV violates the obscenity laws but more importantly about some morally charged acts taking place in the AVs. For instance, in the above cases, the concerns shown about those scenes featuring 'background characters who were using drugs', 'spanking and beating', 'the use of phrase of 138 cm' and the (illegal/inappropriate) use of syringe' – concerns that have nothing to do with obscenity laws but about the preservation of social morality, drug use, violence, and so on – should not normally be considered part of the official duties of Eizōrin. We argue that this is related to Eizōrin's ethics policy. As mentioned above, Eizōrin under Omoiatanarai was attempting to build a new order by adopting the moral high ground in the regulation of adult videos. Under the aegis of this moral high ground, the scene that showed ordinary people operating a syringe had to be cut because ordinary people are legally forbidden from operating syringes; the phrase alluding to a height of 138 cm also had to be removed because it would lead the audience to think (incorrectly) that a real high school girl was performing; and the portrayal of yellow caps in the AV also had to be taken away because it would give a wrong impression that underage children did participate in the movie, even though obviously it was adult male characters who were wearing the caps.

Central to the attempt of Eizōrin to establish a moral high ground over the regulation of adult videos is the reliance of external power or what we might call the 'externalization' of Eizōrin. Here, the external power manifests itself at two different levels. At one level, all inspectors are outsiders, recruited externally rather than appointed from within the industry. As mentioned above, new inspectors are required to declare their absence of conflict of interest to ensure that every inspector will exercise their impartial judgement in the screening of adult videos. The same is also true for Board members, Advisory Board members, and advisors, who are all recruited externally. But external power also manifests itself at the level of the actual inspection process. Recall that every single adult video has to be reviewed by two inspectors and that a third (truly a third person) inspector will become involved to see if there is any problem, especially when their reports contradict each other. In case of any serious conflicts between the reports or dispute over certain problematic scenes, the issue will then be *externalized* first to the monthly Meeting of Inspection Verification, and then to the Committee of Third Person Inspection Verification for final judgement.

If inspectors, Board members, Advisory Board members, and advisors are all recruited *externally* and the process of inspection itself is likewise *externalized*, it is not too much to say that what are being externalized are the 'decision-makers' and 'the process of decision-making'. It is by externalizing the 'decision-makers' and the process of decision-making that Eizōrin aims to settle internal conflicts or disagreements and establish legitimacy within the adult video industry by taking the moral high ground.

Indeed, Eizōrin has managed to establish itself as one of the most 'prestigious' and 'credible' self-regulatory agencies within the Japanese AV industry since its inception in 2010. According to internal data we received from Omoiatanarai, the number of AV titles submitted to Eizōrin for inspection reached almost 9,000 in 2011 – just one year after it was founded. The prominence of, and prestige enjoyed by, Eizōrin can be further seen in terms of the market share of the major self-regulatory agencies. Presently, there are six major self-regulatory agencies specializing in the regulation and inspection of adult videos, namely Eizōrin, Visual Software Contents Industry Coop (VSIC), Japan Video Produce and Sell (JVPS), All Japan Video Shinsa (AJVS), East Japan Contents Soft (EJCS) and Association of Computer Software Ethics (Sofurin). According to internal data provided by Omoiatanarai, Eizōrin has captured 60 to 70 per cent of the market share in the AV field.

But why have external powers or the externalization of decision-makers and the process of decision-making worked and why do they continue to work? Here, we are going to propose a very strange, if not totally bizarre, argument: that

Sahlins' idea of alterity of power in general, and stranger-king in particular, are remarkably illustrative in explicating Eizōrin's strategies.

In his analysis of Austronesian societies, Sahlins delved into the alterity of power. Inspired by Firth's brilliant ethnography of the Tikopia where the locals ascribed tremendous powers to the missionaries, other foreigners and the leading chiefs of overseas origins, Sahlins argued that similar phenomena can be widely found in Austronesian and numerous other societies all over the world.[11] While the indigenous people claim precedence over the land as its 'owners', bestowed with the right of first occupancy, they nonetheless do not enthrone any natives to be their ruler but choose to subsume themselves to foreign rulers: hence the universal reliance of human beings on exteriority. Indeed, this reliance on exteriority has a lot to do with the generic predicament of the human condition. To explain this, allow us to include a long quotation from Sahlins:

> I take Viveiros de Castro's points that, 'If human beings are immortal, perhaps society would be confounded with the cosmos. Since death exists, it is necessary for society to be linked with something that is outside itself – and that it be linked *socially* to this exterior' (1992: 190–91). Ranging from beasts, spirits, and gods to ineffable forces, by the way of the generic dead or the ancestors, and of other peoples with their remarkable gifts, the extraordinary agents that control the human fate live outside the space of human control ... I take the rather positivist and Malinowskian view that people must in reality depend for their existence on external conditions not of their own making – hence and whence the spirits.... If people really were in control of their own existence, they would not die.... Or, notably, the other peoples of their ken: peoples whose cultural existence may be enviable or scandalous to them. But in either case, by the very difference from themselves, ken are strangers who thus offer proof of a transcendent capacity for life. It is as if nothing foreign were merely human to them. Endowed with transcendental powers of life and death, the foreign becomes an ambiguous object of desire and danger. Hence the ubiquity – and ambiguity – of the aforementioned stranger-king formations.
> (Sahlins 2012: 139–40; italics in original)

Here, we can see that the capacity of external powers – the so-called third person status including lawyers, scholars, feminists and laymen inspectors – employed by Eizōrin in establishing the moral high ground over the regulation of Japanese AVs bears a striking similarity to the power of the immigrant chiefs in trumping the native people's rights by transgressive demonstrations of superior might. Not unlike the immigrant kings, outsiders – including lawyers, feminists, scholars and laymen inspectors in our case – can work to resolve internal conflicts and disagreements because of their ambiguous and stranger nature which offers proof of a transcendental capacity. Endowed with transcendent power outside the industry, the outsiders here are not just objects of danger but also of desire, functioning to create order and hence prosperity in the chaotic situation of the adult video industry, particularly after the arrest of the members of Biderin in 2008.

This argument will become more convincing if we take into account the fact that Eizōrin, not unlike its counterparts, is nothing more than a non-governmental self-regulatory agency. If Eizōrin can beat its competitors and take 70 per cent of the market share, then it is not too much to say that the external status of its decision-makers and externalizing process of decision-making, not unlike the foreign and ambiguous nature of the stranger-kings, has conferred on Eizōrin a certain transcendental power and so allowed it to be recognized by the people within the industry.

Consequences for AV production

The obvious consequence for AV production is that AV makers have to pay close attention not just to the erotic scenes of their AVs but also to any scene that might be seen as offending the morality of society or harming the social good. Eizōrin's policy of ethicization, therefore, has further expanded its inspection criteria to cover anything that is considered harmful to the social morality of Japanese society – as we can see from the above cases of the use of yellow caps, terms such as 138 cm, a fake sex toy or a syringe, and so on that were all prohibited in the movies in which they appeared.

The second consequence concerns the authenticity of the problematic scenes in the above cases. We have to emphasize that the problematic in the above scenes lies at two different levels. The first concerns the authenticity of the actress, as illustrated in the above case in which Eizōrin ordered an AV maker not to reveal the true identity of the AV actress who was a former idol. Second, the authenticity of the story should also be avoided, as we can see from the inspectors' comments on a case mentioned above that the settings of the characters evoked the impression that 'real' underage or school girls participated, or that the acts themselves were 'real' and therefore problematic.

But why? There is a long tradition among censorship advocates in Japan that does not trust that readers/spectators can maintain a distance from the story and its characters in literature or films, which is also to say that readers/spectators might easily imitate the behaviour of such characters (Cather 2004: 38) and mimic the story in which they appear (Cather 2004: 167). This is why the courts in postwar Japan have tended to believe that obscenity in reality and its representation are one and the same, and that the latter can even be more harmful than the former. Obscenity in representation should therefore be policed. As Cather, quoting the prosecutor Iida in *In the Realm of the Senses (Ai no Korida*, the film directed by Oshima Nagisa) trial, wrote,

> What the Supreme Court calls the principle of the non-public nature of the sex act is not a principle that applies only to the actual sex act, but is a principle that we must recognize as applying also to the expression of the sex act in prose.... As for the expression of the sex act in prose, based on the way it is expressed, it has a psychological effect on viewers (*miru mono*) that is either equal or greater than if the actual sex act had occurred....

Based on the nature of prose, there is the danger that the effect will extend to an even wider sphere than the actual sex act....

(Cather 2004: 164)

Fully realizing this tradition, Eizōrin asked AV makers to find a way to indicate in their AVs that not only all the potentially problematic acts are just performance and thus not real, but also that the identities of the characters are fake so that they will not be prosecuted by the Police Force. By so doing spectators would not identify with the story, or with the characters in a story, and thus avoid imitation of the characters' behaviour.

But such de-authentication of an AV story and AV characters has a negative impact on *tantai* AVs. Recall that the gist of *tantai* AV production lies in the authenticity of the *tantai* AV actress, in the sense that both actress and female character are one and the same. Eizōrin's emphasis on the necessity of indicating the inauthenticity of the actress in AVs may jeopardize the sales of *tantai* AVs because it runs against the gist of *tantai* AVs: the authentication of the actress. We argue that this is another major reason for the recent decline in production of *tantai* AVs.

In contrast, Eizōrin's emphasis on the inauthenticity of both the AV actresses and the AV story has had a rather complicated impact on *kikaku* AVs. On the one hand, the inauthenticity of the AV actresses required by Eizōrin causes *kikaku* AV makers no problem because the major selling point of *kikaku* AVs, as we mentioned in Chapter 4, is the authenticity of the story and the character in the story that can best express the sexual domination of men over women, rather than the authenticity of the AV actresses which can best reveal women's lack of sexual agency in the case of *tantai* AVs.

On the other hand, *kikaku* AVs might suffer from Eizōrin's emphasis on the inauthenticity of the story because the major selling point of *kikaku* AVs, as we mentioned in Chapter 4, is the authentication of the story. Take the above case study of S&M as an example. While it was understood that the setting of the S&M scenario in the film was fake, the maker produced this S&M movie in a more realistic fashion in order to better appeal to audiences fond of this genre. In other words, the producer strived to produce authenticity in the story out of fakeness, whereas consumers acquired pleasure from a sense of authenticity out of a fake scenario. This thus raises an interesting issue as to the nature of movie authenticity, a topic we shall discuss in the conclusion to this book.

We are now clear that the logic of the inspection conducted by Eizōrin is the de-authentication of the story of, and the actress in, AVs. However, it has never tried to address the salvage ideology that underlines the production of both *tantai* and *kikkau* AVs with the excuse of protecting freedom of expression. It is of importance to note that during the internship we mentioned above, the director alongside our instructors took pride in emphasizing that Eizōrin would never inspect the 'content' of adult videos, for fear that it would violate the AV directors' freedom of expression. Eizōrin's adoption of such moral high grounding thus forecloses any discussions of the gender inequality depicted in the movies, no matter how sexist or misogynist they are, which is also to say that Eizōrin does not consider the biases against women embedded in AV ideology to be immoral and thus problematic. We argue that this has to do with the nature of Eizōrin as a self-regulated agency formed by the AV makers, because if it attempted to criticize the salvage ideology, the production of AVs would not be possible, which must also mean that the AV industry in Japan would not survive, let alone be profitable. More importantly, given the claim that Eizōrin is determined to uphold a moral high ground, those AVs that are endorsed by Eizōrin are seen as morally unproblematic. The general public is then led to believe that the salvage ideology is morally acceptable and it is in this way protected from being challenged or criticized by the general public. In the event, the gender politics *in* the formation of the sexual being of women and men in Japan mentioned in Chapter 7 cannot be openly discussed, criticized or challenged. This points to the final consequence of Eizōrin's inspection: the salvage ideology and the biases against women embedded in it is sustained by Eizōrin in postwar Japan.

Conclusion

Inspired by Victor Turner's idea of social drama and its temporary structure that consists of four phases – breach, crisis, redressive action and reintegration – we have told the story of how the regulatory system of the Japanese AV industry has gone through these four phases. The phase of breach started with the emergence of Medirin and other regulatory bodies that not only challenged the legitimacy of Biderin and the domination of the Big Five AV makers over small AV makers, wholesalers and retailers, but also revolutionized the norm about how Japanese AVs should be circulated and regulated in Japan; and how Japanese AVs were consumed and made sense.

The second phase of crisis was marked by Biderin's consent to reach an agreement with Medirin on inspection criteria and its subsequent relaxation of its own inspection criteria. Inasmuch as the consent and the relaxation themselves symbolized that Medirin had achieved the similar status as Biderin, which further implies the dominant cleavage between the Big Five AV makers and those indie AV makers headed by Takahashi and his Soft On Demand. That is to say, the power structure of the whole industry has changed from singular domination by the Big Five AV makers to a sharing of power between the Big Five AV makers and those indie makers headed by Takahashi and his Soft On Demand. At the same time, Medirin was renamed CSA.

The phase of crisis invited the Japanese Police Force to take redressive action. Biderin was taken to the Tokyo Supreme Court and later to the Tokyo Court of Appeals where it was convicted. This conviction totally defeated Biderin and more importantly ended the dominant cleavage, if not antagonism, between the Big Five AV makers and Soft On Demand and its followers.

Biderin was then dissolved and a new organization named Nichieishin was established by the former Biderin members. However, Nichieishin was soon absorbed and reintegrated into Eizōrin, a new regulatory body formed by CSA. This symbolized the arrival of the final phase: reintegration.

There have been many major changes in this last phase of reintegration, one of which is the way the new Eizōrin operates. We have shown that the new Eizōrin has devised a series of measures to promote itself as a neutral, fair and socially reflexive organization that can represent the views of the wider society on sexual morality. Our ethnography of the inspection process and the minutes of meetings we collected from Eizōrin reveal that the so-called problematic cases found in the inspection process are primarily concerned with the violation of social/moral norm, the portrayal of violence, the portrayal of underage/real characters and the portrayal of male/female sex organs. The major problem underlined in all these cases is the authenticity of a story and the characters in that story, because such pornographic realism might be interpreted as obscene by a court according to a long tradition among censorship advocates in Japan that does not distinguish between obscenity in reality and in its representation. Eizōrin therefore requests those AV makers at issue to de-authenticate their story and the characters in the story – a tactic which is believed to be able to prevent spectators from identifying with the story and the characters in the story.

Such requests have certainly had a bearing on the ways AV makers produce adult videos. For instance, AV makers may self-regulate themselves by avoiding the use of phrases such as 138 cm, the use of a syringe or yellow cap in their videos because they know that they may likely be picked up by Eizōrin. But the impact on the production of *tantai* AVs and *kikaku* AVs is different because their major selling points are different. *Tantai* AV makers have suffered most because the production of *tantai* AVs emphasizes the authenticity of AV actresses. The impact on *kikaku* AVs, however, is not that straightforward because, while Eizōrin's request for a de-authentication of the characters in a story does not affect their video production, the de-authentication of the story itself may cause trouble because the essence of *kikaku* AVs lies in the authenticity of their story.

More importantly, while Eizōrin has been very concerned about the pornographic realism of AVs in Japan since its inception, it has never tried to address the salvage ideology that underlines the production and consumption of AVs under the excuse of freedom of expression. As mentioned in Chapter 7, this failure to address the politics deeply rooted in the formation of the sexual being of men and women prevents the gender inequality embedded in the definition from being challenged and criticized. Any critique that focuses *only* on the pornographic depiction of how men oppress women in and/or through sex therefore can do nothing but perpetuate the gender inequality rooted in the formation of the sexual being of men and women. By the same token, Eizōrin's neglect in addressing the salvage ideology could ironically lead the general Japanese public to believe that the salvage ideology is not problematic, and maybe even acceptable. We can now see how the regulatory body can not only shape the production of the AV industry, but also sustain the salvage ideology that has been, and is still, lingering in Japan's AVs.

Finally, the development of the regulatory system of Japanese AVs seems to have little to do with moral and ideological issues concerning the content of AVs as pornography. What we have witnessed, however, is how the Big Five AV makers used Biderin to establish their domination over the industry; and how they as a cartel imposed a set of 'standard practices' on other AV makers, wholesalers and rental shops. We can also see how Soft On Demand and other indie AV makers as another cartel reacted to the domination of the Big Five AV makers by launching their own regulatory body, Medirin; and how the Japanese Police Force selectively cornered Biderin and took it to court, thereby ending the hegemony of the Big Five AV makers in the industry. The current major AV regulator, Eizōrin, is just a temporary compromise between the Big Five AV makers and the indie AV makers. In other words, the development of the regulatory system of Japanese AVs is not the result of a debate about the moral and ideological issues concerning AVs. Rather, it reveals the power struggle between the two camps over the control of the industry through the regulatory system. Our intent in adopting Turner's idea of social drama and its temporary structure was to highlight the interests, motivations and strategies of the major players involved in this power struggle as the social drama unfolds itself.

Notes

1 As mentioned before, the full name is Nippon Bideo Rinri Kyōkai, Nihon Ethics Video Association.
2 As mentioned before, the full name is Media Rinri Kyōkai, Medirin Media Ethics Association.
3 As mentioned before, the full name is Eizō Rinri Kyōkai, Image Ethics Association, which first emerged as Inspection Centre and was later incorporated under Eizōrin.
4 For instance, Japan Ethics Inspection Association (Nihon Rinri Shinsa Kyokai), All Japan Video Society (Zennihon Eizō Rinri Shinsa Iinkai 2002), and Japan Visual Produce Sell (2005).
5 One of the authors conducted ethnographic fieldwork at Eizōrin in the summer of 2012 and 2015.
6 We have to emphasize that 'third person status' is the single most important rhetoric of Eizōrin that Omoiatanarai repeatedly stressed all through our research interactions.
7 For instance, there are a scholar-cum-lawyer, a lecturer in communication, a lecturer media sociology, and so on (Eizōrin 2011: 3).
8 Apart from us, there were another three intern participants who were in the final years of the undergraduate studies and would like to take this opportunity to understand the nature of inspector work through some practical training.
9 The term 'telop', which is derived from 'Television Opaque Projector', is coined in Japan to refer to text superimposed on a screen, including captions, subtitles and scrolling tickers.
10 Thanks to the director of Eizōrin as of 2011, we obtained the minutes of the meetings of inspection verification held at Eizōrin in 2012.
11 C.f.: Bernart (1977); Hanlon (1988); Lingenfelter (1975); Parmentier (1987); Petersen (1990).

9 Conclusion

The idea of the book is basically very simple. The production of Japanese AVs is never absolute but culturally, and thus socially, relative because the character of the 'use value' of Japanese AVs is symbolically constituted according to a cultural code that is never the only one possible but relative to society. The same cultural code also specifies the sexual desires of the Japanese people and the means to satisfy them, which is also to say that human sexual desires should not be studied in biological terms, but in terms of cultural meanings that are relative to a particular society. Seen in this light, the relation between production and consumption is not as opposed as is commonly regarded. Arguments that either production or consumption provides a better mode of investigation of a cultural good are not only unnecessary, but also misleading, because they presume that production and consumption entail different lines of logic while in fact they follow the same cultural code. Our goal here is to synthesize accounts of production and consumption because, from the perspective of a cultural code, they are two manifestations of the same thing.

Mediation of production and consumption of Japanese AVs by the salvage ideology

As we have demonstrated in this book, both the production and consumption of Japanese adult video are governed by the very same sexual ideology of salvation. By salvation, we refer to the 'noble' duty of men to rescue women from sexual dissatisfactions or dysfunctions by bringing them to ecstasy. We first showed that *tantai* and *kikaku* AVs, the two major styles of production, had their origins in two pornographic traditions, namely *binibon* and pink films. We pointed out that *tantai* AVs tend to focus on the portrayal of AV actresses as girls-next-door who are young, pure, innocent and sexually inexperienced, whereas *kikaku* AVs are inclined to emphasize the storyline rather than the beauty of their AV actresses. More significantly, *tantai* and *kikaku* AVs also represent differential valuations of women's lack of agency and men's status as women's saviours, two major elements of the salvage ideology, with the former emphasizing women's lack of sexual agency and the latter men's skills in saving women sexually, and their domination over women in sex. As women's lack of sexual agency and men's status as women's saviours are two sides of the same coin, it follows that both *tantai* and *kikaku* AVs are underlined by the same salvage ideology, although each of them emphasizes its different elements. Seen in this light, women's lack of sexual agency and men's sexual domination over women of the salvage ideology serve as a cultural code that specifies the sexual needs of the Japanese consumer, as well as the means to satisfy those needs, which in turn makes *tantai bishōjo* and *kikaku* AVs 'useful' to certain groups of Japanese AV consumers. The *meaningful* connections between women's lack of sexual agency or men's sexual domination over women in the salvage ideology and the sexual needs of certain groups of Japanese AV consumers determine the character of the 'use value' of both types of AVs. The oscillation between the two over the last four decades reveals a swaying of valuations between women's lack of sexual agency and men's sexual domination of women among Japanese AV consumers. The salvage ideology is the cultural reason underpinning Japanese AV consumer taste (Chapter 2).

Yet the point is not just of consuming interest; the production system of *tantai* and *kikaku* AVs is also organized by specific valuation of women's lack of sexual agency and men's status as women's saviour respectively in the salvage ideology. Through a detailed analysis of *tantai* and *kikaku* AVs, we showed how the narrative, number of genres, package, cover design, market price, circulation/acquisition method, clientele of *tantai* AVs and *kikaku* AVs correspondingly depended on the differential valuations of women's lack of sexual agency and men's status as women's saviours. In *tantai* AVs, as the property of women's lack of sexual agency was attached a specific significance and thus accorded 'utility' to a certain category of men in Japan, it required that the actress be rendered 'identical' to the female character inside the movie so that her lack of sexual agency would appear 'authentic' to audiences. This requirement in turn gave rise to a specific kind of pornographic realism which revolves around the authenticity of the actress, in the sense that she is simply acting herself in the movie. The centrality of *tantai* AVs as idol in turn determined the number of genres of *tantai* AVs. As the variants of the image of *tantai* AVs actresses were limited, the genres of *tantai* AVs could not as a result be too many. The supremacy of *tantai* AV actresses as idols also prescribed how the cover of *tantai* AVs was designed, how the product itself was promoted and sold at what price, and how many movies a *tantai* AV actress could appear in over a certain period of time and how she should be paid. This in turn specified her motivation in pursuing a career in the industry.

All of these can change if Japanese men change their preference for women's lack of sexual agency. This we saw in the case of *kikaku* AVs whose focus was on how well the storyline could reveal men's sexual domination over women, which in turn prescribed authentication of both the story and the female character so that the stories presented appeared 'real' to audiences. Thus, somewhat differently from the authenticity of actresses in *tantai* AVs, *kikaku* AVs turned on another kind of pornographic realism emphasizing the authenticity of the story and female character. Since there were so many stories that could perform this function, the number of *kikaku* AV genres could extend beyond human imagination, which resulted in a market where the supply of *kikaku* AVs was always overwhelming. *Kikaku* actresses' pay per movie also tended to be much lower than that of *tantai* AV actresses, thereby further accentuating the 'higher' status of the latter over the former in the industry. But it was precisely because emphasis was placed on the storyline rather than on the actresses that *kikaku* actresses could appear in as many AVs as their physical condition permitted them. The total income of a *kikaku* actress, therefore, could be more than her counterpart in *tantai* AVs over a certain period of time, a fact which further structured the career choice of AV actresses in the industry (Chapter 4). In short, the production of Japanese AVs is also shaped by the same cultural code: the salvage ideology.

More importantly, the fact that the salvage ideology, that evolved from *binibon* and pink films of the 1970s and underwent changes in the 1990s, can carry on even in the modern AV industry has much to do with its unique industrial structure. The major stakeholders involved in the AV industry include AV makers, model agencies, production companies, postproduction companies, regulatory associations, dubbing and packaging companies, wholesalers and rental/retail shops. These stakeholders constitute a world of AV production in which they compete for power, control and ultimately profit. This world of AV production highlights how the Big Five AV manufacturers established their domination over the industry by acting as a cartel not only to prescribe what kinds of adult videos were produced and how they were distributed or circulated in the market, but also to excluded their competitors. Given the fact that the production of AVs by the Big Five AV makers was heavily influenced by the *binibon*-style and pink film-style, their domination indeed helped perpetuate the domination of *tantai* and *kikaku* AVs, a fact which further explains why the salvage ideology can continue to be sustained in the AV industry in Japan (Chapter 3).

The emergence of *kikatan* from the late 1990s, a mixture of *tantai* and *kikaku*, not only indicated the changing taste of Japanese AV viewers but also pointed to the socio-cultural situations surrounding the AV girls. We showed that more and more beautiful young Japanese women had become willing to join the AV industry from the early 2000s and some even regarded being an AV actress as a proper, indeed admirable, career opportunity because, in postwar Japan, women in general were still not being given fair treatment in the contemporary job market and were very often prevented from rising up the social ladder. This situation in the labour market further deteriorated when Japan entered a deep economic recession in the 1990s because Japanese companies tended to sacrifice the interest of fresh graduates especially young female graduates to protect the job security of their regular middle-aged male employees by cutting the number of full-time regular employees they took on every year. At the same time, Japanese corporations adopted contingent job arrangements as a strategy to reduce labour costs. Japanese young men and women, especially high school graduates, were therefore forced to take up part-time, temporary and contracted jobs upon graduation. Among men and women with high school certificates, those who graduated from vocational high schools were more likely to get full-time jobs than those from general high schools; and since it is women who tend to attend general high school, they suffered even more. The AV girls in our survey were the worst of the worst because many of them did not even graduate from high school, which made choice of an AV actress career not just one of last resort, but arguably the best choice in terms of making quick money as well as personal fulfilment.

In addition to women's unfair treatment in the contemporary job market, the so-called 'original theory of self-determination of sex' advocated by some public intellectuals in Japan in the late 1990s has played an important role in raising the awareness among young women in Japan of their right to determine their own sexual body – something which serves as an ideological base for Japanese women to engage in a wide range of sex trades, including being an AV actress (Chapter 5).

The fact that more and more 'high-quality' women were willing to become *kikaku* AV actresses further gave rise to *kikatan* AVs and a new cultural economy that gave significance to both the appearance of AV actresses and the storyline. *Kikatan* AV actresses participated in men's everyday life as a subject who, however, had the status of object in the storyline. We can see that the production of *tantai*, *kikaku* and *kikatan* all followed the same cultural code.

In Chapters 6 and 7, we turned to the *actual* production processes of Japanese AVs and saw how they were informed by the salvage ideology. Before actually participating in a movie, each actress has to go through a *mensetsu*, or interview, process. Through analysis of this recruitment process in which the AV casting director of an AV maker in Tokyo interviewed, photographed and videotaped an AV actress, we identified three crucial qualities in AV actresses that AV makers are most concerned with. They are the uniqueness of actresses, their degree of freshness and determination to succeed in the AV industry.

The uniqueness of actresses, regardless of whether it is manifested in her biographical and sexual characteristics or in her bodily and facial peculiarities, helps AV directors either to transform the woman-applicant into a token of a certain genre of AV actresses, or to invent a new genre of AV during the course of which the actress is recreated as a new kind of AV actress. The former amounts to a production process in which a woman is produced as a certain kind of AV actress, in the course of which the genre at issue is reproduced. The latter can be seen as an inventive production process through which a new genre is invented by creating a new kind of AV actress. Both of these processes are organized by the same cultural code that gives significance to either women's lack of sexual agency in *tantai* AVs or to men's sexual domination over women in *kikaku* AVs. Finally, the quality of the determination for success in the AV industry can help towards tackling the high turnover rate of AV actresses (Chapter 6).

The lucky winner in an interview soon enters into a contract with the AV maker who proceeds to contextualize her against the story for any possible upcoming production. Chapter 7 thus turned to the shooting of a specific genre of acme. We showed that the director attempted to bring the female character to sexual ecstasy by using sensuous and uterus massage, love eggs, vibrator, bare hands and modified electric dildo complemented by the sexual ideology of *kotoba-zeme*, and that as a result, the actress was shown to reach a number of orgasms with an increasing degree of intensity. We demonstrated that the fact that the director, and by extension men in general, was the ultimate cause for the female character's orgasms, and those of women in general, implies that the relation between men and women is hierarchal where men have power over women in sex.

But there was a more deep-rooted politics that lay in the formation of the sexual being of men and women. Shiranai's shooting was built on a series of pre-existing assumptions about the sexual being of men and women where women were passive and unable to reach orgasm on their own, and men (in this case the director) were her saviours by bringing her to an infinite number of orgasms. The politics here occurred in the formation of a *specific* version of the sexual being of men and women in Japan, which was never the only one possible, *as well as* in the suppression of any other possible alternative. By pretending to be scientific, Shiranai naturalized this specific version of the sexual being of men and women, rendering it unspoken and thus silent, thereby further protecting it from being challenged. This series of assumptions took us back to two mutually constituted, implied and reinforced elements of the salvage ideology: women's lack of sexual agency and men's sexual domination of women, an ideology that, as we have shown throughout this book, governs the production of the acme AV (Chapter 7). That is to say, what Shiranai did in the shooting was to transform not only the AV as representation into 'reality', but also the arbitrary definition of men and women by the salvage ideology into *the* 'reality'.

Sustaining the salvage ideology in the 'censorship' of Japanese AVs

As we have shown in Chapter 2, the salvage ideology evolved from a number of sexual ideologies widely seen in postwar Japanese sex manuals which were originally meant to advocate sexual equality – especially women's right to sexual happiness. Nevertheless, women's right to sexual satisfaction was (mis) translated in the manuals into a specific kind of sexual being of men and women, where women were *by nature* sexually inexperienced and innocent and men were *by obligation* required to salvage their helpless wives by bringing them to orgasm: that is, salvage ideology itself. As we can see, the continuities between the postwar sexual ideologies and the salvage ideology in modern Japan are particularly obvious. We have also argued in Chapter 8 that the lingering of the salvage ideology in the Japanese pornoscape in the last few decades has had much to do with specific 'censorship' practices in Japan, which has had a long history of self-regulating pornographic materials, including adult videos. Biderin was the first such organization to oversee the AV industry and, from its inception, it positioned itself as the moral guardian of Japanese society. Biderin's prosecution by the police in 2008 made Eizōrin, the next self-regulatory body of AVs, all the more desperate to seize the moral high ground. To promote the body as a neutral, fair and socially reflexive organization, Eizōrin proceeded to implement a series of measures requiring that AV makers de-authenticate the storyline and the characters in each AV's story. Such a requirement certainly had a bearing on the production of both *tantai* and *kikaku* AVs, though this was manifested in different ways and intensity. *Tantai* AV makers suffered most because the production of *tantai* AVs precisely emphasized the authenticity of their AV actresses. The impact on *kikaku* AVs, however, was not that straightforward because while Eizōrin's requirement of de-authentication of the *characters* in the story did them little harm, the de-authentication of *the story itself* may cause manufacturers trouble since the gist of this genre lies in the authenticity of its storyline.

But the sole focus of Eizōrin on pornographic realism to the exclusion of content has an even more important implication for the present study. We showed that AV industry self-regulatory bodies, including Eizōrin, Medirin and Biderin and many others, have long systematically excluded the content of AVs from inspection in the name of protecting freedom of speech, and hence left the salvage ideology embedded in the movies unexamined and unchallenged. More significantly, this very exclusion of AV contents in censorship is tantamount to announcing to the general public that the contents of AVs, alongside their salvage ideology, are acceptable within the moral parameters of Japanese society. In other words, these self-regulatory bodies have been complicit in reinforcing, if not promoting, this specific kind of sexual ideology and gender politics, which in turn explains why salvage ideology remains intact in modern Japanese pornography.

We argued that the complicity of self-regulatory bodies can be better made sense of if we take into account the fact they are after all profit-making organizations relying heavily on the major AV makers for financial survival and therefore compelled to ensure the latter's profitability. By invoking Victor Turner's famous idea of social drama and its temporary structure, we have shown that the self-regulatory bodies in the Japanese AV industry can be seen as an organizational instrument whereby major AV manufacturers formed a cartel and established their domination over the industry. The whole history of Japan's AV regulatory, therefore, is not the result of a debate over the moral issues found in pornography but a continuous struggle among major AV manufacturers over control of the industry.

The importance of the cultural code in organizing the production and consumption of Japanese AVs is all the more distinguishable in intercultural encounters, although it is not unique to them. In a previous article (Wong and Yau 2015), we explored how the (re)production, circulation and consumption of Japanese AVs are mediated by the *different* cultural codes prevalent in Taiwan and Hong Kong. That is to say, the salvage ideology embedded in Japanese AVs is made sense of at the levels of production, circulation and consumption when they settle in Hong Kong and Taiwan which are governed by their own cultural logics. We showed that men's responsibility to women's sexual well-being and women's sexual passivity determined the 'use value' of Japanese *tantai* AVs to Taiwanese men. The utility of Japanese *tantai* AVs in Taiwan, however, did not derive from the famous Japanese salvage ideology because Taiwan's cultural code attached significance to men's responsibility in *taking care of* women during sex rather than their sexual domination over women.

In contrast, the migration of Japanese AVs to Hong Kong was mediated by the cultural logic of the identity of *heung gong yahn* (Hongkongese): an 'in-betweenness' that we illustrated by means of a case study of an AV actress, Yuki Maiko. We showed that the images of Yuki Maiko matched the cultural logic of the identification of the new middle class which rendered Yuki Maiko in particular, and *bishōjo* AVs in general, as an identity maker of Hong Kong people. It was this that explained the popularity of Japanese AVs in Hong Kong. But the utility of Yuki Maiko derived neither from her lack of sexual agency, as was the case in Japan, nor from her sexual passivity as in Taiwan, but from her 'in-between' image. From this we can conclude that different cultural codes have their own form of pornographies. Other cultures, other pornographies. However, we do not propose to put forward an idiographic idea of cultural relativity; instead we wish to argue that the difference in the pornography of different cultures is structural: the symbolic locus of the cultural code in Hong Kong is different from that in Taiwan, the former being located in the class structure while the latter is founded in local gender roles. This further raises a very important question: to what extent can we say that the societies of Hong Kong and Taiwan are the same Chinese society? The answer to this question would probably require another book but the aim of this book is more moderate: it is intended to simply argue that there is always a cultural reason for the production and consumption of pornography.

It follows that culture cannot be dismissed in the study of economies, including the market economy. As Sahlins effectively pointed out, economists tend to assign a minor if not null role to culture in the operation of a market economy,

> where the logical system of objects and social relations proceeds along an unconscious plane, manifested only through market decisions based on price, leaving the impression that production is merely the precipitate of an enlightened rationality.... From all vantages, the process seems one of the material maximization: the famous allocation of scarce means among alternative ends to obtain the greatest possible satisfaction – or, as Veblen put it, getting something for nothing at the cost of whom it may concern. On the productive side, material advantage takes the form of added pecuniary value. For the consumer, it is more vaguely understood as the return in 'utility' to monetary disbursements; but even here the appeal of the product consists in its purported functional superiority to all available alternatives.
> (Sahlins 1976a: 167)

Culture is understood by economists as at best an exogenous factor and thus does not play a decisive role in such processes of material maximization (Sahlins

2013). But as we have demonstrated in this book, the production and consumption of Japanese AVs are governed by a cultural code which specifies, and thus explains, the properties and forms of Japanese AVs. In more concrete terms, the cultural code of women's lack of sexual agency or men's sexual domination over women determines *tantai* AVs or *kikaku* AVs as a particular type of Japanese pornography 'useful' to certain groups of Japanese AV consumers, in the course of which, to paraphrase Sahlins (1976a: 169), certain groups of Japanese AV consumers reciprocally define certain types of Japanese AVs in terms of themselves and themselves in terms of certain types of Japanese AVs. The production and consumption of Japanese AVs are always governed by the cultural code and by extension, economy is always organized by culture which is the decisive reason for the former.

Retrieval of the endangered specificities

In the sections that follow, we are going to spell out the implications of this book to porn studies. We have here made a concerted effort to retrieve what Sahlins (2000: 12) calls the 'endangered specificities' of Japanese AVs as a particular kind of pornography. As mentioned above, we first showed that Japanese AV can be traced to two different pornographic traditions: *binibon* and pink movies. These two pornographic traditions were shown to find their full manifestation in two different styles of AV productions: namely *tantai* and *kikaku* AVs, with the former placing singular emphasis on the beauty of the actress, and the latter revolving around the story and the female character.

The cultural specification of the properties of pornographic texts helps current porn studies which tend to replace concrete arguments and alternative points of views with moral high ground arguments. Morally correct as such argumentation may be, one major problem of this kind of moral analysis is that arguments get evaluated in terms of their moral stances, with the result that morality becomes *the* arguments. In other words, the more moral the argument is, the truer it must be. More importantly, moral laudable analysis often implies a certain form of *apriorism*. As morality itself has become the arguments, all the facts and details discussed are important *only if* they can reconfirm the presupposed arguments. More problematically, the arguments are not only a priori but functional explanations in the sense that the effects of pornography, regardless of whether they act as a form of sexual discrimination against women or as a form of freedom of speech, are taken as its essence. In the event, the details of pornography – not to mention pornography in different cultures and in different times – are destroyed, as it were. This functional explanation of pornography is, 'like all functionalizing arguments, this one bargains away (actual) content for (presumed) effect, what culture is for what it does, thus giving up what we know about it in order to understand it' (Sahlins 2000: 12). Such a functional explanation, as will be shown below, prevents us from investigating how women are objectified in pornography, the gender inequality embedded in the sexual being of men and women, and the social construction of pornographic reality.

Production of the objectification of women in pornography

The objectification of women is a notion central to feminism and is a major part of its approach toward pornography. It can be roughly defined as seeing and/or treating a woman as an object solely for male sexual pleasure. Over the last few decades, the notion of the objectification of women has been widely and extensively discussed in the feminist and porn studies literature, often being used as a variant of, or elaboration for, 'degradation'. As McKee (2005b: 278) notes, non-degrading/degrading is one of the two major axes adopted by social scientists in the early years when examining the contents of pornographic materials – the other axis being the non-violent/violent. Nevertheless, the term 'degradation' is not transparent, and a review of the history of its usage shows that there has been considerable disagreement about what 'degradation' actually means and how it should be codified. Partly because of this, many scholars have resorted to using terms such as dehumanization, objectification and domination as rough synonyms to denote how women are degraded in pornography (Barron and Kimmel 2000; Check and Malamuth 1986; Cowan and Campbell 1994; Cowan and Dunn 1994; Dines *et al.* 1998).

Among these terms, objectification is arguably the most used and discussed concept in the examination of pornography. For instance, McKee (2005b) argues that objectification can better serve as an umbrella term to cover most of the elements identified as indicators of degradation. Meanwhile, there are also scholars who attribute the current usage of objectification to philosopher Immanuel Kant and explore the implication of such usage in pornography critique (Haslanger 1993; Herman 1993; Korsgaard 1996; Papadaki 2007).

Many previous porn studies, however, fail to demonstrate the process, not to mention the mechanism, whereby women are objectified. This failure obviously comes from the fact that this scholarship by and large singularly focuses on content or textual analysis, rather than on the actual production processes of pornography. True, content analysis is 'a research technique for the objective, systematic and quantitative description of the manifest content of communication' (Berelson 1952: 18), but most of these analyses have been conducted independently of the actual contexts in which those texts were produced. But even when scholars have recognized the importance of production processes and have attempted to approach pornography *as* industry, when push comes to shove they either resort to content analysis (Tyler 2010) or turn industry analyses into critiques of sexism inherent in it, or into personal anecdotes (Hawthorne 2011; Farley 2011). However, we do not mean that textual or content analysis is not helpful at all. Quite the contrary, textual or content analysis allows us to grasp the properties and the recurrent themes of pornographic content, but what they leave largely unexamined and unanswered is the burning question of how the objectification of women is actually produced or manufactured at the moment of shooting. It is a burning issue because it deals with the mechanism whereby women are degraded from human being into object, so that clarification of this mechanism should provide important insights to those who are concerned with the problems of pornography.

One of our major contributions in this book, therefore, lies in ethnographically demonstrating the process whereby a woman, both physical and mental, is objectified at the moment of shooting pornography. We showed that enormous effort goes into depicting the *male* director as *the* cause of the female character's orgasm, and that one such effort involves use of the counterfactual to demonstrate what the actress might have looked like without his sexual stimulation. The immediate suspension of the female character's orgasm when the director leapt away from her thus served very well to prove that there was a causal relationship between his sexual stimulation and her orgasm, in the sense that he was the ultimate cause of her orgasm and hence her sexual well-being. Central to this was the asymmetrical power relationship between the director and the female character in which the former had 'power over' the latter.

We have argued that the visual construction of men having *power over* women points to a mechanism whereby women are objectified in the process of shooting. This mechanism happens to intersect with Martha Nussbaum's definition of objectification. Nussbaum (1995: 257), as a prominent philosopher of law and feminism, identifies seven features that are involved in the idea of treating a person as an object:

1 instrumentality: the treatment of a person as a tool for the objectifier's purposes;
2 denial of autonomy: the treatment of a person as lacking in autonomy and self-determination;
3 inertness: the treatment of a person as lacking in agency, and perhaps also in activity;
4 fungibility: the treatment of a person as interchangeable with other objects;
5 violability: the treatment of a person as lacking in boundary-integrity;
6 ownership: the treatment of a person as something that is owned by another (can be bought or sold);
7 denial of subjectivity: the treatment of a person as something whose experiences and feelings (if any) need not be taken into account.

The power of men over women in our case is a perfect illustration of how women are objectified in the AV shooting process. First, our case clearly demonstrates the *instrumentality* of women in the production of pornography, in that the female character exists only for the male director to demonstrate to his audiences how female orgasm can be brought about and how he has power over her. Remember, the sole aim of this movie was to demonstrate how female orgasm could be initiated; this actress was only called upon to replace the original actress who, for some unknown reason, had suddenly became unavailable on the day of shooting. In other words, she not only functioned as an instrument for the director's own purposes, but could be *conveniently exchanged* with another actress. That is to say, she was treated as an *object* that was interchangeable with other women as *objects*.

The power of the director over the female character also implies that he treated the female character as *lacking in autonomy*, in that she had no control over her orgasms, and hence over her body, in the face of the director's stimulation. As we have seen, the director's implementation of power was causal and sequential: he got the female character to have the kind of orgasm he wanted her to have, but which she would not normally have had. This exercise of power can be seen by the empirical proof: her orgasm stopped whenever the director stepped swiftly away from her. In other words, she was not sexually autonomous, as her orgasm and body were entirely controlled by the director during the whole process. If her body was entirely under the director's control, it follows that her body and her capacity for orgasm were indeed *owned* by the director, at least during the shooting. Since she was not sexually autonomous, lacking ownership of her body and could not resist the sexual stimulation imposed by the director, it follows that she did not possess any *boundary integrity* and was subject to violation whenever such stimulation existed.

In a similar vein, the power of the director over the female character points to the latter's *lack of agency* in the context of filming since she was totally incapable of acting independently and of making her own free choices. Throughout the whole filming, the female character was unable to initiate orgasm by herself, but remained inert, waiting to be stimulated, thrust at or into with various instruments, and brought to orgasm. Even during the process of orgasm, she remained passive and inert, as if she were incapable of acting by herself. Relatedly, if she were inert and could not control her own body, it becomes obvious that she was *denied her subjectivity*, in that her experiences and feelings were not taken into account as she did not possess any. As a matter of fact, her feelings and emotions (including screaming) were not taken into consideration by the director. Remember how he simply ignored the female character's responses or feelings during the process of shooting even when she screamed or cried, and suchlike.

If the female character in case was rendered into someone lacking in autonomy, agency, subjectivity and boundary-integrity, into an individual who was exchangeable with another woman in the process of shooting, and as an object temporarily owned by the director, it is not wrong to say that, according to Nussbaum's definition of objectification, she was a perfect example of how a woman is objectified in pornographic representation. By probing into the production process and the very shooting process in this case, then, we not only can retrieve the long-lost process of how the objectification of women is actually produced at the moment of shooting, but also shed some light on the relationship between the exercise of power and the mechanism of producing objectification.

Politics of the sexual being of men and women

Our analysis of the shooting process also revealed that the asymmetrical relationship between men and women portrayed in the movie had much to do with a series of *pre-existing* assumptions about the sexual being of men and women in the cultural context of Japan, in the sense that these assumptions constituted the primordial base on which the director (men) exercised power over the female character (women) in the movie. These assumptions included: (1) orgasm is the only possible form of sexual pleasure for women and those who cannot reach orgasm are therefore considered as nothing but problematic; (2) women are not agentic in achieving orgasm and only men can give women orgasm; (3) problematic women are nothing more than animals or machines waiting to be tamed or fixed by men; and (4) men, therefore, are women's saviours because only men can bring women to orgasm. This series of pre-existing assumptions is parallel to the elements of the salvage ideology, which is also to say that they are informed by the salvage ideology.

The power asymmetry between director and the female character in the movie indeed existed *prior to* the director's power over the female character because a gender asymmetry was already built in the formation of the sexual being of men and women embedded in the above-mentioned assumptions. Understood as such, there are indeed two levels of power politics operating here. At the level of pornographic representation, there exists a power of the male director vis-à-vis the female character. As is patently clear, the gender asymmetry between the director and the female character here is culturally constructed and hence arbitrary. But the gender asymmetry at the level of pornographic representation is, as just mentioned, indeed based on a series of *pre-existing* assumptions about the sexual being of men and women in the cultural context of Japan, for otherwise the exercise of power in the movie would not have been possible. Obviously enough, this sexual being of men and women is not the objective representation of men and women in Japan. Nor does it follow that there is an absolute existence of men and women in Japan. As argued in Chapter 7, this particular definition of the sexual being of men and women is a function of the internal differences among the categories of 'men' and 'women' within a meaningful scheme that is not the only one possible. In other words, it is a culturally intended selection where certain differences (including female sexual passivity) are assigned significance, while others are ignored. Indeed, the relationship between this specific definition of the sexual being of men and women and the worldly object of men and women in Japan bears a striking similarity to Saussure's principle of arbitrariness between sound image (signifier) and concept (signified). According to Saussure, not only the relationship between the signifier and signified, but also that between the signified and the 'objective' world, is arbitrary. It follows that the relationship between this particular sexual being of men and women and the worldly objects of men and women in Japan is also arbitrary. As Jonathan Culler explains,

> Not only does each language produce a different set of signifiers, articulating and dividing the continuum of sound in a distinctive way; each language produces a different set of signifieds; it has a distinctive and thus 'arbitrary' way of organizing the world into concepts or categories.
> (Culler 1986[1976]: 23)

There is no absolute reason why the worldly objects of men and women in Japan should be defined as the above-mentioned *kind* of men and women. They depict this particular *kind* of men and women according to the internal differences among the categories of 'men' and 'women' within a meaningful scheme, which is never the only one possible. More importantly, the relationship between the worldly objects of men and women and the *kind* of men and women is never fixed, but continues to evolve. Power here functions to fix this ever-evolving relationship between the worldly object of men and women and their signs, that is, the particular *kind* of men and women mentioned above. That is also to say, the cultural politics here lies not just in the arbitrary selection or emphasis on certain differences, but more importantly in the fixation of the arbitrary relationship between the worldly objects of men and women in Japan and the particular kind of men and women mentioned above, thus rendering such arbitrariness as *intrinsic* parts of 'reality'.

All of this means that the real politics here is the fact that the gender asymmetry at the level of 'reality' is as cultural and arbitrary as that at the level of pornographic representation. Yet its arbitrariness is silenced and hence goes entirely unnoticed. The result of silencing this arbitrariness is that the gender asymmetry at the level of reality is rendered natural and real, leaving no room for discussion, not to mention critical reflection.

The politics of the formation of the sexual being of men and women has important implications for the study of pornography – especially the recent revival of anti-pornography scholarship and activism since the 2000s (Boyle 2010; Dines 2008; Jensen 2007; Long 2012; Paul 2005; Reist and Bray 2011). Although the study of pornography has undergone what Attwood (2002: 91) calls a 'paradigm shift' in which porn studies have gradually moved away from the 'tired binary' (Juffer 1998: 2) toward the contextualization of pornography, the early 2000s witnessed the resurgence of a similar sort of polarization in porn studies. For example, McKee *et al.* (2008) attempt to debunk the many misconceptions about porn consumers, and in turn imply that pornography does not do any harm to audiences. More recently, Taormino *et al.* (2013) identify pornography as a form of expression and labour in which women and racial and sexual minorities produce power and pleasure. On the other hand, there is, as just mentioned above, a whole set of anti-pornography literature delving into the various kinds of harm with which pornography threatens us. But this time it is not just women who are objectified, dehumanized or sexualized. Rather, the impact of pornography expands to include our everyday lives, our relationships, our families, our sexualities, and our masculinities – culminating in the so-called 'pornification' of our culture (Nikunen *et al.* 2007; Paul 2005).

It is true that pornography is now an integral part of our popular culture and our everyday lives and that our media, culture and environment have immersed us in a pornographic aesthetic; yet it remains to be seen whether an outright ban on pornography can relieve, if not stop, gender inequality or women's oppression in society. More importantly, as we learn from political scientists, power does not exist out there, waiting to be exercised or operated; instead it exists in a concrete relationship between at least two parties. As Jayan Nayer succinctly notes,

> Power, when all the complex networks of the reach are untangled, is, *personal*; power does not exist out there. It only exists *in* relationship. To say the word power is to describe relationship; to acknowledge power is to acknowledge [a certain kind of] subservience in that relationship. There can exist no power if the subservice relationship is refused – then power can only achieve its ambitions through its naked form, as violence.
>
> (Nayer 2002: 128–9; italics ours)

As shown in our study, the power asymmetry existed not only between the director and the female character in the pornographic representation, but also between them in 'reality' – as expressed by the specific form of the sexual being of men and women in Japan: that is, between men and women of a particular kind. It follows that pornography is at best an expression of the configuration of sexual beings of men and women, rather than the cause of women's oppression. Of course, we are not suggesting that pornography is problem-free. Nor do we agree with the liberal feminists claiming that pornography is merely a kind of expression or labour in which women, alongside other minorities, produce power and pleasure. Yet, saying that pornography is constitutive of gender inequality or women's oppression is to ignore the much more complicated, deep-seated gender politics involved in the formation of the sexual being of men and women. As in our case, the asymmetrical power between the director and the female character is, as mentioned above, hinged upon a series of pre-existing assumptions about the sexual being of men and women. That is to say, the director could only exercise his power over the female character *insofar as*: (1) the latter could not achieve orgasm by herself nor solve her own problems; (2) only the former could bring about female orgasm and hence the saviour of the latter; and (3) most importantly, orgasm is seen as the only possible form of female sexual pleasure. In other words, these assumptions are the necessary conditions for the male director to exercise his power over the female character. Without them, the director's power vis-à-vis the female character would be rendered non-operational. The implication here is that in order to have a better understanding of gender politics in pornography, we need to debunk gender asymmetry not only in pornographic representation, but also in the formation of perception, or in what many feminist scholars would call 'reality'. We have to denaturalize the particular form of sexual beings of men and women as 'reality' by exposing its arbitrariness. Porn studies, therefore, have to address the gender inequality in Japanese AVs as pornographic texts *and* as pornographic 'reality' because they are mutually constituted by the same cultural code: the salvage ideology. This leads to the implications in this book about pornographic realism.

Pornographic realism

The cultural constitution of the sexual being of men and women as 'reality' informed by the salvage ideology in Japanese AVs can be best revealed by our discovery that the meaning of 'the real' or 'reality' in pornographic representation is not singular but plural. As we have shown, the meaning of reality in pornographic representation is not just about ordinary, real people making love in front of the camera for the sake of personal pleasure. The different emphases of *tantai* and *kikaku* AVs indeed lead to different representational strategies whereby the former work to authenticate the actress, while the latter the storyline and the female characters therein. These two representational strategies in turn contribute to two different kinds of reality in Japanese AVs. The authentication of the actress in *tantai* AVs is to emphasize that the actress is not performing the female character in the movie but acting herself in reality as someone who is young, pure, innocent and sexually inexperienced, in order to convey a message that the actress's lack of sexual agency is not staged but real. It is the cultural code of the lack of sexual agency that turns on a certain group of AV consumers. The authentication of the story and the female character in *kikaku* AVs, on the other hand, is designed to convey the message that, although the actress may just act out the female character, the story of men's sexual domination over women itself is real. The major task of *kikaku* AV actresses is to authenticate the female character in the movie, and thus the story, by means of their performing skills, in order to present the reality of the story because it is the cultural code of men's sexual domination over women that sexually stimulates another group in the male audience.

The cultural constitution of pornographic reality informed by the salvage ideology also sheds important light on the above debate about whether pornographic representation does or does not threaten women with harm and violence, and whether pornography should be censored – and if so, in what way. First, pornographic representation focusing on the authenticity of the actress differs tremendously from that which focuses on the authenticity of the story and female character. We therefore need to clarify what the pornographic representation is about before we can reach a conclusion that censorship of pornography is necessary. More importantly, since the constitution of pornographic reality is ultimately informed by the salvage ideology, the major target of critique should be the ideology itself rather than its expression, either at the level of representation or that of 'reality'. Otherwise, all critiques are at best superficial, at worst vain, and sometimes can even sustain the gender inequality they are criticizing, as we demonstrated in Chapter 8. This then brings us back to the major theme of this book: salvage ideology. This is also why this book has been all about this ideology.

Chinese glossary

heung gong yahn	香港人	Hongkongese

Japanese glossary

Adaruto bideo	アダルトビデオ	Japanese adult video	
Akume	アクメ	Acume, meaning a peak	
Amakudari	天下り	Descent from heaven	
Asobi	遊び	A play	
Bakufu	幕府	Literally means 'tent office', referring to the headquarter of a field commander in battle.	
Biderin	ビディリン	Nihon Ethics of Video Association	
Binibon	ビニ本	Soft core pornographic magazine	
Binibon-kei	ビニ本系	Binibon-style	
Binyū	美乳	Beautiful breasts	
Bishōjo	美少女	Beautiful young woman	
Bishōjo	美少女AV	Beautiful young woman AV	
Bukkake	ぶかっけ	A variety of fetish that involves repeated ejaculation on a female by many (sometimes up to a hundred) men	
Chijo	痴女	A female groper or pervert	
Chikan	痴漢	A male groper or pervert	
Chōnyū	超乳	Super-huge breasts	
Chō usukeshi	超薄消し	Super see through	
Eirin	映倫	Film classification and rating organization	
Eizōrin	映像倫	Image Ethics Association	
Eroppoi kei	エロっぽい	Erotic or erotic-like	
Ferachio	フェラチオ	Fellatio	
Futamata	二股	Dating two persons at the same time	
Fūzoku	風俗	Entertainment industry	
Gansha	顔射	Facial ejaculation	
Gekijō	劇場	Theatre	
Genba	現場	The film site	
Genryō	原料	Raw produce	
Gibo	義母	One's mother-in-law or stepmother	
Gijiroku	議事録	Minutes	
Gyaru	ギャル	Girl	
Hakenshain	派遣社員	Temporary employee	
Hageshii	激しい	Acute, vehement	
Hamedōri	ハメ撮り	Self photographing of sex	
Hanayome	花嫁	A-wife-to-be	
Harenchi rosen	破廉恥路線	A shameless line	
Hazukashii	恥ずかしい	Ashamed	

Japanese glossary

Hentai	変態	Pervert
Hidoi	酷い	Terrible, harsh
Hinnyū	貧乳	Small breasts
Hisei-shain	非正社員	Non-full-time or non-permanent employee
Hitotsuma	人妻	Wife
Hitozuma-nanpa	人妻ナンパ	Wife scouting
Hiyake	日焼け	Sunburned
Honban	本番	Real sex
Ie seido	家制度	The household system
Ijōseiai rosen	異常性愛路線	A abnormal line
Ikase	イカセ	Bringing one to orgasm
Iya	嫌	Unpleasant, not good
Iya janai	嫌じゃない	It's not that you don't like…
Jihankihon	自販機本	Vending machine pornography
Jikoshōkai	自己紹介	Self introduction
Jukujo	熟女	Mature women
Jimu shoku	事務職	Clerical staff
Kaisha	会社	A company
Kaizoku	海賊	Piracy
Kanchō	浣腸	Enema
Kasutori	カストリ	Literally means 'scouring the dregs', referring to couple-magazines or pulp magazines
Kawaii	可愛い	Cute or adorable
Kazoku ai	家族愛	Family love
Keiretsu	系列	Enterprising groupings
Kikaku	企画	A plan
Kikaku mono	企画もの	A style emphasizing story
Kikatan	キカタン	A truncated Japanese term combining *tantai* and *kikaku*. Coined in the late 1990s, it refers to *kikaku* AV in which the *kikaku* AV actresses are employed as the main and only actress.
Kimochi	気持ち	Feeling
Kimochi ii	気持ちいい	Good feeling
Kintama	金玉	Testicles
Kisu	キス	Kiss
Kogara	小柄	Petite
Kotoba-zeme	言葉攻め	Attack via words
Kyojiri	巨尻	Big buttocks
Kyonyū	巨乳	Big breasts
Makura-e	枕絵	Pillow pictures
Manēja	マネージャ	Manager
Manga	漫画	Comic
Meidirin	メイディリン	Media Ethics Association
Mensetsu	面接	Interview
Mibōjin	未亡人	Widow
Miko	巫女	Priestess
Mozaiku	モザイク	Mosaic
Mo hazure	モ　外れ	Mosaic that is out of place
Mo more	モ　漏れ	Mosaic that is leaking out
Mo usui	モ　薄い	Mosaic that is thin
Nanpa	ナンパ	Scouting

Japanese glossary

Nichieishin	日映審	Japan Image Review
Ninpu	妊婦	Pregnant woman
Nōkanshi	納棺師	A ritual mortician
Nozoki	覗き	Peeping
Nyūsha shiken	入社試験	Entrance examination
Okumade	奥まで	Deeper
Oppabu	オッパブ	A kind of sex service in Japan where young women's breasts can be groped and caressed by the male customers
Paizuri	パイズリ	Breast-sex
Pinku eiga	ピンク映画	Pink film
Pocchari	ぽっちり	Chubby women
Renai	恋愛	Love
Rinri dantai	倫理団体	Ethics organization
Roman poruno	ロマンポルノ	Roman pornography
Rorikon	ロリコン	Lolita complex
Rōshun	ローシュン	Lotion
Roshutsu	露出	Exposure
Rōtā	ローター	Vibrator
Ryōki	猟奇	Hunting for bizarre
Ryūhāfu	リュウハーフ	New half
Sararīman	サラリーマン	Salaryman
Seikan massāji	性感マッサージ	Sensational massage
Sei-shain	正社員	Regular or permanent employee
Sekukyaba	セクキャバ	Sex cabaret
Senzoku	専属	Exclusivity, here referring to exclusive contract
Shigeki rosen	刺激路線	A sensation line
Shikyū massāji	子宮マッサージ	Uterus massage
Shinsa	審査	Inspection
Shinsa kijun	審査基準	Inspection criteria
Shinsain	審査員	Inspectors
Shirōto	素人	Amateur
Shōchū	焼酎	A distilled liquor made from sweet potatoes, rice or buckwheat
Shunga	春画	Spring pictures, i.e. erotic paintings
Sōgō shoku	総合職	Generalist staff
Sukātoman	スカウトマン	A scout
Sukebe	スケベ	A lewd woman or a bitch
Surendā	スレンダー	Slender
Tantai	単体	A single person
Tantai bishōjo	単体美少女	A beautiful young woman
Tantai mono	単体もの	A single-person style
Tonya	問屋	Wholesalers
Tsūnen	通念	Social values
Waisetsu	猥褻	Obscene
Ura	裏	Illegal
Uso	嘘	A lie
Usukeshi	薄消し	Thin mosaic
Yome	嫁	A daughter-in-law

References

Abegglen, James C. 1960[1958]. *The Japanese Factory: Aspects of Its Social Organization*. Glencoe, IL: Free Press.
Abegglen, James C. 1985. *Kaisha, the Japanese Corporation*. New York: Basic Books.
Abel, Jonathan E. 2012. *Redacted: The Archives of Censorship in Transwar Japan*. Berkeley and London: University of California Press.
Adachi, Noriyuki. 1995. *Adaruto nahitobito* [The Various People in the Japanese AV Industry]. Tokyo: Kodansha.
Adorno, Theodor W. 2001[1991]. *The Culture Industry: Selected Essays on Mass Culture*, edited with an introduction by J. M. Bernstein. London: Routledge.
Akagawa, Manabu. 1999. *Sekushuariti no rikishi shakaigaku* [The Historical Sociology of Sexuality]. Tokyo: Kieso Shobo.
Alexander, R. James. 2003. 'Obscenity, Pornography, and the Law in Japan: Reconsidering Oshima's *In the Realm of the Senses*'. *Asian-Pacific Law and Policy Journal* 4(1): 148–68.
Allison, Anne. 1998. 'Cutting the Fringes: Pubic Hair at the Margin of Japanese Censorship Laws'. In A. Hiltebeitel and B. D. Miller, eds, *Hair: Its Power and Meaning in Asian Cultures*, 195–218. Albany: State University of New York Press.
Allison, Anne. 2000. *Permitted and Prohibited Desires: Mothers, Comics, and Censorship in Japan*. Boulder, CO: University of California Press.
Aoyagi, Hiroshi. 1999. 'Islands of Eight Million Smiles: Pop-Idol Performances and the Field of Symbolic Production'. Phd diss., The University of British Columbia (Canada).
Asuka, Barbara. 2005. *Kyo mo AV tottemasu* [Today, We Shoot AV as Well]. Tokyo: Eagle Publishing.
Attwood, Feona. 2002. 'Reading Porn: The Paradigm Shift in Pornography Research'. *Sexualities* 5(1): 91–105.
Attwood, Feona. 2009. 'Intimate Adventure: Sex Blogs, Sex "Blooks" and Women's Sexual Narration'. *European Journal of Cultural Studies* 12(1): 5–20.
Azuma, Noboru. 1998. *Shimamura Yukibiko intabyū* [The Interview of Shimamura Yukibiko]. In Y. Ishida, ed., *Adult Video in the 20th Century*, 93–9. Tokyo: Asupekuto.
Barron, Martin and Kimmel, Michael. 2000. 'Sexual Violence in Three Pornographic Media: Toward a Sociological Explanation'. *The Journal of Sex Research* 37(2): 161–8.
Beer, Lawrence Ward. 1984. *Freedom of Expression in Japan: A Study in Comparative Law, Politics and Society*. Tokyo; New York; San Francisco: Kodansha International Ltd.

Berelson, Bernard. 1952. *Content Analysis in Communication Research*. Glencoe, IL: Free Press.
Bernart, Luelen. 1977. *The Book of Luelen*. Canberra: The Australian National University Press.
Boer, Roland. 2010. 'That Hideous Pagan Idol: Marx, Fetishism and Graven Images'. *Critique* 38(1): 93–116.
Bornoff, Nicholas. 1991. *Pink Samurai: The Pursuit and Politics of Sex in Japan*. London: HarperCollins.
Bosco, Joseph. 2012. 'The Formula as a Managerial Tool: Audit Culture in Hong Kong'. *Journal of Workplace Rights* 16(3–4): 383–403.
Boyle, Karen. 2000. 'The Pornography Debate: Beyond Cause and Effect'. *Women's Studies International Forum* 23(2): 187–95.
Boyle, Karen. 2010. 'Introduction'. In K. Boyle, ed., *Everyday Pornography*, 1–14. London and New York: Routledge.
Braw, Monica. 1991. *The Atomic Bomb Suppressed: American Censorship in Occupied Japan*. Armonk, NY: M.E. Sharpe Inc.
Brinton, Mary C. 1989. 'Gender Stratification in Contemporary Urban Japan'. *American Sociological Review* 54(4): 549–64.
Brinton, Mary C. 2005. 'Trouble in Paradise: Institutions in the Japanese Economy and the Youth Labor Market'. In Victor Nee and Richard Swedberg, eds, *Economic Sociology of Capitalism*, 419–44. Princeton, NJ: Princeton University Press.
Brinton, Mary C. 2011. *Lost in Transition: Youth, Work, and Instability in Postindustrial Japan*. Cambridge: Cambridge University Press.
Buruma, Ian. 1984. *A Japanese Mirror: Heroes and Villains of Japanese Culture*. London: Vintage.
Cabinet Office, Government of Japan. 2016. www.esri.cao.go.jp/jp/sna/sonota/kenmin/kenmin_top.html (accessed 25 July 2017).
Campbell, Colin. 1987. *The Romantic Ethic and the Spirit of Modern Consumerism*. Oxford: B. Blackwell.
Campbell, Colin. 1995. 'The Sociology of Consumption'. In Daniel Miller, ed., *Acknowledging Consumption: A Review of New Studies*, 96–126. London: Routledge.
Cather, Kirsten. 2004. 'The Great Censorship Trials of Literature and Film in Postwar Japan, 1950–1983'. Phd diss., University of California, Berkeley.
Caves, Richard E. 2002. *Creative Industries: Contracts between Art and Commerce*. Cambridge, MA and London: Harvard University Press.
Chancer, Lynn. 2000. 'From Pornography to Sadomasochism: Reconciling Feminist Differences'. *The Annals of the American Academy of Political and Social Science* 571(1): 77–88.
Check, James V. P. and Malamuth, Neil M. 1986. 'Pornography and Sexual Aggression: A Social Learning Theory Analysis'. *Annals of the International Communication Association* 9(1): 181–213.
Chun, Allen. 2001. 'From Text to Context: How Anthropology Makes Its Subject'. *Cultural Anthropology* 15(4): 570–95.
Ciclitira, Karen. 2004. 'Pornography, Women and Feminism: Between Pleasure and Politics'. *Sexualities* 7(3): 281–301.
Clark, Rodney. 1979. *The Japanese Company*. New Haven, CT: Yale University Press.
Coopersmith, J. (2006) 'Does Your Mother Know What You Really Do? The Changing Nature and Image of Computer-based Pornography'. *History and Technology* 22(1): 1–25.

Cowan, Gloria and Campbell, R. Robin. 1994. 'Racism and Sexism in Interracial Pornography: A Content Analysis'. *Psychology of Women Quarterly*, 18(3): 323–38.

Cowan, Gloria and Dunn, Kerri F. 1994. 'What Themes in Pornography Lead to Perceptions of the Degradation of Women?' *The Journal of Sex Research* 31(1): 11–21.

Culler, Jonathan. 1986[1976]. *Ferdinand de Saussure*, revised edition. Ithaca, NY: Cornell University Press.

Cusumano, M.A., Mylonadis, Y. and Rosenbloom, R. S. 1992. 'Strategic Maneuvering and Mass-Market Dynamics: The Triumph of VHS over Beta'. *The Business History Review* 66(1): 51–94.

Dasgupta, Romit. 2009. 'The "Lost Decade" of the 1990s and Shifting Masculinities in Japan'. *Culture, Society and Masculinity* 1(1): 79–95.

Deetz, Stanley. 1992. *Democracy in an Age of Corporate Colonization: Developments in Communication and the Politics of Everyday Life*. New York: State University of New York Press.

Dines, Gail. 2008. 'Penn, Porn and Me'. https://web.archive.org/web/20090330143944/www.counterpunch.org:80/dines06232008.html (accessed on 15 May 2017).

Dines, Gail, Jensen, Robert and Russo, Ann. 1998. *Pornography: The Production and Consumption of Inequality*. New York: Routledge.

Domenig, Roland. 2014. 'The Market of Flesh and the Rise of the "Pink Film"'. In Abe M. Nornes, ed., *The Pink Book, The Japanese Eroduction and its Contexts*, 17–48. Tokyo: A Kinema Club Book.

Dore, Ronald Philips. 1973. *British Factory, Japanese Factory: The Origins of National Diversity in Industrial Relations*. Berkeley and Los Angeles: University of California Press.

du Gay, Paul, Hall, Stuart, Janes, Linda, Mackay, Hugh and Negus, Keith. 1997. *Doing Cultural Studies: The Story of the Sony Walkman*. London: Sage Publication in association with the Open University.

Duggan, Lisa and Hunter, Nan D. 1995. *Sex Wars: Sexual Dissent and Political Culture*. New York: Routledge.

Dworkin, Andrea. 2003[1978]. *Right-Wing Women*. New York: G. P. Putnam's Sons.

Dworkin, Andrea and MacKinnon, Catharine A. 1989[1988]. *Pornography and Civil Rights: A New Day for Women's Equality*. Minneapolis: Organizing Against Pornography.

Dyrberg, Torben Bech. 1997. *The Circular Structure of Power: Politics, Identity and Community*. London and New York: Verso.

Eizōrin. 2011. Eizō Rinri Kikō [Motion Pictures Regulation and Ethics Committee]. Tokyo: N.P.

Farley, Melissa. 2011. 'Pornography is Infinite Prostitution'. In M. T. Reist and A. Bray, eds, *Big Porn Inc.: Exposing the Harms of the Global Pornography Industry*, 150–9. Australia: Spinifex Press Pty Ltd.

Fine, Ben and Saad-Filho, Alfredo. 2004. *Marx's Capital*. London and Sterling, VA: Pluto Press.

Fiske, John. 1989. *Reading the Popular*. London: Unwin Hyman.

Fruhstuck, Sabine. 2003. *Colonizing Sex: Sexology and Social Control in Modern Japan*. Berkeley; Los Angeles; London: University of California Press.

Fujiki, Tadashi. 1998. '*Hamedori: hachi miri bideo ga toraeru rutari no kankseisei*' [Hamedori: The Relationship of the Characters Captured by the 8mm Video]. In Y. Ishida, ed., *Adult Video in the 20th Century*, 198–9. Tokyo: Asupekuto.

Fujiki, Tadashi. 2009. *Adaruto Video Kakumei Shi* [The Revolutionary History of Japanese Adult Video]. Tokyo: Gentōsha.

Fujiki, Tadashi and Osamu Matsui. 1995. '*Seijin eiga no kyojin: ōkura Mitsugi ga nokoshita pinku no isan!*' [The Giant of Adult Movie: The Treasure Left by Ōkura Mitsugi]. In Hiromu Inoue, ed., *Sei media no goshū nen* [The 50 Years of Sex History], 56–67. Tokyo: Takarajima Sha.

Fujimoto, Tetsushi. 1994. 'Job and Pay Satisfaction Among Japanese Office Workers: A Gender Comparison'. *Japanese Journal of Administrative Science* 9(1): 39–49.

Geertz, Clifford. 1973. *The Interpretation of Cultures*. New York: Basic Books.

Gerlach, Michael L. 1992. *Alliance Capitalism: The Social Organization of Japanese Business*. Berkeley: University of California Press.

Goffman, Erving. 1958. *The Presentation of Self in Everyday life*. Edinburgh: University of Edinburgh, Social Sciences Research Centre.

Graff, Gerald. 1983. 'The Pseudo-Politics of Interpretation'. *Critical Inquiry* 9(3): 597–610.

Grindstaff, Laura. 2002. *The Money Shot: Trash, Class, and the Making of TV Talk Shows*. Chicago: University of Chicago Press.

Handa, Ryosuke. 1996. *Hyoku mannin no yoru densetsu* [The Legend of the Night of One Million People]. Tokyo: Jiyukokuminsha.

Hanlon, David. 1988. *Upon a Stone Altar: A History of the Island of Pohnpei to 1890. Pacific Island Monographic Series No. 5*. Honolulu: The University of Hawai'i Press.

Hardy, Simon. 1998. *The Reader, The Author, His Woman and Her Lover: Soft-core Pornography and Heterosexual Men*. London and Washington, DC: Cassell.

Hardy, Simon. 2008. 'The Pornography of Reality'. *Sexualities* 11(1/2): 60–4.

Hashimoto, Atsuko. 2000. 'Young Japanese Female Tourists: An In-depth Understanding of a Market Segment'. *Current Issues in Tourism* 3(1): 35–50.

Hashitsume, Daisaburō. 1995. *Seiairon* [The Theory of Sex]. Tokyo: Iwanami Shoten.

Haslanger, Sally. 1993. 'On Being Objective and Being Objectified'. In Louise M. Antony and Charlotte Witt, eds, *A Mind of One's Own: Feminist Essays on Reason and Objectivity*, 209–53. Boulder, CO; San Francisco; Oxford: Westview Press.

Hawthorne, Susan. 2011. 'Capital and the Crimes of Pornographers: Free to Lynch, Exploit, Rape and Torture'. In M. T. Reist and A. Bray, eds, *Big Porn Inc.: Exposing the Harms of the Global Pornography Industry*, 107–17. Australia: Spinifex Press Pty Ltd.

Hebdige, Dick. 1988. *Hiding in the Light: On Images and Things*. London and New York: Routledge.

Hebdige, Dick. 1991. *Subculture: The Meaning of Style*. London and New York: Routledge.

Herman, Barbara. 1993. 'Could It Be Worth Thinking About Kant on Sex and Marriage?' In Louise M. Antony and Charlotte Witt, eds, *A Mind of One's Own: Feminist Essays on Reason and Objectivity*, 53–72. Boulder, CO; San Francisco; Oxford: Westview Press.

Hirano, Kyoko. 1992. *Mr. Smith Goes to Tokyo: Japanese Cinema Under the American Occupation, 1945–1952*. Washington, DC and London: Smithsonian Institution Press.

Hobbes, Thomas. 1981. *Leviathan*, edited with an introduction by C. B. Macpherson. Harmondsworth: Penguin.

Hoover, William D. 2011. *Historical Dictionary of Postwar Japan*. Lanham, MD; Toronto; Plymouth, UK: The Scarecrow Press Inc.

Horkheimer, Max and Adorno, Theodor W. 1973. *Dialectic of Enlightenment*, translated by John Cumming. London: Allen Lane.

Hunter, Jack. 1998. *Eros in Hell*. London: Creation Books.

Hwang, Shu-ling, Lee, Tony Szu-Hsien and Chao Yun-chih. 2010. 'Shijie zhi jiao Taiwan ren xingxingwei fenxi: shidai, xingbie, jiaoyu ji hunyin zhuangtai zhi jiaoji chayi' [The Analysis of Sexual Behaviour of Taiwanese]. *Taiwan xingxue xuekan* [*The Taiwanese Journal of Sex*] 16(1): 1–28.

Inoue, Setsuko. 2002. *AV sangyō: yichiokuen ichiba no mekanizumu* [AV Industry: The Mechanism of a Trillion's Market]. Tokyo: Shinhyoron.

Ishida, Yoko. 1998. '*Shiritai, karitai, mayowanai: eibui mēkā katarogu*' [Want to Know, Want to Borrow and Want Not to Be Confused: AV Maker Category]. In Y. Ishida, ed., *20 seiji no adaruto bideo* [Adult Video in the 20th Century], 206–14. Tokyo: Asupekuto.

Jackson, Gregory. 2007. 'Employment Adjustment and Distributional Conflict in Japanese Firms'. In Masahiko Aoki, Gregory Jackson and Hideaki Miyajima, eds, *Corporate Governance in Japan: Institutional Change and Organizational Diversity*, 282–309. New York: Oxford University Press.

Japan News Review. 23 August 2007. Adult Movie Producers Raided in Tokyo After Showing Too Much. www.japannewsreview.com/society/kanto/20070823page_id=1698 (accessed 31 March 2013).

Jensen, Robert. 2007. *Getting Off: Pornography and the End of Masculinity*. Cambridge, MA: South End Press.

Juffer, Jane. 1998. *At Home with Pornography: Women, Sex and Everyday Life*. New York and London: New York University Press.

Kajii, Hiroshi. 1998. '*AV sankyo*' ['The AV Industry']. In Y. Ishida, ed., *20 seiji no adaruto bideo* [Adult Video in the 20th Century], 138–42. Tokyo: Asupekuto.

Kawamoto Koji. 2011. *Poruno sasshi no shōwashi* [The History of Pornographic Magazines in Showa Period]. Tokyo: Tsukuma Shobo.

Kawamura, Kunimitsu and Shōgo Takeda. 1995. '*Kindai nipponjin no sekkusu zō ha ikani umaretaka?*' [How Was the Sex Image of Modern Japanese People Born?]. In Hiromu Inoue, ed., *Sei media no goshū nen* [The 50 Years of Sex History], 233–41. Tokyo: Takarajima Sha.

Keene, Donald. 1984. *Dawn to the West: Japanese Literature of the Modern Era*. New York: Holt, Rinehart, and Winston.

Kelsky, Karen. 2001a. 'Who Sleeps with Whom, or How (Not) to Want the West in Japan'. *Qualitative Inquiry* 7(4): 418–35.

Kelsky, Karen. 2001b. *Women on the Verge: Japanese Women, Western Dreams*. Durham, NC: Duke University Press.

Kinsella, Sharon. 2011. 'From Compensating Comfort Women to Compensated Dating'. *U.S.–Japan Women's Journal* 41: 52–71.

Kinsella, Sharon. 2014. *Schoolgirls, Money, and Rebellion in Japan*. London and New York: Routledge.

Kirsch, Griseldis. 2014. 'Next-door Divas: Japanese *Tarento*, Television and Consumption'. *Journal of Japanese and Korean Cinema* 6(1): Special Issue: Diva Symposium: 74–88.

Koh, Yoree. 2011. 'Japanese Women Quit Unrewarding Careers'. Japan Real Time, https://blogs.wsj.com/japanrealtime/2011/11/14/japanese-women-quit-unrewarding-careers/ (accessed on 4 March 2017).

Korsgaard, Christine. 1996. *Creating the Kingdom of Ends*. Cambridge: Cambridge University Press.

Kurata, Masumi. 1998. '*Mensetsu* (Interview)'. In Y. Ishida, ed., *20 seiji no adaruto bideo* [Adult Video in the 20th Century], 188–9. Tokyo: Asupekuto.

Leheny, David Richard. 2006. *Think Global, Fear Local: Sex, Violence, and Anxiety in Contemporary Japan*. Ithaca, NY: Cornell University Press.

Lévi-Strauss, Claude. 1963. *Totemism*, translated from the French by Rodney Needham. Boston, MA: Beacon Press.

Liberman, Rachael. 2013. 'The Politics of Mediating Female Sexual Subjectivity: Feminist Pornography and the Production of Cultural Variation'. Phd diss., Journalism & Mass Communication Graduate, University of Colorado, Boulder.

Liberman, Rachael. 2015. ' "It's a Really Great Tool": Feminist Pornography and the Promotion of Sexual Subjectivity'. *Porn Studies* 2(2–3): 174–91.

Lin, Kai-shuh. 2016. 'What is "Anthropological" about Anthropological Fieldwork?: Reflections on its Epistemology and Ethics'. *Journal of Archaeology and Anthropology* 84: 77–110 (in Chinese).

Lingenfelter, Sherwood. 1975. *Yap, Political Leadership and Culture Change in Anisland Society*. Honolulu: University of Hawai'i Press.

Long, Julia. 2012. *Anti-Porn: The Resurgence of Anti-Pornography Feminism*. London and New York: Zed Books.

Luff, Donna. 2001. ' "The Downright Torture of Women": Moral Lobby Women, Feminists and Pornography'. *The Sociological Review* 49(1): 78–99.

Macias, Patrick. 2001. *TokyoScope: The Japanese Cult Film Companion*. San Francisco: Cadence Books.

MacKinnon, Catharine A. 1983. 'Not a Moral Issue'. *Yale Law & Policy Review* 2(2): 321–45.

MacKinnon, Catharine A. 1993. *Only Words*. Cambridge, MA: Harvard University Press.

Mainichi Shimbun. 1st March 2008. 'Ethics Body Bigwigs Busted for Failing to Blank Out the Dirty Bits in Adult DVDs'. http://web.archive.org/web/20080303053023/http://mdn.mainichi.jp/national/news/20080301p2a00m0na003000c.html (accessed 26 July 2017).

Marx, Karl. 1963. *Karl Marx: Selected Writings in Sociology and Social Philosophy*. Harmondsworth: Penguin.

Marx, Karl. 1994. *Selected Writings/Karl Marx*, edited, with introduction, by Lawrence H. Simon. Indianapolis: Hackett.

Masters, Patricia Lee. 1992. 'The Politics of Memory: Creating Self-understandings in Postwar Japan'. Phd diss., Department of Political Science, University of Hawai'i.

Matsuzawa, Kureichi. 1995. '*Kasutori zasshi to garo no Nagai san*' [Kasutori Magazine and Garo's Mr. Nagai]. In Hiromu Inoue, ed., *Sei media no goshū nen* [The 50 Years of Sex History], 23–31. Tokyo: Takarajima Sha.

Matsuzawa, Kureichi. 1998. '*Shunga kara AV he to tsuduku: seikyogen no houjo*' [The Continuous Move from Shunga to AV: The Fertility of Sexual Presentation]. In Y. Ishida, ed., *20 seiji no adaruto bideo* [Adult Video in the 20th Century], 24–8. Tokyo: Asupekuto.

McKee, Alan. 2004. 'How to Tell the Difference Between Production and Consumption: A Case Study in Doctor Who Fandom'. In S. G. Jones and R. Pearson, eds, *Cult Television*, 167–86. Minneapolis: Minnesota University Press.

McKee, Alan 2005a. 'The Need to Bring the Voices of Pornography Consumers into Public Debates About the Genre and its Effects'. *Australian Journal of Communication* 32(2): 71–94.

McKee, Alan 2005b. 'The Objectification of Women in Mainstream Pornographic Videos in Australia'. *Journal of Sex Research* 42(4): 277–90.

McKee, Alan, Lumby, Catharine and Albury, Katherine. 2008. *The Porn Report*. Carlton, Victoria: Melbourne University Publishing.

McLelland, Mark. 2012. *Love, Sex and Democracy in Japan During the American Occupation.* New York: Palgrave Macmillan.

Mears, Ashley. 2011. *Pricing Beauty: The Making of a Fashion Model.* Berkeley: University of California Press.

Mercer, C. H., Tanton, C. P., Prah, B., Erens, P. S., Clifton, S., Macdowall, W., Lewis, R., Field, N., Datta, J., Copas, A. J., Phelps, A., Wellings, K. and Johnson, A. M. 2013. 'Changes in Sexual Attitudes and Lifestyles in Britain through the Life Course and Over Time: Findings from the National Surveys of Sexual Attitudes and Lifestyles (Natsal)'. *Lancet* 382: 1781–94.

Miller, Daniel. 1987. *Material Culture and Mass Consumption.* Oxford: B. Blackwell.

Miller, Daniel. 1995a. 'Consumption and Commodities'. *Annual Review of Anthropology* 24: 141–61.

Miller, Daniel (ed.). 1995b. *Acknowledging Consumption: A Review of New Studies.* London: Routledge.

Miller, Robbi Louise. 2003. 'The Quiet Revolution: Japanese Women Working Around the Law'. *Harvard Women's Law Journal* 26: 163–215.

Mintz, Sidney. 1985. *Sweetness and Power: The Place of Sugar in Modern History.* INT New York: Viking.

Mitchell, Richard H. 1983. *Censorship in Imperial Japan.* Princeton, NJ: Princeton University Press.

Miura, Mari. 2008. 'Labor Politics in Japan During "The Lost Fifteen Years": From the Politics of Productivity to the Politics of Consumption'. *Labor History* 49(2): 161–76.

Miyada, Shinji, Hayami, Y., Yamamoto, N. et al. 1998. '*Jiko ketei kenro; jiyū to sonkei*' [Original Theory of Sexual Self-determination]. In S. Miyadai, Y. Hayami, N. Yamamoto, Y. Miya, S. Fujii, H. Hirano, F. Kanazumi and Y. Hirano, eds, *Sei no jiko ketei kenro* [The Original Theory of Sexual Self-determination]. Tokyo: Kinokuniya.

Molasky, Michael S. 1999. *The American Occupation of Japan and Okinawa: Literature and Memory.* New York: Routledge.

Motohashi, Nobuhiro. 2012. '*Ano isai taiho kara yonnen: "Biderin" jiken no sonogo*' [Four Years After the Arrest: The Aftermath of the Biderin Incident]. *The Tsukuru*, Combined Issue of 5 and 6, 122–9.

Nakamura, Atsuhiko. 2009. *Namae no nai onna tachi* [Women without Names]. Tokyo: Takarajimasha.

Nakamura, Atsuhiko. 2012. *Shokugyō toshite no AV joyū* [The Career of AV Actresses]. Tokyo: Gentōsha.

Nakamura, Atsuhiko. 2015. *AV Bijinesu no shogeki* [The Shocking Impact of the AV Business]. Tokyo: Gentōsha.

Natsuhara, Takeshi. 1995. '*Binibon to AV teki seiketsu ero no jidai wo musubu ten to senn*' [The Meeting Point and Line Between Binibon and the Clean Eros in AV]. In Hiromu Inoue, ed., *Sei media no goshū nen* [The 50 Years of Sex History], 166–77. Tokyo: Takarajima Sha.

Nayar, Jayan. 2002. 'Orders of Inhumanity'. In R. Falk, L. E. J. Ruiz and R. B. J. Walker, eds, *Reframing the International: Law, Culture, Politics*, 107–35. New York: Routledge.

Nikaidō, Takuya. 2014. *Pinku eigashi* [The History of Pink Film]. Tokyo: Sairyusha.

Nikunen, Kaarina, Susanna Paasonen and Laura Saarenmaa. 2007. *Pornification: Sex and Sexuality in Media Culture.* Oxford and New York: Berg.

Nussbaum, Martha. 1995. 'Objectification'. *Philosophy and Public Affairs* 24(4): 249–91.

Okano, Kaori H. 2009. *Young Women in Japan: Transitions to Adulthood.* New York and London: Routledge.

Okina, Kunio, Masaaki Shirakawa and Shigenori Shiratsuka. 2001. 'The Role of Monetary Policy under Low Inflation: Deflationary Shocks and Policy Responses, Background Paper – The Asset Price Bubble and Monetary Policy: Japan's Experience in the Late 1980s and the Lessons'. *Monetary and Economic Studies* (Special Edition) 19: s–1.

Ōkura, Mitsugi. 1998. *Wagagei to kane to koi* [My Art, Money and Love]. Tokyo: Ōzorasha.

Omoiatanarai. n.d. *Shinsa wo suru soshiki, eizōrinkikou ni itarumade* [Organization that Administers Film Investigations: Road to the Current Eizōrin], unpublished material.

Ortner, Sherry. 1973. 'On Key Symbols'. *American Ethnologist* 75: 1338–46.

Osawa, Machiko. 2005. 'Japan's Changing Economy and Women Workers'. *The Japanese Economy* 32(4): 96–108.

O'Toole, Laurence. 1999. *Pornocopia: Porno, Sex, Technology and Desire*. London: Serpent's Tail.

Otsubo, Kemuta. 2007. *Sekai ga 100 nin no AV jōyu dattara* [The One Hundred AV Actresses in the World]. Tokyo: Fusosha.

Ozawa, Maria. 2009. *Kotoba zeme* [The Speech Scolding]. Tokyo: KK Bestsellers.

Papadaki, Lina. 2007. 'Sexual Objectification: From Kant to Contemporary Feminism'. *Contemporary Political Theory* 6(3): 330–48.

Parmentier, Richard. 1987. *The Sacred Remains: Myth, History, and Polity in Belau*. Chicago: The University of Chicago Press.

Paul, Pamela. 2005. *Pornified: How Pornography Is Transforming Our Lives, Our Relationships, and Our Families*. New York: Times Books.

Petersen, Glenn. 1990. *Lost In the Weeds: Theme and Variation In Pohnpei Political Mythology*. Honolulu: Center of Pacific Studies, University of Hawai'i at Manoa.

Pratt, Andy C. 2004. 'Retail Therapy'. *Geoforum* 35: 519–21.

Raymo, James M. 2003. 'Educational Attainment and the Transition to First Marriage among Japanese Women'. *Demography* 40: 83–103.

Raymo, James M. and Miho Iwasawa. 2005. 'Marriage Market Mismatches in Japan: An Alternative View of the Relationship between Women's Education and Marriage'. *American Sociological Review* 70: 801–22.

Redden, Joseph P. 2008. 'Reducing Satiation: The Role of Categorization Level'. *Journal of Consumer Research* 34(5): 624–34.

Reist, Melinda Tankard and Bray, Abigail (eds). 2011. *Big Porn Inc.: Exposing the Harms of the Global Pornography Industry*. North Melbourne: Spinifex Press Pty Ltd.

Roberts, G. S. 1994. *Staying on the Line: Blue-Collar Women in Contemporary Japan*. Honolulu: University of Hawai'i Press.

Rolls, Barbara J., Rolls, Edmund T., Rowe, Edward A. and Sweeney, Kevin. 1981. 'Sensory Specific Satiety in Man'. *Physiology and Behavior* 27(1): 137–42.

Rolls, Barbara J., Rowe, Edward A. and Rolls, Edmund T. 1982. 'How Sensory Properties of Foods Affect Human Feeding Behavior'. *Physiology and Behavior* 29(3): 409–17.

Rosenberger, Nancy Ross. 2001. *Gambling with Virtue: Japanese Women and the Search for Self in a Changing Nation*. Honolulu: University of Hawai'i Press.

Roy, Subhadip. 2012. 'To Use the Obvious Choice: Investigating the Relative Effectiveness of an Overexposed Celebrity'. *Journal of Research for Consumer* 22: 41–69.

Rubin, Gayle S. 1993a. 'Thinking Sex: Notes for a Radical Theory of the Politics of Sexuality'. In H. Abelove, M. A. Barale and D. M. Halperin, eds, *The Lesbian and Gay Studies Reader*, 3–34. London: Routledge.

Rubin, Gayle S. 1993b. 'Misguided, Dangerous, and Wrong: An Analysis of Antipornography Politics'. In Alison Assiter and Avedon Carol, eds, *Bad Girls and Dirty Pictures: The Challenge to Reclaim Feminism*, 19–40. London and Boulder, CO: Pluto Press.

Rubin, Jay. 1985. 'From Wholesomeness to Decadence: The Censorship of Literature under the Allied Occupation'. *The Journal of Japanese Studies* 11(1): 71–103.

Sahlins, Marshall. 1976a. *Culture and Practical Reason*. Chicago: The University of Chicago Press.

Sahlins, Marshall. 1976b. *Use and Abuse of Biology*. Chicago: The University of Chicago Press.

Sahlins, Marshall. 1985. *Islands of History*. Chicago and London: The University of Chicago Press.

Sahlins, Marshall. 1999. 'What Is Anthropological Enlightenment? Some Lessons of the Twentieth century'. *Annual Review of Anthropology* 28: i–xxiii.

Sahlins, Marshall. 2000. *Culture in Practice: Selected Essays*. New York: Zone Books.

Sahlins, Marshall. 2002. 'Endangered Specificities'. *Journal of Social Archaeology* 2(3): 283–97.

Sahlins, Marshall. 2012. 'Alterity and Autochthony: Austronesian Cosmographies of the Marvelous. The 2008 Raymond Firth Lecture'. *HAU: Journal of Ethnographic Theory* 2(1): 131–60.

Sahlins, Marshall. 2013. 'The Culture of Material Value and the Cosmography of Riches'. *HAU: Journal of Ethnographic Theory* 3(2): 161–95.

Sartre, Jean Paul. 1968. *Search for a Method*, translated from the French with an introduction by Hazel E. Barnes. London: Methuen.

Sato, Tadao. 1982. *Currents in Japanese Cinema: Essay*, translated by Gregory Barrett. Tokyo: Kodansha.

Sawaki, Takehiko. 1995. '*Saraba! Jihankihon kani kouzho*' [Goodbye! Vending Machine Pornography: The Cannery Boat]. In Hiromu Inoue, ed., *Sei media no goshū nen* [The 50 Years of Sex History], 123–35. Tokyo: Takarajima Sha.

Sawaki, Takehiko. 1998. *Reipu* [Rape]. In Yoko Ishida, ed., *20 seiji no adaruto bideo* [Adult Video in the 20th Century], 168–9. Tokyo: Asupekuto.

Schoenherr, Johannes. 2006. 'Company Matsuo and the World of Japanese Adult Video'. www.midnighteye.com/features/company-matsuo-and-the-world-of-japanese-adult-video/ (accessed 26 July 2017)..

Screech, Timon. 1999. *Sex and the Floating World: Erotic Images in Japan 1700–1820*. London: Reaktion Books.

Segal, Lynne and McIntosh, Mary (eds). 1992. *Sex Exposed: Sexuality and the Pornography Debate*. London: Virago.

Senn, Charlene. 1993. 'The Research on Women and Pornography: The Many Faces of Harm'. In D. E. H. Russell, ed., *Making Violence Sexy: Feminist Views on Pornography*, 179–93. Buckingham: Open University Press.

Shimokawa, Kōshi. 1995. '*Hentai no sogō depāto "kitan kurabu" kara "SM serekuto" ubugoe wo agerumade*' [Until 'SM Selection' Gives its First Cry from an Abnormal Overall Department Store 'Kitan Club']. In Hiromu Inoue, ed., *Sei media no goshū nen* [The 50 Years of Sex History], 48–55. Tokyo: Takarajima Sha.

Shōwa Seishiryo Kenkyu Kai and Saito, Osamu. 2014. *Adaruto no genryu: 'binibon no shutsugen*' [The Origin of Adult Video: The Emergence of Binibon]. Tokyo: East Press.

Slater, Don. 1997. *Consumer Culture and Modernity*. Cambridge, MA: Blackwell Publishers.

Smith, Clarissa and Attwood, Feona. 2014. 'Anti/pro/critical Porn Studies'. *Porn Studies* 1(1–2): 7–23.
Sonoda, Hisashi and Hiroshi Dai. 2016. *Erosu to waisetsu no aida: hyogenn to kisei no sengo kōbōshi* [Between Eros and Obscenity: The Battle in Representation and Regulations in Postwar Japan]. Tokyo: Asahi Shinsho.
Strinati, Dominic. 1995. *An Introduction to Theories of Popular Culture*. London: Routledge.
Suitsu, Hiroshi. 1998a. '*Adaruto bideo nenhyō*' [The Chart of Adult Video]. In Y. Ishida, ed., *20 seiji no adaruto bideo* [Adult Video in the 20th Century], 2–8. Tokyo: Asupekuto.
Suitsu, Hiroshi. 1998b. '*Bishōjo aidoru*' [The Idol of Bishōjo]. In Y. Ishida, ed., *20 seiji no adaruto bideo* [Adult Video in the 20th Century], 156–60. Tokyo: Asupekuto.
Suzuki, Suzumi. 2013. *AV joyū no shakaigaku: naze kanojo tachi wa jyōzetsu mizukara wo kataru noka* [The Sociology of Adult Video Actresses: Why These Women Are Eager to Talk About Themselves]. Tokyo: Seidosha.
Szakolczai, Arpad. 2000. *Reflexive Historical Sociology*. New York and London: Routledge.
Szakolczai, Arpad. 2009. 'Liminality and Experience: Structuring Transitory Situations and Transformative Events'. *International Political Anthropology* 2(1): 141–72.
Tachibanaki, Toshiaki and Urakawa Kunio. 2012. *Nihon no chiikikan kakusa: tokyō ikkyoku shūchūgata kara yatsuga takehoshi he* [The Regional Gap in Japan: From Heavy Concentration in Tokyo to Multipolar Systems]. Tokyo: Nihon kyōronsha.
Tameike, Goro. 2013. *AV joyu no oshigoto* [The Job of Adult Video Actresses]. Tokyo: KK Besuto Serāzu.
Tanaka, Aiko. 2014. '"*Kanjisaserareru onna*" to "*kanjiseru otoko*"': The Establishment of the Double Structure of Sexuality'. In S. Koyama, K. Akaeda and E. Imada, eds, *The History of Sexuality in Postwar Japan*, 101–28. Kyoto: The University Press of Kyoto.
Tanaka, Masakazu. 2007. '*Iyashi to iyarashi no porunogurafī: Yoyogi Tadashi kantoku sakuhinn wo megutte*' [Spiritual Eroticism in the Early Works of a Japanese Porn Director]. *Journal of Humanities*, Institute for Research in Humanities, Kyoto University 94: 101–47.
Taormino, Tristan. 2013. 'Calling the Shots: Feminist Porn in Theory and Practice'. In T. Taormino, C. P. Shimizu, C. Penley and M. Miller-Young, eds, *The Feminist Porn Book: The Politics of Producing Pleasure*, 255–64. New York: The Feminist Press at CUNY Dewey.
Taormino, Tristan, Shimizu, Celine Parrenas, Penley, Constance and Miller-Young, Mireille. 2013. *The Feminist Porn Book: The Politics of Producing Pleasure*. New York: The Feminist Press at CUNY Dewey.
Thompson, John B. 2005. *Books in the Digital Age: The Transformation of Academic and Higher Education Publishing in Britain and the United States*. Cambridge: Polity.
Thompson, John B. 2010. *Merchants of Culture: The Publishing Business in the Twenty-first century*. Cambridge and Malden, MA: Polity.
Tōra, Miki. 1998a. '*Kamera = mannenhitsu*' [Camera = Fountain Pen]. In Y. Ishida, ed., *20 seiji no adaruto bideo* [Adult Video in the 20th Century], 28–31. Tokyo: Asupekuto.
Tōra, Miki. 1998b. '*Uchū bishōjo 80's-90's*' [The Cosmo Bishōjo 80's–90's]. In Y. Ishida, ed., *20 seiji no adaruto bideo* [Adult Video in the 20th Century], 119–25. Tokyo: Asupekuto.
Turner, Victor. 1967. 'Betwixt and Between: The Liminal Period in Rites de Passage'. *The Forest of Symbols: Aspects of the Ndembu Ritual*. Ithaca, NY: Cornell University Press.

Turner, Victor. 1969. *The Ritual Process*. London: Routledge.
Turner, Victor. 1974. *Dramas, Fields, and Metaphors: Symbolic Action in Human Society*. Ithaca, NY and London: Cornell University Press.
Tyler, Meagan. 2010. '"Now, That's Pornography!": Violence and Domination in Adult Video News'. In K. Boyle, ed., *Everyday Pornography*, 50–62. Oxford and New York: Routledge.
Ueno, Chizuko. 1990. 'Explanation Three'. In Ogi Shinzō, Kumakura Isao and Ueno Chizuko, eds, *Fūzoku sei* [The Nature of Adult Entertainment]. Tōkyō: Iwanami Shoten.
Ueno, Chizuko. 2003. 'Self-determination on Sexuality? Commercialization of Sex Among Teenage Girls in Japan'. *Inter-Asia Cultural Studies* 4(2): 317–24.
Umeda, Maki, McMunn, A. Cable, N. *et al.* 2015. 'Does an Advantageous Occupational Position Make Women Happier in Contemporary Japan?: Findings from the Japanese Study of Health, Occupation, and Psychological Factors Related Equity'. *SSM-Population Health* 8: 8–15.
Voss, Georgina. 2012. 'Treating It as a Normal Business: Researching the Pornography Industry'. *Sexualities* 25: 391–410.
Weisser, Thomas and Yuko Mihara Weisser. 1998. *Japanese Cinema Encyclopaedia: The Sex Films*. Miami: Vital Books: Asian Cult Cinema Publications.
Willis, Paul E. 1978. *Profane Culture*. London: Routledge & K. Paul.
Willis, Paul E. 1990. *Common Culture: Symbolic Work at Play in the Everyday Cultures of the Young*. Boulder, CO: Westview Press.
Wilson, E. 1989. 'Against Feminist Fundamentalism'. *New Statesman and Society* 2: 30–3.
Wingfield, R. and Scanlon, J. 1992. 'Feminists Against Censorship or a Campaign for Pornography'. *Spare Rib* 233: 50.
Woida, Chloe. 2009. 'International Video Pornography on the Internet: Crossing Digital Borders and the Un/disciplined Gaze'. A paper presented at Digital Arts and Culture 2009. UC Irvine: Digital Arts and Culture 2009.
Wong, Heung-wah. 1999. *Japanese Bosses, Chinese Workers; Power and Control in a Hong Kong Megastore*. Surrey: Curzon Press.
Wong, Heung-wah and Hoi-yan Yau. 2014. '"Don't Like Watching Japanese Adult Videos Because You Like it": The Politics of Pornography Consumption in Taiwan'. *Sage Open* 4: 1–11.
Wong, Heung-wah and Hoi-yan Yau. 2015. 'Japanese Adult Videos in Taiwan and Hong Kong'. In M. McLelland and V. Mackie, eds, *Routledge Handbook of Sexuality Studies in East Asia*, 414–26. Oxon and New York: Routledge.
Wurst, LouAnn and McGuire, Randall. 1999. 'Immaculate Consumption: A Critique of the "Shop Till You Drop"'. *School of Human Behavior* 3(3): 191–9.
Yamamoto, Akira. 1976. *Kasutori zasshi kenkyu: shinboru ni miruru fūzokushi* [Kasutori Magazine: The History of Adult Entertainment as Symbols]. Tokyo: ShuppanNews.
Yasuda, Rio and Amamiya, M. 2006. *Ero no teki: yima, adaruto media ni okori tsutsuaru koto* [The Enemy of Ero: The Ongoing Development of Adult Media]. Tokyo: Shoeisha.
Yau, Hoi-yan. 2001. 'The Domestication of Japanese Adult Videos in Hong Kong'. MPhil thesis, University of Birmingham.
Yau, Hoi-yan and Wong, Heung-wah. 2009. 'The Emergence of a New Sexual Ideal: A Case Study of Yuki Maiko's Pornographic VCDs in Hong Kong'. *Journal of Archaeology and Anthropology* (National Taiwan University, Taiwan) 70: 1–46.
Yau, Hoi-yan and Wong, Heung-wah. 2010. 'Translating Japanese Adult Movies in Taiwan: Transcending the Production-consumption Opposition'. *Asian Studies Review* 34(1): 19–39.

Yau, Hoi-yan and Yoshikazu, Kobori. 2012a. '*AV nvyou mianshi chang: zixu shangpin yuancai de zhudi shichang*' [The Interview Site of Adult Video Actress: The Masturbating Raw Material for the AV]. In H. W. Wong and H. Y. Yau, eds, *Riben AV nvyou: nvxing de wuhua yu mohua* [The Commodification of Women's Bodies: A Critique of Adult Videos Production in Japan], 74–105. Hong Kong: Up Publications (in Chinese).

Yau, Hoi-yan and Yoshikazu, Kobori. 2012b. *AV Xiangchang: zixu shangpin de jinshi lianshi* [The Shooting Scene of AV: The Production Place for AV]. In H. W. Wong and H. Y. Yau, eds, *Riben AV nvyou: nvxing de wuhua yu mohua* [The Commodification of Women's Bodies: A Critique of Adult Videos Production in Japan], 106–23. Hong Kong: Up Publications (in Chinese).

Yip, Paul S. F., Huiping Zhang, Tai-Hing Lam, Kwok Fai Lam, Lee, Antoinette Marie, Chan, John and Fan, Susan. 2013. 'Sex Knowledge, Attitudes, and High-risk Sexual Behaviors Among Unmarried Youth in Hong Kong'. *BMC Public Health* 13(691).

Yoshioka, Tetsukyo. 1999. *80 nendai AV dazen* [The Collection of Japanese AVs in the 1980s]. Tokyo: Futabasha.

Zhou, Yanfei. 2015. 'Career Interruption of Japanese Women: Why Is it So Hard to Balance Work and Childcare?'. *Japan Labor Review* 12(2): 106–23.

Index

Page numbers in *italics* denote tables, those in **bold** denote figures.

actor(s) 15, 20, 22, 53, 61, 72, 74–5, 79, 88–9, 93, 136, 163, 174, 185
acme 43, 163–4, 182–4, 217
akume 43, 164
apriorism 14, 220
asymmetrical view of power 175, 176
authenticity 17, 23, 43, 67, 79, 85, 87, 101, 165, 208, 209, 211, 214, 218, 227
authentication 46, 79, 101, 174, 178–9, 182, 209, 211, 214, 218, 227
of the actress 46, 79, 101, 209, 227
of the female character 85, 179
AV: actress(es) 5, 12, 16, 20, 22, 25, 27, 42, 44–8, 50–7, 68, 71, 85, 87, 89–93, 99, 101–2, 104–7, 110, 113–14, 116, 118, 120–3, 127–34, 139, 152–61, 167, 208–9, 211, 213–16, 218–19, 227; girl(s) 44, 54, 79, 90, 92, 104–8, 110, 121–3, 132–3, 160, 215; idol(s) 41, 62, 91–2; maker(s) 12, 16, 20, 24–5, 27, 41, 43–5, 49, 50–6, 58–64, 66–9, 71, 79, 86–7, 89–91, 93, 99, 102, 104–5, 137, 139, 156–7, 159, 161, 188–90, 192–3, 195–6, 203–5, 208–9, 210–12, 215–16, 218–19, 227
AVs-for-sale 43, 50, 65–7, 187, 193

Biderin 39, 44, 50, 58–67, 69, 186–96, 198, 207, 210, 212, 217–18
Big Five 24–5, 50, 53, 58, 61–4, 68–9, 88, 186, 188–9, 191–3, 210, 212, 215
Binibon 24, 27, 35, 36, 40–2, 46, 51, 68, 69, 85, 100, 213, 215, 220
binibon-style 41, 51, 68, 215
bishōjo 36, 41, 46, 47, 50, 51, 72, 79, 86, 88, 90, 95–6, 100, 214, 219

cartel 24, 50, 61, 64, 68–9, 180, 212, 215, 218
casting directors 20, 52, 55–6, 89, 92, 105, 129, 132–3, 140, 153, 155, 157, 160–1, 216
censorship 13, 16, 24, 30, 57, 58, 61, 186, 191, 208, 211, 217–18, 227
circulation 11, 23, 25, 34, 49, 64–5, 67, 69, 86, 98, 101, 192, 214, 218
consensus building 198, 202
consumption 5, 6, 8–12, 18, 23–5, 40, 102, 156, 160, 163, 183, 184, 211, 213, 218–19, 220
cover design 94, 214
cultural: code 5–6, 12, 18, 24–5, 46, 91, 92, 102, 134, 160–1, 182–3, 213–16, 218–19, 220, 226–7; economy 101, 216; logic 219; reason 12, 47, 71, 214, 219

de-authenticate/de-authentication 209, 211, 218
debut 1, 4, 36, 45, 51, 72, 86, 90–2, 96
degree: of determination 121, *153–4*, 156, 161, 216; of freshness 153, *154–5*, 156, 161, 216
directors 15, 20, 22, 39, 42, 44, 51n8, 52–3, 63, 65–6, 88, 96, 132, 150, 152, 157–61, 165, 183, 185, 187, 209, 216

Eizōrin 186, 187n3, 191–4, 194n5, 195, 195n6–195n7, 196–9, 202–13, 203n10, 204–12
employment system 90, 124
endangered specificities 220
exchange value 6–7, 9, 11, 92, 158–61
exclusivity system 90–1
external power 206–7

externalization 206

female character(s) 15, 17–18, 23–4, 28, 38, 42–3, 46, 72, 79, 84–7, 101, 159, 163–4, 167–83, 203–4, 209, 214, 217, 220, 222–4, 226–7

genba 20, 53
genre(s) 5, 12, 17, 25, 37–9, 42–3, 47, 50–1, 67, 71–2, 79, 79n3, 86–8, 90, 94–5, 100–2, 130, 132, 136, 157–61, 183, 209, 214–16, 218
girl(s)-next-door 36, 41, 46, 213

Hobbesian man 178–9, 182

Ideology: sadist 183; sexist 183
inauthenticity 209
indie AVs 64–5, 67
industry 5, 9, 12, 16, 18–25, 27, 40–1, 41n5, 43–4, 44n7, 45n12, 47, 49–50, 52–3, 53n9, 54–6, 58–69, 71, 85–6, 89–93, 95, 98, 101–2, 104–5, 107–8, 110, 112, 116–17, 120, 122–3, 127–32, 134, 139, 145, 147, 150, 153, *154*, *155*, 155–7, 159, 161, 163n2, 164–7, 180, 185–95, 203, 206–8, 210–12, 214–18, 221
innocent 30, 36, 41, 46–7, 50, 61, 71–3, 78–9, 85, 92, 101, 205, 213, 217, 227
interview 5, 16, 20, 23–5, 52–5, 68, 71, 74, **75**, 89, 92–3, 98, 105, **106**, 108, 114, 120, 129, 132–3, 139–44, 146–7, 150–3, **153**, 155, 157–61, 198, 216
inventive production 132, 160–1, 216

Japanese AVs 5, 12, 16–18, 21, 23, 25, 27, 43, 47, 50, 64–7, 71–2, 94, 98, 102, 122, 147, 158–9, 167, 188, 207, 210, 212–13, 215–20, 226–7

kasutori 27, 31, 34, 36, 46
kawaii 35
kikaku 12, 17–18, 23–5, 27, 41–7, 50–2, 54–5, 65, 68, 71, 79, 79n2, 84–90, 92–4, **95**, 96–7, **97**, 98, **99**, 100–2, 105, **117**, 117–18, **119**, 120, 132, 157, 159–61, 163, 177, 180, 182–3, 193, 203, 209, 211, 213–16, 218, 220, 227
kikatan 27, 45–7, 52, 93, **117**, 117–18, **119**, 120, 130, 215–16
kotoba-zeme 166–7, 179, *180*, 180–3, 213

liminal(ity) 193–4

marital sex 28–9
market price 25, 65n17, *97*, 97, 214
massage: bodily 168, 171; sensual 167–9, 175, 181, 183, 217; uterus 167, 169, 174–5, 179, 181, 183, 217
men's sexual domination over women 5, 12, 32–3, 36, 46–7, 71, 85, 100–2, 161, 182, 214, 216, 220, 227
medirin 66–7, 69, 186, 186n2, 187–90, 192–3, 210, 212, 218
mediation 213
mensetsu 55, 216
model agency 45, 49, 53–6, 89–90
morality 14, 186, 194, 203–5, 208, 211, 220
moral high ground 13, 25, 33, 186, 195, 205–7, 209–10, 218, 220
mosaic 56, 60, 64–7, 187, 189, 191, 193, 199, 201

narrative 12, 23, 25, 33, 36, 47, 71–2, 78–9, 84–5, 100–1, 214

objectification 6, 221–3
obscenity laws 58–60, 65–6, 186–8, 190–1, 203–5
original theory of self-determination of sex 128–9, 131, 216
orgasm: endless 43; female 23, 43, 163, 174–5, 179, 222, 226; multiple 165, 183

package 12, 64, 95, 101, 155, 214
pink film 24, 27, 37–43, 46, 51, 58, 68, 85, 100, 213, 215
pornograph(ies) 4–6, 12–20, 22, 24–5, 27, 31, 33, 219; proto-pornographies 31, 33
pornographic: realism 18, 163, 177–8, 182–4, 211, 214, 218, 226; reality 17, 183, 220, 227; representation 6, 16–18, 223–7
postproduction 24, 49, 52, 56, 68, 215
power: asymmetry 224, 226; politics 16, 18, 24, 224; over 18, 175–7, 183, 217, 222–4, 226
problematic women 43, 181, 184, 224
production process 16, 18, 23, 25, 52, 132, 158, 160–1, 182, 216, 221, 223
production companies 24, 50, 52–3, 59, 68, 71, 88, 96, 215

real/reality 6, 16–18, 25, 30, 46, 57n11, 118, 130, 132, 147, 163, 177–8, 182–4, 191, 207–8, 211, 217, 225–7

recruitment 56, 58–9, 61, **112**, 112, 124–5, 160–1, 195, 216
regulation 11, 41, 49, 86, 192–5, 202, 205–7
rental AVs 61, 66–7
rental shops 43, 60, 63–5, 67, 95, 192, 212
retail shops 24, 49, 64, 66–8, 94, 98, 215

sadist 43, 166–7, 180, 183
salvage ideology 4–5, 12, 16, 18, 23–5, 28, 36–8, 42–3, 46–7, 50, 68, 85, 100, 132, 161, 163, 182–5, 209–11, 213–19, 224, 226–7
self-regulatory 20, 24–5, 63, 64n15, 66, 186–7, 189–93, 206, 208, 218
sex manual 30–3, 217
sexual: being of men and women 6, 18, 25, 178, 183–5, 211, 217, 220, 223–6; desire(s) 15, 32, 42, 61, 92, 102, *117*, 128, 158–9, 213; dissatisfaction 30, 32–3, 37, 166, 213; ecstasy 164, 166–7, 183, 217; freshness 91, 118; happiness 5, 29–30, 32–3, 217; pleasure 5, 14, 28–9, 32–3, 36–7, 43, 165, 169, 177–83, 221, 224, 226; uniqueness 153, *154–5*, 155, 157, 160–1, 216
shooting 5, 18, 20, 23–5, 42, 44, 53–4, 56, 61–3, 68, 72, 88, 91, 93, 95–6, 115–16, **116**, 118, 122–3, 128, 146, 156, 161, 163–5, 167, 170, 173–83, 185, 216–17, 221–3

softcore 32, 35, 37, 61, 65
social drama 187, 189, 192, 210, 212, 218
storyline 17, 38, 42, 44, 47, 71, 79, 89, 93–4, 100, 161, 213–16, 218, 227
subcontracting 50, 88

tantai 12, 17, 20, 23–5, 27, 41–7, 50–2, 55–6, 68, 71–2, 72n1, 79, 84–94, **94**, 95–7, **97**, *97*, 98–102, 105, *117*, 117–18, *119*, 120, 156–7, 159–61, 205, 209, 211, 213–16, 218–20, 227
tantai bishōjo 36, 41, 46–7, 50, 95, 214

use value 6–7, 9, 11, 47, 92, *154–5*, 158–61, 183, 213–14, 219
useful 5, 7, 24, 46, 55, 153, 155, 161, 214, 220
utility 5–7, 12, 101, 158, 160, 183, 214, 219

vinyl cover book 27, 35–8, 41, 50–2, 63
vending machine pornography 34–5

waisetsu 35, 56–7, 190, 196
women's lack of sexual agency 5, 12, 24–5, 33, 36, 38, 41, 46–7, 71, 85, 91–2, 100–2, 161, 182–4, 209, 213–14, 216–17, 220
women's saviour 5, 24–5, 33, 38, 42–3, 47, 101, 181–2, 184, 213–14, 224